ALMOST
VEGETARIAN
Entertaining

ALMOST VEGETARIAN

Entertaining

Simple and Sophisticated
Recipes for
Vegetarians, Nonvegetarians,
and Everyone in Between

DIANA SHAW

CLARKSON POTTER / PUBLISHERS
NEW YORK

Published by Clarkson N. Potter, Inc., 201 East 50th Street, New York, New
York 10022. Member of the Crown Publishing Group.

Random House, Inc. New York, Toronto, London, Sydney, Auckland
www.randomhouse.com

CLARKSON N. POTTER, POTTER and colophon are trademarks of
Clarkson N. Potter, Inc.

Printed in the United States of America

Design by Maggie Hinders

Library of Congress Cataloging-in-Publication Data
Shaw, Diana
    Almost vegetarian entertaining / Diana Shaw. — 1st ed.
    Includes bibliographical references and index. (pb: alk. paper)
    1. Vegetarian cookery. 2. Entertaining. I. Title.
TX837.S46272   1998
641.5'636—dc21   98-4413

ISBN 0-609-80026-4

10 9 8 7 6 5 4 3 2 1

First Edition

For June
A Friend for All Seasons

Contents

ACKNOWLEDGMENTS

I F IT'S TRUE, AS I BELIEVE, that a friend in need is a friend indeed, then Sarah Fritschner is indeed a friend. I called Sarah, food editor and columnist for the *Louisville Courier Journal* and author of the Fast Lane cookbooks (Chapters), in need of help to finish this book. She agreed to write the extensive introduction under extreme deadline pressure, with no help from the putative author. That she came through with such good work is a tribute to her professionalism; that she is still a friend is a tribute to her nature.

Behind everything accomplished by a working mother is a trustworthy person looking after her child. For nearly two years, my son, Michael, has had the benefit of Veronica Brasher's love and energy, while Veronica's good sense and unfailing conscientiousness have given me the peace of mind I've needed to get something done.

My editor, Katie Workman, demonstrated her dedication to this book by taking on much more than the usual ten thousand tasks involved in editing a manuscript. She, her assistant, Erica Youngren, and my agent, Gail Hochman, did all they could and more than might be expected to keep things moving during a difficult pregnancy.

Thanks to my "experts," friends and pros who generously contributed information and advice in the fields they have mastered: Nicholas Troilo (Bacchus to us, cheers!); the Bread Man, Peter Reinhart; Cake Babe Dede Wilson, who, thankfully, doesn't believe in keeping trade secrets; and as always, Ken Skovron, my favorite fromager, whose Darien Cheese and Fine Foods continues to be a warren of the best things in life, particularly the friendship and warmth of proprietor Ken and his wife, Tori. And thanks once again to Ellen Rose of the Cooks Library in Los Angeles, whose occupation is bookseller, but whose real business in life is nurturing everyone who knows her with her vitality and care.

I am grateful in all ways for my husband, Simon, the party of my life, who understood so well when the going got too tough to keep going. It is thanks to him that my goblet, which once seemed half empty, now looks to me more than half full.

HAVE A PARTY, SAVE THE WORLD

I don't know why Hollywood wastes so much time on aliens, disgruntled miscreants, and just plain bad guys plotting to destroy the civilized world when we're doing such a fine job of it ourselves. Now that we shop, bank, and "chat" by machine, only massive system failure brings us face to face. What's more, thanks to fast food, in-store deli counters, and three-star take-out shops, cooking has become completely optional, and sit-down family meals largely do not occur. Some people don't mind this.

I hope you do.

And so I'm urging you . . . quick! Before a dinner party becomes eating microwaved popcorn while sending sweet nothings into cyberspace . . . cook something! And invite someone to your table to share it with you.

The Triumph of the Home Cook, or Don't be Bullied by the Guys in Toques

IF ENTERTAINING DAUNTS YOU, it could be that now that cooking is no longer essential to everyday life, it is considered a Big Deal. It doesn't help that chefs—hardworking, creative once-obscure individuals who made a nice meal for us once in a while—are now Grand Arbiters of Taste. You can't turn on the television without someone in an apron and baggy pants purporting to show you how to make white chocolate mousse but really convincing you it cannot be done.

The Cult of the Professional discourages confidence in our own instincts, inclinations, and common sense. So I was amused when the redoubtable restaurant critic for a major New York City newspaper praised a well-known chef for traveling to a village in Greece to observe how local housewives prepared food for their families. The implications are ironic; no doubt she would not be as enthusiastic if he'd come to watch homemakers in your town or mine, although there may be no difference in our ability to prepare good, honest meals.

Come Over to My Place!

SO IF YOU'RE INTIMIDATED by the Big Time perfectionist pros, take heart and remember that you have people over for the best of most basic reasons: to show that you care about them, and to enjoy the unique, unparalleled pleasure of friendship and companionship.

Finally, you can shrug off any stress related to entertaining simply by defining a successful dinner party as follows: Everyone is glad they came, and you are glad you had them.

INTRODUCTION

We are long past the time when we can assume that everyone will eat everything. People are more informed than they were 20 or even 10 years ago. They know more about how food choices affect their health. And many of them choose to eat prudently as a result. (Or they may have allergies, which are not a matter of choice.) Since basic etiquette calls for trying to please your guests, you'll want to be able to accommodate everyone, within reason. The recipes and menus in this book give you lots of options, making it possible to serve vegetarians and omnivores at the same meal without compromising anything or cheating anyone. There are plenty of dishes and menus that are exclusively vegetarian, and others that feature chicken or fish, all involving fresh, clean flavors, reasonable preparation times, simple techniques, and ingredients that are available everywhere.

Entertaining books such as this can help you plan a party, but only you can decide what's right for you. If you can't imagine setting a table without Grandma's silver and Spode china, you'll probably need to budget to hire the teenager next door to help you polish before the party and hand-wash afterward. If it's a barbecue outside and you have to go back to work after everybody leaves, you'll want the sturdiest possible plasticware and an empty garbage container.

Between the Spode china and those plastic plates, there is lots of latitude for tailoring a party to your taste, timetable, and budget.

Go ahead, plan a party.

First, decide what kind of do it will be. Formal or informal? Is it on a work night? Are you introducing new neighbors, celebrating an occasion, or watching the Academy Awards? Is it a buffet or sit-down, desserts or potluck? Do you want to send invitations? Is there a theme—tree trimming or mystery solving? How much do you want to spend?

Many of these decisions are interdependent. For example, if you decide to have a Superbowl party, then other decisions fall into place. You're pretty sure it's not going to be a multicourse sit-down meal with a bartender mixing Manhattans. You're probably thinking of finger foods such as dips and spreads and meals people can eat in their chairs (chili?). And you'll probably serve straightforward beverages such as soft drinks and microbrews.

Budget

SUCH ARE THE VARIABLES INVOLVED, it's possible to spend more on dinner for four than for two dozen. You can splurge on the wines, ingredients, and centerpieces or get away frugally with a pasta dinner with salad made with greens from your garden.

In general, some types of parties are more expensive than others. Cocktail parties that involve lots of liquor and a substantial buffet will cost more than a family-size dinner with chicken and beer.

Breakfast and brunch generally run cheaper than dinner. Fish usually costs more than chicken. High tea with light dishes or coffee and dessert are often less expensive than a full meal.

When you're on a budget, use expensive ingredients judiciously. If you want to have grilled seafood on the cheap, don't serve whole tuna steaks—cut them into chunks and skewer them with mushrooms and cherry tomatoes. Stretch the exotic flavors of wild mushrooms by combining them with inexpensive domestic mushrooms. And, obviously, seasonal foods such as citrus, kiwi, greens, and potatoes cost less in January than raspberries and asparagus would at that time of year. And shop prudently for beverages. If you're serving wine, tell your purveyor how many people you're having, how much you want to spend overall, what you're serving, and what kind of wines you like. (More advice on choosing wines on page 12.) For a real budget stretcher, consider wine punches that are "extended" with other ingredients, such as sangria and mimosas. And, if it's a casual event, don't hesitate to take someone up on a "what can I bring" offer, even mentioning what you're serving if it seems appropriate so they can bring a suitable wine.

Consider offering one kind of special drink in limited quantities before dinner. If it's your special margarita and you serve one drink to each guest, you've achieved two purposes. First, you've managed your costs. Second, your guests' palates will still be fresh for dinner. (Moreover, everyone will still be upright and coherent at the table.)

I confess, I don't budget per se. However, I'm highly motivated by economic realism (i.e., I'm not rich). I'll splurge on the wines and the entrée, but never on decor or dessert. I haven't ever hired help, though I've been known to pay someone to clean the house before or after a big party.

Invitations

IT GOES WITHOUT SAYING, you'll have to issue invitations to bring people to your party. There are two types: verbal and written.

Verbal invitations, extended wherever you happen to run into people you're inviting, or over the telephone, are informal and have the virtue of letting your guests know from the beginning that this is not a black tie event. That puts them at ease and has the additional benefit of lowering their expectations of you as a host.

When you issue a verbal invitation, you can't expect a reply immediately. Let your friend get back to you. He may have to check with a spouse; she may have to make sure she can get a baby-sitter.

While verbal invitations are fast gaining ground in this day of casual entertaining, I'd like to make a case for written invitations, which are often more practical and occasionally more polite.

Written invitations can help you organize your thoughts, establishing a sort of outline for the party. You can decide it's Saturday from 6 to 10. If you issue the invitation verbally, you might forget to mention an ending time, or the person you invite might forget the date.

If there's a theme to the party—a fund-raiser or mystery party—you can make it clear on the card. You can reach everybody at once and you're not at the mercy of your friend's daughter who cleared the answering machine tape without saving the message. In short, written invitations are a systematic way to invite people to your home, and probably the most efficient if you're planning to invite more than six people.

A written invitation can also be helpful for

your guests. It gives them the opportunity to come up with an excuse (if they don't feel like donating to your candidate). They have a hardcopy reminder that they need to get back to you by a certain date. They can clip the invitation to the calendar so they're certain they have your address—perhaps the map you sent them—and the correct day and time.

The style of a written invitation can indicate what kind of party it's going to be. If it's a card-store invitation with a clown holding a balloon that says, "It's a party," he knows to get his jeans out of the dryer before they get too wrinkled. An engraved invitation implies something else altogether.

A written invitation allows you to request an RSVP. I suggest you specify a "by" date, which would leave you grace time to call the nonresponders to check their status. You *will* have nonresponders—everyone in the etiquette business reports that they are rampant. Don't take it personally; it happens to everyone. Just leave yourself time to call them.

When you get your replies, remember to ask about food allergies so you can adapt your menu, if necessary. But unless you want to make dinner to your guests' orders, it's best not to inquire about preferences and aversions. (See The Main Course, page 104, for more on this.)

Type of Service
ONCE YOU'VE DECIDED WHAT kind of party it will be, you'll know what kind of dishware you'll be using—for example, plastic or china—and whether you'll need to hire help in the kitchen, at the table, or for parking cars. (Remember, even before the most informal, impromptu backyard barbecue, clean your bathrooms and scrub down any surface where food will be prepared or served.) Again, everything you do ought to be done with the comfort of your guests in mind. If you know you won't be able to serve, clear, and clean all of the plates involved without depriving your guests of your company all evening or making them wait forever between courses, you should consider hiring someone to help you. If hiring help would exceed your budget, you might ask one of your friends to cohost with you, sharing the chores before, during, and after the event.

In certain situations, you may find yourself with an "accidental formality." For instance, if you know that your guests will have trouble finding a place nearby to park, you should consider hiring valets to make arrival and departure more convenient for them. What might seem like an affectation would actually be a thoughtful service. Or you might have come into an exquisite set of china. If you tend to entertain informally, but want to use those plates, go ahead and sling your hash onto them. You'll be happier adapting the china to your party style than waiting to work up the energy and inspiration for an uncharacteristically formal affair.

Because I love to talk to friends and to hear the conversation that goes on between them, and because I have an average-sized dining room, I prefer the six- or eight-person dinner party. My dinner table can hold eight comfortably, so once everyone sits, they stay, and conversation is uninterrupted. They can all talk to each other or break off into groups. It's fun for me to match three couples for interests and backgrounds, either similar or complementary.

For a sit-down dinner, six to ten is an ideal number. Of course you've seen movies of Victorian parties where long tables are set up in lavish dining rooms seating twenty, thirty, or forty people. My humble advice is don't try this at home without professional help. If you are the sort of host who can handle that kind of thing on your own, you have my respect. But this book is meant for those with more modest aspirations and abilities.

There are several options for serving six to ten people at the dinner table. You can plate all the food elsewhere and bring it to the table. You can have some food at the table ready to pass and serve some from your seat or the kitchen. You can pass food family style, you can have a buffet with everyone bringing their filled plates back to the table, or any combination that's comfortable for you.

To serve family-style, have your guests pass serving dishes at the table. If that's the style you use, you may want to preplate the first course and have it waiting at the table for your guests when they arrive (it's probably most convenient to serve a cold or room-temperature first course in that case). When you serve family style, make sure there's enough room to set dishes on the table when the guests are done passing and that there's a generous amount of food. You don't want the person sitting nearest the bowl of mashed potatoes to be the only one to get seconds. Also, if you have ten or twelve people at the table, consider having two of each serving dish (two butter plates, bread baskets, salad bowls, and so on) so there's no inordinate waiting while bowls make the circuitous trip around the table. As the first round of eating progresses, but before anyone is actually through, refill the serving dishes with hot food.

If all service takes place from the kitchen to the dining room, arrange with your spouse, your child, or a friend to help you clear (sometimes clearing can be a job of honor, but you have to know the situation pretty well). It's wise to have this worked out ahead of time. That way you can avoid the melee of having everyone jump up and offer to help you. Objecting politely but firmly is easier if you have a plan.

The number of courses you serve depends ultimately on how much energy you have to shop, cook, serve, and clean up. For eight people I usually serve four courses: starter, entrée, salad, and dessert, with bread passed at the table. Sometimes I serve appetizer, then entrée, with salad and bread passed at the table, and salad to be placed on the dinner plate or a separate salad plate (there's rarely room at my table for a separate plate *and* bread plate).

I prefer to avoid serving a lot of food before dinner. First, before-dinner hors d'oeuvres are usually labor-intensive and I usually have my hands full trying to get dinner ready. Second, I've usually gone to a lot of trouble to plan and make dinner, and I prefer that people be hungry when they eat it. It's my experience that appetizers are generally as filling and rich as dessert. I see it as my obligation to get dinner on the table soon after the guests arrive (20 minutes or so) so they do not consume so much food or alcohol that they won't be able to enjoy their meal.

Buffets

A BUFFET HAS MANY ADVANTAGES, not the least of which is dividing the service responsibility equally among the guests rather than relying on the host. Your guests can serve themselves the exact portions they want. A buffet might be a more practical service method if (1) your table space is limited or (2) you're serving a whole lot of people. But it's not inappropriate for smaller parties. If you choose buffet service, remember:

1. Plates belong at the beginning of the table.

2. Your guests will have a plate in one hand, so they have only one free hand to serve themselves. Make the food easy to serve with one hand. Serving oneself a tossed salad is easy with tongs, but not with a conventional salad fork and spoon. Bowls of pasta salad should be made with chunky noodles rather than long stringy ones (again, tongs are useful with long noodles, but service is still time-consuming).

3. Put the napkins, silverware, and glasses at the end of the line so the guests don't have to juggle or butt in line to retrieve these items after serving themselves. You may choose to put glasses and drink options somewhere else—something as simple as a tea cart or side table—to ease crowding and bottlenecks.

4. If you are serving a large number of people for the space, plan two identical buffet lines, perhaps starting at the far right and far left and working toward the center, or set up in two parts of your serving space. Obviously for this option you will need two serving platters of each dish. Or consider serving various foods at various locations in your party space, what caterers call "stations," so that three different salads are here, shrimp and oysters are over there, and huge fruit and vegetable platters are in the corner.

5. Placing the buffet table near the kitchen allows for easier service and replenishing for you and less distracton for your guests.

6. You guests will appreciate having a place to set their drinks and plates. Sometimes buffet service leads guests back to a single dining room table, but if your guests will be seated all over the house or apartment, try to provide enough surfaces that they can rest their dishes on. Rent or borrow a few small tables, clear off coffee tables, and so on. Even if the plates can balance on knees, you and your guests will both appreciate not having to set drinks on the floor.

Planning a Menu

SOME SIMPLE MEAL PLANNING GUIDELINES:

1. Avoid similarity between courses. A custardy quiche shouldn't be followed by a creamy terrine shouldn't be followed by ice cream. Potato soup shouldn't be followed by turnip gratin. Sliced tomatoes shouldn't be followed by pasta with tomato sauce.

2. Vary the textures, tastes, colors, and shapes. If brunch centers on an eggy, cheesy main dish, think about green, sweet, tart, and fresh flavors to round it out (a fresh green salad, fruit salad, marinated asparagus, sliced tomatoes, and the like).

Also . . .

Think about what's in season. If you know the season of excellent homegrown tomatoes, you can confidently offer a delicious salad. Just slice, season, and serve. If you try that with a tomato in

January, you and your guests will be disappointed.

In the spring you would think about mint and sorrel, asparagus and peas, strawberries and rhubarb, lettuce, field greens, early onions, radishes and potatoes. You may have leeks, and the citrus and more tropical fruits and might still be good. Look for artichokes and fresh cheeses. It's also the season when chicken start laying and more fisherman venture out for longer days.

Early summer gardens yield beans and beets, squash and squash blossoms, thyme and oregano, and early raspberries. Warmer weather and longer days yield blackberries, then blueberries, peaches, corn, tomatoes, cucumbers, and greens. Fall and winter bring you hard-shelled squashes, root vegetables that store and hold well (sweet potatoes, turnips, onions, and so on), and some winter greens that grow even under snow, like kale and chard. Dried fruits and mushrooms add flavor to winter meals.

There's always overlap, of course, and there's no reason you can't use some foods that are out of season (I always have bell peppers in the hydrator drawer and apples are a year-round vegetable at my house). But it's fashionable and economical to let the season guide what you serve.

A salad, for instance, will be something quite different in the spring than in midsummer. Tossed salads of mixed greens, lettuces, and early garden vegetables are appropriate for spring. So is marinated asparagus. As the season gets later, you'd marinate green beans or cucumbers. Then you'd slice tomatoes, or make a corn, black bean, and red onion salad with loads of fresh herbs. When cold weather sets in, grilled greens, lightly dressed with vinaigrette and crumbled ricotta salata cheese, would taste great.

Cold weather and short days seem to require long-simmered stews of root vegetables, gratins of beans, pilafs of grains, and dried fruits. Long, warm summer days seem more appropriate for tomatoes tossed with fresh herbs, grilled corn on the cob, and peach cobbler.

If you have a farmers' market nearby, shopping there will inform you what's locally grown and what's in season. In addition, you might find new and unusual foods there (broccoli rabe? a purple-striped heirloom tomato?) that will delight your guests. If you're shopping at a supermarket, go by your instinct and by the prices. In the summer they practically give away bell peppers, while in February they cost several dollars a pound. Also, talk to the farmers, who know growing seasons intimately and often have great cooking tips.

Another rule for planning menus: Resist your impulse to prepare something new when entertaining. People avidly interested in cooking will ignore this rule. For them, the reason for the party is to cook something new. Guests provide an excuse for innovation.

But besides the pesky little problem that a dish you've never practiced might fail abysmally, there's one other problem with new dishes: They require concentration.

You may concentrate best at a quiet times with few other pressures—not in the throes of orchestrating an event that requires cleaning, cooking, and conjuring all the social graces. If I'm preparing a dish in the kitchen surrounded by good friends who are quizzing me about the cheese they are tasting, looking for the tonic, asking me how my children are, it's difficult for me to read and follow a recipe. Better that I've done this risotto a dozen times. If you're a person who plans ahead and wants to attempt that fancy lasagna, do so with a Plan B in mind that can be prepared at the last minute if things don't work out (omelets?).

When planning what food to serve, consider your temperament. Would you be stumped by timing all dishes to arrive at the table at the same time? Do you need to plan most or all of their dinner to avoid last-minute cooking—roasted vegetables, a terrine, or a sauce easily reheated that can be poured over rice or noodles as soon as they're done?

Some hosts, particularly those who have had experience throwing parties, can manage to serve foods that require last-minute preparation, choosing dishes that get prepared on top of the stove or baked just before serving. Even if you're able to do this, make sure you reread each recipe as you go along, taking special note of those last-minute additions, in case you get distracted as the guests arrive and settle in. All in all, I recommend you either do everything in advance, or pace yourself so you have much of the meal prepared and the rest ready for the oven or stove.

If you are accustomed to cooking with meat, learning to cook with little or none may be a challenge at first. Meat provides a lot of flavor, and in its absence you have to learn how to compensate with herbs, spices, grains, legumes, and fresh produce. But with a little practice, substantial vegetarian dishes such as various types of risotto—which may seem daunting at first glance—will become second nature to you and may become "house specials" that you will prepare even on short notice time and again. (See A First Course, page 54.)

Finally, don't feel as if you're cheating your guests by serving something simple. If you know you can make a good roast chicken or chili with beans, serve it—you will be more confident and more likely to put your guests at ease than if you were to try to offer something fancier to impress them.

If You Make a Mistake

THE BEST CHEFS IN THE WORLD may not be those who cook best, but those who recover best.

Mistakes happen. A nation of aspiring home cooks watched Julia Child week after week as she made little and large mistakes, including dropping dinner on the floor. Pick it up, dust it off, and don't tell your guests, she admonished.

Some disasters are really opportunities for a new dish. The cake that's cracked gets scooped into wineglasses and slathered with whipped cream. The too-peppery broth becomes "moules au poivre," served over plain rice. Overcooked vegetables get topped with sauce or blended into a puree. Lentil soup that ends up too thick just needs more broth, or you can bill it as lentil stew.

A quick stand-in is another strategy. One of my early attempts in a gourmet group was a dessert assignment. I went to a lot of trouble and spent a day on an elaborate baked dessert, only to burn it at nearly the last minute. I was panicky. I had some pears at home and part of a bottle of wine. I sweetened the wine with sugar and simmered the pears in it. While they cooked, I melted chocolate chips in some cream. We had poached pears in chocolate sauce. For years it was my signature dish and people requested it. At a fifteen-person brunch, the brioche I had spent hours on never cooked through. It could have been hours, people were arriving, I had no breakfast bread. So I made biscuits with the flour, butter, and milk I always have. (See On Reserve, page 333.)

Keep ice cream on hand in case your dessert fails. It becomes fancier with a sprinkle of toasted nuts and a drizzle of liqueur—any liqueur, from Drambuie to Kahlúa.

If your dish is too sweet, salty, bitter, or sour, the rule of thumb is to add ingredients that will engage the other taste buds. If the dish is too bitter, add sweet (sugar) and sour (lemon juice or vinegar) to it. If it's too sweet, add sour (lemon juice or vinegar) and salt. Pepper will also distract the palate.

If a soup or stew is too salty, add a quartered potato, cook it, and remove it; it will absorb some of the salt. Or add more bland ingredients (like potatoes, bulgur, rice, or noodles). Add sweet ingredients like onions, tomatoes, or carrots. If the dish is too spicy hot, dilute it with yogurt or sour cream, add bland foods, or use the food as condiment, increasing the proportions of cooler and blander parts of the menu.

If you've burned the soup or chili, do not stir or scrape the bottom of the pan. Pour what you can into another receptacle and taste it. Chances are the burned flavor stayed with the burned food.

Finally, even if they are at fault for selling you bad stuff, don't blame your fishmonger, butcher, or green grocer for an inedible meal. It's easier on your guests if you are gracious rather than irate. Either offer to take everyone out (call a reliable restaurant first to make sure they can take you) or order in from a place that you trust.

Shopping

MARKETING CAN BE THE MOST time-consuming chore involved in giving a party. It helps to have a well-organized list. The list might be several lists: for example, one for the liquor store, another for a specialty store, another for a farmers' market, and one for a supermarket.

List everything called for in your recipes. Then walk around your kitchen or glance through your pantry, and cross off everything you already have. Assemble the remaining items by place of purchase.

Complete your list by adding other essential items, ice, for instance, cream if you're serving coffee or for dessert, and special coffee or tea if appropriate. Remember garnishes—fresh herbs, bread for croutons, orange peel for drinks or coffee, and the like. It helps to picture each course, mentally walking through how the pastry will proceed so you can anticipate what food items will be necessary.

Entertaining gives you a chance to check out the little specialty stores that you'd never get to otherwise. Fresh fish is too expensive to buy all the time, and the quality of the fish in the supermarket may not be great. But when you're having company, you can head to the fish market to splurge on fresh mussels, large shrimp, or sea bass. Farmers' markets should have the best-quality seasonal produce. Specialty produce markets will bring you the best from elsewhere in the country and the world, fabulous mustards, excellent olive oils, and if you're lucky, anchovies preserved in salt. Draw up your initial shopping list several days, or even one week, before the party. See more specific suggestions on page 327.

Setting the Table

RULE NUMBER 1: Do everything you possibly can no later than the night before.

That includes cleaning and/or polishing silverware, glassware, and other ware that is used infrequently. If you use only a few wineglasses on a regular basis, the others can get pretty dusty. They need to be washed before they're used, as do all infrequently used dishes.

Rule number 2: Take rule number 1 seriously.

Not only will you get much of the tedious work out of the way, it gives you time to respond to what should remain a minor crisis: You discover you're running low on no-drip candles. You discover a big stain on the napkins you were going to use. You realize the Asian casserole dish has a big crack in it. Setting the table ahead of time allows you to predict glitches (all the serving plates won't fit on the table if you use separate salad plates) and allows you to figure out a solution. At the last minute, such a glitch is an emergency. The day before, it's all part of planning.

Rule number 3: The more formal the meal, the more dishes it will include. A slightly formal meal will start with an appetizer plate set on top of a larger plate, then both are taken away and the next course is served.

Consider the number of dishes you want to use, given your time and ability to serve and clean up. Assess what you own and what you can borrow. Consider how much room you have on the table. All this information will guide you to your table setting. It's possible to reuse plates at different courses during dinner, but you have to make a plan for washing. For instance, you can reuse the appetizer plates for dessert, but you'll need to make sure you can build in time to wash. That's easy if you're dispatching folks to the living room for dessert and they're busy serving themselves coffee from a tray you set up before dinner even started.

Another option: Be unconventional. Use stemmed glassware (when appropriate) to serve dessert instead of the normal dessert plate. You can't do that with layer cake perhaps, but it will do for pudding cake.

When setting a table, flatware belongs about an inch above the edge of the table with forks on the left, knives and spoons on the right. The silverware is placed in the order that it will be used, going from the outside in. That is, the first-course fork will be the farthest left of the forks. Three is the cutoff for pieces of silverware on each side of the plate. After that, you need to lay pieces across the top of the plate (as with dessert) or replenish the silverware with each new course.

Napkins go in the center of the plate or, if there's an appetizer there, to the left of or under the forks.

Basically, knives, spoons, and drinkware go to the right; everything else goes to the left. If you have butter plates and salad plates, they are placed to the left of the main dinner plate. The water glass is at the tip of the dinner knife and auxiliary glasses are staggered down toward the right from there. Again, too many glasses looks more ostentatious than formal. Setting a table, like all manners of etiquette, is supposed to make life easy on the guest. Three glasses is enough— perhaps more than enough: water, then red wine (bulbous), then white wine (more narrow and tulip shaped). Always serve water, keeping an eye out for those who need refills.

About matching dinnerware: You can, but you don't have to. It's rare for anyone to have an absolutely complete set of anything.

Warming or chilling plates is an elegant and thoughtful thing to do, and it becomes even more important when the weather and the food are opposite temperatures. That is, if you're serving salad on a sweltering summer day, put the salad plates in the freezer several hours before using. If you're serving a hot soup on a cold day, warm the bowls before you add the soup.

Take care not to pour hot drinks into freezing cold cups; they may crack. You can fill them with hot water and let them sit for a few minutes prior to filling. Plates and bowls that need warming can be put in a low (180°F.) oven for a few minutes, or you may want to purchase a plate warmer that's made for the purpose. Plates shouldn't be hot to the touch when they come to the table, but warming or chilling the serving dish can extend the time your food stays at an appetizing temperature.

Whether you use placemats or tablecloths depends on what you like and own. Placemats are generally more informal; they seem to work better when there's plenty of room around them. If you've crammed ten people at a table that normally seats eight, you'll find serving platters and glasses sitting partly on, partly off the placemats distracting and sometimes a little hazardous. Also, if you have a wooden table and plan to use lots of glassware, a table pad and tablecloth will best protect the wood. For more on tableware, see page 343.

Centerpieces

CENTERPIECES ARE OPTIONAL.

If you have a small table and it's crowded with tableware, forget about it. If there's room, consider a cluster of votive candles, some pretty wooden fruit, a platter of glass ornaments, or a shallow dish of floating blossoms. Don't choose anything that forces guests to crane their necks or juggle platters.

It's nice to have a centerpiece that reflects your taste and sparks conversation. If you collect primitive art, use one of those treasures on the table. You might have some brightly painted and shellacked paper fruit pieces from some tropical island you visited.

If you decide to go with flowers, you may do best with fresh, seasonal, perhaps locally grown greenery and blossoms. It's nice and homey to use flowers from your garden. But if you don't garden, or if it's the dead of winter, establish a good relationship with a local florist who shares your taste and your environmental concerns.

You can make your centerpiece more personal by using your favorite basket or antique soup tureen to hold the flower arrangement. If you're using a florist, take the tureen with you when you place your order. Discuss the flower possibilities with the florist and keep your budget in mind. If you're strapped for funds, request *lots* of greenery, a few stunning blossoms, and then a fill with a few wildflowers, lilies, or less expensive seasonal items.

Beverages

SETTING UP A BAR CAN BE SIMPLE. Your bar is nothing more than a few hard liquors and some supermarket-level mixers such as soda, tonic, tomato juice, and/or soft drinks.

It is totally acceptable (and preferable if you're pressed for time) to set up a tray with a dark liquor (bourbon or scotch), a clear liquor (gin or vodka), a few mixers, and some lemon and/or lime slices. You don't need a degree in mixology—whoever wants one can make his or her own.

You can go one more step and provide vermouth (for martini drinkers). A larger bar would contain both gin and vodka, both scotch and bourbon, and perhaps rum and tequila for good measure.

Set up this bar area—or more than one if the party is large—away from the food to ease crowding. And if the party is large and people are serving themselves, put beer in a separate place from the drinks, maybe in a big bucket with ice.

If you want to offer more complicated drinks, you can hire a bartender or consult a bartending manual to master them yourself.

Another option is to provide one type of mixed drink. If you're having a Mexican dinner, you might want to start guests off with some homemade margaritas. If you're serving brunch, you may want to provide Bloody Marys and mimosas (orange juice and sparkling wine). If it's a picnic or light hors d'oeuvres, you might consider a wine punch or mulled cider (cider heated with cinnamon sticks and a pinch of cloves and/or nutmeg). If you're in a retro cocktail mood, premix martinis in a clear glass pitcher and refrigerate until serving. If you do serve martinis, renting or borrowing martini glasses will add a festive flair. (Don't say you weren't warned . . . If you're serving martinis, plan dinner to be ready a little before the end of the first round of drinks.)

Whatever you choose, do yourself, your property, and your guests a favor by limiting the time to drink hard liquor. That is, it may be hospitable to provide your guests a libation while everyone arrives and you get organized in the kitchen. It is not hospitable to have normal drinkers indulging in their third martini by the time dinner is served.

In that same spirit, it is hospitable to provide easy access to nonalcoholic beverages. They should be front and center, not confined to your refrigerator. Make sure your guests can see they have an alternative to getting bombed.

No extra effort is required; a small selection of sodas is fine. Provide lemon and lime wedges and the same snazzy glassware you offer for the hard stuff.

WINE

A good wine can be an integral part of your meal, bringing as much pleasure as the food itself. But there are so many choices and so many ways to go wrong, it seems. How do you decide what to drink with what you're serving?

To an extent, wine is like art. You don't have to know anything about it to know what you like. You buy what you like in a price range you can afford. As wine becomes more interesting to you, you may become more curious, more knowledgeable, and more appreciative of the many distinct qualities of a range of wines.

Remember these things when setting out to shop for wine:

1. One half bottle for each person is a generous portion of wine.
2. There's plenty of really good cheap wine; there is plenty of inexpensive wine that will suit your purpose, that is, wine that both you and your guests will enjoy.

   What is inexpensive wine? At this point at the end of the twentieth century, wine drinkers can expect a lifetime of choices of $10 or less. Plenty sell for $6 or $7.
3. Few people know tons more about wine than you do. Period. If you happen to have invited a wine-knowledgeable person to your home, chances are she'll have enough courtesy not to ridicule your choices. An inexpensive Spanish Rioja will be just as interesting to her as it is to you.
4. Drinking wine is fun and should remain fun.

Even a bad wine is a good education, so there's no bad wine-drinking experience, as long as you have a certifiably drinkable wine on hand to replace the bad bottle. This is an argument for finding one wine you really like and keeping several bottles on hand just in case a new kind should fail you.

There are certain rules that apply to matching wine with food. Be advised that rules for wine seem to be broken the minute they're made.

1. You may have heard of white wine with white food and red wine with red food. So what color is chicken cacciatore? White wine would go with the chicken but red wine would go with the garlicky tomato sauce. *Match the wine to the sauce or seasoning*, not what's underneath.
2. Match prices and/or integrity. If you've spent a lot of money on sushi-quality tuna, it's best to buy wine that doesn't have a screw cap. If you're having a get-together for your favorite political candidate, save the prize-winning Chianti for a more intimate affair.
3. Match robust wines to strong-flavored foods. Let's go back to the chicken cacciatore example. Garlicky tomato sauce is complemented by a bold wine—red or white. Pinot noir and salmon are a justly famous team. Assertive salmon holds its own next to a medium-bodied red wine.
4. Spicy foods call for bold, fruity, slightly sweet wines, such as Gewürztraminer or Riesling Spätlese.
5. Finally, there is no single "right" wine for your dinner. (For basic ideas, see Menus and Meal-Planning Tips, page 326.)

Ask My Expert

If you enjoy wine but find that your eyes glaze over whenever you try to get yourself to learn a thing or two about it, then the best thing you can do to ensure a steady flow of good wine to your table is to find an excellent wine merchant.

Arriving at Nicholas Roberts in Darien after a three-year search for a reliable wine merchant was like winning a lottery that pays handsomely on demand. Nicholas Troilo, proprietor, manager, and purveyor, is a caterer, too. His record recommending wines to us for our meals is flawless . . . meaning the wines add fresh flavors that complement and extend the seasonings in the food. (A flawed selection would be a wine that jars you away from the food and makes for a rough transition from plate to glass to plate again.) Here's how, he says, you can tell a good wine shop.

Check the Window Display

- There should be a theme to indicate the merchant's current interest (for example, bottles of various Italian wines with a map of the region where they're made). Only a few bottles should be displayed, and they should not be offered for sale, since the exposure to light and heat will surely damage the wine.
- If you pass the shop often, check to see that the display changes frequently, indicating that the merchant is actively choosing among new wines and has an ongoing interest in offering good stock.
- Ask for help. A good wine shop will have staff who can discuss the merchandise clearly with anyone, even those who know nothing about wine. To get the most from good staff,

describe the meal you're having so they can recommend a wine, or several, to complement the food. Good purveyors will explain their recommendations, helping you to understand the principles involved in matching food and wine. In fact, the best wine merchants are educators, offering seminars and wine-tasting events where you can learn how to distinguish different wines. You ought to feel that the merchant is intent on taking the mystique out of the process of choosing wine rather than holding you in thrall.

- The staff should know all of the wines in stock. Even if they haven't tasted each wine, they should be able to tell you why they're carrying it. Good reasons include the reputation of the wine maker, critical acclaim for the wine, and a vineyard's consistent history of good wine.
- Check how the wine is stored. The cork must be touching the wine to stay moist. Dry corks let air into the bottle where it spoils the wine, so you want to see bottles lying on their sides or well tilted.
- Check that chilled wines are not kept too cold, but just below the proper temperature for serving, ordinarily just below room temperature (65 to 68°F.)
- Good wine sellers are purveyors, not just merchants. Their shops may look sparse compared with other less conscientious wine stores, but this may indicate a proper attention to breadth of inventory rather than depth. By ordering a small amount of a broad variety of wine, the purveyor can always offer you something interesting and fresh (which is half the fun—author's note).

Very Basic Wine Basics

WINES ARE MADE FROM GRAPES. Duh. Sometimes wine makers mix a whole bunch of different grapes, sometimes they put the juice of just one grape—or mostly one grape—into a bottle. That's called a varietal. In the United States and many other countries, wine makers label their bottles by the primary juice in the bottle. Cabernet sauvignon, merlot, pinot noir, and zinfandel are all varietal names of popular American red wines.

But not all good wines are varietal wines. Châteauneuf-du-Pape wines are made near the Avignon region in France and can be a variety of combinations of thirteen different grapes. Some wines are described by the area where they are produced. Rioja wines, both red and white, come from the Rioja area of Spain. Burgundies come from Burgundy, though white Burgundies are made with Chardonnay grapes and red Burgundies are made with pinot noir grapes.

Confused?

Well, it is confusing. But once you start learning a little, you may find that you're not as concerned about what you don't know and more excited about what's just ahead of you.

If you're new and want to start cheap, look for wines from Chile, Spain, South Africa, and Australia. In fact, all of these countries (and others) export high-quality wines that even knowledgeable wine drinkers haven't tasted.

For most Almost Vegetarian cooking, you'll probably find that whites and medium-bodied reds are most appropriate. But dishes with garlic and capers and Mediterranean black olives can take more robust reds such as zinfandel.

It's completely acceptable to start with a white wine and follow with a red, or to start with a less intense red like Beaujolais and move toward a more robust red like Côtes du Rhône. Occasionally, I enjoy matching a wine with each course and plan a dinner around multiple pairings, starting with a dry Champagne, moving to a bolder white, then a medium red, then a dessert wine.

It is my well-considered opinion that Champagne is underused in our culture, reserved for celebrations. We offer it often as an ice-breaker. Genuine Champagne comes from the Champagne region in northern France, but the term is used to describe many sparkling wines, both good and virtually undrinkable. These days, good sparkling wine comes from all over the world and good sparkling wine is sold inexpensively. Again, Spain offers good value. Spanish sparkling wines are called cavas. Try Codorniu or Sumarroca brands. In the United States, check my favorite, Gloria Ferrar, as well as Sharffenberger. Less expensive French Champagnes include Moët et Chandon and Pol Roger. One brand name—say, Moët et Chandon—will have a wide range of selections and prices, so check what you're buying and ask the advice of your wine purveyor.

After-dinner wines are (finally!) catching on in this country. Wines sold as dessert wines are usually very sweet and complement desserts that aren't too saccharine, such as bitter chocolate or fruit-based things. Château d'Yquem Sauternes (from Bordeux) is popular and pricey (and there are some very expensive German sauternes, too). Check out dessert wines from California and Australia, with guidance from your purveyor.

SERVE CHEESE

On the grand scale of human accomplishments, the making of cheese falls somewhere between harnessing electricity and landing men on the moon. As an art, it rivals literature, music, and what you find in museums, which feed merely the soul.

Lots has happened to American-made cheese in the years since Velveeta joined the lineup in the dairy case at your supermarket. Much of it hasn't been good. But much of it has been sublime.

Cheese enthusiasts have proliferated. People travel abroad and come back with interest, knowledge, and commitment. Cheese shops opened, faltered, and got a second wind. Americans started making cheese as good as or better than the stuff imported from Europe. Chefs became interested and established cheese courses or plates in their restaurants. Now we can get great cheese.

Serve cheese at breakfast, lunch, dinner, snack time, and as a separate course at dinner. It should be at room temperature when it is served. Hard cheeses should be left wrapped until just before you serve them; soft cheeses should be unwrapped when you take them from the fridge.

Some Italians serve cheese just prior to dinner and the French just after. Fancy big-city American restaurants tend to mimic the French, and include a cheese course in their menu after the entrée and salad but before dessert.

Serve cheese wherever and whenever you choose, but if you would like to serve it after an almost vegetarian meal, plan the meal so it's not overdoing a type of cheese. For example, if your dinner includes a dish made with ricotta, then serve aged or blue cheeses after dinner. If your salad includes a grilled fresh goat cheese or blue cheese, serve a washed rind cheese after dinner.

If guests are helping themselves to cheese before dinner, make sure each type of cheese is on a plate or cutting board of its own, or widely separated on a large platter or board from a second or third cheese. (Check the supermarket for inexpensive boards you can use as cheese display and cutting boards.) Each cheese should have its own sturdy knife for cutting, too. If the cheese is especially hard or brittle, you should probably precut or shave the slices with a cheese shaver for your company.

If you plan to serve the cheese as the first course of the meal, buy a good one (see page 16) and have it preplated and at the table when guests sit down. You may want to share what you know about its origins and qualities so your guests can enjoy the particulars as much as you do.

Excellent cheese may be the focus of an hors d'oeuvres gathering. Buttery ripe pears are great with salty hard cheeses; crisp, tart apples go well with blues and semisoft cheeses. If you're fixing a tasting plate, consider good-quality olives (imported, brined, or flavored with herbs and/or hot peppers), or even a fruit paste such as quince or guava paste (available in Caribbean markets). If cheese is a substantial part of a meal, serve about $3\frac{1}{2}$ ounces to each person (approximately 1 ounce of 3 cheeses); put them on individual plates separated by the accoutrements (various olives, pear slices, a vegetable terrine).

Finding good cheese is a little more difficult than finding good wine. You don't have to know

Ask My Expert

Ken Skovron is the proprietor and manager of Darien Cheese & Fine Food, a pocket of paradise improbably located in a shopping plaza in lower Fairfield County, Connecticut. Ken, who started his apprenticeship in high school, bought an indifferent cheese store over a decade ago and built it into a business where passion rules. It is a model shop, and to describe it is to tell you what to look for when you're searching for a place to buy cheese.

- Aroma and cleanliness: As you walk in the door, the aroma should transport you to a universe with cheese at its center. The premises should be spotless, and the lighting and display cases should let you scrutinize the merchandise easily.

- Enthusiastic, knowledgeable, informative staff: Selling cheese is not like peddling greeting cards. Some customers may know what they want, ask for it, and leave. But most of us appreciate suggestions and guidance. In the best cheese shops, each clerk knows a good deal about the merchandise— where it comes from, what kind of milk it contains, what type of fermentation was involved, how to serve it, and how to store it. You should have the feeling there is a reason that each cheese is in that shop—that there's nothing haphazard or perfunctory about the selection. The staff should also be able to help you choose cheeses that complement each other, or that go well with a particular wine or type of food. Moreover, there is a science to handling and maintaining cheese, and watching how they cut, wrap, store, and display, you should feel confident they've mastered it.

- You should be offered a sample of everything you consider buying and everything suggested to you. Sampling not only lets you know whether you like the flavor and texture of the cheese, but assures you that it's still fresh. You should feel that they really want you to love it. The point is that people who want you to enjoy the cheese will do their best to carry cheeses that are enjoyable and do their best to maintain them.

- The staff should be willing to say "no." If you have your heart set on Vacherin, for example, but they know it's not ripe, they should tell you when they expect it to be ready, and either send you away until then or offer you a taste of an alternative, such as Abondance. They should care enough to make sure you get only the best, even if it means disappointing you once in a while.

- All cheese should be cut to order. If you want grated cheese, it should be grated and bagged in your presence. As soon as cheese is cut and exposed to air, it begins to lose flavor, which is why the wrapped pieces of cheese at even the fancier supermarkets never rival what you get from a dedicated cheese merchant.

anything about cheese to choose a good one. But you should buy your cheese from someone who does, and who takes pride and pleasure in it.

Only genuine enthusiasts will do the work it takes to run a good cheese shop, surely among the most labor-intensive retail operations. And only genuine enthusiasts will care so much about cheese they'll want to share that pleasure with you by making sure you get the best.

As a rule, cheese is best served with plain crackers or bread. Naturally, there are exceptions. A cheddar on sesame seed crackers or a great semisoft cheese with a musky-flavored olive bread could be delicious, but avoid those herb-flavored crackers you find in the supermarket—the herbs tend to be dried out and musty and detract from the flavor of the cheese.

Your cheese selection and purchase depends on both how and where you plan to serve it and what's available. If cheese is part of a four- or five-course meal, you may need only little bites presented on a plate with a slice of fruit. The magic number of cheeses is three, but that's a little arbitrary. Your taste buds might not keep up with more than that, and it's certainly legitimate to offer less. If you've found an incredibly wonderful English Stilton and know where to get a great Gouda, don't feel compelled to fill out the cheese plate or tray with a grocery store Brie that is as French as a Ford Taurus. The two great cheeses will stand well on their own.

Aim for a complementary selection. That is, something creamy, something sharp and hard, something blue. Or you can do a cow, a goat, and a sheep cheese, or all cheeses from Spain, or all blues—you get the picture.

Be sure to check out domestic cheeses, too. From Alabama and South Carolina to Maine, Minnesota, and the West Coast, American cheesemakers are making cow, goat, and sheep milk cheeses of excellent quality. Some of them are inspired by European cheeses, such as Capriole's Banon (wrapped in brandy-soaked chestnut leaves), made in Indiana, and the Hollow Road Farm's Hudson Valley Camembert from New York. Other cheeses are all-American in their style—Peluso Cheese's Teleme and Vella Cheese Company's dry Jack come from California.

You can find American cheeses made from unpasteurized milk, cheeses made with organic ingredients, cheeses made with vegetable rennet (for the strict vegetarians in your crowd), and on and on. A superb resource for American cheeses (and cheeses of the world) is Steve Jenkins's *Cheese Primer* (New York: Workman Publishing, 1996), or you can call or write the American Cheese Society at 414-728-4458 (fax: 414-728-1658); the address is W7702 County Road X, Darien, Wisconsin 53114.

Hard cheeses keep best. Aging develops their flavor and lowers their moisture, so they're less vulnerable to spoilage or mold. These include Parmesan, Romano, Asiago, Gouda, cheddar, and Gruyère. If you're serving something tomorrow night, go for creamy fresh cheeses.

Prices of cheese don't seem to be as arbitrarily set as prices of wine. Price reflects, first, the cost to the cheesemaker. Some cheesemakers work alone or have small staffs, and must support themselves on the cheese sales. Then supply and demand kicks in. If it's a delicious cheese that everybody wants and it's traveling from Somerset, England, to Dallas, it's likely to cost more than your average supermarket Colby. If you love flavorful cheese, you'll spring for it.

Generally, the higher-priced cheeses ought to be served on their own, not in recipes. Still, if you buy too much English Chaucer or Welsh Llangloffan, go ahead and add it to bean burritos or a pasta dish. A great, strong-flavored cheese goes a long way in an otherwise mundane main course. Even though you've paid a lot for it, you'd use less than a milder supermarket version of the same cheese.

Storing

YOU MUST ALLOW CHEESE TO BREATHE. Wrap the cheese in porous paper; impermeable paper tends to collect stinky gases and pools liquid that will evaporate if allowed to. Cheese experts often but not always have special porous wrapping paper. After I get my cheese home, I usually wrap it in wax paper and then put it in a zipper-style plastic bag to let air circulate around it.

If you allow cheese to breathe and age, it might change for the better, or at least turn into a different cheese. A fresh goat cheese that starts out creamy might just get smelly, but a slightly aged goat cheese with a bloomed rind might go from mild and creamy the first few days and age to a more flinty, chalky texture with a little stronger flavor, and still be delicious, just different.

In European shops, these changes might be exploited. That is, a cheese seller would know to point out the freshest, youngest cheese to you when you enter the shop and, a few weeks later, to show you the same cheese in its aged form. As a beginning cheese buyer, nobody expects you to know which cheeses age into something and which cheeses just get nasty. I only mention it to suggest that there's often no absolute time that a cheese is good or bad.

Cheeses naturally fall into categories. Sometimes they naturally fall into more than one category. Here are some basic categories.

Fresh cheeses are cheeses such as ricotta and fresh

HOW DO THEY DO THAT?

You've seen those photos—the vegetable soups with potatoes, carrots, and two kinds of squash bobbing picturesquely on the surface. Or that exquisite two-toned fish bisque with the caviar floating artfully on top. Before you prepare to reproduce such beauties, think about it. Think about the first thing you learned in physics. Now consider what happens when you put potatoes into broth. And what, short of pumping air into it, could compel caviar to float?

Food stylists work very hard to make dishes look a way that no amount of effort from you could match. They have a terrific advantage, however; they can work with marbles and paste and partially cooked foods (see Note) while you're stuck with what's edible.

In other words, don't believe your eyes. Chances are you will not get results that look exactly like the photo by merely following the recipe. Since you can't predict how it will look, be prepared to improvise your presentation.

NOTE: Clear marbles prop up the vegetables and other submersibles to make them appear to float on soup. Paste not only holds garnishes in place, it makes lovely-looking icing, whipped cream, and such. And undercooked rice, each grain much more distinct than when fully cooked, is used to photograph as ready to eat.

chèvre that are white, creamy, and fairly bland. Bland is not pejorative here. Sometimes a disc of neutral fresh goat cheese, heated under the broiler and set on top of salad greens with fresh herbs and olive oil, makes the best of all summer eating. And only the most stringent waist watchers will contest the beauty of a creamy Italian mascarpone. Fresh cheeses can be used as appetizers (marinated mozzarella), as a salad (goat cheese with tomatoes), in a main dish (ricotta-stuffed pasta), or in dessert (mascarpone or ricotta with barely sweet cookies, cake, or fruit).

Hard cheeses: If you're new at building cheese trays, start with cheddar. Offering cheddar cheese is a good point of departure, especially for people new at the cheese-tasting business. Cheddar is a style of making cheese that originated in England but has been copied all over the world. There are fabulous traditional English cheddars (Keen's and Montgomery's) and fabulous American cheddars made in the old-fashioned way (Shelburne Farms and Grafton Village). English cheddar, Gouda, and Parmigiano-Reggiano are some hard cheeses; Swiss Emmentaler and Gruyère are other examples.

Blue cheeses: Roquefort is the most famous of blues and its reputation has eclipsed any other. But Roquefort doesn't always arrive in the United States in perfect shape. Buy it from a cheese merchant, not a supermarket case.

Or try Valdeon or Cabrales, the great blue cheeses from Spain. No supermarket will be ordering Cabrales. You have to know these cheeses to love them, and chances are good that when you finally get your hands on one, you'll treat it correctly. Stilton is another fabulous blue and easier to get than Cabrales. And a good "naturale" (aged) Gorgonzola is a wonderfully satisfying cheese. Or check out the domestic Maytag blue.

Semisoft cheeses: include washed rinds and bloomed rinds. Rinds are the outside part of the cheese, and manipulating the rind can change the nature of the cheese. Tailage and Pont l'Évêque are the most famous washed rind cheeses. A good one is a domestic cheese called Mount St. Francis, made in southern Indiana. As they ripen, these cheeses are washed with any one of a number of solutions —beer, wine, or saltwater. Bloomed rind cheeses have the culture applied to the outside and ripen inward. Brie and Camembert are most famous bloomed rind cheeses.

The rinds: To eat or not to eat, that is the question. Semisoft cheeses in particular have rinds that are tempting to eat, but are they edible?

Eating rind on cheese is a matter of practicality and taste. Think of fruit. You wouldn't eat the skin on a banana but you probably would on a peach. Ask your cheese vendor about particular cheeses or taste at your own risk (and possible reward).

Appetizers

A Fine Hello

I USED TO RESENT APPETIZERS. And why not? As if it's not enough to clean the house, shop for food, and make a main course, side dish, and dessert, you have to prepare something on top of all that to offer as everyone arrives. I knew my resentment was bound to spill over to my guests sooner or later, so I dealt with it as best I could. I did not serve appetizers. Appetizers were not mentioned in my house, and only inadvertently acknowledged, as when a cookbook should happen to fall open on a particular page.

Then one evening, after a decent interval of marriage, my husband brought home a small tub of exquisitely marinated artichoke hearts. "Just something to have out when our guests come," he said, probably not nearly as accusingly as I imagined. My subsequent insistence on appetizers shows what I learned that night, which I have incorporated into the following:

A Universal Theory of Appetizers

What you serve as appetizers depends on *why* you're serving them. For example:

1. **Why**: Aid to entrée appreciation. If you know that you'll be spending more than 15 minutes after your guests arrive preparing dinner, it's not only right and hospitable to offer them something to eat; it's wise. If they're starving when they sit down, your guests may treat your stuffed salmon wrapped in leeks like a bag of nachos and gobble it down at one go. But if they've had a slice of bread with Bell Pepper Spread with Olives and Feta (page 36), they will eat your salmon with due reverence and relish.

   What: Simple spreads and dips work to subdue hunger and to stoke appetites. And they're

easy for you. Consider Feta and Chive Spread (page 30), Hummus (page 28), or Orange-Infused Baba Ghanouj (page 27).

2. **Why**: Social engineering. If your guests have never met, sharing appetizers in your living room will give them a chance to get to know one another before they sit down to dinner. Conversation over supper will be a lot easier if everyone has some idea whom they're eating with.

   What: "Interesting" food can spark conversation while making everyone feel comfortable in your home and confident they'll be well fed. Try the Bite-Sized Corn Bits (page 38) or the Crab Nori Rolls (page 42).

3. **Why**: You're serving a distinctly ethnic dinner, and the appetizers can serve as an introduction to the flavors of the region.

   What: Whatever goes with it. Kick off a Middle Eastern meal with Stuffed Grape Leaves (page 44) and Hummus (page 28). If it's a Pan-Asian dinner, start with Steamed Vegetable Dumplings (page 40) or Far Eastern Shrimp Cocktail with Cold Peanut Dip (page 35).

4. **Why**: An intimate evening that you want to stretch across as many courses as possible.

What: The most reliable* starter is a rich, ripe, runny cheese (see page 15) served with crusty, chewy "real" bread, either store-bought or homemade (see the Breads introduction, page 210).

What's Appetizing?

Flipping through the many illustrated books on the subject, you might conclude that making appetizers involves knowing something about cooking and a good deal more about architecture and design. If you happen to have the patience and skill to pipe salmon mousse into symmetrically stacked towers of puff pastry, it's not for lack of envy or respect that I contend: The most appetizing food looks like *food*.

Besides, it's a scientific fact that simply prepared foods taste best. If you're going to be fussing food into unnatural shapes and structures, you're going to be exposing it to a lot of air and light, which affect freshness and flavor.

The Food *Is* the Garnish

Yet presentation is important. Your appetizer tray gives your guests their first glimpse at your food; you want it to be inviting and assuring.

The best way to present appetizers that look as good as they taste—and vice versa—is to serve dishes made from such vibrant, colorful ingredients, they virtually garnish themselves. such as those that follow.

_____

* *Translator's note:* Sensual and intoxicating. Trust me.

Tableware: Serve appetizers from plates or bowls of deep, soothing solid colors such as red, green, dark blue, or eggplant. Avoid clear serving bowls because it's impossible to make the food look neat from all angles.

Fresh Herbs: Be careful when you use herbs as garnishes; some decorative herbs, such as rosemary and sage, have such strong flavors, they may overwhelm anything they're meant to festoon. Arrange sprigs to dress up the serving plate rather than to decorate the food itself.

Ties: You can use chives or strips of Roasted Bell Peppers (page 302) to bind little bundles of julienned vegetables for dunking. Use the julienne blade of a food processor to cut very thin strips of carrot and zucchini, which can be briefly blanched in boiling water to brighten the color

NOTE ON SERVINGS

It can be hard to determine how many people a single appetizer recipe will serve, since it depends on whether you'll be offering other appetizers and how soon dinner will be served, if at all. If your party is a cocktail party, with no dinner to follow, be prepared for your guests to eat more.

Consequently, I've included how many pieces each recipe yields and a range of portion sizes: the low number for when the dish will be the only appetizer, or one of two, or when there will be no meal to follow; the higher number for when the appetizer is one of several, to be followed by dinner.

Rule of thumb: If you're going to be serving a meal, plan on about 4 appetizer pieces per person; if you're serving only appetizers, plan on about 10 appetizer pieces per person.

and soften the texture a bit—30 seconds to 1 minute should do it. Make bite-sized bunches and tie with chive or roasted pepper. If the chives are too stiff to tie, dunk them in boiling water for 10 seconds to make them pliable.

Abracadabra, Appetizers!

YOU CAN VIRTUALLY PULL AN AMPLE, delicious hors d'oeuvre array out of a hat by choosing several of the vegetables below, or others that you like that are in season, and one or two of the simple spreads on page 30.

Vegetables to Serve with Dips

Asparagus: Use medium-thick asparagus—you don't want the stems to droop, so they have to be sturdy, but they shouldn't be so thick that they'll be tough to chew. Snap off the tough woody ends before steaming, and for good measure, peel off the outer skin from the bottom half of the asparagus with a vegetable peeler.

To steam, cut off the tough, woody ends. Fit a large pot with a steamer basket. Add enough water to come up to the base of the steamer. Place the asparagus in the steamer, cover, and steam until the spears turn bright green, about 3 minutes. Meanwhile, fill a large bowl with ice or very cold water. Immediately plunge the asparagus into it and toss to stop the cooking. Drain and transfer the asparagus to a plate. Cover with plastic wrap and chill until you're ready to serve them.

Bell Peppers: Heat the oven to 450°F. Cut the peppers in half lengthwise, and remove the stem and the seeds. Place skin side up on a baking sheet. Bake until the skin blackens, about 20 minutes. Remove from the oven and let cool. (You can speed the cooling by placing the peppers in a paper bag and tossing it into the freezer for 5 to 10 minutes.) Peel the peppers and slice them lengthwise into wide strips. Spread lightly with spread or dip, roll up, and secure with a toothpick. Chill until ready to serve, with toothpicks in place.

Broccoli and Cauliflower: Although they turn up on vegetable trays often enough, raw broccoli and cauliflower are highly concentrated sources of fiber and can therefore be a source of discomfort for your guests. Moreover, they tend to have a strong, acrid flavor that few dips can complement. So if you're going to serve broccoli and/or cauliflower, please steam them. Choose firm heads, and trim into pieces with enough stalk to be held and dunked.

To steam, fit a large pot with a steamer basket. Add enough water to come up to the base of the steamer. Place the cut broccoli or cauliflower in the steamer, cover, and bring the water to a simmer over medium-high heat. Steam until cooked through but still crisp, about 2 or 3 minutes for broccoli, about 6 minutes for cauliflower. Meanwhile, fill a large bowl with ice or very cold water. Immediately plunge the broccoli into it and toss to stop the cooking. Drain and transfer to a plate. Cover with plastic wrap and chill until ready to serve.

Carrots: Packaged baby carrots, which do not need peeling or cleaning, are sweet, crunchy, and ready to serve. Alternately you may buy larger carrots, which need to be trimmed, peeled, and cut into slender 3-inch sticks.

Celery: Trim off the leafy end and the widest part at the bottom. If the celery is particularly stringy, scrape it with a vegetable peeler. Rinse thoroughly and cut into 3-inch lengths.

Cherry Tomatoes: Slice off the top and scoop out enough pulp to make a crater without cutting through the bottom or sides. Fill the cherry tomatoes with the dip or spread of your choice (Guacamole, page 39, or Feta and Chives, page 30, are especially good choices). Or just leave the cherry tomatoes whole and use them to scoop up the dip.

Chile Peppers (mild): Heat the oven to 450°F. Place the peppers whole on a baking sheet. Bake until the skin blackens, about 20 minutes. Remove from the oven and let cool. (You can speed the cooling by placing the peppers in a paper bag and tossing it into the freezer for 5 to 10 minutes.) Peel and split in half lengthwise. Scrape away the seeds. Spread each half with the spread or dip of your choice and roll as directed for bell peppers, above.

Endive: Choose firm, crisp heads. Separate the leaves and arrange as dippers around the spread.

Mushrooms: Use sturdy, flavorful mushrooms, such as the chestnut-colored cremini. Rub away the surface dirt with a vegetable brush or a damp paper towel and trim off the bottoms of the stems. Provide toothpicks in a container, if desired, for dipping into the spread. Or you can place the dip in the center of a large serving plate and put the mushrooms around it, caps down, with the toothpicks stuck into them. For color, put a small piece of roasted red, green, or yellow bell pepper at the end of the toothpick before you pierce the mushroom cap with it.

New Potatoes: Steam until cooked through but not mushy, about 10 minutes, depending on size. Slice off the top and scoop out enough of the potato with a teaspoon to make a small crater without cutting through the bottom or sides. (Hint for the well-heeled: Brush the crater with unsalted butter, add a dab of sour cream, and top with a half teaspoon of caviar!)

Snow Peas or Sugar Snap Peas: Fill a saucepan with water and bring it to a boil. Using a large slotted spoon, dunk into the water as many peas as you can fit on the spoon. Leave the peas submerged for 30 seconds for snow peas, 45 seconds for sugar snaps. Lift out the peas in the slotted spoon and transfer to a plate. Chill thoroughly before serving.

And Don't Forget About

Hard-Boiled Eggs: Use jumbo or extra large eggs. Place as many eggs as you'll need (figure $\frac{1}{2}$ egg per person, with other appetizers) on the bottom of a large pot. Fill the pot with cold water and bring it to a boil. Cover and turn off the heat. (If you're using an electric stove, remove the pot from the burner.) Let sit 15 minutes. Drain the hot water and run cold water over the eggs to stop the cooking process. Chill the eggs. Peel and then cut in half lengthwise or crosswise. Scoop out the yolk, and either mash it into the filling you'll be using or discard it (cholesterol, you know) and replace it with the filling alone.

Suggestions for Fillings

    Smoked Salmon Spread, page 30

    Crab Salad from the Crab and Avocado Timbale, page 95

    Peach Buttermilk Dressing, page 180 (Mash the yolks in it.)

THINGS TO SPREAD, SCOOP, AND DIP

Crostini di Polenta

MAKES ABOUT 16 PIECES,
ENOUGH FOR 6 TO 12 PEOPLE

Polenta, until recently known only to Italians and those who wish they were, is now sold ready-made, cello-wrapped and ready for slicing. You can make this dish with prepared polenta; simply start with the next-to-last step and proceed from there. Choose either the thyme-fontina combo or the basil-mozzarella-Parmesan mixture for the topping.

TIME TO PREPARE (HANDS ON): *About 20 minutes*

TIME TO COOK: *Included in the time to prepare*

TOTAL TIME: *About 20 minutes, plus overnight to chill*

4 cups Vegetable Broth (page 286)
1 cup cornmeal, preferably stone-ground

TOPPINGS
1 tablespoon extra virgin olive oil
1 large onion, thinly sliced

1 tablespoon minced fresh thyme
1 1/2 cups shredded or thinly sliced fontina
   cheese
or
1 tablespoon minced fresh basil
1 cup shredded mozzarella cheese
1 1/4 cup grated Parmesan cheese

Pour the vegetable broth into a large, heavy saucepan and bring to a boil over high heat. Gradually add the cornmeal and stir until it becomes too thick to stir any longer, about 15 minutes. Remove from the heat and let cool slightly. Meanwhile, line a baking sheet with a piece of parchment paper.

Spread the polenta on the paper and smooth into an even layer. Roll up the paper like a jelly roll, allowing the paper to be rolled up into the polenta, and enclose in a piece of foil. Refrigerate overnight.

Heat the oil in a pan and sauté the onion and either the thyme or the basil until the onion is soft, about 7 minutes.

Preheat the broiler. Unroll the polenta, remove the parchment paper, and roll it up again. Slice it into rounds about 1/2 inch thick. Top each with a portion of sautéed onion and fontina or mozzarella and Parmesan, depending on which topping is being used. Place under the broiler until bubbly, about 1 minute. Serve hot.

Make the polenta roll up to 3 days ahead.
- *Wrap tightly in plastic and refrigerate.*
- *Slice, top, and bake just before serving.*

Menu

CROSTINI DI POLENTA
PENNE WITH TOMATO AND FENNEL SAUCE (PAGE 82)
SFORMATA DI FRITTATA (PAGE 251)

Orange-Infused Baba Ghanouj

MAKES ABOUT 1 CUP,
ENOUGH FOR 6 TO 10 PEOPLE

Now that you can buy everything from hummus to tabbouleh at most major supermarkets, it's getting harder to serve something your guests didn't have for dinner just last night. This orange-infused version of a popular dip is just different enough from any commercial kind that you can serve it confident it won't be redundant.

TIME TO PREPARE (HANDS ON): *About 10 minutes*

TIME TO COOK: *About 20 minutes*

TOTAL TIME: *Under 30 minutes*

2 large eggplants
2 tablespoons tahini
½ cup plain nonfat yogurt
1 tablespoon sesame seeds
2 tablespoons fresh orange juice
2 tablespoons fresh lemon juice
3 tablespoons minced fresh cilantro
2 teaspoons ground cumin
1 teaspoon finely grated fresh garlic
Coarse salt (optional)
1 teaspoon paprika

Heat the oven to 450°F. Pierce the eggplants in several places with a fork. Wrap the eggplants in foil and bake until they're soft, about 30 minutes. Unwrap the foil and let the eggplants cool.

Meanwhile, in a mixing bowl, combine the tahini, yogurt, sesame seeds, orange juice, lemon juice, cilantro, cumin, and garlic. When the eggplants are cool enough to handle, peel them and discard as many of the seeds as you can. Chop the pulp very fine and stir it into the rest of the mixture. Season with salt to taste, if desired. Transfer to a serving bowl and garnish with paprika.

Make up to 3 days ahead.
• *Cover and refrigerate.*
• *Take out of the refrigerator about 2 hours beforehand and serve at room temperature.*

Bruschetta

(Garlic Toast)

MAKES 16 TO 20 PIECES,

ENOUGH FOR 6 TO 14 PEOPLE

This is one of the easiest appetizers and easily one of the best.

TIME TO PREPARE (HANDS ON): *About 10 minutes*

TIME TO COOK: *About 5 minutes*

TOTAL TIME: *About 15 minutes*

- 1 loaf good day-old French or sourdough bread
- 1 large garlic clove, cut in half
- Approximately 2 tablespoons extra virgin olive oil
- 2 large ripe tomatoes, minced, or ½ cup minced sun-dried tomatoes, drained and patted dry
- ¼ cup minced fresh basil
- Coarse salt and freshly ground black pepper to taste

Heat the oven to 350°F. Cut the bread into thin slices and place in a single layer on a baking sheet. Bake until lightly toasted, about 3 to 5 minutes.

Rub the cut end of the garlic clove over the slices of bread and brush lightly with olive oil. Put the toasts on a serving platter. In a small mixing bowl, combine the minced fresh or dried tomato, basil, and salt and pepper. Stir well and distribute evenly over the toast. Serve at once.

- *You can't make this ahead. Prepare it just before serving.*

Hummus

MAKES ABOUT 1 CUP,

ENOUGH FOR 6 TO 10 PEOPLE

Commercial hummus is everywhere, and some is very good. If you've found a brand you like, you may not want to make your own. But if you'd like to see what the difference would be, here's the way to go. There may be no way back. This is one recipe where canned chickpeas are practically as good as cooked dried chickpeas. Just be sure to rinse them well.

TIME TO PREPARE (HANDS ON): *About 5 minutes*

TIME TO COOK: *None*

TOTAL TIME: *About 5 minutes*

- 1 cup cooked chickpeas, rinsed and drained
- 2 tablespoons tahini
- 1 garlic clove, crushed and minced
- 2 tablespoons fresh lemon juice
- 1 tablespoon fresh orange juice
- ¼ cup minced fresh cilantro
- 2 teaspoons ground cumin
- 1 teaspoon ground ginger (optional)
- Coarse salt (optional)
- ½ teaspoon paprika

In a food processor or blender, combine the chickpeas, tahini, garlic, lemon juice, orange juice, cilantro, cumin, and ginger. Season with salt to taste, if desired. Transfer to a serving bowl and sprinkle the paprika evenly on top.

Make up to 5 days ahead.
- *Seal in a tightly covered container and refrigerate.*
- *Take out of the refrigerator about 2 hours before serving, transfer to a serving bowl, cover with plastic wrap, and let come to room temperature. Or serve cold.*

Make a sandwich: Spread inside a pita pocket or piece of Lavash (page 228) and stuff with tomatoes, cucumber, and sprouts.

Make a wrap: Spread on Lavash, add steamed vegetables and cooked brown rice, fold in the sides, and roll it up.

FROM DRAB TO DAZZLING, OR
WHAT TO DO ABOUT DULL-LOOKING DIPS
Put the spread in a brightly colored bowl. Sprinkle the top with minced fresh cilantro and parsley. Or, for a fancier presentation, you can use a small diamond or circular cookie cutter as a stencil for the herbs. Flatten the spread with a spatula and rest the cookie cutter in the center, filling it with the minced herbs or with finely shredded carrot or beet. Lift the cookie cutter. Place the serving bowl in the center of a large plate, and arrange bread and/or vegetables for dipping around it

Cold Peanut Dip

SERVES 8

In a popular television ad campaign, adults shrouded in shadow confess to craving a certain sugary brand of breakfast cereal hitherto marketed to children. Adults who eat peanut butter may feel they have to be just as furtive about it . . . unless it's in something foreign, such as this addictive dip. Serve it with cold boiled shrimp (page 34), or with broiled tofu (page 33).

TIME TO PREPARE (HANDS ON): *Under 10 minutes*

TIME TO COOK: *About 3 minutes*

TOTAL TIME: *A little over 3 hours, including time to chill*

1 cup rice vinegar or white vinegar
$\frac{2}{3}$ cup granulated sugar
$\frac{1}{3}$ cup brown sugar
1 teaspoon soy sauce
1 tablespoon grated fresh ginger
1 teaspoon minced garlic
2 small serrano chilies, seeded and minced (optional)
$\frac{1}{3}$ cup smooth unsalted peanut butter
$\frac{1}{4}$ cup minced fresh cilantro

In a small saucepan, combine the vinegar, granulated sugar, brown sugar, and soy sauce. Bring to a simmer, uncovered, over medium-low heat, stirring until the sugars dissolve, about 3 minutes. Remove from the heat.

Transfer the mixture to a large mixing bowl and stir in the ginger, garlic, chilies if using peanut butter and cilantro. Refrigerate until chilled through, about 3 hours. Or put it in the freezer to chill quickly, stirring often to prevent icing.

Make up to 5 days ahead.
* *Wrap or cover tightly, preferably in a glass container, and refrigerate.*
* *Serve cold or at room temperature.*

LOVE THOSE LEFTOVERS!
Make pasta: Toss leftover sauce with hot pasta. Serve right away, chilled, or at room temperature.

Or, serve leftover sauce over steamed vegetables and rice.

Spreads

Having been out of fashion for a while, canapé spreads are back, but in a different style than when they last made the rounds with predinner drinks: They're leaner now, and they've lost that mayonnaise luster. The goop has given way to good, true flavors.

The word canapé *comes from the French for "sofa," referring to something on which something else rests. Typically this has meant toast, bread, or crackers. But you can use vegetables instead, such as cherry tomatoes (hollowed out for filling), new potatoes (insides scooped out to leave room for dips or spreads), or carrot or celery sticks (see pages 24–25).*

You can spread or fill the canapés ahead of time, or fill a bowl with dip or spread and arrange the toast, crackers, and/or vegetables on a plate—along with several spreading knives—so your guests can help themselves.

Leftover spread? Use it for sandwiches or to top bagels or baked potatoes. Or thin it with plain yogurt and serve over steamed vegetables.

TIME TO PREPARE (HANDS ON): *About 5 minutes*

TIME TO COOK: *None*

TOTAL TIME: *About 5 minutes*

Smoked Salmon

Spread this on bagel chips, pita toasts, or melba toast. Or use it to fill hollowed-out cherry tomatoes (see page 25).

- 8 ounces Neufchâtel cheese, softened
- 3 tablespoons nonfat plain yogurt or buttermilk
- 1/4 cup minced fresh chives
- 1 tablespoon fresh lemon juice
- 1/4 to 1/3 pound Nova Scotia smoked salmon, minced
- 2 tablespoons minced red onion
- 2 tablespoon minced fresh parsley

Place the Neufchâtel cheese and yogurt or buttermilk in the work bowl of a food processor or blender. Process until smooth but not liquid. Transfer to a mixing bowl.

Stir in the chives, lemon juice, salmon, onion, and parsley.

Feta and Chive

Spread this on pita triangles or Lavash (see page 228), or use to fill new potatoes or celery stalks (see page 25).

- 1/2 cup crumbled feta cheese
- 8 ounces Neufchâtel cheese, softened
- 4 tablespoons nonfat plain yogurt or buttermilk
- 1/4 cup minced fresh chives, or more to taste
- 6 oil-cured black olives, pitted and minced (optional)

Place the feta, Neufchâtel, and yogurt or butter-milk in the work bowl of a food processor or blender. Process until smooth but not liquid. Transfer to a mixing bowl. Stir in the chives and minced olives, if using.

Cream Cheese and Pineapple

Spread on a small square of toast or use to fill hard-boiled eggs (see page 25) (see Note).

8 ounces Neufchâtel cheese, softened
4 tablespoons nonfat plain yogurt or buttermilk
1 tablespoon honey
One 8-ounce can pineapple chunks in their own juice, drained
¼ cup minced fresh chives
Coarse salt

Place the Neufchâtel, yogurt or buttermilk, and honey in the work bowl of a food processor or blender. Process until smooth but not liquid. Add the pineapple and pulse to distribute it evenly. Do not overdo it, or the mixture will liquefy. Transfer to a mixing bowl. Stir in the chives and season with salt.

NOTE: Do not make this one ahead, it will get runny.

Additional Canapés

Coat thin slices of bread with a layer of spread and cut with small cookie cutters. Or spread thin slices of bread with softened butter, cut with cookie cutters, and top with:

Thinly sliced smoked salmon
Thinly sliced hard-boiled egg, sprinkled with chives
Caviar (and *butter* that bread! if only lightly)
Minced oil-cured black olives, cream cheese, and chives blended together

Make up to 3 days ahead.
• *Seal in a tightly covered container and refrigerate. Serve cold, or take out of the refrigerator about 2 hours before serving, transfer to a serving bowl, cover with plastic wrap, and let come to room temperature.*

Caponata
(Tangy Chopped Eggplant Salad)

MAKES ABOUT 1 1/2 CUPS, ENOUGH FOR 4
TO 8 PEOPLE

*Serve with wedges of pita bread for scooping and a sharp,
medium soft cheese.*

TIME TO PREPARE (HANDS ON): *About 15 minutes*

TIME TO COOK: *About 35 minutes*

TOTAL TIME: *Close to 4 hours, including time to chill*

2 medium eggplants

2 tablespoons extra virgin olive oil, divided

1 large onion, chopped

1 celery stalk, chopped

3 red bell peppers, cored, seeded, and
    chopped

2 tablespoons minced fresh oregano or 1
    tablespoon crumbled dried

1 large ripe tomato, peeled, seeded, and
    chopped

2 tablespoons balsamic vinegar

1 teaspoon capers, rinsed and drained

1/4 cup raisins

1/4 cup minced oil-cured black olives

1 tablespoon sugar

Coarse salt and freshly ground black pepper

Heat the oven to 450°F. Pierce the eggplants in
several places with a fork. Wrap the eggplants in
foil and bake until soft, about 30 minutes. Unwrap the foil and let the eggplants cool.

Meanwhile, heat 1 tablespoon of the oil in a
nonstick skillet over medium-high heat. When
hot, add the onion, celery, bell peppers, and
oregano. Reduce the heat to medium-low and
sauté, stirring often, until the vegetables are soft
and limp, about 10 minutes. Stir in the tomato
and continue cooking over medium heat until it
breaks down into a sauce, about 5 minutes. Add
the balsamic vinegar, turn up the heat to
medium-high, and stir for 1 minute. Remove
from the heat.

Peel the eggplants and chop the pulp, separating out as many seeds as possible. Return the skillet to medium heat, and stir in the eggplant,
capers, raisins, olives, and sugar. Stir until the
sugar has dissolved, about 1 to 2 minutes. Remove from the heat and transfer to a large mixing
bowl. Stir in the remaining tablespoon of olive
oil. Season with salt and pepper. Cover and refrigerate until chilled through, about 3 hours.
Serve chilled or at room temperature.

Make up to 3 days ahead.
* *Wrap or cover tightly, preferably in a glass container,
  and refrigerate.*
* *Serve cold or take out of the refrigerator about 2 hours
  before serving, transfer to a serving bowl, cover with
  plastic wrap, and let come to room temperature.*

Menu
CAPONATA
ROAST CHICKEN (PAGE 157) WITH
MASHED POTATOES (PAGE 191)
OR
FRITTATA CREPES (PAGE 112)
CAULIFLOWER BROILED WITH CHEESE (PAGE 199)

Fromage de Soya Grille, Asian Style

(Broiled Tofu)

MAKES ABOUT 24 PIECES,
ENOUGH FOR 6 TO 10 PEOPLE

One of the most renowned episodes in food history was the passionate campaign, waged by Parisian Auguste Parmentier in the late eighteenth century, to popularize the potato. Thanks to him (and the ongoing bread shortage in France), people developed a taste for potatoes, thought until then to be poisonous. Now we need a Parmentier for tofu, someone whose efforts would eliminate, once and for all, the little wince you get when you mention it.

TIME TO PREPARE (HANDS ON): *About 5 minutes*

TIME TO COOK: *About 10 minutes*

TOTAL TIME: *A little over 2 hours, including time to press and marinate the tofu*

1 tablespoon mirin (rice wine; see Note)
1 tablespoon rice vinegar
1 tablespoon grated peeled fresh ginger
2 garlic cloves, crushed and minced
2 tablespoons hoisin sauce (see Note)
2 teaspoons dark sesame oil (see Note)
1 pound extra firm tofu, cut into 4 slices

Cold Peanut Dip (page 29)

To prepare the tofu for broiling, an hour ahead, wrap each slice of tofu in several layers of paper towels and place in a single layer on a wide plate. Put a large heavy saucepan on top, covering all the slices, then put something heavy inside it (like a can of tomatoes) to weight it down. After an hour, lift up the weight, drain the water from the dish, and unwrap the tofu, which should be much compressed.

In a large mixing bowl, combine the mirin, rice vinegar, ginger, garlic, hoisin sauce, and sesame oil. Add the tofu and turn to coat with the mixture. Cover with plastic wrap, and refrigerate for 30 minutes. Turn the tofu over, replace the wrap and chill for 30 minutes more.

Heat the broiler. Lightly grease the broiler pan with sesame oil or peanut oil, and spread the tofu evenly on it in a single layer. Broil until lightly browned, about 5 minutes.

Turn over, spread with the remaining marinade, and broil the other side until lightly browned, about 4 minutes. Cut each piece into 6 cubes.

To serve, pour the Cold Peanut Dip into a small bowl and place in the center of a large plate. Arrange the tofu pieces around the bowl, and provide plenty of toothpicks for dipping, as well as a small plate for discarding the used toothpicks.

NOTE: Mirin, hoisin sauce, and sesame oil are available at Asian specialty stores or the Asian foods section of most major supermarkets.

Make the marinade up to 3 days ahead. Refrigerate in a glass bowl covered with plastic wrap.

Shrimp Cocktails

*Shrimp go fast, so to give all of your guests a fair shot at
these, wait until everyone's arrived, then let 'em at 'em.*

*You can buy cooked shrimp (taste one before you com-
mit yourself) to serve with one, two, or all of the sauces that
follow. But if you have the time, boil fresh shrimp in a broth
seasoned to complement the sauce you've chosen, as described in the recipes. Or, if you don't have time to boil up
one of these tailored broths, but want to cook your shrimp
fresh at home, bring a large pot of water to a boil, add the
shrimp in their shells, and simmer until they turn pink,
about 4 to 7 minutes. Drain the shrimp, plunge them into a
bowl of waiting ice water to stop the cooking, then peel and
chill the shrimp.*

*If you like, you may leave the tails on the shrimp to use
as a "handle" for dipping, but don't forget to provide a little
dish to toss them in.*

TIME TO PREPARE (HANDS ON): *About 15 minutes*

TIME TO COOK: *About 25 minutes*

TOTAL TIME: *About 40 minutes*

Shrimp Cocktail with Mango Chutney

FOR BOILING THE SHRIMP (NOT NECESSARY
IF YOU'LL BE BUYING COOKED SHRIMP)

    16 jumbo shrimp
    1 leek, white part plus 1 inch of green,
       thinly sliced
    1 shallot, sliced
    3 thinly sliced rounds peeled fresh ginger
    One 2-inch strip lemon peel

    Mango Chutney (recipe follows)

Shell the shrimp and put the shells in a large
saucepan. Add the leek, shallot, ginger, lemon
peel, and 1 cup water. Cover and bring to a boil
over medium-high-heat. Reduce the heat to
medium-low and simmer for 15 to 20 minutes to
infuse the water with flavor. Strain the broth into
a separate saucepan. Bring to a boil over medium-
high heat. Add the shrimp, cover, and simmer
gently until they turn bright pink, about 5 to 6
minutes.

Meanwhile, get a large bowl of ice water
ready. When the shrimp are cooked, drain them
and plunge them into the ice water to stop the
cooking process. Drain them well and refrigerate.

Serve the shrimp and chutney in separate
bowls. Arrange the shrimp decoratively on a
serving platter with chutney bowls tucked amidst
the shrimp.

Mango Chutney

    1 large ripe mango, peeled and chopped
    1 large ripe tomato, chopped
    1 small red onion, chopped
    Juice of 1 lime
    Juice of 1 lemon
    2 teaspoons grated peeled fresh ginger
    1 teaspoon brown sugar
    1/4 cup minced fresh cilantro
    2 tablespoons minced fresh mint
    Coarse salt

Place the mango, tomato, onion, lime juice,
lemon juice, ginger, brown sugar, cilantro, and
mint in a food processor or blender. Pulse to chop
and combine but not puree, about 3 to 4 pulses.

Transfer to a serving bowl and season with
salt.

Southwestern Shrimp Cocktail with Guacamole and Salsa

FOR BOILING THE SHRIMP (NOT NECESSARY IF YOU'LL BE BUYING COOKED SHRIMP)

16 jumbo shrimp

1 onion, sliced

1 garlic clove, crushed

1 celery stalk, including leaves, chopped

$\frac{1}{2}$ cup coarsely chopped cilantro stems

2 tablespoons dry white wine or cider vinegar

Guacamole (page 39)

Salsa, store-bought

Shell the shrimp and put the shells in a large saucepan. Add the onion, garlic, celery, cilantro stems, wine or vinegar, and 1 cup water. Cover and bring to a boil over medium-high heat. Reduce the heat to medium-low and simmer for 15 to 20 minutes to infuse the water with flavor. Strain the broth into a separate saucepan. Bring to a boil over medium-high heat. Add the shrimp, cover, and simmer gently until they turn bright pink, about 5 to 8 minutes.

Meanwhile, get a large bowl of ice water ready. When the shrimp are cooked, drain them and plunge them into the ice water to stop the cooking process. Drain them well.

Serve the guacamole and salsa in separate serving bowls. Arrange the shrimp decoratively on a serving platter. The bowls may be tucked amidst the shrimp on the serving platter.

Far Eastern Shrimp Cocktail with Cold Peanut Dip

FOR BOILING THE SHRIMP (NOT NECESSARY IF YOU'LL BE BUYING COOKED SHRIMP)

16 jumbo shrimp

3 thinly sliced rounds peeled fresh ginger

1 leek, white part plus 1 inch of green, thinly sliced

2 scallions, including green part, chopped

2 garlic cloves, crushed

1 tablespoon mirin (rice wine) or rice vinegar

Cold Peanut Dip (page 29)

Shell the shrimp and put the shells in a large saucepan. Add the ginger, leek, scallions, garlic, wine or vinegar, and 1 cup water. Cover and bring to a boil over medium-high heat. Reduce the heat to medium-low and simmer for 15 to 20 minutes to infuse the water with flavor. Strain the broth into a separate saucepan. Bring to a boil over medium-high heat. Add the shrimp, cover, and simmer gently until they turn bright pink, about 5 to 6 minutes.

Meanwhile, get a large bowl of ice water ready. When the shrimp are cooked, drain them and plunge them into the ice water to stop the cooking process. Drain them well and refrigerate.

Arrange the shrimp on a platter and serve with the Cold Peanut Dip.

- *You can boil the shrimp up to 2 days ahead (provided they were very fresh when you bought them).*
- *Make any of the sauces—except guacamole—up to 3 days in advance.*
- *Seal in a tightly covered container and refrigerate.*

Mediterranean Shrimp Cocktail with Fresh Tomato Vinaigrette

FOR BOILING THE SHRIMP (NOT NECESSARY IF YOU'LL BE BUYING COOKED SHRIMP)

16 jumbo shrimp
1 large shallot, thinly sliced
1 celery stalk, including leaves, chopped
1/2 cup chopped parsley stems
2 tablespoons dry white wine or balsamic vinegar

Fresh Tomato Vinaigrette (recipe follows)

Shell the shrimp and put the shells in a large saucepan. Add the shallot, celery, parsley stems, wine or vinegar, and 1 cup water. Cover and bring to a boil over medium-high heat. Reduce the heat to medium-low and simmer for 15 to 20 minutes to infuse the water with flavor. Strain the broth into a separate saucepan. Bring to a boil over medium-high heat. Add the shrimp, cover, and simmer gently until they turn bright pink, about 5 to 6 minutes.

Meanwhile, get a large bowl of ice water ready. When the shrimp are cooked, drain them and plunge them into the ice water to stop the cooking process. Drain them well and refrigerate.

Fresh Tomato Vinaigrette

2 tablespoons extra virgin olive oil
1 tablespoon balsamic vinegar
1 garlic clove, crushed and minced
1 teaspoon Dijon mustard
2 large ripe tomatoes, peeled, seeded, and chopped
1/4 cup minced fresh basil
Coarse salt and freshly ground black pepper

In a blender or food processor (or using an immersion blender), combine the oil, vinegar, garlic, and mustard until blended. Add the tomatoes and basil, and pulse to combine, about 4 pulses. Season with salt and pepper.

TO SERVE SHRIMP COCKTAIL
Place the dipping sauce in a wide bowl and place in the center of a large dish. "Hook" the shrimp onto the rim of the bowl, spacing them evenly. Or lay them in a circle on the platter around the bowl. Provide toothpicks for dunking, or encourage your guests to use their fingers.

Bell Pepper Spread with Olives and Feta

SERVES 4 TO 6

This never fails. Made with feta cheese or canned tuna, it's versatile enough to serve before just about any kind of dinner (except curries, stir-fries, and other Asian-style entrées.) And it's easy enough to make on short notice.

TIME TO PREPARE (HANDS ON):	*About 5 minutes*
TIME TO COOK:	*About 20 minutes*
TOTAL TIME:	*Under 30 minutes*

1 medium eggplant

1 red bell pepper

10 large oil-cured olives

1 teaspoon capers, drained

$\frac{1}{2}$ cup crumbled feta cheese or 1 6-ounce
   can water-packed tuna, drained

2 garlic cloves, crushed and minced

$\frac{1}{4}$ cup minced fresh basil

$\frac{1}{4}$ cup minced fresh parsley

Coarse salt (optional)

Heat the oven to 450°F.

Pierce the eggplant in several places with a fork. Wrap the eggplant in foil. Cut the red pepper in half lengthwise, and remove the stem and the seeds. Place skin side up on a baking sheet. Put the eggplant on the baking sheet, too.

Bake the eggplant until it is soft, about 20 minutes. Bake the peppers until the skin blackens, which should take about 20 minutes as well. (If they're not done at the same time, remove whichever is done from the oven and let cool).

Unwrap the eggplant, and let it sit along with the peppers until both are cool enough to handle.(You can speed the process by putting both in a paper bag and tossing it in the refrigerator for 5 to 10 minutes).

Peel the eggplant, cut off the gnarly top, and discard as many of the seeds as you can.

In a food processor or blender, combine the olives, capers, feta or tuna, garlic, basil, parsley, eggplant, and red pepper. Process in short spurts to combine. Be careful not to over-process, or the mixture will be mushy. Taste to see if it needs salt.

Make up to 3 days ahead.

- *Wrap or cover tightly, preferably in a glass container, and refrigerate.*
- *Take out of the refrigerator about 2 hours before serving, transfer to a serving bowl, cover with plastic wrap, and let come to room temperature.*

Freeze up to 6 months, well wrapped in a glass or firm plastic container.

- *To defrost, transfer to the refrigerator overnight. Then let sit at room temperature for several hours. Do not refreeze.*
- *To speed defrosting, put in a microwavable bowl (do not microwave in plastic), place a damp paper towel on top, and zap at medium strength, stirring each time, until no longer icy. Transfer to a serving bowl and let come to room temperature.*

LOVE THOSE LEFTOVERS!

Make a sandwich: Heap leftover feta or tuna spread on a roll, cover with a paper towel or wax paper, and put a heavy saucepan on top. Sounds gooey? It is . . . and good!

Make pasta: Toss leftover spread with hot pasta. Serve right away, chilled or at room temperature.

Make a frittata: Beat the leftover spread with a few eggs and some milk (2 eggs and 2 tablespoons milk for an 8- or 9-inch pan). Heat 1 to 2 teaspoons of extra virgin olive oil in a nonstick omelet pan or skillet, or squirt with nonstick spray. Add the egg mixture and cook until the bottom is firm. Either put it into the oven at 350°F until the top is firm, about 4 minutes, or lift up the edge of the frittata and tilt the pan so the uncooked egg runs underneath. Repeat until cooked through.

Bite-Sized Corn Bits

MAKES ABOUT 16 NUGGETS, ENOUGH FOR 4 TO 8 PEOPLE

These are novel, delicious tamale-style nuggets to make when you can get fresh corn. Serve with the Cumin-Lime Dipping Sauce (below) and/or Guacamole (page 39) or salsa.

TIME TO PREPARE (HANDS ON): *About 30 minutes*

TIME TO COOK: *About 1 hour*

TOTAL TIME: *About 1½ hours*

3 ears corn, shucked

1 cup yellow cornmeal, preferably stone-ground

2 teaspoons sugar

1 teaspoon ground cumin

2 tablespoons buttermilk or nonfat plain yogurt

⅓ cup shredded sharp cheddar cheese

⅓ cup shredded Monterey Jack cheese

¼ cup minced fresh cilantro

Salt and freshly ground black pepper

CUMIN-LIME DIPPING SAUCE

½ cup reduced-fat sour cream

Juice of 1 lime

1 tablespoon ground cumin

Coarse salt to taste

Scrape the corn kernels off the cob into a food processor, and process in short pulses until coarsely chopped, about 6 pulses. Add the cornmeal, sugar, cumin, and buttermilk or yogurt. Pulse again to combine, about 6 pulses.

Transfer the mixture to a large bowl. Add the cheddar cheese, Jack cheese, and cilantro. Season with salt and pepper.

Cut a large piece of cheesecloth into eight 5-inch squares. Place 2 tablespoons of the corn mixture into the center of each square. Fold the sides over the filling, then fold down the top and roll over to make a seam underneath.

Fit a large pot with a steamer basket. Add enough water to come up to the base of the steamer. Place the packets in the steamer, seam side down. Cover and bring the water to a simmer over medium-high heat. Reduce the heat to medium-low and steam until the cornmeal filling is set, about 1 hour. Check the water level often to make sure there's enough to keep the pan from burning. Remove the packets with tongs, and let cool before unwrapping.

You can also steam the packets in a pressure cooker. Fit the cooker with a steaming rack (one should have come with your cooker). Add enough water to come up the base of the steamer. Place the packets in the steamer, cover, and bring the cooker to full pressure. Cook at full pressure for 15 minutes. Let the pressure come down on its own. Tilt the cooker away from you when you open the lid. Remove the packets with tongs and let cool to warm or room temperature before unwrapping.

For the Cumin-Lime Dipping Sauce. In a medium mixing bowl, combine the sour cream, lime juice, cumin, and salt. Whisk together to blend.

To serve, pour the dipping sauce into a small bowl. Place the bowl in the center of a large plate. Arrange the nuggets around the bowl. The nuggets may be too delicate for toothpicks; encourage guests to dip them by hand.

*Make up to 3 days ahead. Remove the cheesecloth before
storing.*

- *Wrap or cover tightly, preferably in a glass container,
  and refrigerate.*
- *Take out of the refrigerator about 2 hours before serving,
  transfer to a serving bowl, cover with plastic wrap, and
  let come to room temperature.*
- *Or wrap in foil and heat in a 350° F. oven until
  warmed through.*

Guacamole

MAKES ABOUT 1 CUP,

ENOUGH FOR 4 TO 6 PEOPLE

*There's little point in offering a precise recipe for something
that should be left to personal taste and anyway depends
entirely on the quality of the main ingredient. If you're
lucky enough to have a good avocado, that ought to be the
end of the recipe, or nearly:*

Mash the avocado in a bowl, as chunky or
smooth as you like. Add a teaspoon or two of
fresh lemon or lime juice and a large pinch of salt,
and stir to blend.

Taste and adjust any of those seasonings.

If you want to spice it up, add as much minced
jalapeño pepper or ground cayenne pepper as
you'd like, along with minced onion, tomato, or
scallion and some minced fresh cilantro. You can
add grated garlic, too, but at your peril.

To make a guacamole dip, proceed as follows.

MAKES ABOUT 2 CUPS,

ENOUGH FOR 6 TO 12 PEOPLE

TIME TO PREPARE (HANDS ON):	*About 5 minutes*
TIME TO COOK:	*None*
TOTAL TIME:	*About 5 minutes*

> 1 large ripe avocado, peeled and chopped
> 2 tablespoons fresh lemon juice
> 1/2 teaspoon finely grated fresh garlic, or to
>   taste
> 1/2 cup reduced-fat sour cream
> 1/2 cup nonfat plain yogurt
> 2 tablespoon minced fresh cilantro
> Salt and freshly ground black pepper

In a blender or food processor, combine the avocado, lemon juice, garlic, sour cream, yogurt, and
cilantro. Process until smooth. Season with salt
and pepper and serve right away.

- *You can't make this ahead. Prepare it just before serving.*

FILLED THINGS

Steamed Vegetable Dumplings

MAKES ABOUT 60 DUMPLINGS, ENOUGH
FOR 12 TO 20 PEOPLE

The excellent prepared wrappers available at most supermarkets (check the Asian food aisle or the produce section) make it possible to prepare delicious dumplings on very short notice. For the die-hard do-it-yourselfer, I offer a dumpling dough recipe on page 294. If you're going to be making these often, you'll want to get a plastic dumpling mold, which helps you shape and seal them perfectly in one step (available at kitchen supply stores and by mail; see page 347).

TIME TO PREPARE (HANDS ON): *About 40 minutes, with store-bought or previously prepared dough*

TIME TO COOK: *About 15 minutes*

TOTAL TIME: *About 2 hours*

4 dried shiitake mushrooms
1 cup chopped green cabbage
1 cup shredded carrot
2 tablespoons minced scallions
2 tablespoons minced bamboo shoots,
    wrapped in paper towel and squeezed dry
1 tablespoon minced water chestnuts,
    wrapped in paper towel and squeezed dry
1 tablespoon grated peeled fresh ginger
1 tablespoon mirin (rice wine; see Note)
2 teaspoons soy sauce
1 teaspoon dark sesame oil (See Note)
1 tablespoon cornstarch
60 dumpling wrappers

Ginger-Soy Dipping Sauce (recipe follows)
Minced scallions for garnish

Place the mushrooms in a bowl. Add warm water to cover, and let rest until the mushrooms have softened, about 30 minutes. Drain, wrap in paper towels, and squeeze dry. Mince the mushrooms with kitchen shears.

In a large mixing bowl, combine the minced mushrooms, cabbage, carrot, scallions, bamboo shoots, and water chestnuts.

In a separate bowl, stir together the ginger, mirin, soy sauce, and sesame oil. Add the cornstarch, stirring constantly to make a paste.

Stir the seasoning paste into the vegetables. Blend thoroughly. Refrigerate 1 hour to let the flavors blend.

To fill the dumplings, hold a round dumpling wrapper in the palm of your hand (if you're right-handed, use your left hand; if left-handed, use your right). Put a heaping teaspoon of filling in the center of the wrapper. Using the fingers of your free hand, push the filling inside while you close the other hand so the dough folds over it, making a little sack. Close by pressing the top edges together, pleating to make a seal. Repeat until you've used up all of the filling. Or you can make a half-moon shape by placing the wrapper on a flat surface and putting a heaping teaspoon of filling in the center. Fold the wrapper over the filling, then pinch the edges together like pleats, shaping the dumpling into a crescent as you go.

To steam the dumplings (you'll probably have to steam them in several batches), brush a steamer basket lightly with sesame oil. Fit the basket in a large pot. Add enough water to come up to the base of the steamer. Place the dumplings in the steamer, cover, and bring the water to a simmer over medium-high heat. Turn the heat down to medium-low and steam the dumplings until they are cooked through, about 15 minutes per batch.

You can also boil the dumplings. Fill a large pot with water and bring it to a boil. Add about 8 dumplings at a time and simmer gently, uncovered, for about 7 minutes. Remove with a slotted spoon, draining off the water over the pan.

To serve, pour the Ginger-Soy Dipping Sauce into a small wide-brimmed bowl, and place in the center of a large plate. Arrange the dumplings around the bowl. Provide toothpicks for dunking the dumplings, or encourage everyone to use their hands. Decorate the edges of the platter with a sprinkling of minced scallions.

You can make the filling, dough, or entire dumplings, cooked or uncooked, up to 2 days ahead.
- *Dust the dumplings or the dough well with flour or cornstarch, wrap, and refrigerate.*
- *To reheat, place in a lightly greased steamer basket over simmering water just until heated through, about 2 minutes.*

Freeze uncooked up to 3 months.
- *Instead of defrosting, cook directly from frozen, following the directions above and adding an extra minute or two.*

Ginger-Soy Dipping Sauce
  3 tablespoons soy sauce
  1 tablespoon rice vinegar
  1 teaspoon honey
  1 tablespoon grated peeled fresh ginger
  1 teaspoon finely grated garlic

In a small mixing bowl, combine the soy sauce, rice vinegar, honey, ginger, and garlic.

NOTE: Mirin and sesame oil are available at Asian specialty stores or the Asian foods section of most major supermarkets.

Crab Nori Rolls

MAKES ABOUT 42 PIECES, ENOUGH FOR
10 TO 16 PEOPLE

This version of California roll includes all of the standard ingredients—crabmeat, avocado, and rice—but is easier to prepare and tastes more of crab. You can substitute a thin frittata for the seaweed wrapper, following directions given for the Vegetable Fritatta Roll (page 45).

TIME TO PREPARE (HANDS ON): *About 20 minutes, 40 if making fritatta wrapper*

TIME TO COOK: *About 10 minutes*

TOTAL TIME: *About 30 minutes*

CRAB FILLING

   1 pound crabmeat
   2 tablespoons mayonnaise
   2 scallions, white and green part, minced
   8 sheets nori (seaweed; see Note)
   1 recipe Suschi Rice (recipe follows)
   $\frac{1}{2}$ ripe avocado, cut into 8 thin slices

In a mixing bowl, stir together the crabmeat, mayonnaise, and scallions. Place a bamboo mat (see Note) or a sheet of aluminum foil or wax paper flat on your work surface. Hold a sheet of nori briefly (about 10 seconds) over a hot burner about 3 inches above the flame (or burner if using an electric stove) just to heat. Turn the sheet and heat for about 5 seconds more. Place the nori on your bamboo mat. Wet your hands and use them to spread $\frac{1}{8}$ of the rice over the surface of the nori, leaving a margin of 1 inch at the top. Spread $\frac{1}{8}$ of the crab mixture in a horizontal strip across the rice. Spread one slice of avocado on top. Roll up the nori into a roll, using the mat as a grip and guide. Let the roll rest while making the others in the same way.

Wet the blade of a serrated knife and slice the rolls into pieces $\frac{1}{2}$ inch thick, or as thick as you'd like. Continue to wet the knife as often as necessary to cut smoothly.

NOTE: Nori is available at Asian food markets or in the Asian specialty section of many major supermarkets. Bamboo mats are available at Asian food markets. Both are also available by mail; see page 347.

- *You can't make these ahead. Prepare them shortly before serving.*

Sushi Rice

   2 cups short-grain white rice (sushi rice if available)
   $\frac{1}{2}$ cup rice vinegar
   2 tablespoons sugar
   2 teaspoons coarse salt

Place the rice in a heavy saucepan. Add $2\frac{1}{4}$ cups water and bring to a simmer. Cover the pan, turn the heat to low, and cook until the rice is plump and the water has been absorbed, about 10 minutes. Meanwhile, combine the vinegar, sugar, and salt in a small bowl.

When the rice has cooked, remove the lid and stir in the vinegar dressing while fanning the rice with a piece of cardboard in the other hand. Stir well to distribute the dressing thoroughly.

Quesadilla Strips

MAKES ABOUT 24 STRIPS, ENOUGH FOR 6 TO 8 PEOPLE

Here's a good reason to keep a stack of flour tortillas handy. Improvise freely with the filling.

TIME TO PREPARE (HANDS ON): *About 15 minutes*

TIME TO COOK: *About 5 minutes*

TOTAL TIME: *About 20 minutes*

8 large flour tortillas

FILLING

1 cup kidney beans or black beans, rinsed and drained

¼ cup reduced-fat sour cream

1 garlic clove, crushed and minced

1 cup shredded cheese (cheddar, Monterey Jack, or any containing jalapeño peppers)

1 ripe avocado

½ cup red or green salsa

1 cup shredded cooked chicken (optional)

Heat the oven to 375°F.

Place the kidney beans or black beans, sour cream, and garlic in the work bowl of a food processor or blender. Process until smooth. Transfer to a mixing bowl and stir in the cheese.

Wash out the bowl of the food processor or blender, and puree the avocado. Transfer to a small mixing bowl.

Place a tortilla on a flat work surface. Spread it with ¼ of the salsa, ¼ of the avocado, and ¼ of the bean mixture, plus ¼ of the chicken, if you're using it. Place another tortilla on top and set aside. Repeat with the remaining tortillas and filling. Line a baking sheet with aluminum foil. Place the 4 quesadillas on top, and cover with another sheet of foil. Bake until softened and the cheese melts, about 5 minutes.

Using a pizza cutter, knife, or kitchen shears, slice into strips (about 6 per tortilla). Serve promptly, with plenty of napkins.

- *You can't make these ahead. Prepare them just before you serve them.*

Menu

BITE-SIZED CORN BITS
WITH CUMIN-LIME DIPPING SAUCE (PAGE 38)
QUESADILLA STRIPS
ALL KINDS OF CHILI (PAGE 106)
RICE (PAGE 181)

Stuffed Grape Leaves

MAKES ABOUT 36, ENOUGH FOR
12 TO 16 PEOPLE

*How often have you found yourself with an entire after-
noon free, wishing you had a time-consuming appetizer to
prepare? Never? Then you're probably wondering what
leisure-laden planet this recipe comes from. But if you're
able to beg, borrow, or steal the hour or two you'll need to
try it, I guarantee you'd readily make these again, even if it
were to take you twice as long.*

TIME TO PREPARE (HANDS ON): *About 45 minutes*

TIME TO COOK: *About 1½ hours*

TOTAL TIME: *About 2¼ hours*

¼ cup pine nuts

2 tablespoons extra virgin olive oil, divided

4 large onions, chopped

1 tablespoon ground cumin

2 teaspoons ground cinnamon

1 teaspoon ground allspice

2 cups long-grain white rice

1 tablespoon tomato paste

¼ cup currants

One 17-ounce jar grape leaves, rinsed and
    drained

Juice of 1 lemon

2 cups Vegetable Broth (page 286)

Spread the pine nuts in a single layer on a sheet
of aluminum foil on a toaster tray. Place in the
toaster oven and toast on "light" setting, watching
carefully to make sure they don't burn. Remove
from the oven when golden brown.

Heat 1 tablespoon of the oil in a large nonstick
skillet over medium-high heat. When hot, add the
onions, cumin, cinnamon, and allspice. Lower the
heat to medium-low and sauté, stirring often, until
the onions are soft and limp, about 10 minutes.

Stir in the rice, tomato paste, currants, and
pine nuts, and stir to blend evenly. Add 3 cups of
water, stir well, cover, and bring to a simmer over
medium-high heat. Reduce the heat to medium-
low and continue cooking, covered, until the
water has been absorbed, about 20 minutes.

Place a grape leaf glossy side down with the
tip pointing up and the stem toward you. Place a
heaping tablespoon of filling in the center of the
leaf, then bring the lower portion up over it, then
fold the sides over that. Roll it up toward the tip
to make a little packet. Repeat until you've used
up all of the filling.

Place the filled grape leaves inside a large lid-
ded skillet, seam side down. In a small bowl,
whisk together the lemon juice and the remaining tablespoon olive oil, and pour evenly over the
grape leaves. Pour the vegetable broth on top.
Place a heavy heatproof dish (such as a Pyrex pie
plate) over the grape leaves, and cover the pan
with the lid. Bring it to a boil over medium-high
heat, then lower the heat and simmer until the
grape leaves are tender, about 1 hour.

Let cool completely before serving at room
temperature. Or refrigerate overnight and serve
chilled.

Make up to 3 days ahead.

- *Wrap or cover tightly, preferably in a glass container,
  and refrigerate.*
- *Take out of the refrigerator about 2 hours before serving,
  transfer to a serving bowl, cover with plastic wrap, and
  let come to room temperature. Do not reheat; serve cold
  or at room temperature.*

Freeze up to 6 months, well wrapped in a glass or firm plastic container.

- *To defrost, transfer to the refrigerator overnight. Then let sit at room temperature for several hours. Do not refreeze.*
- *To speed defrosting, put in a microwavable bowl (do not microwave in plastic), place a damp paper towel on top, and zap at medium strength, gently turning the rolls each time, until no longer icy. Transfer to a serving bowl and let come to room temperature.*

Vegetable Frittata Roll

SERVES 8 TO 12

Here's a distinctly unorthodox (and delicious) sushi roll.

TIME TO PREPARE (HANDS ON): *About 45 minutes*

TIME TO COOK: *About 1 hour*

TOTAL TIME: *About 1¾ hours*

1 large sweet potato
1 recipe Sushi Rice (page 42)
8 large eggs
½ cup nonfat milk
1 recipe Broiled Tofu (page 33)
Ginger-Soy Dipping Sauce (page 41)

Heat the oven to 450°F.

Wrap the sweet potato in foil and bake until tender, about 40 minutes. Unwrap and let cool. When cool enough to handle, peel it, place it in a bowl, and mash it. While the potato bakes, make the rice.

Lower the heat to 375°F.

In a large mixing bowl, beat together the eggs and milk. Squirt a 10-inch ovenproof nonstick skillet or omelet pan with nonstick cooking spray. Heat the pan over medium heat. When hot, add ¼ of the egg mixture. Cook over medium heat until the bottom sets. Place the pan in the oven and continue cooking until the top is dry and the frittata is springy. Gently slide the spatula underneath to loosen it, and turn the frittata out onto a cutting board. Trim the sides to make it into a rectangle. Transfer to a large sheet of plastic wrap. Repeat 3 times with the remaining ¾ of the mixture.

Cut the slices of tofu into ⅓-inch wide strips.

For each roll, wet your hands and spread the rice in an even layer on top, leaving a ¾-inch margin around the sides. Spread ¼ of the sweet potato over it and lay ¼ of the strips of tofu on top. Using the plastic wrap as a guide, roll up the frittata, enclosing the rice and tofu. Seal the wrap firmly around the roll and let sit for 30 minutes, until set. Unwrap, taking care not to unroll. Slice into ½-inch-thick pieces with a serrated knife. Place the dipping sauce in a small bowl and place the bowl on a large platter. Surround the bowl with overlapping slices of the frittata roll.

Make the tofu up to 3 days ahead. Refrigerate wrapped in plastic.

Salmon-Stuffed Grape Leaves

MAKES ABOUT 22, ENOUGH FOR
8 TO 14 PEOPLE

*If you're pressed for time, I apologize for tempting you with
this recipe, which isn't speedy but is terrific.*

TIME TO PREPARE (HANDS ON): *About 40 minutes*

TIME TO COOK: *About 1 hour*

TOTAL TIME: *About 2 hours*

1 large garlic clove, crushed and minced

1 tablespoon grated lemon zest

$1/4$ cup minced fresh parsley

1 tablespoon minced fresh basil or
    2 teaspoons crumbled dried

1 tablespoon minced fresh oregano or
    2 teaspoons crumbled dried

2 pounds salmon fillets

1 large egg

$1/3$ cup sour cream

Coarse salt

Extra virgin olive oil, for brushing the leaves

One 17-ounce jar grape leaves, rinsed and
    drained

Seasoned mayonnaise (see page 301)

In a mixing bowl, combine the garlic, lemon zest, parsley, basil, and oregano. Sprinkle over the fish.

Fit a large pot with a steamer basket. Add enough water to come up to the base of the steamer. Place the fish in the steamer, cover, and bring the water to a simmer over medium-high heat. Reduce the heat to medium-low and steam the until the fish is cooked through, about 5 min-

utes. Remove from the heat and set aside to cool. Leave the steamer set up and ready for use again.

In a large mixing bowl, beat together the egg and sour cream. Cut the fish into small pieces and add it to the bowl. Mash it with the egg mixture. Season with salt.

Fill a custard cup or small bowl with olive oil. For each roll, place a grape leaf flat on your work surface glossy side down with the tip pointing up and the stem toward you. Brush the grape leaf lightly with olive oil. Put a heaping spoonful of the fish mixture in the lower center. Fold the sides over the filling, then fold the top down so it overlaps. Roll the leaf up from the bottom, and place seam side down in the steamer. Repeat with the rest. Bring the water in the steamer to a simmer over medium heat. Cover and steam for 45 minutes, until the rolls are soft and the grape leaves are tender. Let cool and serve with seasoned mayonnaise.

Make up to 3 days ahead.
- *Wrap or cover tightly, preferably in a glass container, and refrigerate.*
- *Take out of the refrigerator about 2 hours before serving, transfer to a serving plate, cover with plastic wrap, and let come to room temperature.*

Freeze up to 3 months, well wrapped in foil.
- *To defrost, unwrap the foil and rewrap in plastic. Transfer to the refrigerator overnight. Then let sit at room temperature for several hours until thoroughly thawed. Do not refreeze.*
- *To speed defrosting, put in a single layer on a microwavable plate. Place a damp paper towel on top, and zap at medium strength, rotating the plate 180 degrees each time, until no longer icy in the center. Let sit at room temperature for at least 10 minutes before serving.*

Shrimp Toast

MAKES ABOUT 18 SANDWICHES, ENOUGH
FOR 6 TO 8 PEOPLE

Not to be confused with those pale pink Styrofoamy things you get at cheap Chinese restaurants, these toasted shrimp sandwiches live up to the warm, comforting promise of their name.

TIME TO PREPARE (HANDS ON): *About 20 minutes*

TIME TO COOK: *About 15 minutes*

TOTAL TIME: *About 35 minutes*

$^{1}\!/_{2}$ cup dry white wine

1 pound medium shrimp, shells on

3 large eggs, separated (2 yolks should be
     reserved for another purpose)

1 tablespoon grated peeled fresh ginger

2 tablespoons minced fresh thyme or
     1 tablespoon crumbled dried

Salt and freshly ground black pepper

12 slices firm white bread, crusts removed

$^{1}\!/_{4}$ cup sesame seeds

1 tablespoon extra virgin olive oil

Chopped fresh parsley for garnish

Bring the wine plus 1 cup water to a boil in a medium saucepan. Add the shrimp and boil until they turn bright pink, about 3 minutes. Remove from the heat. Leave the shrimp to cool in the cooking liquid.

When cool enough to handle, peel the shrimp. Place the shrimp in the work bowl of a food processor, along with one of the egg yolks. Process in short pulses until chunky (about 4 pulses). Transfer to a mixing bowl and stir in the ginger and thyme. Season with salt and pepper.

Heat the oven to 400° F.

Using a biscuit cutter 3 inches in diameter, cut 2 rounds out of each slice of bread.

Spread 12 of the circles with the shrimp mixture. Top with the remaining rounds, making 12 sandwiches. Put the egg whites in a wide shallow bowl, and blend with a fork. Put the sesame seeds in another. Dip each sandwich in the egg white, then in the seeds. Place on a nonstick baking sheet. Brush each sandwich lightly with olive oil. Bake until lightly browned, about 10 minutes. Transfer to a serving dish and sprinkle the entire dish lightly with chopped parsley. Pass the shrimp toast while still warm.

- *You can't make these ahead. Prepare them just before you serve them.*

Pizzettes

*Equal parts project and appetizer, these bite-sized pizzas
lend themselves to the Tom Sawyer approach to preparation. Give one of your guests the "opportunity" to come
early to share the pleasure of making them with you.*

TIME TO PREPARE (HANDS ON): *About 15 minutes for each topping*

TIME TO COOK: *About 20 minutes*

TOTAL TIME: *About 35 minutes, using store-bought or previously
prepared dough*

Extra virgin olive oil
1 **recipe Pizza Dough (page 292), or 1
pound store-bought**
1 **recipe topping of choice (recipes follow)**

To make the Pizzettes, preheat the oven to 450°F.
Generously oil twelve 2-inch tartlet pans with
extra virgin olive oil.

Divide the pizza dough into 12 equal-size
pieces and press a piece of dough into each tartlet pan. Cut 12 pieces of parchment paper or tin-
foil to fit over the tart pans and oil each with
extra virgin olive oil. Fit them, oiled side down,
over the pizza dough and hold in place by pouring dried beans or pastry weights on top. Bake for
10 minutes, until the dough sets. Remove the
weights and parchment paper from the dough.
Top the pizzettes with the topping of your
choice. Return to the oven and bake until the
dough has browned and the cheese has melted,
about another 10 minutes.

Zucchini and Smoked Cheese

1 **zucchini**
2 **teaspoons extra virgin olive oil**
1 **garlic clove, crushed and minced**
½ **pound cherry tomatoes, cut in half**
2 **tablespoons minced fresh mint**
⅓ **cup shredded smoked scamorza or
provolone cheese**

Fill a medium pot with water and bring it to a
boil. Put the whole zucchini in the boiling water
and simmer over medium heat for 5 minutes, until
just soft but not mushy. Remove with a slotted
spoon and put in the refrigerator to cool slightly,
about 5 minutes. Slice it lengthwise into thin
slices. Cut each slice into 4 quarters.

Heat the oil in a small heavy saucepan over
medium-high heat. When hot, add the garlic,
lower the heat to medium-low, and swish the garlic through the oil until it starts to color. Quickly
remove the garlic with a slotted spoon and discard. Toss in the tomatoes and stir briskly over
medium heat until they break down into pulp,
about 3 minutes. Remove from the heat. Stir in
the mint.

Using a large spoon, drizzle the sauce over the
prepared pizza dough. Top each with an equal
amount of zucchini and cheese.

Mushroom and Bell Pepper

1 red bell pepper

1 yellow bell pepper

2 teaspoons extra virgin olive oil

1 medium onion, chopped

$\frac{1}{2}$ pound mixed mushrooms (such as cremini, white button, portobello, shiitake), chopped

$\frac{1}{3}$ cup shredded fontina cheese

Heat the oven to 450°F. Cut the bell peppers in half lengthwise, remove the stem, core, and seeds, and place, skin side up, on a nonstick baking sheet. Bake until the skin on the peppers blackens, about 20 minutes. Transfer to a paper bag and toss into the refrigerator to cool for 5 minutes. Peel the peppers and slice them into thin strips.

Meanwhile, heat the oil in a nonstick skillet over medium-high heat. When hot, add the onion, lower the heat to medium-low, and sauté, stirring often, until the onion is soft, about 7 minutes. Add the mushrooms and continue stirring over medium heat until they soften and give up their liquid, about 5 minutes. Continue cooking until the liquid from the mushrooms evaporates, about 3 minutes more.

Distribute the peppers and the mushroom mixture evenly over the prepared pizza dough. Sprinkle an equal amount of cheese on top of each.

Classic Tomato and Mozzarella

1 tablespoon extra virgin olive oil

1 garlic clove, crushed

$1\frac{1}{2}$ pounds tomatoes, peeled, seeded, and chopped

$\frac{1}{4}$ cup minced fresh basil

$\frac{2}{3}$ cup shredded mozzarella cheese

Heat the oil in a small heavy saucepan over medium-high heat. When hot, add the garlic, reduce the heat to medium-low, and swish the garlic through the oil until it starts to color. Quickly remove the garlic with a slotted spoon and discard. Toss in the tomatoes and stir briskly over medium heat until they break down into pulp, about 3 to 5 minutes. Remove from the heat. Stir in the basil. Using a large spoon, drizzle the sauce evenly over the prepared pizza dough. Top each with an equal amount of cheese.

Make up to 3 days ahead.
- *Refrigerate fully baked pizzettes wrapped in plastic or in zip-lock bags. Press out the air before you seal the bags.*
- *To reheat, wrap in foil and heat at 350° F. until warmed through, 10 to 20 minutes. Check after 10 minutes.*

Freeze leftovers up to 3 months.
- *To defrost, wrap in foil and heat at 350° F. until warmed through, about 30 minutes.*

Broiled Mushrooms

These always work. Use firm, unblemished mushroom caps, very good oil, a reliable oven timer, and don't wander away from the oven.

TIME TO PREPARE (HANDS ON): *About 10 minutes*

TIME TO COOK: *About 5 minutes*

TOTAL TIME: *About 1¼ hours, including time to marinate*

2 tablespoons extra virgin olive oil
2 tablespoons fresh lemon juice
¼ cup minced fresh parsley
1 garlic clove, crushed and minced
12 medium mushroom caps
6 ounces shaved or finely cubed taleggio,
    mozzarella, or smoked mozzarella cheese
½ roasted bell pepper, chopped (optional;
    see page 302)

In a large mixing bowl, whisk together the olive oil, lemon juice, parsley, and garlic.

Add the mushrooms, toss well, and let marinate about 1 hour.

Heat the broiler. Line a broiler tray with aluminum foil.

Toss the mushrooms again and place, smooth side up, on the broiler tray. Broil 2 inches from the heat until soft, about 3 minutes.

Turn over and fill the mushrooms with any of the cheeses and the roasted bell pepper, if used.

Broil 2 inches from the heat until the cheese is bubbly, about 1½ minutes. Serve right away.

NOTE: *If you have an extra 5 minutes, tear up 2 slices of white bread, crusts removed. Pulverize in a blender or food processor and sprinkle on top of the mushrooms. Drip a bit of olive oil on top (neat trick: use a small clean medicine dropper for this!), then broil as directed.*

• *Fill the mushrooms up to 4 hours ahead. Refrigerate in a single layer until ready to broil.*

Savory Puff Pastry

All you need to make these gems is a six-week course at the culinary academy covering the fundamentals of puff pastry . . . or a box of dough from your supermarket's freezer.

TIME TO PREPARE (HANDS ON): *About 40 minutes*

TIME TO COOK: *About 12 minutes*

TOTAL TIME: *About 45 minutes*

1 tablespoon extra virgin olive oil
2 leeks, white part only, sliced
2 carrots, peeled and thinly sliced
1 yellow or orange bell pepper, cored,
    seeded, and thinly sliced
2 medium zucchini, peeled and thinly sliced
2 cups coarsely chopped washed fresh
    spinach or chard
1 pound frozen puff pastry dough, thawed
1 egg, lightly beaten

Heat the oil in a skillet over medium-high heat. When hot, add the leeks, carrots, bell pepper, and zucchini. Lower the heat to medium-low and sauté, stirring often, until the vegetables are soft and limp, about 8 minutes. Add the spinach or chard and continue stirring until the greens wilt, about 2 minutes.

Heat the oven to 425°F.

Place 1 sheet of pastry on a clean flat surface. Spread the vegetables over the dough, leaving a ½-inch border all around. Cover with the other sheet of pastry. Lightly roll a rolling pin over the dough to seal the sheets together and encase the filling.

Use a 2-inch biscuit cutter to cut out rounds of dough. Place on a baking sheet. Brush with the beaten egg. Bake until puffy and golden, about 12 minutes. Serve hot.

- *Up to 3 days ahead, you can roast, peel, and slice the peppers. Otherwise, this is strictly last minute. Make it when you've prepared the rest of the meal in advance.*

Ricotta-Filled Figs

MAKES 8 FIGS, ENOUGH FOR
6 TO 8 PEOPLE

These will go fast. Serve them as part of an ample cheese plate before a light supper. Make sure to allow enough time to let them chill through before serving, about 3 hours.

TIME TO PREPARE (HANDS ON): *About 15 minutes*

TIME TO COOK: *Just under 1 hour*

TOTAL TIME: *About 4¼ hours, including time to chill*

2 tablespoons red wine
1 whole cinnamon stick
One 2-inch slice lemon peel, yellow part only
8 large dried Mission figs
2 tablespoons pine nuts
1 cup ricotta cheese
1 tablespoon honey
1 teaspoon grated lemon zest

Put the wine, cinnamon stick, and lemon peel in a medium saucepan and add 2 cups of water. Cover and bring to a boil over medium-high heat. Reduce the heat to medium-low and simmer 15 minutes to allow the cinnamon and lemon to steep.

Add the figs and bring back to a gentle simmer, uncovered, over medium heat. Remove from the heat, cover, and let sit until the figs have softened, about 40 minutes. Drain and let cool.

Meanwhile, spread the pine nuts in a single layer on a sheet of aluminum foil on a toaster tray. Place in the toaster oven and toast on "light" setting, watching carefully to make sure they don't burn. Remove from the oven when golden brown, about 2 minutes.

In a small mixing bowl, combine the ricotta, honey, lemon zest, and pine nuts.

Carefully slice off the top (stem end) of each fig. Using a teaspoon, stuff as much filling into the center of each as you can without forcing it to split. Refrigerate until chilled through, about 3 hours.

Make up to 3 days ahead.
- *Place in a single layer on a tray or plate. Wrap tightly with plastic and refrigerate.*
- *Take out of the refrigerator about 2 hours before serving and let come to room temperature.*

Starters

A First Course

▶ ## Soups

Zucchini Soup
Sweet Bell Pepper Soup with Rice
Spinach and Rice Soup
Artichoke and Spinach Soup
Simple Broth with Gnocchi di Pane
Mushroom Soup with Gnocchi
Lentil Soup with Pumpkin
Curried Lentil Soup with Mango
Carrot-Ginger Soup
Cold Cream of Vegetable Soup
Peach and Cantaloupe Soup
Corn and Sweet Potato Chowder
Scallop and Potato Soup
Sweet Potato Peanut Soup
Creamy Lobster and Potato Soup

▶ ## Risotto

Blueberry Risotto
Apple Risotto
Grape Risotto
Lemon Risotto
Pumpkin and Mushroom Risotto
Risotto with Fennel, Saffron, and
    Tomato
Lobster Risotto
Rice Roulade with Spinach or Bell
    Peppers

▶ ## Pasta and Gnocchi

Tomato and Fennel Sauce
Pumpkin Ravioli
Potato-Spinach Ravioli
Ravioli with Artichokes
Rich Tomato and Spinach Sauce
Ricotta Cheese Gnocchi Two Ways
Pumpkin Gnocchi

▶ ## Terrines, Tartare, and More

Three Terrines: Salmon and Shrimp
    Terrine, Three-Vegetable Terrine,
    and Black Olive–Bell Pepper Terrine
Crab and Avocado Timbales
Seafood Salad
Tartare and Ceviche: Salmon Tartare
    with Orange, Scallop Ceviche, Tuna
    Ceviche, Tuna Tartare
Crepes with Ricotta and Spices
Vegetable Torta

A First Course

MORE THAN A FIRST COURSE is missing from a dinner where one is not offered, such as the particular types of foods that serve as starters and the extra time to enjoy the company of your guests. While it may be unrealistic to assume you have the time to prepare a first course, here are three good reasons to try to make the time.

Reason #1: *Gastronomic.* Some of the best dishes are too unwieldy to eat as appetizers, too "light" as entrées, and too much like soup (in fact, they *are* soup) to serve on the side. So, if you're going to have the chance to enjoy these things, you've got to serve them as a course.

#2: *Social.* When you serve a first course, everyone's able to enjoy more time with one another at the table without having to sit over empty plates.

#3: *Philosophical.* Everyone's moving too fast. We're all too eager to jump up from the table and get on to the next thing. Here's your chance to impose a little leisure; get everyone to sit down and savor the risotto.

A Simple No-Fail Method for Choosing a First Course

Run the possibilities through your mind quickly. Stop at the one that makes you hungry.

Harmony and Balance: Matching the First Course with the Entrée

Harmony of Seasonings: Much as you love foods of all kinds, moving from garlicky toast with tomatoes and basil to cauliflower curry might be as jarring as switching from a classical station to heavy metal in midnote. Once you've taken to the particular harmony of a flavor group, the distinctive flavors of another—even one you love— will come as a shock.

Balance of Substance: If you're serving a rich entrée, make a light first course. And if you've chosen a substantial first course, make the entrée light.

And consider consistency: If you're serving a stew as an entrée, soup is too similar to serve as a first course. Serve something firm, such as a terrine (page 91) or a roulade (page 119), instead. And if you're serving calzone, then something that must be spread on bread, such as a vegetable pâte, would be too similar. Soup or salad would be just right.

TIRED, HASSLED, AND OTHERWISE OVER-WHELMED PARTY GIVERS WANT TO KNOW

"Is it ever all right not to serve a first course?"
   Yes!

- When you're serving lots of appetizers, or one that's substantial, such as Crab Nori Rolls (page 42), Steamed Vegetable Dumplings (page 40), or Salmon-Stuffed Grape Leaves (page 46)

- When it's a barbecue or casual meal outdoors

- When it's a family-style dinner among friends where all of the food will be served on one plate

- When it's a last-minute, spur-of-the-moment dinner

SOUPS

There isn't much in medieval dining practices to guide and instruct the contemporary host. Let's say you want to feed soup to a crowd. You can't take your cue from the Middle Ages, when guests helped themselves directly from a trough in the middle of the table.

But serving hot soup to more than six people in these relatively fastidious times is tricky, unless you recruit a guest to help you carry out each serving. Or, if the occasion is informal enough, have each guest troop to the stove to pick up their bowl as you ladle it out, and bring their own to the table. Or another option is to bring the soup to the table in its pot or a serving bowl, ladle it out yourself, and have your guests pass it down.

Zucchini Soup

SERVES 4

It seems implausible that zucchini, which is mostly water, would yield a soup as full-bodied and full-flavored as this . . . but here it does.

TIME TO PREPARE (HANDS ON): *About 10 minutes*

TIME TO COOK: *About 30 minutes*

TOTAL TIME: *About 40 minutes*

1 tablespoon extra virgin olive oil
1 medium red onion
3 medium zucchini, peeled and chopped
3 cups Vegetable Broth (page 286), Chicken Broth (page 285), or water
1 large egg
¼ cup grated Parmesan cheese
¼ cup minced fresh parsley
¼ cup minced fresh basil or 2 tablespoons crumbled dried
Coarse salt and freshly ground black pepper
4 slices bread, toasted

Heat the oil in a medium, heavy saucepan over medium-high heat. When hot, add the onion and zucchini and sauté until tender, about 6 minutes. Add broth or water to cover and simmer 30 minutes, until the zucchini is soft enough to puree.

Using a food processor, or an immersion blender, puree. If using a food processor, pour the soup back into the saucepan over medium heat.

In a mixing bowl, whisk together the egg, Parmesan cheese, parsley, and basil. Then whisk the mixture into the hot soup. If it looks as though it's curdling, you haven't done anything wrong. This is how it's supposed to look. Season with salt and pepper.

Serve with toast.

• *You can't make this ahead. Prepare it just before serving.*

Sweet Bell Pepper Soup with Rice

SERVES 4 TO 6

Sentiment is a good thing in a cook, a seasoning of sorts. Here's a soup to prepare when you're full of good feeling: one that you'll render to the delight of all.

TIME TO PREPARE (HANDS ON): *About 20 minutes*

TIME TO COOK: *About 1 hour*

TOTAL TIME: *Under 1 1/2 hours*

- 1 tablespoon extra virgin olive oil
- 2 onions, chopped
- 2 garlic cloves, crushed and minced
- 2 leeks, white part plus 1 inch of green, thinly sliced
- 1 celery stalk, chopped
- 2 carrots, peeled and chopped
- 2 red bell peppers, cored, seeded, and chopped
- 2 teaspoons crumbled dried oregano
- 2 teaspoons crumbled dried basil
- 1/4 cup minced fresh parsley
- 1 bay leaf
- 1 medium red or white potato, peeled and chopped
- 1 medium rutabaga (yellow turnip), peeled and chopped
- 4 cups Vegetable Broth (page 286)
- 1/2 cup long-grain white rice
- Coarse salt and freshly ground black pepper

Heat the olive oil in a large saucepan or pressure cooker over medium-high heat. When hot, add the onions, garlic, leeks, celery, carrots, bell pep-pers, oregano, basil, parsley, and bay leaf. Turn the heat down to medium-low and sauté until the vegetables are soft, about 12 minutes. Add the potato and rutabaga and stir to coat with the vegetables. Add the broth and bring to a gentle boil. If using a saucepan, cover and reduce the heat to low. Simmer until the potato is soft enough to puree, about 20 minutes.

If you're using a pressure cooker, lock on the lid and bring to full pressure. Cook at full pressure for 10 minutes, then let the pressure fall on its own. Tilt the cooker away from you and un-lock the lid.

Remove the bay leaf and set aside. Using an immersion blender, or transferring the mixture to a food processor or blender, puree. Return to the saucepan or pressure cooker, if necessary. Stir in the rice, along with 1 cup of water, and bring to a simmer. If using a saucepan, cover and continue to simmer over medium-low heat until the rice is cooked, about 20 minutes. If the soup seems to be getting too thick, or the rice hasn't cooked, add another 1/2 cup of water or vegetable broth. Season with salt and pepper.

If using a pressure cooker, after adding the rice and water, lock on the lid, bring back up to full pressure, and cook for 7 minutes. Remove from the heat and allow the pressure to come down on its own. Tilt the cooker away from yourself and remove the lid.

Make up to 3 days ahead.
- *Seal in a tightly covered container and refrigerate.*
- *To reheat, transfer to a heavy saucepan and stir over medium heat until warmed through. Or transfer to a microwavable bowl and microwave at full power, turning the bowl at 2-minute intervals, until heated through.*

Freeze up to 6 months, well wrapped in a glass or firm plastic container.

- *To defrost, see reheating instructions above.*

Spinach and Rice Soup

SERVES 4

VEGETARIAN ENTRÉE!
Serve with Caponata (page 32)
and Real Bread (page 212).

This soup, along with a salad of some kind, is sufficient—and heartening—as a spur-of-the-moment wintertime supper. So go ahead and invite your friends in after a day of skating, sledding, or slogging through a cold day downtown; the soup is so easy to make, you won't feel stressed, and it's so good, they'll be glad you offered it.

TIME TO PREPARE (HANDS ON): *About 15 minutes*

TIME TO COOK: *About 20 minutes*

TOTAL TIME: *About 45 minutes*

1 tablespoon extra virgin olive oil

1 onion, chopped

1 celery stalk, chopped

2 sage leaves, minced

1/4 cup minced fresh parsley

10 ounces chopped fresh washed spinach or
    one 10-ounce package frozen chopped
    spinach, defrosted and squeezed dry

1/2 cup white rice

4 cups Vegetable or Chicken Broth
    (pages 286, 285)

1 cup milk

1 large egg

1 large egg yolk

3 tablespoons grated Parmesan cheese

Pinch ground nutmeg

Coarse salt and freshly ground black pepper

Heat the oil in a large saucepan over medium-high heat. When hot, add the onion, celery, sage, and parsley, reduce the heat to medium-low, and sauté, stirring often, until the vegetables are soft and limp, about 7 minutes. Add the spinach and rice, and stir to blend with the other ingredients. Add the broth, raise the heat to medium-high, and bring to a boil. Cover, reduce the heat to medium-low, and simmer gently until the rice is getting tender, about 10 minutes. Remove from the heat.

Place the milk in a mixing bowl and add a portion of the hot soup to the milk. Continue adding little by little, stirring, until the milk is very warm. Stir the milk into the remaining soup in the saucepan. Return to the stove on medium-low heat, and continue cooking, uncovered, until the rice is cooked through, about 10 minutes more. Make sure to stir often and keep the soup from boiling.

In a mixing bowl, combine the egg, egg yolk, and grated cheese. Pour into the hot soup and stir well to blend. If it looks as though it's curdling, you haven't done anything wrong. It's supposed to look that way. Sprinkle with nutmeg and season with salt and pepper.

- *You can't make this ahead. Prepare it just before serving.*

Artichoke and Spinach Soup

SERVES 6

Eating whole artichokes leaf by leaf isn't pretty, and it's unfair to expect guests to sacrifice their dignity for the sake of your first course. It's a good thing there are plenty of wonderful alternatives to serving them whole—this, for instance. It's particularly good in early spring, when the first fresh artichokes arrive and the air is still cool enough for hot soup.

The finishing touch of grated lemon zest, minced parsley, and grated Parmesan cheese makes it taste, as well as look, wonderful.

TIME TO PREPARE (HANDS ON): *About 20 minutes*

TIME TO COOK: *About 50 minutes*

TOTAL TIME: *About 1 hour, 10 minutes*

---

4 artichokes
Juice of 1 lemon
1 tablespoon extra virgin olive oil
2 garlic cloves, crushed and minced
2 leeks, white part plus 1 inch of green,
   thinly sliced
1/4 cup barley
1 1/2 cups tomato puree
3 cups Vegetable Broth (page 286)
10 ounces washed fresh spinach, coarsely
   chopped, or one 10-ounce box frozen
   spinach, defrosted and chopped
1 tablespoon grated lemon zest
3 tablespoons minced fresh parsley
2 tablespoons grated Parmesan cheese
Coarse salt and freshly ground black pepper

To prepare the artichokes, cut away the stem and snap off the tough outer leaves. (This will amount to more than half the artichoke.) Once you're down to the light green tender leaves, cut the artichoke in half lengthwise. With a melon scoop, paring knife, or teaspoon, scoop out the fuzz and prickly leaves at the center. Finally, cut the artichoke into quarters lengthwise, then cut each quarter in half lengthwise again. Place them in a bowl of water with the lemon juice and set aside.

Heat the oil in a heavy saucepan over medium-high heat. When hot, add the garlic and leeks. Reduce the heat to medium and sauté until the leeks are soft, about 7 minutes. Add the barley and artichokes, and stir well to coat with the garlic and leeks. Stir in the tomato puree and broth. Bring to a simmer. Cover and simmer until the artichokes and barley are cooked, about 50 minutes.

Add the spinach, lemon zest, parsley, and Parmesan cheese, and stir until the spinach is cooked, about 3 minutes. Season with salt and pepper.

In a pressure cooker, proceed as directed above up through the point where you add the tomato puree and broth. Bring to a gentle boil, lock on the lid, and allow the cooker to come to full pressure. Maintain the pressure for 20 minutes. Remove from the heat, and allow the pressure to come down on its own.

When the pressure comes all the way down, tilt the cooker away from yourself and remove the lid. Add the spinach, lemon zest, parsley, and Parmesan cheese, and stir until the spinach is cooked, about 3 minutes. Season with salt and pepper.

Make up to 3 days ahead.

- *Wrap or cover tightly, preferably in a glass container, and refrigerate.*
- *To reheat, transfer to a heavy saucepan and stir over medium heat until warmed through. Or transfer to a microwavable bowl and microwave at full power, turning the bowl at 2-minute intervals, stirring after each, until heated through.*

Freeze up to 6 months, well wrapped in a glass or firm plastic container.

- *To defrost, see reheating instructions above.*

Simple Broth with Gnocchi di Pane

SERVES 4

Here's a light start to a rich meal, or something to have with salad at lunch.

TIME TO PREPARE (HANDS ON): *About 15 minutes (using previously prepared broth)*

TIME TO COOK: *About 5 minutes*

TOTAL TIME: *Just about 45 minutes, including time to soak the bread*

1 cup milk
4 cups loosely packed day-old chunks of bread without crust
2 large eggs
Approximately 1 ⅓ cups unbleached all-purpose flour
2 tablespoons grated Parmesan cheese
¼ teaspoon ground nutmeg

3 cups Vegetable Broth (page 286) or Chicken Broth (page 285)
Pinch salt
Minced fresh parsley and/or basil for garnish

Place the milk in a deep bowl and add the bread. Let the bread soak for 15 minutes. In a separate bowl, beat together the eggs, flour, cheese, and nutmeg.

Squeeze the bread as dry as possible and crumble it to bits. Drain the milk and return the crumbled bread to the bowl. Add the egg mixture and mix well with your hands. Shape into about 12 small torpedoes.

Bring the broth to a gentle simmer in a medium saucepan. Add the salt and the gnocchi, and boil until they rise to the surface, about 2 minutes. Using a slotted spoon, transfer them to a plate. When you've cooked all of the gnocchi, strain the broth and return it to the saucepan on medium heat. Distribute the gnocchi evenly among serving bowls, and ladle the warm broth on top.

Sprinkle each serving with an equal amount of minced fresh parsley and/or basil.

- *You can't make this ahead. Prepare it just before serving.*

Mushroom Soup with Gnocchi

SERVES 6

Compound recipes are annoying, I know, so I don't offer many, making exceptions only for the exceptional, such as this soup, which calls for pumpkin or bread gnocchi.

TIME TO PREPARE (HANDS ON): *About 40 minutes, including time to make gnocchi*

TIME TO COOK: *Between 1¼ and 2 hours, depending upon which gnocchi you choose*

TOTAL TIME: *Up to 2 hours, 40 minutes*

1 recipe Pumpkin Gnocchi (page 90) or
    Gnocchi di Pane (page 59)
4 cups Vegetable Broth (page 286) or
    Chicken Broth (page 285)
4 dried porcini mushrooms
1 tablespoon extra virgin olive oil
1 onion, chopped
2 garlic cloves, crushed and minced
1 celery stalk, chopped
1 carrot, peeled and chopped
1 pound firm mushrooms, such as cremini or
    portobello, trimmed and chopped
Coarse salt and freshly ground black pepper
¼ cup grated Parmesan cheese
Tiny pinch ground nutmeg for each serving

If you're using gnocchi di pane, make them, then boil them in the vegetable broth you're using for this soup. This will take about 45 minutes. Set the gnocchi aside in a lightly greased baking dish, strain the broth, adding additional broth if necessary to make 4 cups, and proceed with this recipe.

(You can make the gnocchi up to a day ahead. When cool, cover with plastic wrap and refrigerate. Refrigerate the strained broth separately.)

If you're making the pumpkin gnocchi, boil them as directed in the recipe. This will take about 1½ hours total. Set aside in a lightly greased baking dish while you make the soup. (You can make the gnocchi up to a day ahead. Refrigerate as directed above.)

Put the porcini in a small bowl and add hot water to cover. Let sit until soft, about 30 minutes. Strain the soaking water and add to the vegetable or chicken broth. Chop the mushrooms and set aside.

In a large saucepan or pressure cooker, heat the oil over medium-high heat. When hot, add the onion, garlic, celery, and carrot. Lower the heat to medium-low and sauté, stirring often, until the vegetables are soft and limp, about 7 minutes. Add the porcini and the chopped fresh mushrooms. Continue sautéing until the mushrooms darken and become tender, about 5 minutes.

Add the vegetable broth and bring to a simmer. If you're using a saucepan, cover and simmer for 45 minutes. If you're using a pressure cooker, lock on the lid and allow the cooker to come to full pressure. Maintain the pressure for 15 minutes.

Remove from the heat and allow the pressure to come down on its own. Tilt the cooker away from yourself and remove the lid.

Season with salt and pepper.

Place 3 to 4 gnocchi in individual soup bowls and pour the hot soup on top. Sprinkle each serving with an equal amount of grated Parmesan cheese and a tiny pinch of nutmeg.

Make and boil the gnocchi up to 1 day ahead.
- *Wrap or cover tightly, preferably in a glass container, and refrigerate.*
- *Take out of the refrigerator about 2 hours before serving and let come to room temperature. The hot soup will warm them at serving time.*

Lentil Soup with Pumpkin

SERVES 6 TO 8

VEGETARIAN ENTRÉE!
Serve with Stuffed Grape Leaves (page 44)
and Orange-Infused Baba Ghanouj (page 27).

If you're at all like me, just when you think you've found your all-time favorite lentil soup, you taste another that's better still. Here's a current favorite.

TIME TO PREPARE (HANDS ON): *About 15 minutes*

TIME TO COOK: *About 45 minutes*

TOTAL TIME: *About 1 hour*

1 tablespoon extra virgin olive oil
2 onions, 1 chopped and 1 cut into quarters
1 celery stalk, chopped
1 carrot, peeled and chopped
2 cups shredded cabbage
1 pound fresh pumpkin, peeled, seeded, and
  cut into chunks
4 cups Vegetable Broth (page 286)
1 whole clove
1 cup lentils, rinsed
Coarse salt and freshly ground black pepper
Pinch ground nutmeg
¼ cup grated Parmesan cheese

Heat the oil in a large saucepan, stockpot, or pressure cooker. When hot, add the chopped onion, celery, carrot, and cabbage, and sauté until soft, about 10 minutes. Add the pumpkin and stir to combine with the other vegetables, about 2 minutes. Add the vegetable broth and bring to a boil. If you're using a saucepan or stockpot, cover and simmer until the pumpkin is soft enough to puree, about 25 minutes. If you're using a pressure cooker, lock on the lid and bring to full pressure. Cook at full pressure for 10 minutes, then let the pressure fall on its own. Tilt the cooker away from yourself when you unlock the lid.

Meanwhile, stick the clove into one of the onion quarters. Place all 4 quarters in a medium saucepan with the lentils. Add water to cover by 1 inch, bring to a simmer, cover, and cook until the lentils are soft, about 20 minutes. Drain in a fine sieve. Remove and discard the clove and as much of the onion as you can.

Puree the pumpkin mixture and stir in the lentils. Season with nutmeg and sprinkle with Parmesan cheese. Serve hot.

Make up to 3 days ahead.
- *Seal in a tightly covered container and refrigerate.*
- *To reheat, transfer to a heavy saucepan and stir over medium heat until warmed through. Or transfer to a microwavable bowl and microwave at full power, turning the bowl at 2-minute intervals, until heated through.*

Freeze up to 6 months, well wrapped in a firm plastic container.
- *To defrost, see reheating instructions above.*

Curried Lentil Soup with Mango

SERVES 4

VEGETARIAN ENTRÉE!
Serve with Crepes with Ricotta and Spices
(page 100), Naan (page 226) or Lavash
(page 228), and rice.

*You might think that a soup made with mango would be
unbearably sweet. In fact, with tomato to temper the fruc-
tose, it's unequivocally delicious. Choose a big, pulpy
mango, with a bright orange blush.*

TIME TO PREPARE (HANDS ON): *About 15 minutes*

TIME TO COOK: *About 45 minutes*

TOTAL TIME: *About 1 hour*

---

1 cup lentils

1 large potato, peeled and sliced

1 teaspoon crumbled dried thyme

1 red bell pepper

1 tablespoon extra virgin olive oil

1 onion, chopped

2 tablespoons grated peeled fresh ginger

1 cup tomato puree

1 large ripe mango, peeled and chopped

1 tablespoon curry powder

Coarse salt and cayenne pepper

2 tablespoons minced fresh cilantro

Place the lentils in a heavy saucepan along with
the potato and thyme. Add water to cover by 3
inches, bring to a simmer, cover, and simmer
gently until the lentils are cooked, about 30
minutes.

Meanwhile, heat a toaster oven or oven to
450°F. and line a small baking sheet with aluminum foil. Slice the red pepper in half lengthwise and remove the core and seeds. Place, skin
side up, on the foil-lined sheet. Bake until the
skin blackens, about 15 minutes. Remove and let
cool. (You can speed the cooling by putting the
pepper in a paper bag and throwing it into the refrigerator for 5 minutes.)

Peel the skin off the pepper and coarsely chop
it. While the lentils finish cooking, heat the olive
oil in a heavy saucepan. Sauté the onion, ginger,
and peeled roasted pepper until the onion is soft
and limp, about 15 minutes. Stir in the tomato
puree and mix to blend. Remove from the heat.

Using a food processor or blender, puree the
lentils in their cooking liquid, or use an immersion blender right in the saucepan. Add the
chopped mango and process again until smooth.
Season with curry powder, salt, and cayenne pepper, and return to the saucepan. Stir in the
minced cilantro and heat through before serving.

Make up to 3 days ahead.
- *Seal in a tightly covered container and refrigerate.*
- *To reheat, transfer to a heavy saucepan and stir over
  medium heat until warmed through. Or transfer to a microwavable bowl and microwave at full power, turning
  the bowl at 2-minute intervals, until heated through.*

*Freeze up to 6 months, well wrapped in a firm plastic
container.*
- *To defrost, see reheating instructions above.*

LOVE THOSE LEFTOVERS!
The soup will thicken as it cools. Heat gently
and serve warm over brown rice.

Carrot-Ginger Soup

SERVES 4 TO 6

There are countless versions of carrot and ginger soup; whether that makes it a classic or a cliché depends, of course, on how you feel about it. This one is soothing and sweet.

TIME TO PREPARE (HANDS ON): *About 15 minutes*

TIME TO COOK: *About 30 minutes*

TOTAL TIME: *About 45 minutes*

---

1 tablespoon extra virgin olive oil

1 leek, white part plus 1 inch of green, thinly sliced

1 Vidalia onion, thinly sliced

1 tablespoon grated peeled fresh ginger

1 pound carrots, peeled and chopped

1 potato, peeled and sliced

1 bay leaf

2 cups Vegetable Broth (page 286)

Ground nutmeg

Coarse salt and freshly ground black pepper

GARNISH

Heavy cream

Finely grated orange zest and minced fresh parsley

Heat the olive oil in a heavy saucepan over medium-high heat. When hot, add the leek, onion, ginger, and carrots. Reduce the heat to medium-low, and sauté until the vegetables are soft, about 12 minutes. Stir in the potato, bay leaf, and vegetable broth. Bring to a gentle boil. Cover, reduce the heat to low, and simmer until the carrots and potatoes are soft enough to puree, about 20 minutes. Remove the bay leaf, transfer the mixture, in batches, to a food processor or blender (or use an immersion blender right in the pot), and puree. Return to the saucepan to reheat. Season with nutmeg, salt, and pepper.

In a pressure cooker, heat the olive oil and proceed as above to the point where you add the broth. (On an electric stove, move to a separate burner on low heat.) Bring to a gentle boil, lock on the lid, and allow the cooker to come to full pressure. Maintain the pressure for 10 minutes.

Remove from the heat and allow the pressure to come down on its own. Tilt the cooker away from yourself and remove the lid. Remove and discard the bay leaf, transfer the mixture, in batches, to a food processor or blender (or use an immersion blender right in the pot), and puree. Return to the pressure cooker to reheat, uncovered. Season with nutmeg, salt, and pepper.

To garnish the soup, use a medicine dropper or baster and squeeze drops of cream in a pattern on top. Sprinkle a bit of the orange zest and parsley in the middle of each serving.

Make up to 3 days ahead.
- *Wrap or cover tightly, preferably in a glass container, and refrigerate.*
- *To reheat, transfer to a heavy saucepan and stir over medium heat until warmed through. Or transfer to a microwavable bowl and microwave at full power, turning the bowl at 2-minute intervals, until heated through.*

Freeze up to 6 months, well wrapped in a firm plastic container.
- *To defrost, see reheating instructions above.*

LOVE THOSE LEFTOVERS!

Make pasta: Heat gently and toss with hot pasta and grated Parmesan or Asiago cheese.

Cold Cream of Vegetable Soup

SERVES 6

The produce options in midsummer are mind-boggling. Everything from zucchini and sweet onions to eggplant and bell peppers is appealing, and a resolve to make ratatouille may yield to a craving for grilled vegetables, then an urge for pasta sauce, and then stifling confusion. Here's yet another dish to consider when summer produce is at its peak— a cold soup, calling for firm, fresh eggplant and brilliant bell peppers.

TIME TO PREPARE (HANDS ON): *About 20 minutes*

TIME TO COOK: *About 45 minutes*

TOTAL TIME: *About 1 hour*

2 medium eggplants, washed
1 red bell pepper
1 yellow bell pepper
1 tablespoon extra virgin olive oil
1 onion, chopped
1 garlic clove, crushed and minced
2 tablespoons balsamic vinegar
2 cups Vegetable Broth (page 286)
Coarse salt and freshly ground black pepper
¼ cup nonfat plain yogurt
Small sprigs of fresh basil for garnish

Heat the oven to 400° F. Wash the eggplants, pierce them with a knife in several places, then wrap them in foil. Cut the red and yellow bell peppers in half lengthwise, remove the seeds and core, and place, skin side up, on a nonstick baking sheet along with the eggplants. Bake until the skin of the peppers char and the eggplants are very soft, about 20 minutes for the peppers, 40 minutes for the eggplants. Place the peppers in a brown paper bag and put it in the refrigerator to cool for 5 minutes. Unwrap the eggplants and set them aside, leaving the peppers in the bag.

Meanwhile, heat the oil in a medium saucepan over medium-high heat. When hot, add the onion and garlic, lower the heat to medium-low and sauté, stirring often, until the onion is soft, about 10 minutes.

Peel and chop the cooled peppers. Add them to the saucepan along with the balsamic vinegar, and continue cooking for 5 minutes, stirring often. Add the broth and bring to a simmer over medium-high heat. Reduce the heat to keep the broth at a simmer. Meanwhile, slice the eggplants in half and scoop out as many seeds as possible. Peel off the skin and chop the pulp finely. Stir it into the soup. Season with salt and pepper.

If you want a chunky soup, continue to simmer until the mixture thickens, about 10 minutes. Remove from the heat and chill. Stir in the yogurt.

If you want a smooth soup, transfer the mixture in batches to the work bowl of a food processor or blender. Or use an immersion blender right in the saucepan. Process until smooth. Pour into a clean bowl and chill. Stir in the yogurt.

To speed chilling, plug the sink and fill ⅓ with cold water and as many ice cubes as you can spare. Pour the soup into a large bowl and place the bowl in the sink with the ice water. Stir the soup until it stops steaming. Cover and refrigerate.

Garnish each serving with a sprig of fresh basil. If you have no basil leaves small enough, cut larger leaves into shreds and place in the center of each serving.

Make up to 3 days ahead.
- *Seal in a tightly covered container and refrigerate.*

Peach and Cantaloupe Soup

SERVES 6

Here's a treat for the sultriest days of summer . . . and a good way to get the best taste from highly perishable fruit. The lemon and lime juice will kick up the flavors, while the soup itself will revitalize spirits and appetites all around. A sprig of mint makes a pretty garnish.

TIME TO PREPARE (HANDS ON):	*About 10 minutes*
TIME TO COOK:	*About 1 minute*
TOTAL TIME:	*About 3¼ hours, including time to chill*

1 cup fresh orange juice, plus 1 cup additional for ice cube garnish

1 cup buttermilk, plus 1 cup additional for ice cube garnish

4 large ripe peaches

1 large ripe cantaloupe

1 tablespoon fresh lime juice

2 tablespoons fresh lemon juice

One day to 6 hours in advance, pour 1 cup of orange juice into the cups of a mini muffin tin or round ice "cube" tray, filling the cups no more than ¼ full. Make another set of ice cubes with 1 cup of buttermilk. Freeze solid.

Fill a large pot with water and bring it to a boil. Add the peaches and let simmer 30 seconds. Drain and set the peaches aside to cool.

Slice the cantaloupe into quarters; scoop out the seeds and discard them. Cut out the fruit, chop it coarsely, and place it in the work bowl of a food processor or blender.

Peel the peaches and chop them. Add to the cantaloupe in the food processor. Process in short pulses to blend.

Add 1 cup orange juice and the lime and lemon juices to the fruit mixture, and process again until smooth. Transfer to a large bowl and stir in the buttermilk. Cover the bowl and refrigerate at least 3 hours.

To serve, fill each serving bowl with soup, then add 1 juice cube and 1 buttermilk cube to each bowl. Serve right away.

Make up to 2 days ahead.
- *Seal in a tightly covered container and refrigerate.*

Corn and Sweet Potato Chowder

Serves 6 to 8

Vegetarian Entrée!
Serve in Bread Bowls (page 230) with
Beet and Radish Salad (page 178).

*Good corn and sweet potatoes don't share the same season.
No problem! Even early or late season fresh produce tastes
terrific in this hearty soup. It's best at the very end of the
corn season, when the first sweet potatoes arrive and it's
cooling off at night.*

TIME TO PREPARE (HANDS ON): *About 15 minutes*

TIME TO COOK: *Just under 1 hour*

TOTAL TIME: *About 1¼ hours*

---

1 tablespoon vegetable oil, such as canola or
    corn

1 leek, white part plus 1 inch of green,
    thinly sliced

1 onion, chopped

1 tablespoon grated peeled fresh ginger

1 whole clove

2 ears fresh corn

4 medium sweet potatoes, peeled and
    chopped

¼ cup yellow cornmeal, preferably stone-
    ground

4 cups Vegetable Broth (page 286) or
    Chicken Broth (page 285)

½ cup buttermilk (optional)

2 teaspoons maple syrup

1 teaspoon ground cinnamon

Pinch ground nutmeg

Coarse salt and freshly ground black pepper

Heat the oil in a large pot over medium-high heat. When hot, add the leek, onion, ginger, and clove. Reduce the heat to medium-low and sauté, stirring often, until the vegetables are soft and limp, about 7 minutes.

Scrape the kernels off the corn, and add along with the sweet potatoes and cornmeal; continue stirring to blend. Add the broth, stir, and bring to a boil over medium-high heat. Cover and reduce the heat to medium-low. Simmer until the potatoes are soft enough to puree, about 15 to 20 minutes. Transfer in batches to the work bowl of a food processor or blender, or insert an immersion blender into the pot. Puree until smooth. Return to the stove and stir in the buttermilk, if using, maple syrup, cinnamon, nutmeg, and salt and pepper to taste. Warm gently on medium heat, about 10 minutes, taking care not to let it boil. Serve warm.

In a pressure cooker, heat the olive oil in the pressure cooker and proceed as directed above to the point where you add the broth. Bring to a boil, lock the lid on the cooker, and allow it to come to full pressure. Maintain the pressure for 20 minutes.

Remove from the heat, and allow the pressure to come down on its own. When the pressure comes all the way down, tilt the cooker away from yourself and remove the lid.

Puree and proceed as directed above.

Make up to 3 days ahead.
- *Wrap or cover tightly, preferably in a glass container, and refrigerate.*
- *To reheat, transfer to a heavy saucepan and stir over medium heat until warmed through. Or transfer to a microwavable bowl and microwave at full power, turning*

the bowl at 2-minute intervals, stirring each time, until heated through.

Freeze up to 3 months, well wrapped in a glass or firm plastic container.

- *To defrost, see reheating instructions above.*

Scallop and Potato Soup

S ERVES 4

Maybe you don't want to mention this in polite company, but just so you know, scallops are hermaphrodites. Since we eat only the muscle, we see no evidence of sex of either kind. But in Europe, where they tend to be less squeamish about these things, everyone enjoys the roe and the, uh, male bit, as well.

Never mind. This marvelous soup extends the flavor of precious fresh sea scallops, stretching a relatively small amount to cover your first course.

TIME TO PREPARE (HANDS ON): *About 20 minutes*

TIME TO COOK: *About 15 minutes*

TOTAL TIME: *About 40 minutes*

---

1 large red or white potato, peeled, halved if large

1 tablespoon extra virgin olive oil

1 medium onion, chopped

1 leek, white part only, thinly sliced

1 head Belgian endive, trimmed and chopped

2 tablespoons dry sherry

3 cups Vegetable Broth (page 286)

3 tablespoons half-and-half

1 pound sea scallops, cut in half

2 tablespoons minced fresh chives

2 tablespoons minced fresh parsley

Pinch paprika

Coarse salt and freshly ground black pepper

Fit a large pot with a steamer basket. Add enough water to come up to the base of the steamer. Place the potato in the steamer, cover, and bring the water to a simmer over medium-high heat. Reduce the heat to medium-low and steam until the potato is cooked through, about 15 to 20 minutes. Let cool.

Meanwhile, heat the olive oil in a heavy saucepan. When hot, add the onion and leek, and sauté until soft. Add the endive and continue to sauté until wilted. Add the sherry and stir until it evaporates, about 2 minutes.

Drain and mash the potato and add it to the endive mixture. Add enough broth to cover and stir to make a thick puree. Thin with half-and-half and additional broth. Add the scallops and simmer gently until just cooked through, about 4 minutes.

Ladle the soup into warm individual serving bowls. Sprinkle each serving with chives, parsley, and paprika, and season with salt and pepper.

Make up to 3 days ahead.

- *Seal in a tightly covered container and refrigerate.*
- *To reheat, transfer to a heavy saucepan and stir over medium heat until warmed through. Or transfer to a microwavable bowl and microwave at full power, turning the bowl at 2-minute intervals, until heated through.*

Freeze up to 3 months, well wrapped in a glass or firm plastic container.

- *To defrost, see reheating instructions above.*

Sweet Potato Peanut Soup

SERVES 6

VEGETARIAN ENTRÉE!
Serve with Naan (page 226) and
Sweet and Nutty Bulgur Salad (page 182).

*Rich tasting and ultra thick, this hearty soup is best served
in winter when such things are welcome. Peanut butter
comes in degrees of adulteration; choose the purest.*

TIME TO PREPARE (HANDS ON): *About 15 minutes*

TIME TO COOK: *About 1 hour 10 minutes*

TOTAL TIME: *About 1 hour, 40 minutes, plus you must soak the
    chickpeas overnight*

1 cup dried chickpeas, soaked overnight
1 tablespoon peanut oil
1 large leek, white part plus 2 inches of
    green, thinly sliced
1 shallot, minced
2 tablespoons grated peeled fresh ginger
4 medium sweet potatoes, peeled and thinly
    sliced
2 tablespoons smooth unsalted peanut butter
4 cups Vegetable Broth (page 286)
1 bay leaf
2 tablespoons fresh lemon juice
1 tablespoon curry powder
1 teaspoon ground cardamom
Coarse salt and freshly ground black pepper

Place the chickpeas in a large heavy pot or a pressure cooker. Add 2 cups of water and bring to a simmer. If using a pot, reduce the heat to medium-low, cover with the lid slightly ajar (this will keep the water from boiling over), and simmer until the beans are cooked through, about 45 minutes. If using a pressure cooker, cover and bring to full pressure. Maintain full pressure for 20 minutes, then turn off the heat and let the pressure come down on its own. Tilt the cooker away from you when you open it.

Reserve 1 cup of cooking water, draining off the rest.

Meanwhile, heat the oil in a large heavy saucepan over medium-high heat. When hot, add the leek, shallot, and ginger. Reduce the heat to medium-low and sauté until the leek is soft and limp, about 10 minutes. Add the sweet potatoes, chickpeas, reserved cooking water, peanut butter, vegetable broth, and bay leaf. Cover and simmer until the potatoes are cooked and soft enough to puree, about 20 minutes.

Transfer to a food processor or blender, in batches if necessary (or use an immersion blender right in the pot), and puree the soup. Stir in the lemon juice, curry powder, and cardamom, and season with salt and pepper.

Make up to 3 days ahead.
- *Seal in a tightly covered container and refrigerate.*
- *To reheat, transfer to a heavy saucepan and stir over medium heat until warmed through. Or transfer to a microwavable bowl and microwave at full power, turning the bowl at 2-minute intervals, until heated through.*

Freeze up to 6 months, well wrapped in a glass or firm plastic container.
- *To defrost, see reheating instructions above.*

LOVE THOSE LEFTOVERS!
The soup will thicken when cool; serve cold over chilled cooked soba noodles.

Creamy Lobster and Potato Soup

SERVES 4 TO 6

This dish is offered with exceptional enthusiasm. While other specialty foods have become less special, thanks to cultivation or aggressive marketing, lobster is as desirable a delicacy as it ever was.

TIME TO PREPARE (HANDS ON): *About 20 minutes*

TIME TO COOK: *About 40 minutes*

TOTAL TIME: *About 1 hour*

One 1½-pound boiled lobster (have your
   fish market cook it for you)

4 cups Vegetable Broth (page 286)

2 whole artichokes

1 tablespoon extra virgin olive oil

¼ cup minced shallots

2 medium red or white potatoes, peeled

¼ teaspoon powdered saffron

½ cup reduced-fat sour cream

Coarse salt and freshly ground black pepper

Remove the meat from the lobster shell, chop, and set aside.

Place the lobster shell in a large stockpot or pressure cooker. Add the vegetable broth and bring to a boil over medium-high heat. If you're using a stockpot, cover, reduce the heat to medium-low, and simmer, covered, for 40 minutes.

If you're using a pressure cooker, lock on the lid and bring to full pressure. Cook at full pressure for 15 minutes, then let the pressure fall on its own. Tilt the cooker away from you and unlock the lid.

Set a colander over a large bowl and pour the broth through it. Discard the lobster shell.

Meanwhile, prepare the artichokes. Cut away the stem and snap off the tough outer leaves. (This will amount to more than half the artichoke.) Once you're down to the light green, tender leaves, cut the artichoke in half lengthwise. With a melon scoop, paring knife, or teaspoon, scoop out the fuzz at the center. Finally, cut the artichoke into quarters lengthwise, then cut each quarter in half lengthwise again.

Heat the oil in a large saucepan over medium-high heat. When hot, add the shallots and sauté until golden, about 4 minutes. Add the broth, potatoes, artichokes, and saffron. Simmer gently until the potatoes and artichokes are cooked through.

Puree the soup in a food processor or blender (or with an immersion blender right in the pot) in batches if necessary. Stir in the sour cream and the lobster meat. Heat through, stirring frequently, but do not let it come to a full simmer.

Season with salt and pepper.

Make up to 3 days ahead.
- *Seal in a tightly covered container and refrigerate.*
- *To reheat, transfer to a heavy saucepan and stir over medium heat until warmed through. Or transfer to a microwavable bowl and microwave at full power, turning the bowl at 2-minute intervals, until heated through.*

Freeze up to 3 months, well wrapped in a glass or firm plastic container.
- *To defrost, see reheating instructions above.*

RISOTTO

If you're going have a "house special," a dish you want to be known for among everyone who has the privilege of eating at your home, I recommend risotto. Just as the rice takes on the flavor of whatever you cook with it, the dish itself becomes whatever the occasion demands. For family, it's comforting. For more formal company, it's elegant. And for, well, you know who, it's appropriately beguiling.

For risotto you need arborio rice and very good broth. Arborio's uncommonly high starch content gives the final dish its distinctive character; no other rice becomes as creamy and chewy as it cooks. Arborio rice used to come from Italy exclusively, but it now grows in abundance in Texas and California. We get two benefits from this. First, homegrown rice costs less, and, second, it's often better than imported brands. It's better because it's fresher. Fresh rice cooks faster and tastes sweeter than grain that's been sitting around for a while. Try Rice Select Arborio from Texas (available at most supermarket chains nationwide) or Lundberg's California arborio, available at most natural and health foods markets.

Broth is critical because the rice absorbs it as it cooks, becoming infused with its flavor. If you can't make the time to boil broth from scratch (see page 284), taste around to find a commercial brand you like. Look for one that's low in sodium, so you can adjust the salt to taste before serving. *Reheating risotto:* There is a persistent myth to the effect that risotto must be eaten promptly and never reheated. First, I prefer to let mine sit for 5 to 10 minutes before serving to give the flavors a chance to settle. As long as it doesn't get cold, it will not become gummy, as many cooks fear. Second, as long as it is warmed gently over moist heat, most risotto can survive reheating with excellent flavor and texture. See the reheating instructions with each risotto recipe.

Finally, if you love serving risotto but find that the thrill of standing over it and stirring for 20 to 30 minutes at a time wears off after a while, consider buying a pressure cooker. In fact, I rarely make risotto without one anymore. It's not only faster and easier, but the risotto is creamier and more flavorful. You can also make the broth in it in less than half the time it would take you in a stockpot . . . and it will taste better, too. See About Those Appliances (page 340) for more.

Blueberry Risotto

SERVES 4

Looking for something new? Be the first person on your block (guaranteed!) to serve this savory Blueberry Risotto. It's not just different . . . it's delicious, especially before or alongside an entrée of grilled vegetables or fish.

TIME TO PREPARE (HANDS ON): *About 30 minutes*

TIME TO COOK: *Included in the preparation time*

TOTAL TIME: *About 30 minutes*

> 3 cups Vegetable Broth, page 286 (2 cups if you're using a pressure cooker)
> 1 tablespoon unsalted butter
> 1 Vidalia or other sweet onion, coarsely chopped
> 1 leek, white part only, thinly sliced

¼ cup dry white wine

1 cup arborio rice

2 cups blueberries, washed

3 tablespoons sour cream or mascarpone
cheese

Salt

Pour the broth into a heavy saucepan and bring to a simmer over medium-high heat. Reduce the heat to low, keeping the broth hot.

Melt the butter in a heavy saucepan over medium heat. When hot, add the onion and leek, and sauté until soft, about 7 minutes. Add the wine and stir until most of it has evaporated, about 2 minutes. Add the rice and stir to coat with the vegetables. Pour in enough vegetable broth to cover by about an inch and stir until it's been absorbed. Continue to add broth about ⅓ cup at a time, stirring often until the rice is cooked through and the mixture is creamy, about 20 minutes altogether. Add the blueberries and continue stirring until they begin to burst, about 3 minutes. Remove from the heat and stir in the sour cream or mascarpone. Season lightly with salt.

To make it in a pressure cooker, heat the butter in the pressure cooker and proceed as directed above up to the point where you begin adding broth. (If you're using an electric stove, turn on a separate burner to low.) Add 2 cups of broth and bring to a boil. Lock on the lid and bring to moderate pressure. Maintain the pressure for 7 minutes; if you're using a gas stove, you can do this by turning the heat down as far as it will go. If you're using an electric stove, transfer the cooker to the preheated burner. After 7 minutes, remove from the heat.

When the pressure comes all the way down, tilt the cooker away from yourself and remove the lid. (If there's any liquid left, return the cooker to the stove and turn the heat to low, stirring until it is absorbed and the rice is creamy.) Add the blueberries, turn the heat to low, and stir until the berries begin to burst, about 3 minutes. Remove from the heat and stir in the sour cream or mascarpone. Season lightly with salt.

Make up to 1 day ahead.

- *Wrap or cover tightly, preferably in a glass container, and refrigerate.*
- *Take out of the refrigerator about 2 hours before serving, transfer to a serving bowl, cover with plastic wrap, and let come to room temperature.*
- *Do not reheat. If you're not serving the risotto right away, serve it cold or at room temperature.*
- *This dish doesn't keep well for more than 1 day; encourage your guests to polish it off at one sitting.*

Menu

BLUEBERRY RISOTTO

SALMON AND SHRIMP TERRINES (PAGE 91)

ARTICHOKES IN LEMON SAUCE (PAGE 196)

ANGEL FOOD LOAF (PAGE 303) WITH

LEMON GLACE (PAGE 279)

Apple Risotto

SERVES 4

In pie, sure. In salad . . . well, okay. But in rice? Apple-solutely! With savory seasonings and cheddar cheese, it's a great starter for an autumn supper.

TIME TO PREPARE (HANDS ON): *About 40 minutes*

TIME TO COOK: *Included in the preparation time*

TOTAL TIME: *About 40 minutes*

3 to 4 cups Vegetable Broth, page 286
   (2 cups if you're using a pressure cooker)
1 tablespoon extra virgin olive oil
1 red onion, chopped
2 teaspoons crumbled dried oregano
1 cup arborio rice
2 tablespoons dry white wine
2 Granny Smith apples, peeled and finely
   chopped
1/4 cup shredded cheddar cheese
Salt

Pour the broth into a heavy saucepan and bring to a simmer over medium-high heat. Reduce the heat to low, keeping the broth hot.

Meanwhile, heat the oil over medium heat in a separate heavy saucepan, swirling the pan to coat the bottom. When hot, add the onion and oregano and sauté until the onion is soft, about 7 minutes. Add the rice and stir to coat with the onion. Add the wine and stir for about 30 seconds, until it is almost evaporated.

Using a ladle, add about 1 cup of the hot broth. Stir often over medium heat until the liquid is absorbed, 3 to 5 minutes. Add another ladleful and stir until this too has been absorbed.

Continue the process, adding broth about 1/3 cup at a time until the rice is plump and chewy and no longer hard and chalk white in the center, about 20 minutes. Stir in the apples and the cheddar cheese. Season with salt to taste and let sit about 5 minutes before serving.

To make it in a pressure cooker, heat the olive oil and proceed as above to the point where you begin adding broth. (On an electric stove, move to a separate burner on low heat.) Add 2 cups of broth and bring to a boil. Lock on the lid and bring to moderate pressure. Maintain the pressure for 7 minutes; if you're using a gas stove, you can do this by turning the heat down as far as it will go. If you're using an electric stove, transfer the cooker to the preheated burner. After 7 minutes, turn off the heat. If you're using an electric stove, take the cooker off the stove.

When the pressure comes all the way down, tilt the cooker away from yourself and remove the lid. (If there's any liquid left, return the cooker to the stove and turn the heat to low, stirring until it is absorbed and the rice is creamy.) Stir in the apples and cheese and serve.

Make up to 1 day ahead.
- *Wrap or cover tightly and refrigerate.*
- *Take out of the refrigerator about 2 hours before serving, transfer to a serving bowl, cover with plastic wrap, and let come to room temperature.*
- *To reheat, place the risotto in a heat-resistant dish or bowl, such as Pyrex. Cover loosely with foil and place inside a large baking dish. Add water to the outer dish until it comes halfway up the side of the one with the risotto. Heat in a preheated 325° F. oven for 20 minutes, stirring occasionally and adding water as necessary to maintain the level.*

Grape Risotto

SERVES 4

If this combination seems eccentric, it bears explaining that it's not a case of California-style creative overkill, but a genuine Tuscan dish. The mellow flavor is distinctly autumnal, and a good match for highly seasoned entrées.

TIME TO PREPARE (HANDS ON): *About 45 minutes*

TIME TO COOK: *Included in the preparation time*

TOTAL TIME: *About 45 minutes*

3 cups Vegetable Broth, page 286 (2 cups if
     you're using a pressure cooker)
1 tablespoon unsalted butter
1 shallot, finely chopped
$1/4$ cup minced fresh parsley
$1 1/2$ cups white button mushrooms,
     quartered
1 cup arborio rice
$1/4$ cup dry white wine
1 cup seedless green grapes
1 cup seedless red grapes
2 tablespoons sour cream, reduced-fat sour
     cream, or half-and-half
Salt and freshly ground black pepper

Pour the broth into a heavy saucepan and bring to a simmer over medium-high heat. Turn the heat down to low, keeping the broth hot.

Melt the butter in a heavy saucepan over medium heat. Add the shallot and stir until soft, about 6 minutes. Add the parsley and mushrooms and continue stirring until the mushrooms darken and begin to give up their liquid. Add the rice and the wine, and stir until the wine has been absorbed, about 2 minutes. Add vegetable broth to cover by about an inch and stir until it's been absorbed. Continue to add broth about $1/3$ cup at a time, stirring often until the rice is cooked through and the mixture is creamy, about 20 minutes altogether.

Stir in the grapes along with the sour cream or half-and-half. Continue stirring over low heat until thoroughly blended. Season lightly with salt and pepper and serve.

To make it in a pressure cooker, proceed as above to the point where you add the broth. Add 2 cups of broth and bring to a simmer. Lock on the lid and bring to moderate pressure. Maintain the pressure for 7 minutes. If you're using a gas stove, turn the heat down as far as it will go. On an electric stove, move to a separate burner on low heat. Remove from the heat.

When the pressure comes all the way down, tilt the cooker away from yourself and remove the lid. (If there's any liquid left, return the cooker to the stove and turn the heat to low, stirring until it is absorbed and the rice is creamy.) Over low heat, stir in the grapes and sour cream or half-and-half. Continue stirring over low heat until well blended. Season lightly with salt and pepper.

Make up to 1 day ahead.
- *Wrap or cover tightly, preferably in a glass container, and refrigerate.*
- *Take out of the refrigerator about 2 hours before serving, transfer to a serving bowl, cover with plastic wrap, and let come to room temperature. Or, to reheat, place the risotto in a heat-resistant bowl. Cover loosely with foil and place inside a large baking dish. Add water to the outer dish until it comes halfway up the side of the inner one. Heat for 20 minutes, stirring occasionally and adding water as necessary to maintain the level.*

Lemon Risotto

SERVES 4 TO 6

"The fruit of the poor lemon is impossible to eat," goes an old folk song.

"Not true," goes you, once you've made this risotto, which calls for lemon, not for mere accent, but for fundamental flavor. And there won't be a pucker in the place when you serve it, either. Parmesan cheese and egg yolk tame the tart taste, so all can appreciate the delicious essence of lemon.

TIME TO PREPARE (HANDS ON): *About 40 minutes*

TIME TO COOK: *Included in the preparation time*

TOTAL TIME: *About 40 minutes*

3 cups Vegetable Broth, page 286 (2 cups if
    you're using a pressure cooker)
1 tablespoon extra virgin olive oil
1 red onion, chopped
1/4 cup minced fresh parsley
1 cup arborio rice
1 large egg yolk
1/4 cup nonfat milk
Grated zest and juice of 1 lemon
1/2 cup grated Parmesan cheese
Salt and freshly ground black pepper
Additional finely chopped parsley for
    garnish

Pour the broth into a heavy saucepan and bring to a simmer over medium-high heat. Reduce the heat to low, keeping the broth hot.

Heat the olive oil in a heavy saucepan over medium heat. When hot, add the onion and parsley and sauté until the onion is soft, about 6 minutes. Add the rice and stir to coat with the onion and parsley. Add vegetable broth to cover by about an inch and stir until it's been absorbed. Continue to add broth about 1/3 cup at a time, stirring often until the rice is cooked through and the mixture is creamy, about 20 minutes altogether. Turn down the heat as low as it will go.

In a small bowl, stir the egg yolk into the milk. Add the lemon juice, and add slowly to the rice mixture, stirring constantly so the mixture won't curdle. Add the cheese and grated lemon zest, and stir to blend. The rice should be very creamy, with no puddles on the surface. Season lightly with salt and pepper, and serve right away, sprinkled with additional parsley.

To make it in a pressure cooker, proceed as above to the point where you add the broth. Add 2 cups of broth and bring to a boil. Lock on the lid and bring to moderate pressure. Maintain the pressure for 7 minutes. If you're using a gas stove, you can do this by turning the heat down as far as it will go. If you're using an electric stove, transfer the cooker to a burner preheated to low. Remove from the heat.

When the pressure comes all the way down, tilt the cooker away from yourself and remove the lid. (If there's any liquid left, return the cooker to the stove and turn the heat to low, stirring until it is absorbed and the rice is creamy.)

Stir the egg yolk into the milk. Add the lemon juice, and add slowly to the rice mixture, stirring constantly so the mixture won't curdle. Add the cheese and lemon zest and stir to blend. The rice should be very creamy. Season lightly with salt and pepper and serve right away, sprinkled with additional parsley.

Make up to 2 days ahead.

- *Wrap or cover tightly, preferably in a glass container, and refrigerate.*
- *Take out of the refrigerator about 2 hours before serving, transfer to a serving bowl, cover with plastic wrap, and let come to room temperature.*
- *To reheat, place the risotto in a heat-resistant dish or bowl. Cover loosely with foil and place inside a large baking dish. Add water to the outer dish until it comes halfway up the side of the one with the risotto. Heat for 20 minutes, stirring occasionally and adding water as necessary to maintain the level.*

Pumpkin and Mushroom Risotto

SERVES 4 TO 6

VEGETARIAN ENTRÉE!
Serve with Savory Puff Pastry (page 50) and Beets and Sour Cream (page 178).

This is an autumn treat as a first course or entrée. You can use it to fill winter squash in place of the bread stuffing (page 185), or omit the cheese and use it to stuff a turkey or chicken.

TIME TO PREPARE (HANDS ON): *About 45 minutes*

TIME TO COOK: *Included in the preparation time*

TOTAL TIME: *About 45 minutes*

About 3 cups Vegetable Broth, page 286
   (2 cups if you're using a pressure cooker)
1 tablespoon extra virgin olive oil
1 onion, chopped
2 teaspoons minced fresh sage or crumbled dried
1 cup chopped firm mushrooms, such as cremini or portobello
1 cup diced fresh pumpkin or butternut squash
1 cup arborio rice
2 tablespoons dry white wine, or
   1 tablespoon white wine vinegar or Champagne vinegar
1/4 cup grated Parmesan cheese
1/2 teaspoon ground nutmeg, or to taste
Salt and freshly ground black pepper

Pour the broth into a heavy saucepan and bring to a simmer over medium-high heat. Turn the heat down to low, keeping the broth hot.

Heat the olive oil in a heavy saucepan over medium heat. When hot, add the onion and sage, and sauté until the onion is soft, about 6 minutes. Add the mushrooms and continue stirring until they darken and the liquid they give off has evaporated, about 7 minutes. Add the pumpkin and rice, and stir to coat with the rest. Add the wine or vinegar and stir until most of it has evaporated, about 1 minute.

Add vegetable broth to cover by about an inch and stir until it's been absorbed. Continue to add broth about 1/3 cup at a time, stirring often until the rice is cooked through and the mixture is creamy, about 20 minutes altogether. Stir in the cheese (if you're not using this for stuffing) and nutmeg. Season with salt and pepper.

In a pressure cooker, proceed as directed above to the point where you add the broth. Add 2 cups of broth and bring to a boil. Lock on the lid and let come to moderate pressure. Maintain moderate pressure for 7 minutes. If you're using a gas stove, you can do this by turning the heat down as far as it will go. If you're using an electric stove, transfer the cooker to a burner preheated to low. Remove from the heat. When the pressure has come all the way down, tilt the cooker away from yourself and remove the lid. If excess liquid remains, return to medium-low heat and stir until it's gone, usually about 1 to 2 minutes. Stir in the cheese and nutmeg. Season with salt and pepper.

Make up to 2 days ahead.
- *Wrap or cover tightly, preferably in a glass container, and refrigerate*
- *Take out of the refrigerator about 2 hours before serving, transfer to a serving bowl, cover with plastic wrap, and let come to room temperature.*
- *To reheat, place the risotto in a heat-resistant dish or bowl. Cover loosely with foil and place inside a large baking dish. Add water to the outer dish until it comes halfway up the side of the one with the risotto. Heat for 20 minutes, stirring occasionally and adding water as necessary to maintain the level.*

▶

Risotto with Fennel, Saffron, and Tomato

SERVES 4 TO 6

VEGETARIAN ENTRÉE!
Make a well in the center of each serving and fill with Tomato and Fennel Sauce (page 128). Serve with Asparagus Packets (page 198).

Amply flavorful as it is, this first course or vegetarian entrée becomes prettier and tastier still served with Tomato and Fennel Sauce. Make a well in the center of each serving of this risotto, and fill with the sauce, then sprinkle with grated Parmesan or Asiago cheese. You won't be overdoing the fennel by any means. It's so subtle, it will echo pleasantly from sauce to rice and back.

TIME TO PREPARE (HANDS ON): *About 40 minutes*

TIME TO COOK: *Included in the preparation time*

TOTAL TIME: *About 40 minutes*

About 3 cups Vegetable Broth (page 286),
Chicken Broth (page 285), Shrimp Broth
(page 286), or Lobster Broth (page 287),
2 cups if using a pressure cooker
1 tablespoon extra virgin olive oil
1 onion, chopped
1 fennel bulb, cored, fronds removed, thinly
sliced
1 cup arborio rice
¼ cup dry white wine
1 tomato, peeled and chopped (fresh or
canned)
2 tablespoons half-and-half or reduced-fat
sour cream
¼ cup grated Parmesan cheese
½ teaspoon powdered saffron (or saffron
threads soaked in 1 tablespoon warm
broth)
Salt and freshly ground black pepper

Pour the broth into a heavy saucepan and bring
to a simmer over medium-high heat. Turn the
heat to low, keeping the broth hot.

Heat the olive oil in a heavy saucepan over
medium heat. When hot, add the onion and fennel, and sauté until soft, about 10 minutes. Add
the rice and stir to coat with the vegetables. Add
the wine and stir briskly until most of it evaporates, about 2 minutes. Add broth to cover by
about an inch and stir until it's been absorbed.
Continue to add broth about ⅓ cup at a time,
stirring often until the rice is cooked through and
the mixture is creamy, about 30 minutes altogether. Remove from the heat. Stir in the tomato,
half-and-half or sour cream, cheese, and saffron
(including soaking broth, if you're using threads).
Stir well until thoroughly blended.

If it seems too liquid, return to medium-low
heat and stir until set, about 1 minute. Season
with salt and pepper.

In a pressure cooker, proceed as above until the
point where you add the broth. Add 2 cups of
broth, lock on the lid, and bring to moderate pressure. Maintain moderate pressure for 7 minutes. If
you're using a gas stove, you can do this by turning the heat down as far as it will go. If you're
using an electric stove, transfer the cooker to a
burner preheated to low. Remove from the heat.

When the pressure has come all the way
down, tilt the cooker away from you and remove
the lid. Stir in the half-and-half or sour cream,
cheese, and saffron (including soaking broth, if
you're using threads). Stir well until thoroughly
blended. If it seems too liquid, return to medium-
low heat and stir until set, probably about 1
minute. Season with salt and pepper.

Make up to 2 days ahead.
- *Wrap or cover tightly, preferably in a glass container,
  and refrigerate.*
- *Take out of the refrigerator about 2 hours before serving,
  transfer to a serving bowl, cover with plastic wrap, and
  let come to room temperature.*
- *To reheat, place the risotto in a heat-resistant dish or
  bowl. Cover loosely with foil and place inside a large
  baking dish. Add water to the outer dish until it comes
  halfway up the side of the one with the risotto. Heat for
  20 minutes, stirring occasionally and adding water as
  necessary to maintain the level.*

Lobster Risotto

SERVES 4

Your basic magician is not a very practical person. Pulling a rabbit out of a hat may be an impressive trick, but what then? And sawing someone in half may be good for a thrill, but so? Here's magic that matters . . . a way of feeding 4 people with one average-sized lobster, amplifying the flavor rather than diluting it.

TIME TO PREPARE (HANDS ON): *About 50 minutes*

TIME TO COOK: *1 hour for the broth, which you can make up to*
   3 days ahead

TOTAL TIME: *About 1 hour, 50 minutes*

1½ to 2-pound lobster, boiled or steamed
   (have your fish market do this for you)
1 large onion, peeled and quartered
2 leeks, white and green parts, thinly sliced
2 carrots, peeled and chopped
2 celery stalks, including leaves, chopped
1 tablespoon extra virgin olive oil
2 shallots, minced
2 tablespoons minced fresh parsley
1 cup arborio rice
¼ cup dry white wine
1 medium tomato, peeled, seeded, and
   chopped
2 tablespoons reduced-fat sour cream
   (optional)
Coarse salt and freshly ground black pepper

GARNISH
   Minced fresh chives
   Whole flat-leaf parsley sprigs

Crack the lobster shell and remove all of the meat. Wrap the meat well and refrigerate. Put the shell, including the head, in a large stockpot or pressure cooker. Add the onion, leeks, carrots, and celery. Add water to cover by about 2 inches and bring to a boil over medium-high heat.

Cover and turn the heat down to medium-low. Simmer until you have a strong broth, about 1 hour. If you're using a pressure cooker, lock on the lid and bring to moderate pressure. Cook at moderate pressure for 15 minutes, then let the pressure fall on its own. Tilt the cooker away from you and unlock the lid.

Strain the mixture through a colander into a large saucepan, and discard the vegetables and shell. Bring the broth to a simmer over medium heat and keep warm over low heat while you make the risotto.

Heat the olive oil in a heavy saucepan. When hot, add the shallots and parsley and sauté until the shallots are soft, about 6 minutes. Add the rice and stir to coat with the shallots. Add the wine and continue stirring until some of it evaporates, about 1 minute. Add lobster broth to cover by about an inch and stir until it's been absorbed. Continue to add broth about ⅓ cup at a time, stirring often until the rice is nearly cooked through (you'll be able to see that the center of the kernels is almost completely translucent, with just a bit of hard white remaining), about 15 minutes altogether. Stir in the lobster meat and the tomato, and continue stirring until the rice is cooked through (the center should be completely translucent and smooth, with no hard white). The kernels should be bound together like a thick rice pudding, and there shouldn't be any liquid pools on the surface. Remove from the heat and stir in the sour cream, if you're using it. Season with salt and pepper, and serve right away.

To make it in a pressure cooker, proceed as above up to the addition of broth. Add 2 cups of broth and bring to a boil. Lock on the lid and bring to high pressure. Maintain the pressure for 7 minutes. If you're using a gas stove, you can do this by turning the heat down as far as it will go. If you're using an electric stove, transfer the cooker to a burner preheated to low. Remove from the heat.

When the pressure comes all the way down, tilt the cooker away from yourself and remove the lid. (If there's any liquid left, return the cooker to the stove and turn the heat to low, stirring until it is absorbed and the rice is creamy.) Stir in the sour cream, if you're using it. Season with salt and pepper.

Make up to 3 days ahead.
- *Wrap or cover tightly, preferably in a glass container, and refrigerate.*
- *Take out of the refrigerator about 2 hours before serving, transfer to a serving bowl, cover with plastic wrap, and let come to room temperature.*
- *To reheat, place the risotto in a heat-resistant dish or bowl. Cover loosely with foil and place inside a large baking dish. Add water to the outer dish until it comes halfway up the side of the one with the risotto. Heat for 20 minutes, stirring occasionally and adding water as necessary to maintain the level.*

Neat Trick

Lightly grease 6 custard cups, ramekins, or muffin tins with unsalted butter or olive oil. Pat an equal portion of hot risotto into each and smooth the tops. Turn the ramekins or custard cups out onto individual serving plates. Turn the muffin tin out onto a large sheet of wax or parchment paper and lift each mound carefully with a wide spatula and place on serving plates.

Garnish with minced chives and parsley sprigs.

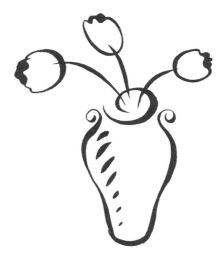

Rice Roulade with Spinach or Bell Peppers

SERVES 4 AS A STARTER

VEGETARIAN ENTRÉE!
Serve the spinach version with
Corn and Sweet Potato Chowder (page 66).

This is rice artfully rolled around the filling of your choice;
call it roulade and command some respect. Serve it sliced,
displaying the swirls in the center.

TIME TO PREPARE (HANDS ON): *About 30 minutes*	
TIME TO COOK: *About 1 hour*	
TOTAL TIME: *About 1½ hours*	

ROULADE
1 cup short-grain rice, such as arborio,
   cooked (see page 181)
One 10-ounce package fresh spinach leaves
Spinach Filling (recipe follows) or Bell
   Pepper Filling (recipe follows)

To make the roulade, spread the rice evenly into a 10 × 4-inch rectangle over a large piece of cheesecloth, double thickness, on a flat work surface. Lay the fresh spinach leaves evenly over the surface, leaving a 1½-inch margin. Spread the filling on top, leaving a 1-inch margin.

Starting at a narrow end, roll it up, taking care not to tuck the cheesecloth into the roulade. Wrap the cheesecloth around the roulade.

If you have a large steamer basket, put it in a large pot, then add enough water to come up to the base of the steamer. Place the roulade in the steamer, cover, and bring the water to a simmer over medium-high heat. Turn the heat down to medium-low and steam for 25 minutes. (There isn't any firm indication that it's done; 25 minutes should do it.) Check the water level frequently during that time and add water as necessary to maintain it.

If you don't have a steamer big enough, place a cooling rack in a flame-resistant roasting pan. Add water until it comes within ⅛ inch of the rack and set over 1 or 2 burners on the stove. Place the roulade on the rack, cover with foil, and steam as directed above.

Remove from the heat and let cool for 20 minutes. Unwrap, slice, and serve.

Spinach Filling
1 tablespoon extra virgin olive oil
1 onion, chopped
1 egg, lightly beaten
1 cup part-skim ricotta cheese
½ cup dry breadcrumbs
½ cup shredded Gruyère cheese
10 ounces fresh spinach, chopped, or one
   10-ounce package frozen chopped
   spinach, thawed and squeezed dry
Coarse salt and freshly ground black pepper
Pinch grated nutmeg

Heat the oil in a skillet over medium-high heat. When hot, add the onion, lower the heat to medium-low, and sauté, stirring often, until the onion is soft and limp, about 7 minutes. Remove from the heat.

In a large mixing bowl, combine the egg, ricotta, breadcrumbs, and cheese. Stir in the spinach and season with salt, pepper, and nutmeg. Stir well to combine.

Bell Pepper Filling

You may use all red or all yellow peppers in this filling, if both colors aren't available.

1 $\frac{1}{2}$ cups part-skim ricotta cheese
1 large egg, lightly beaten
$\frac{1}{2}$ cup dry breadcrumbs
$\frac{1}{4}$ cup grated Asiago or Parmesan cheese
2 roasted red bell peppers, cored, seeded, peeled, and sliced (see page 302)
2 roasted yellow bell peppers, cored, seeded, peeled, and sliced (see page 302)
2 teaspoons crumbled dried oregano
Coarse salt and freshly ground black pepper to taste

In a large mixing bowl, combine the ricotta, egg, breadcrumbs, Asiago or Parmesan cheese, bell peppers, oregano, salt, and pepper. Stir well to blend.

Make either filling up to 3 days ahead.
- *Wrap or cover tightly, preferably in a glass container, and refrigerate.*
- *Take out of the refrigerator about 2 hours before filling the roulade and let come to room temperature.*

VEGETARIAN
Menu
FOR ROULADE WITH BELL PEPPER FILLING
FETA AND CHIVE SPREAD (PAGE 30) WITH TOAST ROUNDS
RICE ROULADE WITH BELL PEPPER FILLING
CHICKPEAS WITH ONIONS, SPINACH, AND RAISINS
BEETS AND SOUR CREAM (PAGE 178)

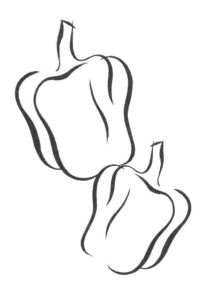

PASTA AND GNOCCHI

Tomato and Fennel Sauce

SERVES 4 TO 6

Sweet and simple. Serve it over penne or orzo, cheese-filled Potato-Spinach Ravioli (page 84), gnocchi (page 88), or Chicken Sformata (page 161).

TIME TO PREPARE (HANDS ON): *About 20 minutes*

TIME TO COOK: *Included in the preparation time*

TOTAL TIME: *About 20 minutes, plus about 15 minutes to cool*

1 tablespoon extra virgin olive oil
1 large onion, thinly sliced
1 fennel bulb, trimmed and thinly sliced
1 bay leaf
1 tablespoon crumbled dried oregano or
  2 tablespoons minced fresh
$\frac{1}{4}$ cup dry white wine
3 cups fresh or canned chopped peeled
  tomatoes
$\frac{1}{2}$ teaspoon powdered saffron
$\frac{1}{4}$ cup low-fat sour cream
Coarse salt and freshly ground black pepper

Heat the oil in a deep nonstick skillet. When hot, add the onion, fennel, bay leaf, and oregano, and sauté over medium heat until the fennel softens a bit, about 7 minutes. Add the wine and stir until most of it evaporates, about 2 minutes.

Stir in the tomatoes and saffron, and simmer gently until they break down into a sauce, about

7 minutes. Cover, remove from the heat, and let sit for 15 minutes.

Stir in the sour cream and reheat gently, taking care not to boil, until warmed through. Season with salt and pepper. Remove the bay leaf before serving.

Make up to 3 days ahead.
- *Seal in a tightly covered container and refrigerate.*
- *To reheat, transfer to a heavy saucepan and stir over medium heat until warmed through. Or transfer to a microwavable bowl and microwave at full power, turning the bowl at 2-minute intervals and stirring occasionally, until heated through.*

Freeze up to 6 months, well wrapped in a firm plastic container
- *To defrost, see reheating instructions above.*

Pumpkin Ravioli

SERVES 4

VEGETARIAN ENTRÉE!
Serve with Avocado and Apple Salad (page 174).

Here's one of several excellent reminders that pumpkin is a vegetable (along with Pumpkin and Mushroom Risotto, page 75, Pumpkin Gnocchi, page 90, and Lentil Soup with Pumpkin, page 61). It's an ideal opener for an autumn dinner, unexpected and exceptional. If you are serving this as an entrée, toss the ravioli with Bechamel Sauce with Cheese (page 290).

TIME TO PREPARE (HANDS ON): *About 40 minutes to make the pasta; about 5 minutes to make the filling*

TIME TO COOK: *About 5 minutes*

TOTAL TIME: *Under 1 hour*

1 $\frac{3}{4}$ cups unbleached all-purpose flour

Pinch salt

2 large eggs

1 cup canned or fresh pumpkin puree

$\frac{2}{3}$ cup low-fat or nonfat ricotta cheese

3 tablespoons grated Asiago cheese

$\frac{1}{4}$ cup plus 2 tablespoons dry breadcrumbs

1 teaspoon ground ginger

1 teaspoon ground cinnamon

$\frac{1}{2}$ teaspoon freshly ground nutmeg, or to taste

1 tablespoon minced fresh sage, divided

Pinch coarse salt

1 $\frac{1}{2}$ tablespoons unsalted butter or extra virgin olive oil

To make the pasta by hand, on a clean, flat work surface, make a mound of flour. Sprinkle with salt, then stir with a fork and make a well in the center of the mound. Drop the eggs into the well and beat them lightly with a fork. Gradually incorporate the flour, using your hand to guide it into the eggs as you beat them. Continue mixing until you have a firm, stiff dough. Knead the dough until it's smooth. Wrap in plastic and set aside for 30 minutes.

Or to make the pasta in a food processor, beat the eggs together lightly, in a mixing bowl. Put the flour and salt into a food processor and pulse to combine. With the motor running, pour the eggs in slowly, allowing them to be incorporated into a stiff dough. Take the dough out of the food processor, and knead it by hand until it's smooth and supple. Shape it into a ball, wrap in plastic, and let it rest for 30 minutes.

Meanwhile, make the filling. In a large mixing bowl, combine the pumpkin, ricotta and Asiago cheeses, breadcrumbs, ginger, cinnamon, nutmeg, and 2 teaspoons of sage. Season with salt.

Divide the dough into 4 pieces. Take 1 piece and flatten it with your hands. Generously flour it on each side. Put it through a hand-cranked pasta maker at the widest setting. Fold the dough in half and pass it through again. Adjust the setting 2 notches down and pass the dough through again. Fold it in half and pass through again. Adjust the setting 1 notch down and repeat. Cover the sheet of pasta with plastic wrap while you roll out the rest of the dough. Alternatively, you may roll it out on a lightly floured surface using a rolling pin. Fold it in half several times as you roll.

Place the pasta on a lightly floured surface and cut with a 3-inch biscuit cutter. Put a teaspoon of filling in the lower half of each circle and fold the top over to enclose the filling. Dip a long-tined fork in water and press along the edges to seal. Transfer to wax paper and cover loosely with plastic wrap while you complete the batch.

Melt the butter and put it into a large glass bowl, or put the olive oil in the bowl. Stir in the remaining 1 teaspoon of sage.

Fill a large pot with water and bring it to a boil. Add the ravioli, no more than 8 at a time, and simmer gently until cooked through, about 2 minutes. Remove with a slotted spoon and transfer to the prepared bowl. Toss well and serve warm.

Make the dough up to 3 days ahead.

- *Flour lightly, wrap in wax paper, then plastic, and refrigerate.*
- *Take out of the refrigerator about 30 minutes before rolling and filling.*

Make the filling up to 3 days ahead.

- *Seal in a tightly covered container and refrigerate.*

Freeze the cooked ravioli up to 6 months.

- *Reheat by plunging the frozen ravioli into boiling water for 1 minute.*

Menu

PUMPKIN RAVIOLI
ROAST CHICKEN (PAGE 157)
YELLOW TURNIPS WITH POTATOES AND CHEESE
(PAGE 189)

Potato-Spinach Ravioli

SERVES 4 TO 6

A little hard wheat flour (semolina) makes this pliant dough firm enough to shape and fill, while potato gives it ample body and subtle flavor. You can pace the preparation by making the filling a few days in advance, the sauce the day after that, and then the dough. Put it all together on the day you're going to serve it.

TIME TO PREPARE (HANDS ON): *About 40 minutes*

TIME TO COOK: *About 35 minutes*

TOTAL TIME: *About 1 hour, 15 minutes*

1 pound potatoes, preferably medium-starch, such as Yukon Gold, halved if large
1 large egg
1 cup semolina flour
1 cup unbleached all-purpose flour
1/2 teaspoon coarse salt

FILLING
Two 10-ounce packages frozen chopped spinach, thawed and squeezed dry
2 1/2 cups nonfat or reduced-fat ricotta cheese
1/2 cup grated Parmesan cheese
Pinch ground nutmeg
Coarse salt

SAUCE (OPTIONAL; YOU CAN USE A GOOD COMMERCIAL TOMATO SAUCE)
4 to 6 large ripe tomatoes or 3 cups canned whole or chopped tomatoes
2 tablespoons extra virgin olive oil
1 onion, chopped
1 garlic clove, crushed and minced
2 tablespoons dry white wine
2 tablespoons minced fresh basil or 1 tablespoon crumbled dried
2 tablespoons minced fresh oregano or 1 tablespoon crumbled dried (optional)
Coarse salt and freshly ground black pepper

Unsalted butter or extra virgin olive oil

For the pasta, fit a large pot with a steamer basket. Add enough water to come up to the base of the steamer. Place the potatoes in the steamer, cover, and bring the water to a simmer over medium-high-heat. Reduce the heat to medium-low and steam the potatoes until they're cooked though, about 20 to 30 minutes. Remove the potatoes from the heat. When they're cool enough, peel them.

Using a long-tined fork, mash together the egg and potatoes. Add the semolina flour, unbleached flour, and salt, and use your hands to blend into a dough that is soft but firm. (Do not use a food processor or other electric gadget for this, or the mixture will be sticky and mushy). Place in a glass or ceramic bowl, cover with plastic wrap, and refrigerate while you make the filling and sauce.

For the filling, in a mixing bowl, combine the spinach, ricotta and Parmesan cheeses, and nutmeg. Season with salt.

For the sauce, if using fresh tomatoes, fill a large pot with water and bring it to a boil. Add the tomatoes and bring to a boil again. Let boil for 30 seconds. Drain the water. When the tomatoes are cool enough to handle, peel them and cut into quarters. Squeeze out as many seeds as possible. If using canned whole tomatoes, chop them coarsely.

Heat the oil in a nonstick skillet over medium-high heat. When hot, add the onion and garlic, lower the heat to medium-low, and sauté until the onion is soft and limp, about 7 minutes. Add the

wine and stir until most of it evaporates, about 1 minute.

Add the tomatoes and basil and/or oregano, stirring until the tomatoes cook down into a sauce, about 7 minutes. Transfer to a blender or food processor and gently puree, or use an immersion blender right in the skillet. Season with salt and pepper. Keep warm while you cook the ravioli.

Lightly flour a work surface. Divide the dough into 4 pieces. Working with 1 piece at a time, roll each piece into a circle or square about $\frac{1}{4}$ inch thick. Using a large biscuit cutter or a cleaned empty tuna can, cut as many circles as you can. Gather the scraps of dough into a ball, roll out again, and cut as many as you can from this. Repeat until you've used up all of the dough.

To make the ravioli, place a teaspoon of filling in the center of 1 round. Place another round on top. Use a long-tined fork to press the edges, sealing them. Transfer to a well-floured plate or baking sheet.

Lightly grease a bowl with the butter or olive oil. Fill a large pot with water and bring to a boil. Add salt, then add the ravioli, about 8 at a time. When they rise to the surface, after about 2 minutes, remove with a slotted spoon and transfer to the prepared bowl. Add the sauce and toss well to coat the ravioli. Serve right away.

Make the dough up to 3 days ahead.
- *Flour lightly, wrap in wax paper, then plastic, and refrigerate.*
- *Take out of the refrigerator about 30 minutes before rolling and filling.*

Freeze the dough up to 6 months, well wrapped as above.
- *To defrost, transfer to the refrigerator overnight.*

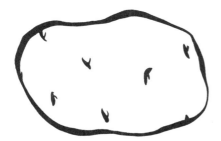

Ravioli with Artichokes

SERVES 4 TO 6

Paring an artichoke down to its edible essence can be depressing. You buy these big, beautiful globes and then reduce them, leaf by leaf, to less than ½ of their size. But after you mix them with garlic, shallots, and some good cheeses, wrap them in lemony dough, and then serve them under a creamy sauce, you will feel a whole lot better.

TIME TO PREPARE (HANDS ON): *About 40 minutes to make the pasta; about 20 minutes to make the sauce*

TIME TO COOK: *About 5 minutes*

TOTAL TIME: *About 1¼ hours; for prepared pasta, about 25 minutes*

PASTA (OPTIONAL; YOU CAN USE PREPARED FRESH PASTA)

1½ cups unbleached all-purpose flour
Pinch salt
2 large eggs
1 tablespoon grated lemon zest

FILLING AND SAUCE

4 medium artichokes
2 tablespoons extra virgin olive oil, divided
1 shallot, minced
2 tablespoons dry white wine
⅔ cup part-skim or nonfat ricotta cheese
3 tablespoons grated Parmesan cheese, divided
Coarse salt and freshly ground black pepper
1 tablespoon unbleached all-purpose flour
1 cup Vegetable Broth (page 286)
2 tablespoons sour cream or reduced-fat sour cream
Pinch ground nutmeg

Unsalted butter or extra virgin olive oil

To make the pasta by hand, on a clean, flat work surface, make a mound of flour and sprinkle with salt. Stir with a fork, then make a well in the center of the mound. Drop the eggs and lemon zest into the well, and beat lightly with a fork. Gradually incorporate the flour, using your hand to guide it into the eggs as you beat them. Continue mixing until you have a firm, stiff dough. Knead the dough until it's smooth. Wrap in plastic and set aside for 30 minutes.

To make the pasta in a food processor, beat the eggs together lightly in a mixing bowl. Put the flour and salt into a food processor and pulse to combine. With the motor running, pour the eggs in slowly, allowing them to be incorporated into a stiff dough. Take the dough out of the food processor, and knead it by hand on a lightly floured surface until it's smooth and supple. Shape it into a ball and place it in a glass or ceramic bowl. Cover with plastic wrap and let it rest for 20 to 30 minutes.

Meanwhile, make the filling and sauce. To prepare the artichokes, cut away the stem and snap off the tough outer leaves. (This will amount to more than half the artichoke.) Once you're down to the light green, tender leaves, cut the artichoke in half lengthwise. With a melon scoop, paring knife, or teaspoon, scoop out the fuzz at the center. Finally, cut the artichoke into quarters lengthwise, then cut each quarter in half lengthwise again.

Heat 1 tablespoon of the oil in a nonstick skillet over medium-high heat. When hot, add the shallot, reduce the heat to medium-low, and sauté, stirring often, until soft, about 6 minutes. Add the wine and continue stirring until it evaporates, about 2 minutes. Add the artichokes and stir to coat with the shallot. Add enough water to keep the artichokes from sticking to the pan, about ¼ cup. Cover and steam the artichokes until tender, about 10 minutes (check the water often, adding more as needed). Break up the artichokes with the back of a large spoon, leaving small chunks.

In a large mixing bowl, combine the ricotta, 1 tablespoon of the Parmesan, and the artichokes. Stir well to blend. Season with salt and pepper.

Divide the dough into 4 pieces. Take 1 piece, flatten it with your hands, and generously flour it on each side. Put it through a hand-cranked pasta maker at the widest setting. Fold the dough in half and pass it through again. Adjust the setting 2 notches down and pass the dough through again. Fold it in half and pass through again. Adjust the setting 1 notch down and repeat. Cover the sheet of pasta with plastic wrap while you roll out the rest of the dough. Alternatively, you may roll the dough out on a lightly floured surface using a rolling pin. Fold it in half several times as you roll.

Place the pasta on a lightly floured surface and cut as many rounds as possible with a 3-inch biscuit cutter. Put a teaspoon of filling in the lower half of each circle and fold the top over to enclose the filling. Dip a long-tined fork in water and press along the edges to seal. Transfer to wax paper and cover loosely with plastic while you complete the batch.

To make the sauce, heat the remaining tablespoon of olive oil in a nonstick skillet and add the flour. Stir over medium heat until the flour starts to color, about 4 minutes. Whisk in the broth and continue whisking over medium heat until it thickens, about 5 minutes. Remove from the heat and let cool for 10 minutes. Put the sour cream in

a large bowl and starting with just a few drops, gradually add the broth mixture. Stir in the remaining 2 tablespoons of Parmesan and the nutmeg. Season with salt and pepper.

Meanwhile, fill a large pot with water and bring it to a boil. Lightly oil or butter a large serving bowl. Add the ravioli, no more than 8 at a time, and simmer gently until cooked through, about 2 minutes. Remove with a slotted spoon and transfer to the prepared bowl.

Pour the sauce over the ravioli and serve warm.

Make the dough up to 3 days ahead.
- *Flour lightly, wrap in wax paper, then plastic, and refrigerate.*
- *Take out of the refrigerator about 30 minutes before rolling and filling.*

Make the filling up to 3 days ahead.
- *Seal in a tightly covered container and refrigerate*

Freeze the cooked ravioli up to 6 months.
- *Reheat by plunging frozen ravioli into boiling water for 1 minute.*

LOVE THOSE LEFTOVERS!

Make pasta: Toss leftover filling with hot pasta and additional grated cheese.

Make a frittata: Beat the leftover filling with 2–3 eggs, 2 tablespoons milk, and additional grated Parmesan cheese. Heat 1 to 2 teaspoons olive oil over medium heat in a nonstick skillet, or squirt with nonstick spray. Add the egg mixture and cook until the bottom is firm. Put into a preheated 350°F. oven until the top is firm, about 4 minutes.

Rich Tomato and Spinach Sauce

SERVES 4 TO 6

VEGETARIAN ENTRÉE!
Serve inside Cheese-Filled Risotto Ring
(page 184) with tossed salad with Vinaigrette
(page 299) and Real Bread (page 212).

*This dense blanket of a sauce also makes a hearty starter.
Serve it over sturdy pasta such as radiatore or perciatelli, or
over the Ricotta Cheese Gnocchi, following, and adjust the
portion size depending on which course you're serving it for.*

TIME TO PREPARE (HANDS ON): *About 30 minutes*

TIME TO COOK: *Included in the preparation time*

TOTAL TIME: *About 30 minutes*

---

1 tablespoon extra virgin olive oil

1 onion, chopped

3 tablespoons minced fresh basil or
   1 tablespoon crumbled dried

3 tablespoons minced fresh oregano or
   1 tablespoon crumbled dried

2 teaspoons ground cinnamon

2 cups fresh or canned peeled, seeded, and
   chopped tomatoes

3 tablespoons dried currants

1 tablespoon pine nuts, toasted

1 tablespoon unsalted butter

2 tablespoons unbleached all-purpose flour

½ cup nonfat milk

½ cup grated Parmesan cheese

10 ounces chopped fresh spinach, or one
   10-ounce package frozen spinach,
   thawed, squeezed dry, and chopped

½ teaspoon ground nutmeg

Heat the oil in a medium saucepan over medium-high heat. When hot, add the onion, basil, oregano, and cinnamon. Turn the heat down to medium-low and sauté until the onion is soft, about 7 minutes. Add the tomatoes, currants, and pine nuts, and continue cooking until the sauce thickens, about 10 minutes.

Melt the butter in a medium saucepan over medium-low heat. Stir in the flour and continue stirring to make a golden paste, about 2 minutes. Stir in the milk and whisk until smooth and thickened. Add the cheese and keep stirring to make a thick, smooth sauce. Add the spinach and nutmeg. Stir over low heat until warmed through, about 3 minutes.

Make up to 2 days in advance. Refrigerate, covered. Reheat in a saucepan over low heat, stirring often.

Ricotta Cheese Gnocchi Two Ways

SERVES 4

Cheese gnocchi demands tough aesthetic choices. You can make pretty good gnocchi, or gnocchi that's not so pretty but very, very good. The trade-off has to do with flour: Although lots of flour helps gnocchi hold their shape, it also blunts their flavor. You can have it both ways by covering imperfectly shaped gnocchi with a vibrant sauce.

TIME TO PREPARE (HANDS ON): *About 20 minutes*

TIME TO COOK: *About 5 minutes*

TOTAL TIME: *About 30 minutes*

---

2 cups part-skim ricotta cheese

½ to ¾ cup unbleached all-purpose flour

1 large egg

1 large egg yolk

2 tablespoons grated Parmesan cheese

Pinch ground nutmeg

Coarse salt

Cheese and Asparagus Topping (recipe
   follows) or Tomato and Pesto Sauce
   (recipe follows)

In a mixing bowl, combine the ricotta, ½ cup flour, egg, egg yolk, Parmesan cheese and nutmeg. Scoop up a spoonful. If the mixture isn't stiff enough to hold its shape, stir in more flour. It should be the consistency of mashed potatoes.

Bring a large pot of water to a boil. Add 1 tablespoon salt. Using a soup spoon, scoop up enough of the ricotta mixture to fill the spoon. Use another soup spoon to smooth it into a mound. Gently push the ricotta off the spoon so it slides in the water. Add the rest and simmer until they rise to the surface. Lift out with a slotted spoon and let drain briefly on paper towels before tossing with the topping of your choice.

Cheese and Asparagus Topping

   1 pound skinny asparagus

   2 tablespoons unsalted butter

   2 tablespoons grated Parmesan cheese

   Coarse salt and freshly ground black pepper
      to taste

Fit a large pot with a steamer basket. Add enough water to come up to the base of the steamer. Place the asparagus in the steamer in a single layer, cover, and bring the water to a simmer over medium-high heat. Turn the heat down to medium-low and steam the asparagus until bright green and cooked through, 2 to 4 minutes depending how thick they are.

In the microwave, melt the butter in a large microwaveproof glass or ceramic bowl. Toss the asparagus with the butter. Add the gnocchi, cheese, salt, and pepper and toss again gently. Serve right away.

Tomato and Pesto Sauce

   3 medium ripe tomatoes

   3 tablespoons extra virgin olive oil, divided

   1 cup loosely packed basil leaves

   1 tablespoon pine nuts

   1 tablespoon ricotta cheese, part-skim if
      you'd like

   2 tablespoons grated Parmesan cheese

   1 garlic clove, crushed and minced

   Coarse salt and freshly ground black pepper

To peel the tomatoes, fill a medium saucepan with water and bring it to a boil. Add the tomatoes and allow the water to return to a boil. Boil for 30 seconds. Remove the tomatoes with a slotted spoon. When cool enough to handle, strip off the peel. Chop the tomatoes and discard as many of the seeds as possible. Place the tomato pulp in a mixing bowl and toss with 1 tablespoon of olive oil. Set aside.

In a blender or a food processor, place the basil, pine nuts, ricotta, Parmesan, garlic, and remaining 2 tablespoons of olive oil. Process into a paste. Stir into the tomatoes. Season with salt and pepper. Toss gently with the gnocchi.

Make the gnocchi 1 day ahead.

- *Seal in a tightly covered container and refrigerate.*
- *To reheat, place in a single layer in a buttered baking dish. Cover the dish with aluminum foil. Place the dish inside a larger baking dish. Add water to the outer dish until it comes halfway up the side of the inner one. Bake at 450° F. for 15 minutes, until the gnocchi are heated through.*

Make the tomato sauce up to 5 days ahead.

- *Seal in a tightly covered container and refrigerate.*

Pumpkin Gnocchi

SERVES 4

Your guests will express wonder and delight when you serve these sweet and chewy dumplings, guaranteed.

TIME TO PREPARE (HANDS ON): *About 30 minutes*

TIME TO COOK: *About 45 minutes*

TOTAL TIME: *About 1½ hours*

---

1 fresh pumpkin, approximately 1 pound

1 pound medium starch potatoes, such as russet or Yukon Gold

Approximately 1½ cups unbleached all-purpose flour (you may need up to twice as much, depending how watery your pumpkin is)

3 tablespoons grated Parmesan cheese, divided

½ teaspoon ground nutmeg, or to taste

Unsalted butter or extra virgin olive oil

Pinch coarse salt

Heat the oven to 450° F.

Cut the pumpkin in half across the width and remove the seeds. Wrap each half in foil.

Wrap the potatoes in foil.

Bake the pumpkin and potatoes until both are soft enough to puree, about 40 minutes. If one is ready before the other, remove it from the oven. Let cool and scoop the pulp out of both.

Using a long-tined fork, mash together the pumpkin and potatoes. Add the flour, 1 tablespoon of the cheese, and nutmeg, and use your hands to blend into a dough that is soft but firm. (Do not use a food processor or other electric gadget for this, or the mixture will be too mushy to mold.)

Lightly flour a work surface. Cut the dough into 6 pieces. Working with 1 piece at a time, roll each into a rope about 8 inches long and as thick as your thumb. Cut each rope into inch-long pieces. Transfer to a well-floured dish or baking sheet.

Lightly grease a baking dish with butter or olive oil, pour a thin layer of sauce on the bottom, and set it aside. Heat the oven to 375° F.

Fill a large pot with water and bring to a boil. Add salt, then add the gnocchi, about 8 at a time. When they rise to the surface, after about 5 minutes, remove with a slotted spoon and transfer to the prepared baking dish. Drizzle the rest of the sauce evenly on top and sprinkle with the remaining 2 tablespoons of cheese.

Bake until the cheese melts, about 6 minutes.

Make the gnocchi up to 3 days ahead.

- *Wrap or cover tightly, preferably in a glass container, and refrigerate.*
- *To reheat, transfer to a lightly greased baking dish and place in a 350° F. oven until warmed through.*

TERRINES, TARTARE, AND MORE

Three Terrines

Dying to show off? Try one of these. Each looks as if it calls for exceptional skill, when all that's really required is the patience to rinse out the food processor bowl a half dozen times.

Salmon and Shrimp Terrine

SERVES 8

TIME TO PREPARE (HANDS ON): *About 30 minutes*

TIME TO COOK: *About 50 minutes*

TOTAL TIME: *About 1 hour, 20 minutes*

$^3/_4$ cup white wine, divided

Grated zest and juice of 1 lemon

1 bay leaf

1 pound unshelled shrimp

2 tablespoons unsalted butter, divided, plus extra for greasing pan

1 large onion, chopped

1 pound monkfish, cut into 1-inch cubes

3 large eggs

1 cup soft fresh breadcrumbs, divided

1$^1/_2$ cups half-and-half, divided

2 teaspoons crumbled dried tarragon

4 fresh or frozen artichoke hearts, cooked

1 pound salmon fillet

$^1/_4$ cup minced fresh chives

2 teaspoons ground ginger

2 teaspoon crumbled dried oregano

2 leeks, white part only, thinly sliced

1 tablespoon all-purpose flour or rice flour (available at Asian markets and some supermarkets)

1 cup milk

Coarse salt and freshly ground black pepper

In a medium saucepan, combine $^1/_4$ cup of the white wine, the lemon zest, lemon juice, bay leaf, and 1 cup of water. Bring to a boil over medium-high heat. Turn the heat down to medium and add the shrimp in their shells. Cover and simmer until the shrimp turn pink, about 5 minutes. Remove from the heat and transfer the shrimp to a bowl, using a slotted spoon. Set aside to cool.

In a large nonstick skillet, melt 1 tablespoon of butter over medium-low heat. Add the onion and sauté until soft and limp, about 7 minutes. Add $^1/_4$ cup of wine, turn up the heat to medium-high, and continue stirring until most of it evaporates, about 2 minutes. Turn the heat down to medium, add the monkfish, cover, and cook until lightly browned, about 2 minutes. Remove from the heat.

In a food processor, combine 1 egg, $^1/_2$ cup breadcrumbs, $^1/_4$ cup half-and-half, tarragon, artichoke hearts, and monkfish. Process in short spurts to combine. *Careful, now . . . do not overprocess into a paste!* Transfer to a bowl and clean out the work bowl of the food processor.

Place the salmon, chives, ginger, and 1 egg in the work bowl of a food processor. Process in short pulses to combine. *Careful, now . . . do not overprocess into a paste!* Transfer to a bowl and clean out the work bowl of the food processor.

In the work bowl of a food processor, combine the shrimp, oregano, $^1/_4$ cup of half-and-half, the remaining egg and breadcrumbs. *Careful, now . . . do not overprocess into a paste!*

Lightly grease an 8-inch loaf pan with butter. Spread the salmon mixture on the bottom, spread the shrimp layer on top, and finish with the monkfish mixture. Cover loosely with foil.

Place the loaf pan in a baking dish. Add enough water to the baking dish to come halfway up the side of the loaf pan. Bake until set, about 40 minutes. Remove the foil and continue baking until the top is firm, about 10 minutes.

Meanwhile, make the sauce. Melt the remaining tablespoon of butter in a medium saucepan over medium-high heat. Turn down the heat, add the leeks and sauté until the leeks are soft and limp, about 7 minutes. Add the remaining $1/4$ cup wine, turn up the heat, and stir until the wine evaporates, about 2 minutes. Turn down the heat to medium and stir in the flour or rice flour to make a paste. Stir in the milk and the remaining cup of half-and-half. Continue stirring over medium heat until the sauce thickens. Season with salt and pepper.

Transfer the loaf pan to a cooling rack and let sit for 20 minutes. Refrigerate to chill through. Invert onto a serving plate. Slice and drizzle each portion with sauce.

Make up to 2 days ahead.
- *Wrap tightly in plastic and refrigerate.*
- *Take out of the refrigerator about 2 hours before serving and let come to room temperature. Do not reheat; serve at room temperature*

Freeze leftovers up to 1 month.
- *To defrost, place, wrapped, in the refrigerator overnight. If still frozen, leave out at room temperature. Don't microwave; it dries out easily.*

Three-Vegetable Terrine
S E R V E S   6   T O   8

This is so pretty and good, you'll want to eat your terrine and display it, too. But you'd better get something else to decorate your table . . . one taste of this, and you'll opt for eating it. Serve it with wedges of wheat toast.

TIME TO PREPARE (HANDS ON): *Just under 1 hour*

TIME TO COOK: *About 1 1/2 hours*

TOTAL TIME: *About 6 hours, including time to cool*

$1/2$ pound carrots, peeled and thinly sliced
8 dried apricots
1 bay leaf
$1/3$ cup fresh orange juice
2 tablespoons extra virgin olive oil
1 medium red onion
2 teaspoons crumbled dried thyme
10 ounces chopped fresh spinach, or one 10-ounce package frozen spinach, thawed and squeezed dry
$1/2$ teaspoon ground nutmeg
1 shallot, minced
12 ounces white button mushrooms, chopped
3 tablespoons minced fresh chives
2 tablespoons balsamic vinegar
3 large eggs
$1/2$ cup shredded Gruyère cheese
$2/3$ cup soft breadcrumbs
2 teaspoons ground ginger
Coarse salt and freshly ground black pepper
2 tablespoons low-fat sour cream
$1/3$ cup grated Asiago or Parmesan cheese
Unsalted butter

Put the carrots, apricots, bay leaf, and orange juice in a medium saucepan or a pressure cooker. Add as much water as needed to cover by about 2 inches and bring to a simmer over medium-high heat. If you're using a saucepan, cover and turn the heat down to medium-low. Simmer until the carrots are soft enough to puree, about 40 minutes. If you're using a pressure cooker, lock on the lid and bring it up to full pressure. Cook at full pressure for 10 minutes. Remove from the heat. Let the pressure come down on its own. Tilt the cooker away from you as you unlock the lid.

Strain through a colander. Discard the bay leaf.

Transfer the carrots and apricots to a food processor or blender and puree in short pulses, taking care not to overdo it and liquefy. Set aside to cool.

Heat 1 tablespoon of the olive oil in a medium nonstick skillet over medium-high heat. When hot, add the onion and thyme, turn the heat down to medium-low, and sauté until the onion is soft, about 7 minutes. Add the spinach and stir to combine. Turn off the heat, stir in the nutmeg, and set aside.

Clean the skillet and add the remaining tablespoon of olive oil. Heat over medium-high heat. When hot, add the shallot, turn the heat down to medium-low, and sauté until the shallot turns translucent, about 3 minutes. Add the mushrooms and chives, and continue to cook, stirring often, until the mushrooms darken and begin to give up their liquid. Add the balsamic vinegar, turn the heat up to medium-high, and continue to cook until the liquid from the mushrooms and vinegar evaporate, about 5 minutes (it will get more watery first). Remove from the heat.

In a medium mixing bowl, beat 1 egg lightly with a fork. Stir in the Gruyère cheese and bread-crumbs. Add the carrot puree and stir well to blend. Add the ginger and season with salt and pepper.

In a separate mixing bowl, beat another egg lightly with a fork. Add the spinach mixture, half of the sour cream, $1/3$ of the breadcrumbs, and the Asiago cheese.

In the work bowl of a food processor or blender, place the mushrooms with the remaining egg, sour cream, and breadcrumbs. Process in short spurts to combine, being careful not to overprocess and liquefy.

Lightly grease an 8-inch loaf pan with butter. Spread the carrot mixture on the bottom of the pan, spread the mushroom mixture on top, and spread the spinach mixture on top of that. Cover loosely with foil.

Place the loaf pan inside a baking dish. Add water to the outer dish so it comes halfway up the side of the loaf pan. Bake until set, about 30 minutes. Remove the foil and continue baking until the top is firm and no longer runny, about 10 minutes.

Transfer the loaf pan to a cooling rack and let sit about 20 minutes. Cover tightly with foil and refrigerate to chill through, at least 6 hours.

Make up to 3 days ahead.
- *Wrap tightly in plastic and refrigerate.*
- *Take out of the refrigerator about 2 hours before serving and let come to room temperature. Do not reheat.*

Freeze leftovers up to 3 months.
- *To defrost, place, wrapped, in the refrigerator overnight. If still frozen, leave out at room temperature. Don't microwave.*

Black Olive–Bell Pepper Terrine

SERVES 6

Light and creamy, with a neutral taste, pureed eggplant extends some potent Mediterranean flavors in this, a favorite first course of mine. Leave out the anchovies to make this a vegetarian terrine.

TIME TO PREPARE (HANDS ON): *About 5 minutes*

TIME TO COOK: *About 1 hour 10 minutes*

TOTAL TIME: *About 1¼ hours*

---

2 medium red bell peppers

1 large eggplant

3 anchovy fillets, rinsed and patted dry (optional, but encouraged)

⅔ cup chopped pitted oil-cured olives

1 teaspoon capers, rinsed

½ cup minced fresh parsley

½ cup dry breadcrumbs

1 garlic clove, crushed and minced

2 tablespoons minced fresh basil or 2 teaspoons crumbled dried

1 large egg

Heat the oven to 450°F. Line a baking sheet with foil.

Slice the bell peppers in half and remove the core and seeds. Place, cut side down, on the baking sheet. Pierce the eggplant with a fork in several places. Place on the baking sheet. Bake until the skin on the peppers blackens and pulls away easily, and the eggplant is very soft, 30 to 40 minutes. (Remove each when it is done.) Turn down the oven to 350°F. Lightly grease 6 custard cups.

When they are cool enough to handle, remove the skin from the peppers, and slice one of the halves into 12 very thin slices (if you have to slice part of another half to get 12, that's fine). Place 2 strips in an X inside each custard cup and set aside.

Peel the eggplant, remove as many seeds as possible, and coarsely chop the pulp. Place the remaining bell pepper and the eggplant in a food processor along with the anchovies, olives, capers, parsley, breadcrumbs, garlic, basil, and egg. Process in short pulses to combine, but do not puree. Pour the mixture into the prepared custard cups, distributing it evenly.

Place the custard cups inside a large baking dish. Add water to the outer dish until it comes halfway up the cups. Cover the outer dish loosely with foil. Bake until firm, about 30 minutes. Remove the foil and continue baking until the tops are set and no longer runny, about 7 minutes more.

Remove the custard cups from the water bath and let cool on a rack. To serve, invert on a plate. If you're making them ahead, do not turn them out until it's time to serve.

Make up to 3 days ahead.
- *Wrap tightly in plastic and refrigerate.*
- *Take out of the refrigerator about 2 hours before serving, transfer to a serving bowl, cover with plastic wrap, and let come to room temperature. Serve at room temperature. To reheat, place the ramekins in a heat-resistant dish or bowl. Cover loosely with foil and place inside a large baking dish. Add water to the outer dish until it comes halfway up the ramekins. Heat in a preheated 325°F. oven for 20 minutes, adding water as necessary to maintain the level.*

Crab and Avocado Timbales

SERVES 4

One thing's for sure. No one is going to say, "Oh, no, not Crab and Avocado Timbales again!" A neatly shaped mound of rice topped with avocado and crab salad, it's a beautiful beginning to a summer supper or a lavish lunch. Lump crabmeat is expensive, but an excellent choice for a splurge.

TIME TO PREPARE (HANDS ON): *About 20 minutes*

TIME TO COOK: *About 15 minutes*

TOTAL TIME: *About 45 minutes, including time for the rice to cool*

½ cup short-grain brown or white rice

2 tablespoons mayonnaise

¼ cup nonfat plain yogurt

3 tablespoons fresh lemon juice

3 tablespoons minced fresh chives, plus
   additional whole chives for garnish

½ pound lump crabmeat, picked over for
   shells

2 hard-boiled eggs, shells removed, finely
   chopped

Coarse salt and freshly ground black pepper

1 ripe avocado, peeled, pitted, and chopped

2 tablespoons rice vinegar or 1 tablespoon
   cider vinegar

2 teaspoons sugar

1 teaspoon coarse salt

Cook the rice (see page 181 or follow package or rice cooker instructions). Let it sit for 15 minutes, covered, off the heat.

Meanwhile, in a mixing bowl, combine the mayonnaise, yogurt, lemon juice, and chives. Add the crabmeat and chopped eggs, and stir well with a fork to blend. Season with salt and pepper.

In a separate mixing bowl, mash the avocado with the back of a spoon to make a pulpy paste.

In a large mixing bowl, combine the vinegar, sugar, and salt. Add the warm rice and stir well to coat with the dressing.

On an individual serving plate, place an English muffin ring or a ring made by cutting both ends off a cleaned tuna can. Place ¼ of the rice in the center and smooth it down to fill the ring. Spread ¼ of the avocado pulp on top. Place ¼ of the crabmeat on top, patting it gently. Lift up the ring. You should have a circular timbale.

* *You can't make these ahead. Prepare just before serving.*

Garnish the timbales by sticking long chives in the center so they poke out like antennae.

Seafood Salad

Serves 4

There are three secrets to good seafood salad: (1) excellent olive oil (see page 334 for suggestions), (2) fresh shellfish, and (3) a long tenderizing boil for the squid. Don't debeard the mussels until just before cooking or they'll spoil.

TIME TO PREPARE (HANDS ON): *About 10 minutes*

TIME TO COOK: *About 20 minutes*

TOTAL TIME: *3½ hours, including time to chill*

1 pound shrimp
½ cup white wine, divided
2 garlic cloves, crushed and minced
2 pounds mussels in their shells, scrubbed
  and debearded
Grated zest and juice of 1 lemon
1 pound squid bodies (no tentacles),
  cleaned and sliced
3 tablespoons extra virgin olive oil
1 tablespoon balsamic vinegar
2 tablespoons minced fresh chives
Coarse salt and freshly ground black pepper

GARNISH
Minced chives and parsley
Lemon wedges

Shell the shrimp and put the shells in a large saucepan. Add 2 cups of water and 2 tablespoons of wine. Cover and bring to a boil over medium-high heat. Turn the heat down to medium-low and simmer for 10 minutes to infuse the water with flavor. Strain the broth into a separate saucepan. Bring to a boil over medium-high heat.

Add the shrimp, cover, and simmer gently until they turn bright pink, about 5 to 8 minutes. Remove from the heat and drain right away. Transfer the shrimp to a clean bowl and set aside.

Put 2 inches of water in a large pot and bring it to a boil. Add the garlic and ¼ cup of the wine. Let simmer for 3 minutes. Add the mussels. Cover and steam until they open, about 7 minutes. Remove from the heat. Discard any that haven't opened and remove the rest from their shells. Add to the shrimp in the bowl.

In a deep skillet, add 3 inches of water, the remaining 2 tablespoons of wine, and the lemon zest. Bring to a simmer. Add the squid and simmer, covered, until tender, about 10 minutes. Drain and add to bowl with shrimp and mussels.

Mix together the olive oil, vinegar, chives, and lemon juice. Pour over the seafood and toss well. Season with salt and pepper and toss again. Chill, covered, for 3 hours.

Toss again before serving, garnished with minced chives and parsley and lemon wedges.

Make up to 2 days ahead.
• *Seal in a tightly covered container and refrigerate. Serve cold.*

Tartare and Ceviche

Some people are plain squeamish when it comes to raw fish, and no amount or degree of assurances from you will persuade them to try it. But surely you have friends who would appreciate these dishes and love you that much more for serving them. Loosely defined and distinguished, tartare is minced raw fish, while ceviche is chunks of fish marinated in citrus juice. Once it's been marinated, ceviche will seem to have been cooked by the citrus; the pieces will be firm yet tender, and opaque in color. But the action of the citrus juice will not have killed any bacteria that might be in the fish, as heat cooking would. Consequently, it's critical that you buy fish for tartare and ceviche at a spanking clean fish counter with brisk daily turnover, managed by someone who can be trusted to sell you the best (sushi-grade) fresh fish.

Salmon Tartare with Orange

SERVES 6

These are torpedo-shaped mounds of minced fresh salmon, seasoned with orange. (Be sure that your salmon is ultra fresh, with no odor, a clear, vibrant color, and springy flesh.)

TIME TO PREPARE (HANDS ON): *About 10 minutes*

TIME TO COOK: *None*

TOTAL TIME: *About 6 hours, 10 minutes, including time to chill*

2 pounds sushi-grade skinless salmon fillets
1 $\frac{1}{2}$ teaspoons sugar
1 $\frac{1}{2}$ teaspoons sea salt
$\frac{1}{4}$ cup grated peeled carrots
2 tablespoon minced scallions, white and green parts

2 tablespoons minced fresh chives
2 tablespoons minced fresh parsley
2 navel oranges (seedless), 1 peeled and thinly sliced and 1 juiced

In a baking dish, coat the salmon with sugar and salt. Cover with plastic wrap and refrigerate for 6 hours. Rinse off the sugar and salt, and mince the salmon by hand. In a large mixing bowl, combine the carrots, scallions, chives, parsley, sliced orange, and orange juice. Toss well with the salmon. (The mixture may be covered and chilled for up to 2 hours at this point.)

Lightly grease 6 small custard cups with extra virgin olive oil. Pat an equal amount of salmon into each. Invert each onto a serving plate.

- *The tartare mixture may be chilled, covered, for up to 2 hours before serving, either in a bowl or in individual custard cups.*

Scallop Ceviche

SERVES 6

TIME TO PREPARE (HANDS ON): *About 10 minutes*

TIME TO COOK: *None*

TOTAL TIME: *About 3 hours, 10 minutes, including time to chill*

Juice of 1 lemon
Juice of 1 lime
2 tablespoons extra virgin olive oil
2 teaspoons capers, rinsed
1/4 cup minced fresh basil
1 pound fresh scallops, skin and dark brown
    spots removed
Freshly ground black pepper

FOR SERVING

4 medium or 6 small new potatoes
3 tablespoons extra virgin olive oil
2 tablespoons fresh lemon juice
1/2 teaspoon Dijon mustard
Pinch salt
1 ripe tomato, seeded and chopped
Minced fresh chives

In a glass or ceramic bowl, whisk together the lemon juice, lime juice, and olive oil. Stir in the capers and basil. Mince the scallops by hand as finely as you can. Stir into the bowl thoroughly to coat with the mixture and season with black pepper. Cover with plastic wrap and refrigerate for 3 hours, stirring at least once during that time.

While the scallops are marinating, fit a large pot with a steamer basket. Add enough water to come up to the base of the steamer. Place the potatoes in the steamer, cover, and bring the water to a simmer over medium-high heat. Turn the heat down to medium-low and steam until the potatoes are tender but firm enough to slice, 10 to 15 minutes, depending on size. Remove from the heat and let sit until cool enough to handle, about 5 minutes. Peel and slice. Place on a lightly oiled plate, cover with plastic wrap, and refrigerate until time to serve.

In a blender or with an immersion blender, process the olive oil, lemon juice, and mustard to blend. Season with salt.

Stir the tomato into the scallop mixture. Place a spoonful of scallop ceviche in the center of each serving plate and arrange the potato slices around it. Drizzle the potatoes with the vinaigrette and sprinkle with the chives. Serve right away.

Tuna Ceviche

SERVES 6

TIME TO PREPARE (HANDS ON): *About 5 minutes*

TIME TO COOK: *None*

TOTAL TIME: *About 3 hours to marinate*

Juice of 1 lemon

Juice of 1 lime

1 teaspoon soy sauce

3 tablespoons minced fresh cilantro

2 tablespoons minced fresh parsley

1 Vidalia onion, chopped

1 pound fresh sushi-grade tuna, cut into tiny cubes

2 fresh tomatoes, peeled, seeded, and chopped

6 boiled new potatoes, peeled and sliced

In a large glass bowl, combine the lemon juice, lime juice, soy sauce, cilantro, parsley, and onion. Stir in the tuna and coat well with the other ingredients. Cover with plastic wrap and chill for 3 hours.

Just before serving, stir in the tomatoes. Serve in small mounds on appetizer plates with sliced potato arranged around it.

Tuna Tartare

SERVES 4 TO 6

TIME TO PREPARE (HANDS ON): *About 15 minutes*

TIME TO COOK: *None*

TOTAL TIME: *About 15 minutes*

$1\frac{1}{2}$ pounds fresh sushi-grade tuna

2 tablespoons minced scallions, white and green parts

2 tablespoons minced fresh chives, plus additional for garnish

1 tablespoon grated lemon zest

1 tablespoon fresh lemon juice

$\frac{1}{2}$ teaspoon light soy sauce

Mince the fish very fine. (Although it may be tedious, do it by hand. A food processor or blender will make mush of it.)

Place the minced fish in a mixing bowl along with the scallions, chives, lemon zest, lemon juice, and soy sauce. Mix well.

Use an elongated soup spoon to shape. Place about 2 tablespoons of the mixture into the spoon and pat it into the curve. Invert the spoon over a plate to make a mound. Place 3 to a plate, pointing toward the center. Garnish with additional minced chives.

- *Do not make any of these further ahead than specified in the recipe.*

Crepes with Ricotta and Spices

SERVES 6

VEGETARIAN ENTRÉE!
Serve with Curried Lentil Soup with
Mango (page 62), Cucumber Raita (page 177),
and Naan (page 226).

*There's fusion and there's confusion . . . and at a time when
no one would be shocked to see jalapeño egg foo yung on a
menu, it can be hard to know the difference. These crepes,
with a curry-seasoned cheese and pepper filling, are on the
sane side of the trend.*

TIME TO PREPARE (HANDS ON): *About 15 minutes to make the
crepes; about 20 minutes to make the filling*

TIME TO COOK: *About 20 minutes*

TOTAL TIME: *About 2 hours*

CREPES

1 cup unbleached all-purpose flour

$\frac{1}{2}$ cup nonfat milk

1 large egg

1 tablespoon safflower or vegetable oil

1 onion, chopped

1 red bell pepper, cored, seeded, and thinly
   sliced

$\frac{1}{2}$ teaspoon whole fennel seeds

2 teaspoons ground cumin

$\frac{1}{3}$ cup canned crushed tomatoes

1$\frac{1}{2}$ cups nonfat or reduced-fat ricotta cheese

$\frac{1}{3}$ cup shredded Monterey Jack cheese

$\frac{1}{2}$ cup minced fresh cilantro

Salt and freshly ground black pepper

Unsalted butter or vegetable oil

To make the crepes, in a large mixing bowl, whisk
together $\frac{1}{2}$ cup water, the flour, milk, and egg to
make a smooth batter. Cover and refrigerate for
at least an hour.

Heat the oil in a medium nonstick skillet over
medium-high heat. When hot, add the onion, red
pepper, fennel seeds, and cumin. Turn down the
heat to medium-low and sauté until the onion
and pepper are soft and limp, about 15 minutes.
Add the tomatoes and continue cooking until
much of the juice evaporates and the mixture
thickens, about 5 minutes. Remove from the heat.

In a mixing bowl, combine the ricotta, Monterey Jack cheese, and cilantro. Stir in the tomato
mixture and mix well. Season with salt and pepper.

Remove the crepe batter from the refrigerator
and whisk a few times. Lightly grease a nonstick
crepe pan or 8-inch omelet pan with unsalted
butter or vegetable oil. Heat the pan over
medium heat until hot. Using a $\frac{1}{4}$-cup measuring
cup or a ladle that holds $\frac{1}{4}$ cup, pour a little less
than $\frac{1}{4}$ cup batter onto the pan. Quickly rotate
the pan to try to spread the batter evenly over
the surface. Cook the crepe for 1 minute, then
flip the crepe using a spatula and helping with
your fingers. Cook the second side for 30 seconds (see Note).

Lay a crepe on your work surface. Place about
3 tablespoons of the filling in the center and fold
all 4 sides of the crepe into the center to form an
envelope. Serve immediately, or make a stack of
the filled crepes and wrap in foil. Store and reheat at 250°F. for 15 minutes.

NOTE: This takes practice, and if your crepes
turn out lopsided or lumpy, you can console
yourself with two facts: (1) They will be used as

wrappers, so no one will notice their shape, and (2) symmetry has no effect on flavor.

Make the unfilled crepes up to 3 days ahead.
• *Wrap tightly in plastic wrap and refrigerate.*
Don't make the filling ahead; it will get runny.

Vegetable Torta

SERVES 6

VEGETARIAN ENTRÉE!
Serve with Carrot-Ginger Soup (page 63) or Corn and Sweet Potato Chowder (page 66).

It's alarming for some of us to realize that most people alive today were not yet around, or of an age to remember, when quiche was chic. Well, let me tell you, it was: spinach, mushroom, tomato and onion, ham and Swiss . . . it was such a relentless, ubiquitous phenomenon that most people who lived through that time reflexively avoid quiche altogether. It was so much of a good thing, we forgot it was a good thing. Here's a fresh taste of a once (and future?) favorite.

TIME TO PREPARE (HANDS ON): *About 20 minutes*

TIME TO COOK: *About 35 minutes*

TOTAL TIME: *Just under 1 hour*

One 1-pound package frozen puff pastry, thawed
1 tablespoon extra virgin olive oil
4 shallots, minced
1 red bell pepper, cored, seeded, and chopped
1 zucchini, minced

1 large egg
1 large egg yolk
$1/2$ cup half-and-half
$1/4$ cup plus 2 tablespoons grated Emmentaler cheese
1 tablespoon unbleached all-purpose flour
1 tablespoon minced fresh parsley

Heat the oven to 375°F.

Lightly grease six 4-inch tartlet pans with unsalted butter or squirt with nonstick cooking spray. Roll out the puff pastry, one sheet at a time, on a lightly floured surface until just slightly larger than original size. Cut the pastry to fit the tart pans. Prick the bottom of the tarts in several places with a fork. Bake for 15 minutes; the pastry will puff slightly.

Meanwhile, heat the oil in a nonstick skillet over medium-high heat. When hot, add the shallots and red pepper, reduce the heat to medium-low, and sauté, stirring often, until soft, about 7 minutes. Add the zucchini and continue stirring and sautéing until cooked through but still firm, about 3 minutes. Remove from the heat.

In a large mixing bowl, beat together the egg, egg yolk, half-and-half, cheese, flour, and parsley. Stir in the vegetable mixture and distribute evenly among the tart shells. (Use a ladle and scoop from the bottom of the bowl.)

Bake until set, when a knife inserted in the center comes out clean, and the tops are golden, about 20 minutes. Let cool on a rack. Serve warm or at room temperature.

Refrigerate leftovers up to 3 days.
• *Wrap in foil and heat in a 350°F. oven until warmed through.*

Entrées

Vegetarian and Adaptable

All Kinds of Caesar-Style Salad
All Kinds of Chili
All Kinds of Curry
Baked Falafel with Sweet Potato
Chickpeas in Tomato Sauce with Feta
    and Wine
Frittata Crepes
Piperade
Corona di Riso with Minced Ratatouille
    or Mussels
Eggplant Casserole with Spinach,
    Tomato, and Béchamel
Grilled Vegetable Salad
Vegetables Stewed in Peanut Sauce
Two Omelet Roulades
Stuffed Baked Potatoes
Cheese Fondue

Fish and Seafood

Baking Fillets, Steaks, and Whole Fish
Broiling Fillets and Steaks
Grilling Fish
Multipurpose Seasonings for Fish
Poached Salmon
Mussels . . . in Minutes!
Three Never-Fail Mussel Steaming
    Sauces
Serving Shrimp
Three Fast Never-Fail Sauces for Shrimp
Shrimp Tabbouleh
Calamari Filled with Fish
Calamari with Polenta
Simple Baked Fish in Foil
Sea Bass with Clams

Stuffed Snapper with Spiced Sauce
Monkfish in Coconut Milk
Shellfish in Orange Bowls
Pasta Packets with Sea Bass
Spinach Lasagna with Fish
Paella
Scallop and Potato Salad
Salmon with Mussels and Cream
Leek-Wrapped Salmon Stuffed with
    Shrimp
Fish Fillets with Mango Sauce
Tuna Spread for Sandwiches
Sole and Salmon Terrines with Spinach
Sole with Fresh Tomatoes
Grilled Fish Steaks in Sweet Soy
    Marinade
Steamed Salmon Medallions
Tender Ginger-Flavored Steamed Fish
    Fillets
Seafood Stew with Spinach and Saffron
Tonnato Sauce

Chicken and Turkey

Roast Chicken
Seasonings for Roast Chicken
Chicken Baked in Parchment
Poached Chicken Breasts
Chicken Breasts Steamed in Lettuce
Chicken in Wine
Chicken Sformata
Vegetable-Filled Chicken Breasts
Chicken with Apricots and Pine Nuts
Grilled Spiced Ground Chicken
Grilled Chicken in Yogurt Marinade
Borscht with Chicken Dumplings
Roast Turkey
Turkey Roulade

The Main Course

As ungracious as it sounds, I advocate the My House Is *My* House principle of entrée selection. While it smacks of selfishness, this credo is not at all at odds with the fundamental rules of etiquette calling for generosity toward and consideration for your guests. Here's why.

Whenever you cook something that you enjoy making and that you look forward to eating, you'll prepare a far better meal than you would if you were to make something to impress or appease the people you've invited. While it's important to keep your friends' preferences in mind, you may come to regret allowing yourself to be dictated to by them. Consider this: making a dish merely because you think you should is like kissing a relative you don't know very well. What ought to be an act of warmth becomes perfunctory. Inevitably, it shows.

However, like most sound philosophical principles, this one is more easily stated than applied. You may have found that when you invite certain people to dinner, they respond with a list of things they'd rather not eat. You can decide to accommodate them—and ought to if they are constrained by allergies or religious principles—or you might just tell them what you're planning to prepare and let them decide whether they want to come. If their preferences would require shopping at far-flung specialty stores or buying special cookbooks, you might agree to go out for a meal together on some other occasion.

Never Lose Your Nerve (or Mind) Again!
Keeping Your Composure with a House Special
Choose a particular dish as a House Special, something you can prepare well, even on short notice. Your choice may change with the seasons or remain constant over many years. For optimum flexibility, consider a versatile dish such as All Kinds of Chili (page 106) or All Kinds of Curry (page 108). Once you've mastered the basic dish, you'll be able to adapt it to make use of fresh seasonal ingredients and to suit your guests, vegetarian or not. Or you may want to become known among your friends for something distinctive such as Corona di Riso (page 114) or Calamari Filled with Fish (page 131).

Although some party-givers would shrink in shame from serving the same thing to repeat guests, others find that their friends look forward to enjoying a reliably good meal at their house time and again (after all, you don't think twice about ordering a favorite dish at your favorite restaurant).

When you're planning what to serve, consider how many other courses you'll include in the meal. If you're going to serve appetizers and a starter beforehand and a salad and dessert afterward, you'll want a lighter entrée than you would if you were planning to serve less. (See the menus given throughout and beginning on page 328 for specific suggestions). Also, if one or more of your guests are vegetarian and the rest are not, you might offer a relatively light chicken or fish entrée and substantial vegetable and grain side dishes. For a one-plate family-style dinner, a substantial one-dish entrée, such as chili or seafood lasagna, works best. Or try a combination of simple foods, such as roast chicken, mashed potatoes, and a salad of some kind.

VEGETARIAN AND ADAPTABLE

All Kinds of Caesar-Style Salad

SERVES 4

Anchovy is a defining ingredient in authentic Caesar salad, but you can substitute olives if you'd like. If you and your guests do eat anchovies, toss them in, too, and shrimp or chicken, for additional substance. Boiling the egg eliminates the minuscule risk of salmonella poisoning that haunts those wary of traditional Caesar salad, which calls for raw eggs, known to carry the pernicious bacteria.

TIME TO PREPARE (HANDS ON): *About 10 minutes*

TIME TO COOK: *Under 5 minutes*

TOTAL TIME: *About 15 minutes*

CREAM-STYLE DRESSING
1 large egg
½ cup part-skim ricotta cheese
½ cup buttermilk
2 anchovy fillets, rinsed, patted dry, and minced, or 6 oil-cured black olives, minced
¼ cup plus 2 tablespoons grated Parmesan cheese
2 tablespoons fresh lemon juice
½ teaspoon Dijon mustard
2 tablespoons minced fresh chives

SALAD
2 to 3 hearts of romaine lettuce, leaves washed and thoroughly dried
6 thick slices substantial bread, crusts removed
1 garlic clove, sliced in half lengthwise

OPTIONAL
1 to 2 cups diced cooked chicken or turkey
or
1 pound boiled peeled shrimp (page 127)

Coarse salt and freshly ground black pepper

Fill a small saucepan with water and bring it to a boil. Place the egg on a spoon and gently lower it into the boiling water. Cover and remove from the heat. Let sit 3 minutes, then drain and set aside to cool.

Meanwhile, with a blender, immersion blender or food processor, combine the remaining dressing ingredients. Remove the shell from the egg and add the egg. Process until smooth.

Tear the romaine leaves and put them into a large salad bowl. Rub the bread with the cut end of the garlic clove. (Toast the bread first, if you'd like.) Tear the bread into chunks and add it. Toss with your optional ingredient, if using. Pour the dressing on top and toss thoroughly. Season with salt and pepper and toss again.

• *You can't make this ahead. Prepare it just before serving.*

All Kinds of Chili

The concept of authenticity is tyranny in the kitchen. So it's nice to know that despite the regional pride it inspires, chili is native to nowhere. Self-proclaimed purists, I suspect, are profoundly self-serving. "The real thing" is whatever they say it is, and you can hardly expect them to say that it's made of things they can't stand. So you have the meat lovers insisting on beef and no beans, and those with more eclectic appetites allowing a few legumes into the mix, or maybe even ditching the meat altogether. Well here's MY authentic version—all three of it.

TIME TO PREPARE (HANDS ON): *About 15 minutes*

TIME TO COOK: *Between 20 and 40 minutes, depending which main ingredient you choose*

TOTAL TIME: *Between 35 minutes and 1 hour, depending which main ingredient you choose*

CHILI BASE (AND VEGETARIAN CHILI)

1 tablespoon canola or vegetable oil

2 large onions, chopped

3 garlic cloves, crushed and minced

1 red bell pepper, cored, seeded, and sliced

1 green bell pepper, cored, seeded, and sliced

2 tomatillos, papery skin removed and minced (optional)

$1/4$ cup minced fresh cilantro

2 tablespoons minced fresh oregano or 1 tablespoon crumbled dried

1 tablespoon chili powder

2 teaspoons ground cumin

2 teaspoons chipotle pepper flakes, or to taste (optional; see Note)

$1/4$ cup red wine or dry white wine

1 bay leaf

2 cups fresh or canned chopped peeled tomatoes

1 cup cooked kidney beans or black beans, rinsed and drained

Coarse salt to taste

TO SERVE

6 cups cooked long-grain or medium-grain white rice (1 $1/2$ cups dry)

GARNISHES

Shredded sharp cheddar and/or Monterey Jack cheese

Sour cream

Minced fresh cilantro

Minced onions

Heat the oil in a large heavy saucepan over medium-high heat. When hot, add the onions, garlic, red and green bell peppers, tomatillos, cilantro, oregano, chili powder, cumin, and chipotle pepper flakes. Lower the heat to medium-low and sauté, stirring often, until the onions and peppers are soft and limp, about 10 minutes. Add the wine, turn up the heat to medium-high, and stir until most of it evaporates, about 2 minutes. Add the bay leaf and tomatoes, turn the heat down to medium, and simmer gently, covered, until the sauce thickens, about 20 minutes. Stir in the beans and add the additional ingredient(s) from below, if desired. Continue according to the specific directions. Season with salt. Serve with rice (about 1 cup cooked rice per serving). Put the garnishes in separate bowls and place them on the table so that guests can help themselves.

Chicken Chili

Chili Base

4 boneless, skinless chicken breast halves, cubed

Add the chicken to the simmering Chili Base and cook, stirring often, until no longer pink in the center, about 20 minutes. Serve with rice (about 1 cup cooked rice per serving). Put the garnishes in separate bowls and place them on the table.

Mushroom Chili

Chili Base

Additional 1 cup cooked kidney beans or black beans

1 tablespoon corn, canola, or vegetable oil

1 shallot, minced

1 pound portobello or cremini mushrooms, quartered

Add the additional cup of beans to the simmering Chili Base and stir to blend.

Heat the oil in a nonstick skillet over medium-high heat. When hot, add the shallot, reduce the heat to medium-low, and sauté, stirring often, until softened, about 6 minutes. Add the mushrooms and sauté, stirring often, until they're dark and tender, about 8 minutes.

Add to the Chili Base and stir well to blend. Serve with rice (about 1 cup cooked rice per serving). Place the garnishes in separate bowls and place them on the table so that guests can help themselves.

Seafood Chili

Chili Base

$1/2$ pound minced clams, drained

$1/2$ pound shrimp, shells removed

$1/2$ pound sea scallops, rinsed, patted dry, and cut into halves or quarters, depending on size

Add the clams, shrimp, and scallops to the simmering Chili Base and cook *just* until the shrimp are bright pink and the scallops are white and no longer glossy, about 5 minutes. Serve with rice (about 1 cup cooked rice per serving). Put the garnishes in separate bowls and place them on the table so that guests can help themselves.

NOTE: Chipotle pepper flakes add a distinct smoky flavor to the chili. They can be found in specialty and gourmet stores, or in the spice or Mexican section of good supermarkets. See source guide (page 347) for mail-order information.

Make up to 3 days ahead.
- *Seal in a tightly covered container and refrigerate.*
- *To reheat, transfer to a heavy saucepan and stir over medium heat until warmed through. Or transfer to a microwavable bowl and microwave at full power, turning the bowl at 2-minute intervals, until heated through.*

Freeze up to 6 months, * *well wrapped in a glass or firm plastic container.*
- *To defrost, see reheating instructions above.*

---

* With seafood, only 1 month.

All Kinds of Curry

SERVES 4

Curry means nothing more specific than highly seasoned stew. The seasonings vary from country to country in the Near and Far East, and from region to region and household to household within those countries. This versatile curry base calls for seasonings most common to Southern India, or at least to Southern Indian restaurants in the West. Prepare plenty of long-grain white rice or basmati (a smoky long-grain rice available wherever there is a good selection of eastern and/or health foods—see sources, page 347) to serve along with it.

TIME TO PREPARE (HANDS ON): *About 15 minutes*

TIME TO COOK: *Between 20 and 40 minutes, depending which main ingredient you choose*

TOTAL TIME: *Between 35 minutes and 1 hour, depending which main ingredient you choose*

---

1 $\frac{1}{2}$ tablespoons peanut or vegetable oil

2 large white onions, chopped

1 leek, white part only, thinly sliced

4 garlic cloves, crushed and minced

1 tablespoon grated peeled fresh ginger

2 green medium-hot chili peppers, such as jalapeño or anaheim, seeded and minced (optional)

1 tablespoon ground cumin

2 teaspoons ground coriander

2 whole cloves

One 1-inch cinnamon stick

$\frac{1}{2}$ teaspoon turmeric

$\frac{1}{2}$ teaspoon whole cumin seeds

Generous pinch mustard seeds

Generous pinch ground fenugreek

1 large potato, preferably yellow flesh, such as Yukon Gold or Yellow Finn, peeled and cubed

1 sweet potato, peeled and cubed

2 large fresh or canned tomatoes, peeled, seeded, and chopped

1 $\frac{1}{2}$ cups light coconut milk or $\frac{1}{2}$ cup coconut milk diluted with 1 cup water

2 tablespoons fresh lime juice

3 tablespoons unsweetened shredded coconut

Coarse salt

4 cups cooked long-grain or basmati rice (1 cup raw)

GARNISHES

Plain nonfat yogurt

Minced fresh cilantro

Minced red onions

Heat the oil in a large nonstick skillet over medium-high heat. When hot, add the onions, leek, garlic, ginger, chilies, if using, cumin, coriander, cloves, cinnamon, turmeric, cumin seeds, mustard seeds, and fenugreek. Reduce the heat to medium-low and sauté, stirring often, until the onions and leek are soft and limp, about 7 minutes.

Add the yellow and sweet potatoes and stir to coat with the spices. Add about 3 tablespoons water to keep them from sticking. Add the tomatoes and cook, stirring, until they start to break into a sauce, about 3 minutes.

Add the coconut milk and lime juice, and stir to blend. Add any of the ingredient groups below, stir to coat, cover the skillet, and cook on low heat until done (see approximate times following).

Meanwhile, put the shredded coconut into a dry skillet and place over medium-high heat. Stir the coconut until evenly browned. Stir into the curry before serving, or sprinkle some over each serving as a garnish. Season the curry with salt, and remove the cloves and cinnamon stick before serving with rice. Place the garnishes in separate bowls and pass at the table.

Cauliflower

    1 pound cauliflower, cut into florets
    1 $\frac{1}{2}$ cups cooked chickpeas, rinsed and drained

Cook over medium-low heat until the cauliflower is tender, about 20 minutes.

Egg

    $\frac{1}{4}$ cup almonds or dry-roasted cashews
    $\frac{1}{4}$ cup plus 2 tablespoons minced dried apple
    8 hard-boiled eggs, peeled and sliced in half lengthwise

Pulverize the almonds or cashews in a blender or food processor. Stir into the simmering curry sauce when you add the coconut milk, along with the diced dried apple. Simmer over low heat until the apples soften, about 10 minutes.

    Place the eggs, yolk side up, in the curry, and spoon the curry sauce over them.

Chicken

    4 boneless, skinless chicken breast halves (about 1 pound), cubed

Cook over medium-low heat until the chicken is no longer pink in the center, about 20 minutes.

Fish

    1 pound firm white fish fillet, such as haddock, snapper, or monkfish, cubed

Cook over medium-low heat until the fish is flaky, about 8 minutes.

Shellfish

    $\frac{1}{2}$ pound shrimp, shells removed
    $\frac{1}{2}$ pound sea scallops, rinsed and patted dry, halved or quartered if large

Cook until the shrimp turns bright pink and the scallops are white, not glossy, about 7 minutes.

Make up to 3 days ahead.
- *Seal in a tightly covered container and refrigerate.*
- *To reheat, transfer to a heavy saucepan and stir over medium heat until warmed through. Or transfer to a microwavable bowl and microwave at full power, turning the bowl at 2-minute intervals, until heated through.*

Freeze up to 6 months, well wrapped in a glass or firm plastic container.*
- *To defrost, see reheating instructions above.*

---

* With seafood, only 1 month.

Baked Falafel with Sweet Potato

SERVES 4

Sweet potato adds flavor and texture to a familiar Middle Eastern treat. (If falafel isn't familiar to you . . . make this, quick! And enjoy the fruits of enlightenment.) Enjoy it for lunch or a casual light supper.

TIME TO PREPARE (HANDS ON): *About 10 minutes*

TIME TO COOK: *About 50 minutes*

TOTAL TIME: *About 1 hour*

1 medium sweet potato
2 cups cooked chickpeas, rinsed and drained
2 tablespoons tahini
2 tablespoons nonfat plain yogurt
1 tablespoon fresh lemon juice
2 tablespoons fresh orange juice
1 garlic clove, crushed and minced
2 teaspoons ground cumin
1 teaspoon paprika
Pinch salt

FOR SERVING
Pita Bread (page 224)
Tahini Sauce (recipe follows)
Mild onion, minced
Alfalfa sprouts

Heat the oven to 450°F.

Wrap the sweet potato in foil and bake until soft, about 30 minutes. Leave the oven on. Unwrap the potato and let it cool. When cool enough to handle, peel and mash with a fork.

Place the sweet potato, chickpeas, tahini, yogurt, lemon juice, orange juice, garlic, cumin, paprika, and salt in the work bowl of a food processor or blender. Process in spurts to make a chunky paste.

Pat the mixture into 6 nonstick muffin tins and bake until firm on top, about 20 minutes (It will be soft in the middle.) Run a wet butter knife around each and turn out of the muffin tins. Mash each on a piece of pita, drizzle with tahini sauce, and top with onion and sprouts.

Tahini Sauce

1 cup nonfat plain yogurt
1 tablespoon tahini
Juice of 1 lime
Generous pinch ground cumin
Coarse salt to taste

In a large mixing bowl, combine the yogurt, tahini, lime juice, cumin, and salt. Whisk well to blend.

Make up to 3 days ahead.
- *Wrap in plastic or store in zip-lock bags, pressing out the air before you seal. Refrigerate.*
- *Serve cold or at room temperature.*

Chickpeas in Tomato Sauce with Feta and Wine

SERVES 4

Nothing worth sharing for supper could be easier or more pleasing. If you have first-time hosting jitters, this is the dish to serve. Even if you're well seasoned at serving guests, you can count on this whenever you're too tired or busy to cope with anything complicated.

TIME TO PREPARE (HANDS ON): *About 25 minutes*

TIME TO COOK: *Included in the preparation time*

TOTAL TIME: *About 40 minutes, including time to rest*

---

1 tablespoon plus 1 teaspoon extra virgin
    olive oil
1 onion, chopped
2 garlic cloves, crushed and minced
2 tablespoons minced fresh oregano or
    1 tablespoon crumbled dried
6 tomatoes, peeled, seeded, and chopped,
    or 2$\frac{1}{2}$ cups canned chopped tomatoes,
    drained
$\frac{1}{2}$ cup dry white wine
2 cups cooked chickpeas, rinsed and drained
$\frac{3}{4}$ cup crumbled feta cheese
Salt and freshly ground black pepper

Heat the oil in a nonstick skillet over medium-high heat. When hot, add the onion, garlic, and oregano. Reduce the heat to medium-low and sauté, stirring often, until the onion is soft, about 7 minutes. Add the tomatoes and stir until bubbly. Add the wine and continue to simmer, stirring occasionally until the mixture thickens into a sauce, about 15 minutes. Stir in the chickpeas and feta cheese. Continue stirring until the cheese melts, about 4 minutes. Season with salt and pepper.

Remove from the heat and let sit for 10 minutes before serving.

Make up to 3 days ahead.
- *Seal in a tightly covered container and refrigerate.*
- *To reheat, transfer to a heavy saucepan and stir over medium heat until warmed through. Or transfer to a microwavable bowl and microwave at full power, turning the bowl at 2-minute intervals, until heated through.*

Menu

ORANGE-INFUSED BABA GHANOUJ (PAGE 27)
STUFFED GRAPE LEAVES (PAGE 44)
CHICKPEAS IN TOMATO SAUCE WITH FETA AND WINE
SWEET AND NUTTY BULGUR SALAD (PAGE 182)
BEETS AND SOUR CREAM (PAGE 178)
PITA BREAD (PAGE 224)

Frittata Crepes

SERVES 6 TO 8

Thinner than frittatas, thicker than crepes, these are not quite one or the other, but they are quite perfect layered, stacked, and served for brunch.

TIME TO PREPARE (HANDS ON): *About 30 minutes*

TIME TO COOK: *About 20 minutes*

TOTAL TIME: *2 hours, including time for crepe batter to rest*

6 large eggs

1 cup unbleached all-purpose flour

²⁄₃ cup milk

Pinch salt

Two 10-ounce packages frozen chopped spinach, thawed and squeezed dry

2¹⁄₂ cups nonfat or reduced-fat ricotta cheese

¹⁄₂ cup grated Parmesan cheese

Salt and freshly ground black pepper

1 tablespoon extra virgin olive oil

1 onion, chopped

4 cups fresh or canned peeled, seeded, and chopped tomatoes

1 bay leaf

¹⁄₄ cup reduced-fat sour cream

To make the crepes, whisk together the eggs, flour, milk, and salt. Cover with plastic wrap and refrigerate for at least an hour.

In a mixing bowl, combine the spinach, ricotta, and Parmesan cheese. Season with salt and pepper.

Heat the olive oil in a medium skillet over medium-high heat. When hot, add the onion, turn the heat down to medium-low, and sauté until the onion is soft, about 7 minutes.

Add the tomatoes and bay leaf, and continue cooking until the tomatoes thicken into a sauce, about 7 minutes. Stir in the sour cream and remove from the heat.

Heat the oven to 350° F.

Lightly grease a nonstick omelet pan with vegetable oil or unsalted butter and heat over medium heat. Pour in ¹⁄₄ of the batter and rotate the pan to coat it evenly. When the underside is nearly set, 1 to 2 minutes, gently loosen the edge with a plastic spatula, and, using your fingers, quickly flip the crepe to set the other side, about 1 minute more. Transfer to a plate and repeat until you've used up all of the batter.

Lightly grease a pie plate or gratin dish, then pour about ¹⁄₄ cup of the tomato sauce into the bottom of the dish. Place 1 crepe in the dish and spread with ¹⁄₃ of the spinach mixture. Top with another crepe and then another layer of spinach. Repeat, ending with a crepe. Pour the rest of the tomato sauce on top and cover loosely with foil. Bake for 20 minutes.

Remove the foil and invert a serving plate on top. Turn the dish with the crepes over so the crepes end up on the serving plate in a neat stack. Let sit for 10 minutes with the pan still on before lifting off the pan and slicing. Serve warm or room temperature.

Make the sauce up to 3 days ahead (or use prepared sauce).
* *Seal in a tightly covered container and refrigerate.*
Make the crepes up to 2 days ahead.
* *Wrap tightly in plastic and refrigerate.*
Wrap the leftovers in a dish covered with plastic. Refrigerate. Serve cold or at room temperature. This dish gets a bit tough when reheated.

Piperade

SERVES 2

There are times—and it's probably not necessary to get too specific here—when you want to invite someone in for a late supper. You may not have to mention any specific food as enticement, but having nothing to serve would make the already obvious a little too plain. Even if your intentions are in fact merely to have something to eat, there's nothing better after hours than a creamy piperade.

TIME TO PREPARE (HANDS ON): *About 15 minutes*

TIME TO COOK: *Included in the preparation time*

TOTAL TIME: *About 15 minutes*

1 tablespoon extra virgin olive oil
1 large onion, thinly sliced
1 garlic clove, crushed and minced
1 large red bell pepper, cored, seeded, and thinly sliced
1 large green bell pepper, cored, seeded, and thinly sliced
1 tablespoon crumbled dried oregano
2 fresh or canned peeled and chopped tomatoes
4 large eggs, lightly beaten
2 tablespoons half-and-half or reduced-fat sour cream
Coarse salt and freshly ground black pepper

FOR SERVING
Cooked rice, toast, or garlic bread
Minced fresh parsley

Heat the oil in a large nonstick skillet over medium-high heat. When hot, add the onion, garlic, bell peppers, and oregano. Reduce the heat to medium-low and sauté, stirring often, until the vegetables are soft and limp, about 10 minutes. Raise the heat to medium-high and add the tomatoes, stirring until bubbly. Turn the heat down to medium-low and continue stirring until they break down into a sauce, about 3 minutes.

In a small mixing bowl, beat together the eggs and half-and-half or sour cream. Stir into the skillet, turn the heat down to low, and continue stirring until creamy. Try not to let the eggs reach the scrambled stage. (If they do, it's okay—it will still taste very good.)

Season with salt and pepper, and serve over rice or with toast or garlic bread. Sprinkle the piperade with minced parsley to serve.

• *You can't make this ahead. Prepare it just before serving.*

Corona di Riso with Minced Ratatouille or Mussels

SERVES 4

Whether you fill the center with ratatouille or steamed mussels, this ring of spinach risotto is a stunning main course.

TIME TO PREPARE (HANDS ON): *About 45 minutes*

TIME TO COOK: *Included in the preparation time*

TOTAL TIME: *About 45 minutes, plus time to prepare the vegetables or mussels*

1 tablespoon extra virgin olive oil

1 onion, chopped

1 garlic clove, crushed and minced

2 tablespoons minced fresh oregano or
   1 tablespoon crumbled dried

2 tablespoons minced fresh basil or
   1 tablespoon crumbled dried

1 $\frac{1}{2}$ cups arborio rice

2 tablespoon dry white wine

Approximately 3 $\frac{1}{2}$ cups Vegetable Broth
   (page 286) or 2 cups if using a pressure
   cooker

10 ounces fresh spinach, coarsely chopped,
   or one 10-ounce package frozen chopped
   spinach, defrosted and squeezed dry

$\frac{1}{4}$ cup grated Parmesan cheese

1 recipe Minced Ratatouille (page 207)

1 recipe Mussels Steamed in Wine with
   Herbs (page 125) (optional)

Heat the olive oil in a heavy saucepan or pressure cooker. When hot, add the onion, garlic, oregano, and basil, and sauté until the onion is soft, about 7 minutes. Remove and discard the garlic when it starts to brown, after about 3 minutes. Add the rice and stir to coat with the onion and herbs. Add the wine and stir until most of it evaporates, about 1 minute.

Bring the broth to a simmer in a saucepan. If cooking the rice in a saucepan, add the broth to cover by about an inch and stir until it's been absorbed. Continue to add broth about $\frac{1}{2}$ cup at a time, stirring often until the rice is cooked through and the mixture is creamy, about 20 minutes altogether. Most or all of the broth should have been used at this time. Stir in the spinach and cheese.

In a pressure cooker, stir in 2 cups of broth and bring to a boil. Cover and bring to moderate pressure. Maintain the pressure for 7 minutes; if you're using a gas stove, you can do this by turning the heat down as far as it will go. If you're using an electric stove, transfer the cooker to a burner heated to low. After 7 minutes, remove from the heat.

When the pressure comes all the way down, tilt the cooker away from yourself and remove the lid. (If there's any liquid left, return the cooker to the stove and turn the heat to low, stirring until it is absorbed and the rice is creamy.) Stir in the spinach and cheese.

Grease a circular tube mold lightly with vegetable oil or squirt it with nonstick spray. Spoon the risotto into it and press firmly. Let sit for 10 to 15 minutes. Turn over onto a large serving plate. If you're serving the minced ratatouille and mussels, stir together to blend. Fill the center of the ring with the mixture or fill with Minced Ratatouille alone. Serve warm or at room temperature.

Make the Minced Ratatouille up to 3 days ahead.

- *Seal in a tightly covered container and refrigerate.*

Make the risotto for the corona up to 1 day ahead.

- *Seal in a tightly covered container and refrigerate. Press into the circular mold as directed, then cover loosely with foil and place inside a large baking dish. Add water to the other dish until it comes halfway up the side of the mold. Heat in a preheated 450° F oven until warmed through, about 20 minutes, adding water as necessary to maintain the level.*

Eggplant Casserole with Spinach, Tomato, and Béchamel

SERVES 6

Eggplant is uncommonly accommodating. In summer, its peak season, you can enjoy it in simple dishes hot or cool. And in winter, when most summer produce is best forgotten until next year, eggplant is still most useful, as in this hearty one-dish dinner.

TIME TO PREPARE (HANDS ON): *About 45 minutes*

TIME TO COOK: *About 40 minutes*

TOTAL TIME: *About 1 1/2 hours*

Extra virgin olive oil
2 large eggplants, sliced 3/4 inch thick
1 onion, chopped
3 tablespoons minced fresh basil or
   1 tablespoon crumbled dried
3 tablespoons minced fresh oregano or
   1 tablespoon crumbled dried
2 teaspoons ground cinnamon
2 cups fresh or canned peeled, seeded, and
   chopped tomatoes
3 tablespoons dried currants
1 tablespoon pine nuts, toasted
1 tablespoon unsalted butter
2 tablespoons unbleached all-purpose flour
1/3 cup nonfat milk
1/2 cup grated Parmesan cheese
1/2 teaspoon ground nutmeg, or to taste
10 ounces chopped fresh spinach, or one
   10-ounce package frozen chopped
   spinach, thawed and squeezed dry

Heat the oven to 425° F. Lightly grease 2 nonstick baking sheets with olive oil. (If you only have one, do this in 2 batches).

Place the eggplant in a single layer on the baking sheets. Bake until lightly browned on top, about 12 minutes. Turn the slices over and brown the other side, about 5 to 7 minutes.

Heat 1 tablespoon of oil in a medium saucepan over medium-high heat. When hot, add the onion, basil, oregano, and cinnamon. Turn the heat down to medium-low and sauté until the onion is soft, about 7 minutes. Add the tomatoes, currants, and pine nuts, and continue cooking until the sauce thickens, about 10 minutes.

Melt the butter in a medium saucepan over medium-low heat. Stir in the flour and continue stirring to make a golden paste, about 2 minutes. Stir in the milk and whisk until smooth and thickened. Add the cheese and keep stirring to make a thick, smooth sauce. Add the nutmeg and spinach and stir to blend. Cook for 2 minutes to heat through.

Lightly grease a baking dish. Pour some tomato sauce on the bottom. Place a layer of eggplant on top. Spread a third of the spinach sauce over the eggplant, then top with another layer of eggplant. Drizzle the tomato sauce over the eggplant, then spread another third of the spinach sauce over it. Repeat with the remaining ingredients, ending with a layer of spinach sauce.

Bake until bubbly and golden, about 40 minutes.

• *Wrap the leftovers in a dish covered with plastic. Refrigerate. To reheat, replace the plastic with foil and place in a 350° F. oven until warmed through.*

LOVE THOSE LEFTOVERS!
Make pasta: Toss leftover sauce with hot pasta, or stir it into warm brown rice.

Menu

CARROT-GINGER SOUP (PAGE 63)
EGGPLANT CASSEROLE WITH SPINACH, TOMATO, AND BÉCHAMEL
AVOCADO AND APPLE SALAD (PAGE 174)
LEMON ANGEL FOOD LOAF (PAGE 303) WITH LEMON GLACE (PAGE 279)

Grilled Vegetable Salad

SERVES 4

Does anyone else have this problem? It's high summer and you're doing nothing with all that fresh produce but hoarding it. The tomatoes, the eggplant, the peppers, squash, and corn—they're all so staggeringly perfect, recipes spin through your head until your mind goes blank. Next time you find yourself at a loss, mix this marinade and grill whatever you've got. The marinade works well with any and all seasonal produce well into autumn.

NOTE: The vexing truth for anyone short on time is that most vegetables must be blanched (partially cooked) before you grill them. Blanching makes them softer and more absorbent, so they soak up the marinade and cook evenly and quickly on the grill. Fortunately, you can blanch most vegetables hours before you grill them so you can pace meal preparation.

TIME TO PREPARE (HANDS ON): *About 15 minutes*

TIME TO COOK: *About 10 minutes, depending on the vegetables*

TOTAL TIME: *About 1 hour*

---

1 large eggplant
1 pound asparagus
1 red bell pepper
1 yellow bell pepper
2 large Vidalia onions, peeled
8 ounces portobello mushrooms
2 tablespoons extra virgin olive oil
2 tablespoons balsamic vinegar
1 garlic clove, crushed and minced
2 tablespoons minced fresh basil
Tahini Dressing (recipe follows)

Peel the eggplant and cut it in half lengthwise. Cut each half lengthwise into quarters.

Trim the asparagus to remove the tough ends of the stems.

Cut the red and yellow peppers in half lengthwise and remove the stem, core, and seeds. Cut each half in half.

Fill a large pot with water and bring to a boil. Add the onions and boil until they are soft but not mushy and the layers separate easily, about 5 minutes. Remove with a slotted spoon and set aside.

Add the eggplant and boil until just tender, about 3 minutes. Remove with a slotted spoon and set aside.

Add the asparagus and boil until bright green, about 1 minute. Remove with a slotted spoon and set aside.

In a shallow baking dish, combine the olive oil, vinegar, garlic, and basil. Stir well. Separate the layers of the onions. Hold each onion and push the center; it will separate into hollow rounds. Place the rounds in the baking dish. Add the eggplant, asparagus, and mushrooms, and stir well to coat with the oil and vinegar. Cover the dish with plastic wrap and let marinate for 30 minutes, stirring after 15 minutes.

Heat the grill. When the heat is very hot, grease a fine-mesh grate with olive oil and place on top. Place the bell peppers, skin side down, on the grate, and arrange the vegetables so that all of the asparagus is together, all of the onion rings together, and all of the eggplant together on the grate. Turn the vegetables occasionally so they cook evenly. As each vegetable is cooked, re-move from the grate, transferring to a deep bowl. Cover the bowl with foil.

Toss with Tahini Dressing before serving.

Tahini Dressing

$\frac{1}{2}$ cup crumbled feta cheese (see Note)
1 $\frac{1}{2}$ cups nonfat plain yogurt
1 tablespoon tahini
2 tablespoons fresh lemon juice
$\frac{1}{2}$ teaspoon salt
2 teaspoons ground cumin
1 teaspoon paprika

In a food processor or blender, combine the feta cheese, yogurt, tahini, lemon juice, salt, cumin, and paprika. Process in short spurts until smooth.

NOTE: If any of your guests are vegan, substitute soft tofu for the yogurt, double the amount of tahini, and omit the feta cheese.

Make the tahini dressing up to 3 days ahead.
• Seal in a tightly covered container and refrigerate.
Wrap the leftovers in a dish covered with plastic. Refrigerate. Serve cold or at room temperature.

LOVE THOSE LEFTOVERS!
Make a wrap! Fill Lavash (page 228) or a large flour tortilla with vegetables, sauce, and rice. Fold into an envelope or roll up.

Vegetables Stewed in Peanut Sauce

SERVES 4

New vegetarians can be shy about cooking for their omnivorous friends, concerned they'll affirm the obsolete yet persistent stereotype of the soy-sodden ascetic. They become bolder as they realize that there are many dishes such as this that will satisfy everyone without compromising vegetarianism, gastronomy, or hospitality. Serve over couscous or rice.

TIME TO PREPARE (HANDS ON): *About 20 minutes*

TIME TO COOK: *About 40 minutes*

TOTAL TIME: *About 1 hour*

1 tablespoon peanut oil

1 large onion, chopped

3 garlic cloves, crushed and minced

1 tablespoon grated peeled fresh ginger

1 fresh jalapeño or anaheim chili pepper, seeded and minced

2 tablespoons minced fresh cilantro

1 tablespoon ground cinnamon

1 tablespoon ground cumin

½ teaspoon ground cardamom

1 bay leaf

1 teaspoon ground coriander

3 cups shredded cabbage

10 ounces chopped fresh spinach, or one 10-ounce package frozen chopped spinach, thawed and squeezed dry

4 medium potatoes, such as Yukon Gold, peeled and cut into bite-sized chunks, or 8 small new potatoes, peeled and left whole

4 medium sweet potatoes, peeled and cut into bite-sized chunks

2 yellow turnips (rutabagas), peeled and cut into bite-sized chunks

1 cup fresh or canned peeled, seeded, and chopped tomato

3 tablespoons unsalted peanut butter

¼ cup fresh lemon juice

Coarse salt and freshly ground black pepper

4 cups cooked rice or couscous to serve

Heat the oil in a large deep nonstick skillet or a pressure cooker. When hot, add the onion, garlic, ginger, chili pepper, cilantro, cinnamon, cumin, cardamom, bay leaf, and coriander. Turn the heat down to medium-low and sauté until the onion is soft and limp, about 15 minutes.

Add the cabbage and spinach and stir until they wilt, about 4 minutes. Stir in both the potatoes, the turnips, tomato, peanut butter, and lemon juice and bring to a simmer over medium-high heat.

Turn the heat down to medium-low. If you're using a skillet, cover and cook until the rutabaga, potato, and sweet potato are tender all the way through, about 40 minutes, adding water 2 tablespoons at a time if necessary to prevent sticking. If you're using a pressure cooker, lock on the lid and bring it up to full pressure. Cook for 10 minutes, then let the pressure come down on its own. Tilt the cooker away from yourself when you unlock the lid.

Season with salt and pepper and serve over rice or couscous.

Make up to 3 days ahead.
* *Seal in a tightly covered container and refrigerate.*

- To reheat, transfer to a heavy saucepan and stir over medium heat until warmed through. Or transfer to a microwavable bowl and microwave at full power, turning the bowl at 2-minute intervals, until heated through.

Freeze up to 6 months, well wrapped in a glass or firm plastic container.

- To defrost, see reheating instructions above.

LOVE THOSE LEFTOVERS!

Make a wrap! Mix the leftovers with brown rice and wrap in Lavash (page 228) for a substantial sandwich.

Two Omelet Roulades

SERVES 4 TO 6

They say you can't make a silk purse out of a sow's ear, but that's hardly going to cramp your party style. What really matters is that you can make an elegant main course out of half a dozen eggs: a light, puffy omelet rolled around a cheese and vegetable spread, sliced to show off colorful swirls of filling.

TIME TO PREPARE (HANDS ON): *About 20 minutes*

TIME TO COOK: *About 15 minutes*

TOTAL TIME: *About 1 hour, including time to cool*

1 cup soft fresh breadcrumbs
⅓ cup half-and-half
½ cup shredded cheese, such as sharp
　　cheddar, Gruyère, or Parmesan
6 large eggs, separated
Coarse salt and freshly ground black pepper
¼ cup grated Parmesan cheese

Filling of your choice (recipes follow)
Béchamel sauce to serve (if using Spinach
　　Filling; optional)

Heat the oven to 400° F.

Line a jelly roll pan with parchment paper.

In a mixing bowl, combine the breadcrumbs, half-and-half, shredded cheese, and egg yolks. Season with salt and pepper and beat well to blend.

In a separate bowl, whip the egg whites until stiff with an electric mixer or a whisk. Fold them into the yolk mixture until evenly incorporated. Gently spread it over the parchment paper in an even layer. Bake until set, 10 to 15 minutes.

Wet a clean, lightweight dish towel and wring it out. (Sniff the towel first to make sure it doesn't have residue from fabric softener or laundry detergent.) Lay the towel over the omelet while it cools. Leave the oven on.

Meanwhile, make a filling.

Sprinkle another clean kitchen towel with the grated Parmesan cheese. Take the damp cloth off the omelet, and turn it out onto the prepared towel. Spread the filling on the center of the omelet, leaving a ½-inch margin all around. Carefully roll up the omelet, using the towel as a guide (but being sure not to roll the end of the towel into the omelet!)

For the spinach filling, turn the oven down to 350° F. Once you've rolled the omelet, return it to the baking sheet and wrap a sheet of parchment paper around it. Bake until heated through, about 10 minutes. Take it out of the oven and let it rest 10 minutes before slicing and serving, with Béchamel Sauce if you'd like.

For the crabmeat filling, after you've rolled the filling into the omelet, put it on a cutting board, seam side down. Trim the edges and cut into slices 2 inches thick. Lay on serving plates to display the swirls, and garnish with the additional chives.

Spinach Filling

10 ounces chopped fresh spinach or one 10-ounce package frozen chopped spinach, thawed and squeezed dry

1 1/2 cups part-skim ricotta cheese

1/3 cup shredded cheese, such as sharp cheddar, Gruyère, or Parmesan

1/2 cup dry breadcrumbs

Pinch ground nutmeg

Coarse salt and freshly ground black pepper

Steam the fresh spinach, if using, in a steamer basket placed over a pot of simmering water until bright green and wilted, about 2 minutes. In a large mixing bowl, combine the spinach, ricotta, shredded cheese, breadcrumbs, and nutmeg. Season with salt and pepper.

Crab and Avocado Filling

2 tablespoons mayonnaise

1/4 cup nonfat plain yogurt

3 tablespoons fresh lemon juice

3 tablespoons minced fresh chives, plus additional whole chives for garnish

1/2 pound crabmeat, picked over for shells

1 ripe avocado, peeled, pitted, and chopped

Coarse salt and freshly ground black pepper

In a large mixing bowl, combine the mayonnaise, yogurt, lemon juice, chives, and crabmeat. Mash

the avocado and stir it into the crab mixture, blending well. Season with salt and pepper.

- *Make the spinach filling up to 2 days ahead. Seal in a tightly covered container and refrigerate.*

▶

Stuffed Baked Potatoes
(A TV or Video Dinner)

SERVES 2 (MAY BE MULTIPLIED)

Here it is . . . a couch potato! Something simple to eat during the play-offs or your customized Fred-and-Ginger retrospective.

TIME TO PREPARE (HANDS ON): *About 10 minutes*	
TIME TO COOK: *About 45 minutes*	
TOTAL TIME: *About 1 hour, including time to cool*	

2 very large russet potatoes, scrubbed

1 cup chopped fresh vegetable of your choice (such as spinach or broccoli)

1/2 cup low-fat cottage cheese

4 tablespoons buttermilk or milk

1/2 cup shredded cheddar cheese

Coarse salt and freshly ground black pepper

2 large eggs

Heat the oven to 450°F. Carve an X at each end of each potato, place on a baking sheet, and bake until tender, about 40 minutes.

Meanwhile, fit a saucepan with a steamer basket. Add water up to the base of the steamer and bring to a boil. Place the vegetables in the steamer, cover the saucepan, and steam until just cooked through, about 1 1/2 minutes for spinach, 3 minutes for broccoli. In a mixing bowl, combine the cottage cheese, buttermilk, cheddar cheese, and vegetable. Season with salt and pepper and stir well to blend.

When the potatoes have cooked and cooled slightly, split them open. Scoop out the insides and mash with the cheese mixture. Place the potato shells on a foil-lined baking sheet and fill them with the mixture, patting it down, then making a well at the top with the back of a spoon. Crack the eggs into the well. Bake until set, about 7 minutes.

• *You can't make this ahead. Prepare it just before serving.*

Cheese Fondue

SERVES 4

One of the great things about fondue is that once you've bought the pot, forks, and bottle of kirsch, you're committed to making it more than once. And you will make it again and again, because it's implausibly easy. Have all the ingredients assembled ahead of time, but wait until your guests have arrived before you start to make it.

TIME TO PREPARE (HANDS ON): *About 15 minutes*

TIME TO COOK: *About 5 minutes*

TOTAL TIME: *About 20 minutes*

6 ounces Gruyère cheese, shredded (about 1 $\frac{1}{2}$ cups)

6 ounces Emmentaler cheese, shredded (about 1 $\frac{1}{2}$ cups)

2 ounces appenzeller cheese, shredded (about $\frac{1}{2}$ cup)

3 tablespoons all-purpose flour

1 garlic clove, sliced in half lengthwise

1 cup very dry white wine, such as Swiss Fendant, Dezaley, or a Riesling

2 teaspoons fresh lemon juice

2 tablespoons kirsch (cherry liqueur)

Coarse salt and freshly ground black pepper

Pinch ground nutmeg

FOR SERVING

1 large basket substantial white bread (store-bought or homemade, page 212) crusts removed, cut into bite-sized chunks

Steamed vegetables (steamed until tender-crisp, so you can spear them with a fork without having them fall apart), such as broccoli, cauliflower, and new potatoes

Boiled Shrimp, shells removed (see page 127, optional)

In a large mixing bowl, combine the Gruyère, Emmentaler, and appenzeller cheeses. Add the flour and mix well with your fingers until the flour is well distributed.

Rub the inside of the fondue pot with the cut sides of the garlic clove, then discard the garlic. Pour in the wine and heat on the stove over medium heat. When hot but not boiling, add the lemon juice and kirsch.

Stir in the cheese a handful at a time. Stir well after each addition, waiting until it has melted to add the next batch.

Light the fondue pot burner and place the pot over it. Season with salt and pepper, and sprinkle with nutmeg. Serve at once.

• *You can't make this ahead. Prepare it just before serving.*

FISH AND SEAFOOD

Fish is easy.

Porous, with faint flavor of its own, most fish take to simple seasoning, requiring little from you but a sharp eye on the clock.

There can be complications, of course, such as when you have your heart set on swordfish and the only piece left at the market looks as if it's been there all year. Or you see that salmon's on special this week, but get to the store to find the truck's been delayed and there is none in stock.

CONTENTED COOKS WANT YOU TO KNOW

- Never set your heart on something without a backup that will do as well. Since many fish have similar flavors and textures, this is often easy.
- Know several seasoning combinations that work with a variety of fish (see below).
- Be *extra super nice* to the folks where you buy seafood, and let them know you appreciate candid guidance and advice so they will tell you what came in today, and when it's worth waiting for the next catch.

Checking Out the Fish Counter

Do you want to buy fish from this place? You're looking for:

Ice: clean and packed solid, not seeping.

Trimmings (such as parsley, cut lemons—anything used to decorate the case): sprightly, not drooping, artfully and deliberately arranged. If the person managing the fish counter cares about how it looks, chances are that person cares about what it carries.

Fish: Whole fish should have sparkling skin and clear eyes. Steaks and fillets should have a bright luster and clear color. Ask the clerk to poke one for you—(and check whether that clerk puts on gloves first). It should spring right back.

Attitude: Look for enthusiastic and knowledgeable clerks. They should know the origin of everything they carry, and whether it arrived fresh or frozen. If they don't have the fish you want, they should ask what you'd planned to do with it, then recommend a good substitute. If they have fish you're not familiar with, they should be able to suggest ways to prepare it.

Can't Find That Fish?

Frustrated fish shoppers need to know . . .

Fish with similar fat content and density are often interchangeable.

In other words, fish fillets and steaks that look and feel like the one you have in mind can take its place. Any recipe that calls for swordfish, for example, can also be made with halibut or tuna. Salmon can be switched with snapper and haddock, for another example; roughy or bass for monkfish and scrod.

And there are many seasonings that complement nearly all kinds of fish (see below), so you can choose your seasoning before you go shopping, fairly certain it will go well with whatever you find when you get to the store.

Basic Preparation for Fish

Baking Fillets, Steaks, and Whole Fish

Heat the oven to 400°F. Lightly grease a baking dish with olive oil or unsalted butter.

Season the fish according to a recipe or your own bright idea, and wrap it in parchment paper or place it directly in the dish.

Bake for 10 minutes per inch of thickness. (Check a few minutes before the estimated cooking time is up.)

Broiling Fillets and Steaks

Heat the broiler. Lightly grease the broiler tray with olive oil or unsalted butter.

Season the fish and place it on the broiler tray, then into the broiler. Place fish less than 1 inch thick roughly 2 inches from the heat. Place fish 1 inch thick—more or less—4 inches from the heat.

Broil thin fish (under 1 inch) 2 minutes on each side. Broil thicker fish 4 minutes on each side.

Grilling Fish

Heat the grill. Lightly grease a grilling grate or special fish basket (available at hardware or home stores) that will hold your fish.

When the fire is hot, place the fish 4 to 6 inches from the coals.

Grill 10 minutes for each inch of thickness, turning after 4 minutes and checking after 7.

Multipurpose Seasonings for Fish

Gremolata (Lemon and Garlic) for Baking, Broiling, or Grilling

FOR EACH POUND OF FISH

    1 teaspoon sea salt
    2 garlic cloves, crushed and minced
    1 tablespoon lemon zest
    ¼ cup plus 2 tablespoons minced fresh
      parsley

Rub the salt evenly over the fish.

Combine the garlic, lemon zest, and parsley in a small mixing bowl and mash with the back of a spoon to make a paste. Or use a mortar and pestle if you have one.

Rub into the fish. Bake, broil, or grill according to the directions above.

Olive and Caper for Baking

FOR EACH POUND OF FISH

    2 teaspoons extra virgin olive oil
    4 oil-cured back olives, pitted and minced
    1 teaspoon capers, rinsed and minced
    1½ tablespoons minced fresh basil or
      oregano or 2 teaspoons crumbled dried
    1 garlic clove, crushed and minced
    ¼ teaspoon sea salt
    1 large ripe tomato, peeled and chopped

In a mixing bowl, combine the olive oil, olives, capers, basil or oregano, garlic, and salt. Rub it into the fish. Put the fish in a single layer in the center of a large piece of parchment paper. Put the tomato on top of the fish. Wrap the parchment securely around the fish. Bake according to the directions on page 123.

Ginger and Soy for Baking, Broiling, or Grilling

FOR EACH POUND OF FISH

1 tablespoon grated peeled fresh ginger
2 teaspoons honey
2 garlic cloves, crushed and minced
3 tablespoons minced scallion, white and green parts
¼ cup soy sauce

In a mixing bowl, combine the ginger, honey, garlic, scallion, and soy sauce. Place the fish in a shallow dish and pour the mixture over it. Turn the fish over to coat with the mixture. Cover and let rest for 30 minutes. Wrap in parchment paper and bake as directed on page 123. Or broil or grill according to the directions on page 123.

Poached Salmon
(*Boneless Fillets or Whole Fish*)

The price of fresh salmon has plummeted, thanks to prolific fish farms in our hemisphere. But although salmon farmers strive for uniformity among their stock, all cultivated salmon are not equal. Depending on what they're fed, they may be fatty or lean, oily or not. Although fish oil is reported to be good for your health, when it's concentrated on your plate, those benefits may not seem all that significant to you. You may have to taste salmon from several different

sources to find one with a clean taste that matches the pricier wild salmon.

2 to 4 cups Vegetable Broth (page 286), Shrimp Broth (page 286), Lobster Broth (page 287), or water
1 onion, peeled and chopped
2 carrots, peeled and chopped
1 celery stalk, with leaves, chopped
1 whole salmon, or 6 salmon steaks or fillets of similar size (so they'll cook at the same rate)

Fill a deep skillet or fish poacher with broth or water (the amount of liquid you need will depend on the size and depth of your skillet or poacher). Add the onion, carrots, and celery. Bring to a simmer over medium-high heat, cover, and let simmer for 30 minutes.

Add the salmon either directly or on the poacher rack, and simmer until just cooked through, about 7 minutes for fillets, 15 to 20 minutes for whole fish. Turn the whole fish over halfway through cooking.

Variation

For an Asian flavor, instead of the onion, carrots, and celery, add to the broth or water:

3 scallions, chopped
3 tablespoons minced fresh cilantro
4 thin slices fresh ginger
1 garlic clove, crushed

Follow the directions above, simmering the broth for 30 minutes before poaching the salmon.

Mussels . . . in Minutes!

Thanks to a surge in shellfish farming, good, meaty mussels are abundant and affordable. You might not find mussels all that tempting in their bruise-colored shells, but once you discover how quickly and easily they become delicious, you'll be glad they're so plentiful and cheap.

Cultivated mussels aren't only inexpensive, they're safe; aquatic farms protect them from a pernicious bacteria prevalent among mussels in the wild. Plus—BIG plus— cultivated mussels are easier to clean than those hauled up offshore.

Basic Preparation

Rinse the mussels thoroughly, and pull out the "beard," a black fuzzy string that had bound the bivalve to its former home. Cultivated mussels shouldn't be gritty, but if they are, fill a large bowl with cold water and add about 2 tablespoons of cornmeal. Add the mussels and leave them for an hour. The mussels will eat the cornmeal, expelling dirt and grit as they open their shells to ingest. Do not clean mussels more than an hour before you prepare them, or they may start to spoil. Before cooking, discard any mussels that don't close when you tap them, and after cooking discard any mussels that haven't opened.

Three Never-Fail Mussel Steaming Sauces

EACH SAUCE STEAMS 4 POUNDS MUSSELS (SERVES 4 AS A FIRST COURSE, 2 AS AN ENTRÉE)

Wine and Herbs

These are the mussels to use in Corona di Riso with Minced Ratatouille or Mussels (page 114). Or serve them as a starter or an entrée over pasta.

TIME TO PREPARE (HANDS ON): *About 10 minutes*

TIME TO COOK: *About 10 minutes*

TOTAL TIME: *About 20 minutes*

1 tablespoon extra virgin olive oil
2 garlic cloves, crushed and minced
2 cups fresh or canned peeled and chopped
  tomatoes
½ cup dry white wine
¼ cup minced fresh parsley
2 tablespoons minced fresh basil or
  1 tablespoon crumbled dried
Coarse salt and freshly ground black pepper

Heat the oil in a heavy pot over medium-high heat. When hot, add the garlic, reduce the heat to medium-low, and sauté, stirring often, until the garlic colors, about 1 minute. Remove from the heat. Lift out the garlic and discard, leaving the oil in the pot. Return to medium-high heat and add the tomatoes, turn the heat down to medium-low, and stir until the tomatoes start to break down into a sauce. Add the wine, parsley, and basil, and stir until bubbling. Add the mussels, cover, and steam until they open, about 10 minutes. Discard any mussels that haven't opened. Season with salt and pepper.

- *You can't make this ahead. Prepare it just before serving.*

Curry Spices and Tomato
Serve over rice (page 181).

TIME TO PREPARE (HANDS ON): *About 20 minutes*

TIME TO COOK: *About 10 minutes*

TOTAL TIME: *About 30 minutes*

    1 tablespoon vegetable oil
    1 onion, chopped
    2 garlic cloves, crushed and minced
    1 tablespoon grated peeled fresh ginger
    $1/4$ cup minced fresh cilantro
    1 teaspoon ground cumin
    $1/2$ teaspoon ground coriander
    $1/2$ teaspoon turmeric
    $1/4$ cup light coconut milk or coconut milk
    1 large tomato, peeled, seeded, and chopped
    Juice of 1 lemon
    Coarse salt

Heat the oil in a deep heavy pot over medium-high heat. When hot, add the onion, garlic, ginger, cilantro, cumin, coriander, and turmeric. Reduce the heat to medium-low and sauté, stirring often, until the onion is soft, about 7 minutes. Add the coconut milk and tomato, and stir until the tomato breaks down into a sauce, about 3 minutes.

Add the mussels, cover, and steam until they open, about 10 minutes. Discard any mussels that haven't opened. Drizzle lemon juice over them and season with salt.

- *You can't make this ahead. Prepare it just before serving.*

Ginger and Garlic
Serve as a first course with Steamed Vegetable Dumplings (page 40).

TIME TO PREPARE (HANDS ON): *About 10 minutes*

TIME TO COOK: *About 25 minutes*

TOTAL TIME: *About 35 minutes*

    2 cups Vegetable Broth (page 286), Chicken Broth (page 285), or Shrimp Broth (page 286)
    3 tablespoons rice wine (mirin) or dry sherry
    3 thin slices fresh ginger
    2 scallions, thinly sliced
    2 garlic cloves, crushed and minced
    $1/4$ cup minced fresh cilantro

Place the broth, rice wine, ginger, scallions, garlic, and cilantro in a large heavy pot. Bring to a boil over medium-high heat. Reduce the heat to medium and simmer for 15 minutes to steep.

Add the mussels, cover the pot, and steam until they open, about 10 minutes. Discard any mussels that haven't opened.

- *You can't make this ahead. Prepare it just before serving.*

Serving Shrimp

Shrimp come in many sizes, and which you want depends on what you want them for: small for salads; medium for pasta sauces, curries, and stews; large for cocktail; and jumbo for grilling.

Most shrimp is flash frozen at the moment it's caught, then sold still frozen or defrosted. If you're buying frozen shrimp, make sure it hasn't been defrosted, then refrozen. Twice-frozen shrimp tend to be tough, and not have much flavor. Like all fish and seafood, shrimp should smell fresh and clean, not fishy. Buy shrimp the day you're going to cook them, or the day before at most, and store in the coolest part of the refrigerator, well wrapped.

Basic Preparation

Peel the shrimp just before you're going to cook them. If the veins (long black line that follows the curve of the back from the head to the tail) are prominent, use a paring knife to make a slit along the back. Pull out the vein like a thread. Save the shells for broth (page 286.)

If the shrimp you've got are still frozen, you may be able to cook them without defrosting. Just peel off the shell and proceed with the recipe, increasing the cooking time to allow the shrimp to defrost.

BUT if the shrimp is caked with ice, it will dilute your dish. In this case, peel the shrimp, cover with paper towels, and put it in the refrigerator to defrost. Drain away the liquid and pat them dry before proceeding with the recipe.

If you're using frozen cooked shrimp (only as a last resort, please), put it only in highly seasoned dishes, and cook it just to warm through.

Those "ever-helpful" Food Authorities tell us that shrimp taste best when cooked in the shell. That is true. But it's also impractical in most cases. Just try to figure out who's going to remove the shell and at what point. Is it fair to ask your guests to strip them and deal with the empty shells? Or do you really want to make the last moment before serving that hectic as you rush to make every shrimp shell free before the sauce (and the shrimp) get cold?

Cook shrimp swiftly, just until they turn pink. They should "crunch" when you bite into them, feel tender in the center, and taste sweet. This will take anywhere from 2 minutes for small to 7 or 8 minutes for jumbo, depending on the cooking method.

From Not-so-great-moments in Party Giving: What if the shrimp are no good? If they're tough, with a "fishy" flavor, don't serve them. Remove them from the sauce at once. Now taste the sauce. If it hasn't picked up the flavor of the shrimp, put a can of rinsed chickpeas in it, cover, and simmer for 10 to 15 minutes. Stir in some cheese (mild, creamy mozzarella or Monterey Jack for the curry, Parmesan for the tomato and fennel, cheddar for the corn and bell pepper) and serve over rice.

If the sauce *has* taken on the flavor, grab your coat and implement one of the strategies proposed on page 8.

Three Fast Never-Fail Sauces for Shrimp

EACH SAUCE COVERS 2 POUNDS OF SHRIMP, 4 MAIN-COURSE SERVINGS

Curry and Cream

Serve over rice (page 181) or linguine.

TIME TO PREPARE (HANDS ON): *About 30 minutes*

TIME TO COOK: *Included in preparation time*

TOTAL TIME: *About 30 minutes*

1 tablespoon unsalted butter or vegetable oil

1 large onion, chopped

2 leeks, white part plus 1 inch of green, cleaned and thinly sliced

1 tablespoon curry powder

1 cup fresh or canned chopped peeled tomatoes

2 pounds shrimp (medium to extra large), peeled

$\frac{1}{4}$ cup half-and-half or reduced-fat sour cream

Coarse salt and freshly ground black pepper

3 tablespoons unsweetened coconut flakes

Melt the butter or heat the oil in a nonstick skillet over medium-high heat. When hot, add the onion, leeks, and curry powder. Reduce the heat to medium-low and sauté, stirring often, until the onion is soft and limp, about 7 minutes.

Add the tomatoes and stir until they start to break down into a sauce, about 2 minutes. Continue simmering over medium heat until thickened, about 3 minutes more. Add the shrimp and cook until they turn pink, about 5 to 7 minutes, depending on size. Remove from the heat. Stir in the half-and-half or sour cream, and stir to blend. Season with salt and pepper.

Meanwhile, put the coconut into a dry skillet and place over medium-high heat. Stir until evenly browned. Stir into the shrimp before serving or sprinkle some over each serving.

● *Refrigerate leftovers, tightly wrapped. Reheat gently over low heat, stirring often until warmed through.*

Tomato and Fennel

Serve with Lemon Risotto (page 74) or rice (page 181).

TIME TO PREPARE (HANDS ON): *About 30 minutes*

TIME TO COOK: *Included in preparation time*

TOTAL TIME: *About 30 minutes*

1 tablespoon extra virgin olive oil

1 large onion, chopped

1 leek, white part plus 1 inch of green, cleaned and thinly sliced

1 small fennel bulb, trimmed and thinly sliced

1 bay leaf

$\frac{1}{4}$ cup dry white wine

2 cups fresh or canned peeled, seeded, and chopped tomatoes

2 pounds shrimp (medium to large), peeled

$\frac{1}{4}$ cup reduced-fat sour cream

Coarse salt and freshly ground black pepper

Heat the oil in a nonstick skillet over medium-high heat. When hot, add the onion, leek, fennel, and bay leaf. Reduce the heat to medium-low and sauté, stirring often, until the vegetables are soft and limp, about 10 minutes.

Add the wine, turn up the heat to medium-high, and stir until most of it evaporates, about 2 minutes. Add the tomatoes and continue cooking until the sauce thickens, about 4 minutes. Stir in the shrimp. Cook over medium heat until the shrimp turn bright pink, about 5 to 7 minutes, depending on size.

Remove from the heat. Stir in the sour cream, and season with salt and pepper. Remove the bay leaf before serving.

- *Refrigerate leftovers, tightly wrapped. Reheat gently over low heat, stirring often until warmed through. Or serve leftovers at room temperature.*

Corn and Bell Pepper

Serve with rice (page 181) and/or tortillas.

If you have time, make the broth base, which adds another dimension of flavor. If you're short on time, however, just use water and the sauce will be a bit more delicate, but still delicious.

TIME TO PREPARE (HANDS ON): *About 30 minutes (including broth)*

TIME TO COOK: *Included in preparation time*

TOTAL TIME: *About 30 minutes*

BROTH (OPTIONAL; 1 CUP WATER MAY BE USED)

Shrimp shells reserved from 1 pound shrimp
1 onion, peeled and quartered
1 celery stalk
1 bay leaf
1 cup water

1 tablespoon vegetable oil, such as corn or canola
1 large onion, thinly sliced

1 red bell pepper, cored, seeded, and thinly sliced
1 green bell pepper, cored, seeded, and thinly sliced
2 tablespoons minced fresh oregano or 2 teaspoons crumbled dried
1 tablespoon ground cumin
1 teaspoon ground coriander
2 cups fresh or frozen corn kernels
2 pounds shrimp, peeled (shells reserved for broth, above)
Broth (below) or 1 cup water
Coarse salt and freshly ground black pepper

If you're making the broth, put the shrimp shells, onion, celery, bay leaf, and water in a large saucepan. Bring to a boil over medium-high heat. Cover, reduce the heat to medium-low, and simmer for 15 to 20 minutes to steep.

To make the shrimp, heat the oil in a large nonstick skillet over medium-high heat. When hot, add the onion, red and green bell peppers, oregano, cumin, and coriander. Lower the heat to medium-low and sauté, stirring often, until the onion and peppers are soft and limp, about 10 minutes.

Strain the broth, if you're making it.

Add the corn and shrimp, and enough broth or water to keep from sticking, about 3 tablespoons. Stir over medium heat until the corn is cooked through and the shrimp is bright pink, about 7 minutes. Season with salt and pepper.

- *You can make this dish up to 1 day ahead. Cover and refrigerate. Serve cold or at room temperature.*

Shrimp Tabbouleh

SERVES 4

Strictly speaking, tabbouleh is a simple, refreshing salad involving bulgur wheat, olive oil, lemon, and parsley. For the less literal-minded, it can be any cold dish based on bulgur, such as this one with shrimp. It makes a great picnic meal because, unlike most salads, tabbouleh benefits from sitting around soaking in dressing.

TIME TO PREPARE (HANDS ON): *About 15 minutes*

TIME TO COOK: *About 30 minutes*

TOTAL TIME: *About 3 hours, 40 minutes, including time to chill*

---

1 cup bulgur wheat

1 leek, white part plus 1 inch of green, cleaned and thinly sliced

One 2-inch strip lemon zest

1 tablespoon dry white wine or 1 1/2 teaspoons balsamic vinegar

1 pound medium shrimp, peeled

2 limes

1 1/2 tablespoons extra virgin olive oil

1 teaspoon Dijon mustard

2 teaspoons balsamic vinegar

1 cucumber, peeled, seeded, and chopped

2 scallions, white part only, minced

3 tablespoons minced fresh chives

Coarse salt and freshly ground black pepper

Put 1 1/4 cups water in a saucepan. Bring to a boil over high heat and stir in the bulgur. Allow to return to a boil, cover, then remove from the heat. Let sit, covered, for 30 minutes, until the bulgur has absorbed all of the water.

Meanwhile, fill a medium saucepan 1/2 full with water and bring it to a boil. Add the leek, lemon zest, and wine or vinegar, and bring back to a boil. Turn the heat down to keep it at a gentle simmer. Simmer, covered, for 10 minutes to infuse with the flavor of the leek and lemon.

Have a bowl of ice water nearby. Add the shrimp to the simmering liquid, and continue to simmer until they turn bright pink, about 5 minutes. Remove the shrimp with a slotted spoon, and transfer them to the ice water to cool. Drain.

Grate the zest of 1 lime. In a separate bowl, combine the juice of both limes, the olive oil, mustard, and balsamic vinegar. Whisk well. Stir in the bulgur, stirring thoroughly to coat with the dressing. Stir in the shrimp, cucumber, scallions, chives, and lime zest. Season with salt and pepper.

Chill for at least 3 hours.

Make up to 3 days ahead.
- *Seal in a tightly covered container and refrigerate.*

Calamari Filled with Fish

SERVES 4

If you're going to serve squid, it's best to call it "calamari" and put off answering any questions until your guests have had a bite. Chances are the nature of their inquiries will change from "Squid, huh?" as in, "You have got to be kidding," to "Squid, huh?" as in, "This is good."

TIME TO PREPARE (HANDS ON): *About 20 minutes*

TIME TO COOK: *Under 30 minutes*

TOTAL TIME: *Just under 1 hour*

12 large calamari sacks, cleaned
1 tablespoon extra virgin olive oil
1 onion, chopped
2 garlic cloves, crushed and minced
2 teaspoons crumbled dried thyme
¼ cup dry white wine
½ pound shucked baby clams in their juice
2 cups fresh or canned peeled, seeded, and
    chopped tomatoes
1 bay leaf
1 pound swordfish
2 teaspoons grated lemon zest
¼ cup minced fresh chives
Pinch salt

To prepare the calamari, you may be able to buy calamari sacks already cleaned and ready for stuffing. If your only option is whole squid, choose 12 that are uniform in size. Pull off the tentacle portion, which should separate easily from the body. Peel off the skin and place under running water. Stick your finger inside the sack and pull out the stiff quill, which feels like a piece of plastic. Also scoop out any goop that's in there. Rinse well and pat dry.

Frozen calamari is often very good. Defrost in the refrigerator overnight before cleaning and/or stuffing, and smell it to determine whether it's good. As with fish and shellfish of any kind, if it has an odor, it has to go.

Heat the oil in a nonstick skillet over medium-high heat. When hot, add the onion, garlic, and thyme, lower the heat to medium-low, and sauté until the onion is soft, about 7 minutes. Add the wine, raise the heat to medium-high, and continue to cook, stirring constantly, until much of the wine has evaporated, about 2 minutes. Drain the clams, reserving the juice. Add the tomatoes, bay leaf, and clam juice, turn the heat down to medium-low, and continue to sauté, stirring occasionally, until the tomatoes break down into a lumpy sauce, about 15 minutes. Stir in the clams.

Meanwhile, mince the swordfish by hand. Don't use a food processor or the fish will be mushy. Place it in a mixing bowl along with the lemon zest and chives. Salt lightly and mix well with your hands.

Using a small spoon, scoop the fish mixture and place inside the calamari sacks, filling each about halfway, without packing the mixture tightly. If you fill them more than that, the sacks will burst during cooking when the fish expands. Use a toothpick to thread the ends closed.

Place the filled calamari in the skillet with the tomato sauce, cover, and simmer until the underside is white, about 7 minutes. Turn each over and cook for 7 minutes more.

Remove the toothpicks before serving.

Make the sauce up to 3 days ahead.

- Seal in a tightly covered container and refrigerate. After you've filled the calamari, pour the sauce back into the skillet, heat until warmed through, and proceed with the recipe.

Wrap the leftovers in plastic or store in zip-lock bags, pressing out the air before you seal. Refrigerate up to 2 days. Do not reheat; serve cold or at room temperature.

Calamari with Polenta

SERVES 4

Italian may be the most euphonic language, at least regarding food. What we would call "Squid with Cornmeal Mush" and what would go by the relatively discordant "Calmar avec polenta" in France is the sonorous, aptly inviting "Calamari con Polenta" in Italy.

TIME TO PREPARE (HANDS ON):	*About 35 minutes*
TIME TO COOK:	*About 20 minutes*
TOTAL TIME:	*Under 1 hour*

1 tablespoon extra virgin olive oil
1 onion, chopped
1 garlic clove, crushed and minced
1 celery stalk, chopped
1 carrot, peeled and chopped
2 teaspoons ground cumin
1 tablespoon chili powder
1 red bell pepper, cored, seeded, and sliced
1 green bell pepper, cored, seeded, and sliced
1/4 cup dry white wine
1 cup tomato puree

1 bay leaf
2 pounds calamari, cleaned (see page 131) and cut into rings
1 cup Vegetable Broth (page 286)
1/2 cup yellow cornmeal, preferably stone-ground
1/4 cup grated Parmesan cheese

Heat the oil in a large, deep heavy skillet over medium-high heat. When hot, add the onion, garlic, celery, carrot, cumin, and chili powder. Lower the heat to medium-low, and sauté until the vegetables are soft, about 10 minutes. Add the peppers and continue sautéing until they're soft and limp, about 7 minutes more. Add the wine and stir until most of the liquid has evaporated, about 2 minutes. Add the tomato puree, bay leaf, and the squid. Stir well to blend, and simmer until the sauce is very thick and the squid is tender, about 20 minutes.

Meanwhile, bring the vegetable broth to a boil in a medium saucepan. Sprinkle in the cornmeal slowly, whisking constantly to avoid lumps. Once you've added all of the cornmeal, continue stirring until the mixture is very thick, about 15 minutes. Sprinkle in the cheese and stir to blend. Remove from the heat.

To serve, place a portion of the polenta in the center of the plate. Or lightly grease 4 custard cups or ramekins with unsalted butter. Pat an equal portion of polenta into each and smooth the tops. Turn each out onto individual serving plates. Spoon the calamari sauce evenly around it.

Seal the leftovers in a tightly covered container and refrigerate up to 2 days.

- Serve any leftovers at room temperature. Reheating will make the calamari tough.

Simple Baked Fish in Foil

SERVES 6

You meant to make the sauce last Friday and freeze it for tonight, then prepare the rest of your lavish meal bit by bit as the week progressed. But you didn't! And everyone's on their way over.

Use any firm white fish steak or fillet, such as swordfish (see Note), halibut, monkfish, bass, haddock, scrod, or roughy.

TIME TO PREPARE (HANDS ON): *About 5 minutes*

TIME TO COOK: *About 15 minutes*

TOTAL TIME: *About 20 minutes*

> **3 pounds firm fish fillets (see suggestions above)**
> **1 tablespoon extra virgin olive oil**
> **2 tablespoons coarse sea salt**
> **1 tablespoon dry white wine**
> **1 large Vidalia onion, chopped**
> **1 tablespoon grated lemon zest**
> **1 tablespoon minced fresh oregano**
> **1 tablespoon minced fresh basil**
> **1 tablespoon minced fresh thyme**
> **1 tablespoon minced fresh parsley**
> **4 large ripe tomatoes, peeled and chopped**

Heat the oven to 450° F.

Divide the fish inside 2 or 3 large pieces of foil, keeping the fish in a single layer. Drizzle the olive oil evenly over the fish and rub it into it. Sprinkle the salt over the fish and rub it in, too. In a mixing bowl, stir the wine, onion, lemon zest, oregano, basil, thyme, and parsley into the tomatoes, and distribute evenly on top of the fish.

Fold the foil over the fish to seal it inside like a packet. Place the packets in a single layer inside a shallow baking dish, and bake until cooked through, about 8 to 10 minutes. Unwrap, transfer neatly to serving plates or a big serving platter, and serve with the cooking juices.

NOTE: Swordfish is not for the fainthearted. Cook it just right, and you have something special. Keep it in a second too long, and it's so tough and tasteless, you might as well serve canned tuna. Stick strictly to the 10-minute rule, checking 2 minutes before the estimated time.

- *Wrap leftovers in plastic or store individual portions in zip-lock bags, pressing out the air before you seal. Refrigerate. Serve cold or at room temperature. Reheat with caution, wrapped in foil in a 350° F. oven, until warmed through, or microwave in short spurts at medium strength.*

Sea Bass with Clams

SERVES 4

If you get nervous around recipes that warn "avoid over-cooking," here is a fish for you: Chilean sea bass. Even if you bake the fat, buttery fillets somewhat past doneness you will have a moist, delicious dish. Whether you've never cooked with bass or you're already familiar with this mercifully forgiving fish, this dish is a treat.

TIME TO PREPARE (HANDS ON): *About 20 minutes*

TIME TO COOK: *About 30 minutes*

TOTAL TIME: *About 50 minutes*

4 sea bass fillets, about $1/2$ pound each
   (2 pounds of fish total)
3 garlic cloves
$1/2$ cup fresh lemon juice
$1/2$ cup minced fresh parsley, divided, plus
   additional minced parsley for serving
12 clams in their shells, scrubbed
$1/4$ cup dry white wine
1 tablespoon extra virgin olive oil
1 medium onion, chopped
2 leeks, white part plus 1 inch of green,
   cleaned and thinly sliced
$1/4$ teaspoon powdered saffron
1 teaspoon red pepper flakes (optional)
Coarse salt

Place the bass fillets in a single layer in a deep porcelain or Pyrex baking dish. Crush and mince 2 garlic cloves and sprinkle over the fillets. Drizzle the lemon juice on top and scatter half of the parsley over it. Turn the fillets over, cover with plastic wrap, and set aside while you proceed with the recipe.

Place the clams in a heavy saucepan. Mince the remaining garlic clove and add to the saucepan along with the wine and the remaining parsley. Cover and bring to a simmer. When the clams have opened, remove them from the heat and discard any that haven't opened. Let the clams sit, uncovered, while you do the next step.

Heat the oil in a medium skillet over medium-high heat. When hot, add the onion and leeks, reduce the heat to medium-low, and sauté, stirring often, until soft, about 7 minutes. Turn off the heat.

Heat the oven to 350° F.

Strain the cooking liquid from the clams into a measuring cup. Add the saffron and stir well. Remove the clams from their shells and set aside, discarding the shells. Pour the clam juice into the skillet with the onions and leeks, turn up the heat to medium-high, and stir until some of the liquid has evaporated and the sauce reduces by about a quarter, about 4 minutes. Stir in the red pepper flakes, if desired, and season with salt.

Pour the contents of the skillet into the baking dish with the fish. Cover the baking dish with foil and bake until the fillets are flaky, about 20 minutes.

Place each fillet on a serving plate and top each with an equal portion of the clams. Spoon the pan juices over each. Sprinkle parsley over each serving.

• *Wrap the leftovers in a dish covered with plastic. Refrigerate. Take out of the refrigerator 1 hour ahead and serve at room temperature. Do not reheat.*

Stuffed Snapper with Spiced Sauce

SERVES 4

Seasonings have seasons, and nutmeg's is winter. If you tend to think of fish as summer fare, here's one to savor in the cold months.

TIME TO PREPARE (HANDS ON): *About 45 minutes*

TIME TO COOK: *Included in the preparation time, plus 15 minutes*

TOTAL TIME: *About 1 hour*

½ cup long-grain white or brown rice
2 tablespoons extra virgin olive oil, divided
1 onion, chopped
1 carrot, peeled and chopped
1 tablespoon fresh lemon juice
½ teaspoon ground nutmeg, or to taste, divided
4 snapper fillets (about 2 pounds), or other firm fish such as haddock, with no skin
2 tablespoons unbleached all-purpose flour
1½ cups Vegetable Broth (page 286) or Chicken Broth (page 285)
1 tablespoon grated lemon zest
¼ cup dry white wine
1 tablespoon minced fresh parsley
Coarse salt and freshly ground black pepper

To make the filling, cook the rice according to package directions or directions on page 181.

Meanwhile, heat 1 tablespoon oil in a nonstick skillet over medium-high heat. When hot, add the onion and carrot, reduce the heat to medium-low, and sauté, stirring often, until soft, about 10 minutes. Add the lemon juice and ¼ teaspoon nutmeg, and stir well to blend. Stir in the cooked rice and remove from the heat.

Heat the oven to 325°F.

Place the fish fillets on a flat surface. Place ¼ of the filling just below the center of each and pat down lightly. Fold the top over the filling to enclose it. Secure the packet at the bottom with a toothpick. Line a baking sheet with parchment paper and place the fillets on top. Cover loosely with foil and bake until cooked through, 15 to 20 minutes. Begin checking after 13 minutes.

Meanwhile, make the sauce. Heat the remaining 1 tablespoon olive oil in a nonstick skillet. Add the flour, stirring constantly to make a paste, about 3 minutes. Stir in the broth, lemon zest, and remaining ¼ teaspoon nutmeg. Continue stirring over medium heat until the sauce thickens, about 10 minutes. Add the wine and parsley, and stir for 5 minutes more. Season with salt and pepper.

Place each stuffed fish fillet on a serving plate and spoon the sauce over each.

Make the filling up to 3 days ahead.
• *Seal in a tightly covered container and refrigerate.*
Make the sauce up to 2 days ahead.
• *Seal in a tightly covered container and refrigerate. To reheat, transfer to a heavy saucepan, stir in 2 tablespoons dry white wine or broth, and stir over medium heat until warmed through.*

Monkfish in Coconut Milk

SERVES 4

Don't you love guests who, when asked the critical question, reply, "Oh, I eat anything!" This one's for them—highly seasoned fish dumplings in a coconut curry sauce. You'll enjoy making them, too; as it cooks, the sauce sends up an aroma as inviting as anything you will smell in this lifetime.

TIME TO PREPARE (HANDS ON): *About 40 minutes*

TIME TO COOK: *Included in the preparation time*

TOTAL TIME: *About 40 minutes*

1 tablespoon peanut oil

1 leek, white part plus 1 inch of green, cleaned and thinly sliced

2 garlic cloves, crushed and minced, divided

2 tablespoons grated peeled fresh ginger, divided

¼ cup minced fresh cilantro, divided, plus extra for serving

2 tablespoons dry white wine

1 tablespoon cornstarch

¼ cup coconut milk

1 cup nonfat plain yogurt

1 pound monkfish, snapper, or haddock fillet, coarsely chopped

1 tablespoon fresh lemon juice

1 large egg white

Coarse salt and freshly ground black pepper to taste

Heat the oil in a wide saucepan over medium-high heat. When hot, add the leek, half the garlic, half the ginger, and half the cilantro. Reduce the heat to medium-low and sauté, stirring often, until the leek softens, about 7 minutes. Add the wine and stir until it evaporates, about 2 minutes.

Stir the cornstarch into the coconut milk and pour into the saucepan, stirring constantly to make a thick sauce. Remove from the heat and let cool for 10 minutes.

Add the yogurt, a tablespoon at a time at first, stirring well to keep from overheating and curdling.

Place the monkfish in the work bowl of a food processor along with the remaining garlic, ginger, and cilantro, and the lemon juice, egg white, and salt and pepper. Process in short spurts to mince and combine. Shape into golf ball–sized dumplings.

Gently heat the sauce, taking care not to bring it to a boil. Add the fish balls and cook, turning often, until they're cooked through, about 5 minutes. (Check for doneness by sticking the point of a knife into a dumpling. If there's no sheen in there, they're ready.) Try not to overcook them, or they may be tough.

Using a ladle, spoon the monkfish balls and sauce into 4 warmed individual soup bowls. Sprinkle with cilantro and serve immediately.

Make the sauce up to 3 days ahead.
* *Seal in a tightly covered container and refrigerate. Make the monkfish dumplings, then reheat the sauce gently (do not boil) before adding the monkfish.*

Wrap the leftovers in a dish covered with plastic. Refrigerate. To reheat, transfer to a heavy saucepan and stir over medium heat until warmed through. Or transfer to a microwavable bowl and microwave at full power, turning the bowl at 2-minute intervals, until heated through.

Shellfish in Orange Bowls

SERVES 4

If it's your objective to serve a memorable meal, here's one they won't forget. If you can find large, firm navel oranges, you'll have novel bowls for this shellfish and barley dish. Even in ordinary bowls, it's extraordinary. And it's delicious cold, so you can make it ahead if you'd like to serve it that way.

TIME TO PREPARE (HANDS ON): *About 20 minutes*

TIME TO COOK: *About 1 hour*

TOTAL TIME: *About 1 hour 30 minutes*

½ cup barley
½ cup dry white wine
2 garlic cloves, crushed and minced
¼ cup minced fresh parsley
2 pounds mussels, scrubbed and debearded
1 pound medium shrimp, unshelled
1 pound bay scallops
5 jumbo navel oranges or ½ cup fresh
    orange juice
1 tablespoon extra virgin olive oil
1 onion, chopped
2 tablespoons minced fresh thyme or
    1 tablespoon dried
Coarse salt and freshly ground black pepper

Place the barley in a saucepan with 1 cup of water. Bring to a boil over medium-high heat. When it starts to simmer, turn the heat down to low, cover, and let cook until the water has been absorbed and the barley is chewy, about 50 minutes.

To make it in a pressure cooker, put the barley and ¾ cup water in the cooker. (If you're using an electric stove, turn on a separate burner at low.) Bring to a boil. Cover and bring to high pressure. Maintain the pressure for 10 minutes; if you're using a gas stove, you can do this by turning the heat down as far as it will go. If you're using an electric stove, transfer the cooker to the pre-heated burner. After 10 minutes, turn off the heat. If you're using an electric stove, take the cooker off the stove.

When the pressure comes all the way down, tilt the cooker away from yourself and remove the lid. (If there's any liquid left, return the cooker to the stove and turn the heat to low, stirring until it is absorbed.)

Put the wine, garlic, and parsley in a large stockpot. Bring to a boil and simmer, uncovered, for 5 minutes. Add the mussels, cover, and steam until the mussels open, about 10 minutes. Lift out the mussels, then strain the liquid and transfer to a medium saucepan. When cool enough to handle, take the mussels out of their shells and discard the shells.

Bring the strained mussel liquid to a simmer over medium-high heat. Add the shrimp, cover, turn down the heat to medium-low, and cook until they turn bright pink, about 5 minutes. Lift out the shrimp with a slotted spoon and set aside to cool. Add the scallops to the saucepan and simmer gently until cooked through, about 3 minutes. Lift out with a slotted spoon and set aside, reserving the cooking liquid.

If you're using fresh oranges, slice them in half horizontally. Squeeze the juice from 1 orange, or use fresh orange juice, and place in the saucepan

▶

with one half of the seafood cooking liquid and bring to a simmer. Scoop out the fruit from the other 4 oranges and reserve the fruit for salad. Without cutting through the shell, slice off the rounded bottoms of the orange halves so they will sit flat on serving plates.

When the barley is done, heat the oil in a non-stick skillet over medium-high heat. When hot, add the onion and thyme, reduce the heat to medium-low, and sauté, stirring often, until the onion is soft and limp, about 7 minutes. Add the barley and toss well to mix with the onion. Add the seafood cooking liquid and continue cooking, stirring constantly, until there is no more liquid in the pan. Season with salt and pepper.

Remove the shells from the shrimp and discard. Mix the mussels, shrimp and scallops with the barley, and fill the orange shells, using 1 or 2 per serving, or place in individual serving bowls.

Make up to 1 day ahead, if you want to serve it cold.
- *Seal in a tightly covered container and refrigerate. Do not reheat.*

Pasta Packets with Sea Bass

S E R V E S 4

Mention seafood with pasta to most people, and they'll think of linguine with clams, or one of those "Tutti frutti di mare" spaghetti sauces in which everything tastes the same. They will not be thinking of tender packets of pasta filled with subtly seasoned shrimp and sea bass . . . but they'll be glad you were.

TIME TO PREPARE (HANDS ON): *About 45 minutes, including time to make the pasta*

TIME TO COOK: *Included in the preparation time*

TOTAL TIME: *About 1 hour, including time to chill the pasta dough*

FOR THE PASTA
1 $\frac{1}{4}$ cups unbleached all-purpose flour
$\frac{2}{3}$ cup semolina flour
$\frac{1}{4}$ cup minced fresh oregano
$\frac{1}{4}$ cup dry white wine
1 large egg

FOR THE FILLING
1 pound sea bass fillet
6 large shrimp, shelled
1 cup soft breadcrumbs
$\frac{1}{4}$ cup nonfat milk
1 garlic clove, crushed and minced
$\frac{1}{4}$ cup minced fresh chives
1 large egg yolk
Pinch coarse salt
1 tablespoon grated Parmesan cheese
8 long, sturdy chives (if the chives aren't pliant enough to use as ties, dunk them in boiling water for several seconds)

FOR BAKING

2 tablespoons unsalted butter, melted

To make the pasta, put the all-purpose flour, semolina flour, and oregano into a food processor and pulse to combine. In a small mixing bowl, beat together the wine and egg. With the motor running, pour the mixture in slowly, allowing it to be incorporated into a stiff dough. Take the dough out of the food processor, and knead it by hand until it's smooth and supple, about 7 minutes. Shape it into a ball and place it in a glass or ceramic bowl. Cover with plastic wrap and let it rest for 20 to 30 minutes.

To make the filling, if you have a fish poacher, put water into the basin portion, and place the fish and the shrimp on the poaching rack. Bring the water to a boil, then insert the rack. Steam until the shrimp have turned bright pink, about 4 minutes. Remove the shrimp and continue steaming until the bass is flaky all the way through, about 7 minutes more. If you don't have a poacher, you can use a steaming basket instead and follow the same procedure. (You may have to cut the bass into a few pieces to fit in the steamer.) Transfer the bass to a plate to cool.

When cool enough to handle, chop the bass and place in the work bowl of a food processor, along with the breadcrumbs, milk, garlic, chives, egg yolk, salt, and Parmesan cheese. Process in pulses to blend.

Divide the dough into 4 pieces. Take one piece and flatten it with your hands. Generously flour it on each side. Put it through a hand-cranked pasta maker at the widest setting. Fold the dough in half and pass it through again. Adjust the setting 2 notches down and pass the dough through again. Fold it in half and pass through again. Adjust the setting 1 notch down and repeat. Cover the sheet of pasta with plastic wrap while you roll out the rest of the dough.

Place the pasta on a lightly floured surface, and cut it into 8 squares of equal size.

Heat the oven to 375° F.

Fill a large pot with water and bring it to a boil. Add the pasta one sheet at a time and simmer for 4 minutes. Remove with a slotted spoon and transfer to a plate. Spread the fish filling on the pasta and roll it up. Cut each in half and tie with a chive. Lightly grease a Pyrex or other ovenproof baking dish with unsalted butter. Transfer the pasta packets to the dish. Pour the melted butter evenly on top. Cover the dish loosely with foil. Bake 20 minutes, until the filling is set. Serve at once.

Make the dough up to 3 days ahead.
- *Flour lightly, wrap in wax paper, then plastic, and refrigerate.*
- *Take out of the refrigerator about 30 minutes before rolling and filling.*

Freeze the dough up to 6 months, well wrapped as above.
- *To defrost, transfer to the refrigerator overnight.*

Wrap the leftovers in a dish covered with plastic. Refrigerate. To reheat, replace the plastic wrap with foil and place in a 350° F. oven until warmed through.

Menu

ZUCCHINI SOUP (PAGE 55)
PASTA PACKETS WITH SEA BASS
STEAMED BEET, POTATO, AND TURNIP MELON BALLS
(PAGE 173)

Spinach Lasagna with Fish

Those of us who live where fresh fish is abundant and affordable feel really badly for those who have to pay a premium for what little they can find. If you're among the latter, you may resent the suggestion that you spend an exorbitant amount of money on swordfish and snapper, only to treat it like so much cheap ricotta cheese. But that isn't quite the deal here. Supple fresh lasagna noodles make a showcase, not a mere receptacle, for the fish. And the delicate sauce enhances and extends their subtle flavors.

TIME TO PREPARE (HANDS ON): *About 45 minutes*

TIME TO COOK: *About 10 minutes*

TOTAL TIME: *About 1 hour*

10 ounces fresh spinach, tough stems
  removed
3 large eggs
3 cups unbleached all-purpose flour, or
  more if necessary
1/2 pound swordfish
1/2 pound haddock or snapper
1 tablespoon extra virgin olive oil
1 large onion, chopped
1/4 cup dry white wine
2 tomatoes, peeled, seeded, and chopped
1/4 cup minced fresh cilantro
Coarse salt and freshly ground black pepper

Mussel and fennel sauce (see page 144)

  or

WHITE SAUCE
  1 tablespoon unsalted butter
  2 tablespoons unbleached all-purpose flour
  1 cup 1% or 2% milk
  1/4 teaspoon ground nutmeg
  Coarse salt and freshly ground black pepper
    to taste

To make the pasta, rinse the spinach and shake out as much moisture as you can. Put it into a deep saucepan, cover, and turn up the heat to medium. When the spinach has wilted and turned bright green—about 2 minutes—take the pan off the heat. Transfer the spinach to a large plate to let it cool. Drain and put it into a food processor and process until it's finely ground. With the motor running, add the eggs, one at a time, waiting for each to be incorporated. Then add the flour, 1/2 cup at a time, until you have a stiff dough. Take the dough out of the food processor, and knead it by hand until it's smooth and supple. Shape it into a ball and place it in a glass or ceramic bowl. Cover with plastic wrap and let it rest for 20 to 30 minutes.

Meanwhile, dice the fish by hand into very small pieces. (Don't use a food processor or the fish will be mushy. You want it in tiny cubes, not like ground meat.) Cover and set aside.

Tear off a quarter of the pasta dough and dust it lightly with flour. Pat it with your hands to flatten it slightly, then feed it into the pasta machine with the feed slot set to its widest. Roll the dough through, dusting it lightly with flour again. Continue rolling and tightening the slot until the pasta is as thin as you'd like. Be careful not to overdo it, or the dough will tear. (If it does tear, ball it up and run it through from the widest slot again.) Cover with a lightweight towel and repeat with the remaining dough. Using kitchen shears, a pizza cutter, or a serrated knife, cut into noodles between 1½ and 2 inches wide, and long enough to fit into either an 8-inch square or 7×11-inch rectangular ovenproof dish.

Heat the oil in a nonstick skillet over medium-high heat. When hot, add the onion, reduce the heat to medium-low, and sauté, stirring often, until the onion is soft and limp, about 7 minutes. Add the fish and continue to sauté until it colors, about 2 minutes. Using a slotted spoon, transfer the fish mixture to another dish.

Add the wine to the skillet and stir until most of it has evaporated, about 2 minutes. Add the tomatoes and cilantro, and continue cooking, stirring often, until the sauce thickens, about 10 minutes. If the sauce is boiling, turn the heat down to low so it will reduce more slowly. Stir in the fish and remove from the heat right away. Season with salt and pepper.

Fill a large pot with water and bring it to a boil. Add a generous pinch of salt, then stir in the lasagna. Bring the water back to a boil, then cook for 2 minutes, stirring often to keep the sheets from sticking together. Drain and let the sheets dry on a clean cloth towel.

Heat the oven to 375°F.

To prepare the white sauce, melt the butter in a small nonstick skillet or saucepan. Add the flour and stir over medium heat to make a paste. As soon as the paste turns golden, pour in the milk. Using a whisk, continue to stir over medium-high heat until thickened, about 8 minutes. Season with nutmeg, salt, and pepper. If it's too thick, add more milk or a dash of dry white wine.

Combine the fish sauce with the white sauce or mussel sauce. Lightly butter an 8-inch square or 7×11-inch rectangular baking dish. Place a third of the pasta on the bottom, then top with a third of the sauce. Repeat twice with the remaining pasta and sauce.

Cover loosely with foil and bake just until warmed through, about 15 minutes.

Make the dough up to 3 days ahead.
- *Flour lightly, wrap in wax paper, then plastic, and refrigerate.*
- *Take out of the refrigerator about 30 minutes before rolling and filling.*
Freeze the dough up to 3 months, well wrapped as above.
- *To defrost, transfer to the refrigerator overnight.*
Wrap leftovers in a dish covered with plastic. Refrigerate. To reheat, replace the plastic wrap with foil and place in a 350°F. oven until just warmed through. Do not microwave (it will get tough).

Paella

SERVES 8

The excellent and authoritative food writer Penelope Casas tells us there's no paella in the world to compare with what's served in Valencia, the home of this fantastic dish, once described, she tells us, as a "gastronomic miracle." Casas generously adds that one need not aspire to the miraculous to make delicious paella, noting further that few Spaniards agree on what comprises the ideal version. Serve with a simple tossed salad and crusty bread.

TIME TO PREPARE (HANDS ON): *About 15 minutes*

TIME TO COOK: *About 30 minutes*

TOTAL TIME: *About 45 minutes*

6 cups Chicken Broth (page 285), Shrimp Broth (page 286), Lobster Broth (page 287), or Vegetable Broth (page 286)

$\frac{1}{2}$ teaspoon powdered saffron

2 tablespoons extra virgin olive oil

2 whole chicken breasts, skin on, split and halved

$\frac{1}{4}$ pound medium-spicy chicken sausage, thinly sliced

1 large onion, chopped

3 garlic cloves, crushed and minced

1 bay leaf

3 cups short-grain rice (arborio, see page 70, or imported Spanish paella rice)

$\frac{1}{4}$ cup dry white wine

1 pound firm fish, such as halibut, cut into 8 pieces

2 pounds mussels in their shells, scrubbed and debearded

1 pound medium shrimp, shells removed

$1\frac{1}{2}$ cups freshly shelled peas or frozen peas (optional)

$\frac{1}{2}$ pound minced clams, drained

$\frac{1}{4}$ cup minced fresh parsley, plus additional minced parsley for garnish

Coarse salt and freshly ground black pepper

Heat the oven to 325°F.

In a large saucepan, bring the broth to a simmer over medium-high heat. Add the saffron and stir until it dissolves, less than 1 minute. Reduce the heat to low to keep the broth warm.

Heat the olive oil in a large, heavy ovenproof pan about 15 inches in diameter over medium heat. When hot, add the chicken and sausage, and brown, stirring occasionally, allowing the sausage to give up some oil, about 5 minutes. Transfer the chicken and sausage to a plate and cover with foil.

Add the onion, garlic, and bay leaf to the pan and sauté until the onion becomes soft and limp, about 7 minutes. Add the rice and stir to coat with the onion and garlic. Stir in the broth and wine. Add the chicken, sausage, and halibut, and stir well. Bury the mussels in the rice. Place in the oven, uncovered, for 15 minutes.

Remove the pan and stir in the shrimp and peas, if using. Return to the oven for 5 minutes, until the shrimp are no longer translucent.

Place the pan on top of the stove over very low heat, and stir in the clams and parsley. Stir well and cover with foil. Turn off the heat and let sit for 10 minutes.

Season with salt and pepper and sprinkle with additional parsley before serving. Serve the paella from the pan, taking care to remove the bay leaf.

Make up to 3 days ahead.

- *Wrap or cover tightly, preferably in a glass container, and refrigerate.*
- *Take out of the refrigerator about 2 hours before serving, transfer to a serving bowl, cover with plastic wrap, and let come to room temperature.*
- *If you'd like to reheat, place the paella in a heat-resistant dish or bowl. Cover loosely with foil and place inside a large baking dish. Add water to the outer dish until it comes halfway up the side of the one with the paella. Heat for 20 minutes in a preheated 325° F. oven, stirring occasionally and adding water as necessary to maintain the level.*

Scallop and Potato Salad

SERVES 2 TO 4

This is picnic food nonpareil, perhaps best served at dusk, when the sun won't spoil the mayonnaise. It serves 2 as a main course, 4 as part of a larger picnic spread.

TIME TO PREPARE (HANDS ON): *About 10 minutes*

TIME TO COOK: *About 10 minutes*

TOTAL TIME: *About 3 hours, 20 minutes, including time to chill*

1 pound new potatoes, scrubbed and halved or quartered, depending on size
1 leek, white part plus 1 inch of green, cleaned and thinly sliced
One 2-inch piece lemon zest
1 tablespoon dry white wine or
    1 1/2 teaspoons balsamic vinegar
1 pound sea or bay scallops (if you're using large sea scallops, you can cut them in half or quarters)

1 tablespoon mayonnaise
1/4 cup nonfat plain yogurt
2 teaspoons Dijon mustard
1 cucumber, peeled, seeded, and chopped
2 scallions, white part only, minced
2 tablespoons fresh lemon juice
2 tablespoons minced fresh chives
Coarse salt and freshly ground black pepper

Fit a large pot with a steamer basket. Add enough water to come up to the base of the steamer. Place the potatoes in the steamer, cover, and bring the water to a simmer over medium-high heat. Turn the heat down to medium-low and steam the potatoes until they're cooked through, 10 to 15 minutes. Remove them from the steamer and set them aside to cool.

Meanwhile, fill a medium saucepan half full with water and bring it to a boil. Add the leek, lemon zest, and wine or vinegar and bring back to a boil. Turn the heat down to keep it at a gentle simmer. Simmer for 10 minutes to infuse with the flavor of the leek and lemon. Add the scallops and simmer until they are no longer translucent, 5 to 8 minutes, depending on size. Remove the scallops with a slotted spoon and transfer to a bowl to cool.

In a separate bowl, combine the mayonnaise, yogurt, and mustard. Whisk well. Stir in the scallops, potatoes, cucumber, scallions, lemon juice, and chives. Season with salt and pepper. Cover and chill for at least 3 hours.

- *Do not make ahead; this tastes best fresh.*

Salmon with Mussels and Cream

SERVES 4

Fish farms here and abroad have been yielding bumper crops of mussels and salmon in all seasons, so you should be able to get your hands and cream sauce on them whenever you want, wherever you live.

TIME TO PREPARE (HANDS ON): *About 20 minutes*

TIME TO COOK: *About 20 minutes*

TOTAL TIME: *About 40 minutes*

2 garlic cloves, crushed and minced

¼ cup dry white wine

2 pounds mussels, scrubbed and debearded

1 tablespoon unsalted butter or extra virgin olive oil

1 onion, chopped

1 leek, white part plus 1 inch of green, cleaned and thinly sliced

1 small fennel bulb without fronds, chopped

2 tablespoons fresh lemon juice

½ cup sour cream or reduced-fat sour cream

Salt and freshly ground black pepper

1 tablespoon grated lemon zest

1 garlic clove, crushed and minced

2 tablespoons minced fresh parsley

½ teaspoon coarse salt

2 pounds salmon fillets

Put the garlic and wine in a deep pot and bring to a simmer. Add the mussels, cover the pot, and steam until they open, about 5 minutes. Discard any mussels that haven't opened. Let the rest cool until you can handle them.

Meanwhile, melt the butter or heat the oil in a nonstick skillet over medium-high heat. When hot, add the onion, leek, and fennel. Reduce the heat to medium-low and sauté, stirring often, until the vegetables are soft, about 8 minutes. Add the lemon juice and continue to stir until the liquid evaporates, about 2 minutes. Remove from the heat. Allow to cool slightly, then stir in the sour cream.

Heat the oven to 425° F.

Take the mussels out of their shells and stir them into the fennel mixture. Season with salt and pepper.

Line a shallow baking dish with parchment paper so that the paper extends several inches over the sides. Combine the lemon zest, garlic, parsley, and salt. Place the salmon fillets skin side down on top of the parchment and use your fingers to rub the lemon zest mixture into the fish. Bake 10 minutes, or until the fish is flaky and an even soft pink color inside and out. Remove the fish from the parchment with a spatula. Top each serving with the mussel sauce, which can be served at room temperature or gently reheated.

Make the mussel sauce up to 2 days ahead.

- *Seal in a tightly covered container and refrigerate.*
- *To reheat, transfer to a double boiler or place in a Pyrex bowl and place the bowl inside a large saucepan or stockpot. Add enough water to come halfway up the side of the bowl. Bring the water to a simmer, and continue to simmer until the sauce is heated through, about 15 minutes.*

Wrap the leftover salmon in plastic or store in zip-lock bags, pressing out the air before you seal. Refrigerate up to 2 days.

Menu

BLACK OLIVE–BELL PEPPER TERRINE (PAGE 94)

LEMON RISOTTO (PAGE 74)

SALMON WITH MUSSELS AND CREAM

ASPARAGUS PACKETS (PAGE 198)

Leek-Wrapped Salmon Stuffed with Shrimp

SERVES 4

When you last had leeks they may have been bit players in a soup or sauce. Here they have a starring role, as a tender, sweet casing for salmon that's been stuffed with shrimp.

TIME TO PREPARE (HANDS ON): *About 30 minutes*

TIME TO COOK: *About 25 minutes*

TOTAL TIME: *About 1 hour*

6 large leeks, cleaned and ends trimmed
2 cups chopped cleaned Swiss chard
2 pounds salmon fillet, in 4 even-sized pieces
1 pound shrimp, peeled
1 tablespoon extra virgin olive oil
2 scallions, white part only, chopped
3 tablespoons dry white wine
1 tablespoon grated lemon zest
$1/2$ cup minced fresh parsley
Unsalted butter

Trim off the root end of each leek, and cut off as much of the green as necessary to make the leek 6 inches long. Slit lengthwise to clean, taking care not to cut the leeks in half. Rinse thoroughly.

Fit a rack or steamer basket inside a stockpot or deep, wide skillet. Add water to barely touch the bottom of the rack and bring it to a simmer. Place the leeks on the rack, cover the pot, and steam until they're soft and pliable but not mushy, about 7 minutes. Lift out of the steamer and let cool.

Rinse the chard well and put the damp leaves inside a large saucepan. Cover and place over medium heat until the leaves turn bright green, about 4 minutes. Remove from the heat, uncover, and let cool.

Trim a 2-inch piece of fish from each fillet and mince.

Mince the shrimp.

In a medium nonstick skillet, heat the oil over medium-high heat. When hot, add the scallions and reduce the heat to medium-low. Sauté until the scallions soften, about 4 minutes. Add the wine and stir until most of it has evaporated, about 2 minutes.

Transfer to a mixing bowl and add the chard, minced salmon, and shrimp. Stir in the lemon zest and parsley.

Spread the chard mixture on top of 1 salmon fillet, then place the other fillet on top.

Separate the layers of the leeks and wrap them around the salmon "sandwich" widthwise to encase the entire thing.

Lightly butter a baking dish and place the salmon inside, not touching. Cover loosely with foil and bake until the salmon is flaky, about 25 minutes. (You'll have to poke a knife through the leek casing to check for doneness—*that's your portion!*)

Cut each packet in half across the width and serve right away.

- *Wrap the leftovers in a dish covered with plastic. Refrigerate. Do not reheat; serve cold or at room temperature.*

Fish Fillets with Mango Sauce

SERVES 4

The mango mad do not know the meaning of moderation. Not content to eat them in salad (page 174), soup (page 62), and dessert (page 280), they manage to work them into the main course, too. Calling for one succulent mango, some shrimp, and firm fish, this sweet and pungent summertime supper is easy to prepare.

TIME TO PREPARE (HANDS ON): *About 10 minutes*

TIME TO COOK: *About 45 minutes*

TOTAL TIME: *Under 1 hour*

8 large shrimp, shells removed and reserved
Four 2-inch strips fresh lemon zest, divided
Four 2-inch strips fresh lime zest, divided
4 garlic cloves, crushed and minced, divided
3 tablespoons grated peeled fresh ginger, divided
1 large ripe mango, peeled and chopped
2 ripe fresh tomatoes, cored and chopped
1½ teaspoons Thai or Vietnamese fish sauce (nam pla or nuoc mam) or
   1 teaspoon soy sauce
2 pounds thick-cut sea bass, red snapper, or haddock fillets
2 tablespoons minced fresh basil
2 tablespoons fresh lime juice
4 cups cooked white rice (1 cup dry)

Remove the shells from the shrimp and set the shrimp aside.

Place the shrimp shells in a large saucepan along with 2 strips of lemon zest, 2 strips of lime zest, half the garlic, and half the ginger. Add 2 cups of water and bring to a simmer over medium-high heat. Cover and continue to simmer gently for 30 minutes. Strain the broth into a deep skillet.

Bring the broth to a simmer over medium-high heat. Add the remaining strips of lemon zest and lime zest, the remaining garlic and ginger, and the mango and tomatoes. Continue simmering until the mango and tomatoes become soft and pulpy, about 15 minutes. Add the shrimp and cook until they turn bright pink, about 4 to 6 minutes. Remove the shrimp with a slotted spoon and set aside.

Stir the fish sauce or soy sauce into the skillet. Add the fish, skin side down. Cover and let simmer gently over medium-low heat for about 3 minutes. Turn over and cook 2 to 3 minutes more, until the fish flakes easily and the color is no longer translucent. Return the shrimp to the sauce and remove from the heat.

Stir in the basil and lime juice. Serve warm over rice.

Make the shrimp broth up to 3 days ahead.
* *Seal the broth and the shrimp separately in tightly covered containers and refrigerate.*
Don't reheat. Serve leftovers cold or at room temperature.

Menu

STEAMED VEGETABLE DUMPLINGS WITH
GINGER-SOY DIPPING SAUCE (PAGE 40)
FISH FILLETS WITH MANGO SAUCE
RICE (PAGE 181)
STEAMED SNOW PEAS (PAGE 25)

Tuna Spread for Sandwiches

SERVES 2

The next time someone starts to wax rhapsodic about Italian cooking, citing, in particular, its special regard for foods in season, you might remind them about the tuna. Italians have more recipes for canned tuna than most ardent admirers of their cuisine would like to admit. As it happens, many are really very good, this sandwich spread for one, which comes from Milan.

TIME TO PREPARE (HANDS ON): *About 5 minutes*

TIME TO COOK: *About 20 minutes*

TOTAL TIME: *About 40 minutes, including time to chill*

1 Japanese eggplant (small slender eggplant, see Note)
One 6-ounce can tuna packed in water, drained
3 tablespoons fresh lemon juice
2 anchovy fillets, rinsed and patted dry
1 teaspoon capers, rinsed
2 teaspoons mayonnaise
2 tablespoons nonfat plain yogurt
1 teaspoon Dijon mustard
1 whole scallion, including green, minced
$1/4$ cup minced fresh chives
$1/4$ cup minced fresh parsley
Coarse salt and freshly ground black pepper

Heat the oven to 450° F.

Pierce the eggplant in several places with a fork. Wrap the eggplant in foil and bake until it's soft, about 20 minutes. Unwrap the foil and let the eggplant cool. To speed cooling, put into a paper bag and toss into the refrigerator for 5 to 10 minutes.

Peel, and discard as many seeds as possible. (If the eggplant is very fresh, there should be few, if any, seeds.)

In a food processor or blender, combine the tuna, lemon juice, anchovies, capers, eggplant pulp, mayonnaise, yogurt, mustard, scallion, chives, and parsley. Process in short pulses to combine. Be careful not to overprocess, or the mixture will be mushy. Season with salt and pepper.

NOTE: Japanese eggplant, or any small slender eggplant, tends to be far less bitter than the larger eggplant. You can substitute ½ conventional eggplant, but only if the one you're using contains very few seeds, which make it bitter.

Make up to 3 days ahead.
- *Seal in a tightly covered container and refrigerate.*

Sole and Salmon Terrines with Spinach

SERVES 4

Salmon, while distinctive, is subtle enough to allow the milder sole to assert its own sweet flavor in this beautiful dish.

TIME TO PREPARE (HANDS ON): *About 20 minutes*
TIME TO COOK: *About 30 minutes*
TOTAL TIME: *Just under 1 hour*

FISH
4 sole fillets, weighing a total of about 1 pound, each cut in half
1 salmon fillet, weighing about 1 pound, cut lengthwise into 8 strips of roughly the same size
1 garlic clove, crushed and minced
¼ cup minced fresh parsley
1 tablespoon grated lemon zest

FENNEL AND SPINACH FILLING
1 tablespoon unsalted butter or extra virgin olive oil
1 onion, chopped
1 leek, white part plus 1 inch of green, cleaned and thinly sliced
1 small fennel bulb, trimmed and chopped, fronds reserved for garnish if desired
2 tablespoons fresh lemon juice
10 ounces fresh spinach, cleaned, trimmed, and chopped, or one 10-ounce package frozen chopped spinach, thawed and squeezed dry

½ cup sour cream or reduced-fat sour
  cream
Coarse salt and freshly ground black pepper

1 recipe Artichokes in Lemon Sauce, or just
  the lemon sauce from the same recipe
  (optional; page 196)
Chives for garnish (optional)
Thin lemon slices for garnish (optional)

Lay the sole and salmon in a single layer on a
large plate or baking sheet. In a bowl, combine
the garlic, parsley, and lemon zest. Spread evenly
on the fish. Cover with plastic wrap and refrigerate until ready to use.

Melt the butter or heat the oil in a nonstick
skillet over medium-high heat. When hot, add
the onion, leek, and fennel, reduce the heat to
medium-low, and sauté, stirring often, until the
vegetables are soft, about 8 minutes. Add the
lemon juice and continue to stir until the liquid
disappears, about 2 minutes. Stir in the spinach
to blend. If using fresh spinach, continue stirring
until it turns bright green. Remove from the heat.
Stir in the sour cream and season with salt and
pepper.

Heat the oven to 450°F.

Lightly grease 4 ramekins or ovenproof bowls
with unsalted butter or extra virgin olive oil.
Place 1 piece of sole on the bottom of each. Top
with ⅛ of the fennel mixture. Cover with a piece
of salmon, another piece of sole, another ⅛ of
the fennel mixture, ending with a piece of
salmon. In each terrine, there should be 2 pieces
of sole, 2 of salmon, and a total of ¼ of the fennel mixture.

Place the terrines inside a large baking dish.

Add water to the outer dish until it comes
halfway up the side of the terrines. Cover loosely
with foil and bake until the terrine is set, about
20 minutes, checking occasionally, adding water
if necessary to maintain the level. Remove from
the oven. Let cool on a rack at least 5 minutes before turning out onto a serving plate. Serve drizzled with lemon sauce, if you'd like. Otherwise,
garnish with reserved fennel fronds, chives, and
lemon slices.

- *You can make the filling up to 2 days in advance. Refrigerate, covered, until ready to use.*

Sole with Fresh Tomatoes

SERVES 4

We've become so distracted by the splashier things at the fish counter—swordfish, monkfish, squid, and what have you—it's easy to forget about simple unassuming sole. But don't. Its delicate sweet taste makes it easy to prepare well, as here, with a handful of fresh ingredients.

TIME TO PREPARE (HANDS ON): *About 20 minutes*

TIME TO COOK: *About 6 minutes*

TOTAL TIME: *About 30 minutes*

1 tablespoon plus 1 teaspoon extra virgin olive oil, divided

2 pounds sole fillets

2 garlic cloves, crushed and minced, divided

2 tablespoons minced fresh oregano or 1 tablespoon crumbled dried

2 tablespoons minced fresh parsley

2 teaspoons grated lemon zest

2 shallots, minced

4 fresh sage leaves, minced, or 1 tablespoon crumbled dried

1 tablespoon unbleached all-purpose flour

1 cup dry white wine, divided

6 tomatoes, peeled, seeded, and chopped, or 2½ cups canned

½ cup half-and-half or reduced-fat sour cream

Coarse salt and freshly ground black pepper

Heat the oven to 425°F.

Grease a large baking dish with 1 teaspoon olive oil. Lay the fillets inside the dish in as close to a single layer as possible. In a small mixing bowl, combine half of the minced garlic, the oregano, parsley, and lemon zest. Spread evenly on the fish fillets and set aside.

Heat the remaining 1 tablespoon oil in a wide saucepan over medium-high heat. When hot, add the remaining garlic and the shallots and sage. Reduce the heat to medium-low and sauté, stirring often, until the shallots are soft, about 7 minutes. Sprinkle the flour over the mixture and continue stirring to make a paste. Add half of the wine and continue to stir until thick. Turn up the heat and add the tomatoes and the remaining wine. Turn the heat down to medium-low and simmer, stirring often, until the tomatoes break down into a thick sauce, about 7 minutes. Transfer to a food processor or blender to puree, or puree in the saucepan with an immersion blender.

Place the fish in the oven and bake until flaky, about 6 minutes.

Stir the half-and-half or sour cream into the sauce. Season with salt and pepper. Place the fillets on serving plates and spoon the sauce over them.

Wrap the leftovers in a dish covered with plastic. Refrigerate.
- *To reheat, transfer to a skillet and warm over medium heat, stirring gently. Do not allow to boil. Or separate the fish from the sauce. Put the sauce in a microwavable bowl and zap at medium strength, stirring each time, until heated through. Pour over the fish and let sit for several minutes to warm it.*

LOVE THOSE LEFTOVERS!

Make pasta: Toss any leftover sauce with hot pasta, chickpeas, and grated Parmesan cheese or crumbled feta cheese. Serve right away.

Grilled Fish Steaks in Sweet Soy Marinade

SERVES 4 TO 6

This works beautifully on any fatty fish. Serve with rice.

TIME TO PREPARE (HANDS ON): *About 5 minutes*

TIME TO COOK: *About 10 minutes*

TOTAL TIME: *About 15 minutes*

1/2 cup soy sauce

1/4 cup plus 2 tablespoons mirin (rice wine)

1/4 cup rice vinegar

2 tablespoons grated peeled fresh ginger

4 garlic cloves, crushed and minced

1 tablespoon grated orange zest

1 tablespoon honey

4 to 6 salmon or halibut steaks, or 2 pounds tuna or swordfish, 1 inch thick

In a deep Pyrex or other heavy baking dish, combine the soy sauce, mirin, rice vinegar, ginger, garlic, orange zest, and honey. Stir well.

Add the fish and turn once to coat with the marinade. Cover the dish with plastic wrap and refrigerate. Marinate for 30 minutes to 6 hours, turning at least once.

Heat the fire. When hot, grill the fish for 5 minutes. Brush the fish with the remaining marinade, turn, and grill the other side for 3 to 5 minutes. Using a sharp knife, poke into the thickest part of the fish to test for doneness. The flesh should be a solid color with a slight bit still translucent. (The translucent part is undercooked but will finish cooking once the fish is off the grill.) If most of the inside is still translucent, allow it to cook for 2 minutes more before checking again.

Remove from the grill and let stand for a few minutes before serving.

Make the marinade up to 3 days ahead.
* *Seal in a tightly covered container and refrigerate.*
Wrap the leftovers in a dish covered with plastic. Refrigerate. Take out of the refrigerator 2 hours ahead and serve at room temperature. Or reheat with caution, wrapped in foil, in a 350° F. oven until warmed through, or microwave in short spurts at medium strength.

Steamed Salmon Medallions

SERVES 4

Never much of a food stylist, I was immoderately and immodestly pleased with myself when I turned out a perfect medallion on my very first try. My success had nothing to do with either native skill or beginner's luck, but with the fact that shaping salmon steaks into these boneless beauties is simple. Serve them as follows with sculpted steamed root vegetables.

HOW TO MAKE SALMON MEDALLIONS

Place a salmon steak on a flat work surface so that the rounded edge is on the bottom.

Cut the V-shaped center bone from the salmon. Cut away the backbone, taking care not to cut through the skin.

Hold the thin upper left portion in your hand and slide the knife under the outer skin. Carefully slice about 2 inches of skin back from the flesh, so you have a loose strip of skin attachd to a flap of flesh.

Fold the flap of salmon in toward the center, and the other flap over that, making a tight spiral. Use the strip of skin to overlap the other side, making a round. Tie securely with kitchen twine.

Once you've cooked the salmon, the skin and twine will strip off easily, and the medallions will hold their shape.

TIME TO PREPARE (HANDS ON): *About 30 minutes*

TIME TO COOK: *About 40 minutes*

TOTAL TIME: *About 1 1/4 hours*

12 asparagus spears, trimmed
8 new potatoes, peeled and carved into torpedoes (see page 172)
2 yellow turnips (rutabagas), carved into torpedoes (see page 172)
1 yellow bell pepper
1 red bell pepper
4 salmon steaks
1 garlic clove, thinly sliced
2 teaspoons grated lemon zest
1 head butterhead lettuce (Boston lettuce)
2 tablespoons extra virgin olive oil
1 tablespoon fresh lemon juice
2 tablespoon minced fresh chives
Coarse salt and freshly ground black pepper to taste

Fit a large pot with a steamer basket. Add enough water to come up to the base of the steamer. Cover and bring the water to a simmer over medium-high heat. Place the asparagus in the steamer, cover, and steam until it turns bright green, 2 to 4 minutes, depending how thick it is. Take it out of the steamer and let cool. Check the water level in the pot, adding more if necessary to reach the base of the steamer.

Place the potatoes and yellow turnips in the steamer and steam until just cooked through, 15 to 20 minutes.

Meanwhile, heat the broiler. Line a broiling tray with aluminum foil. Slice the bell peppers in half, remove the core and seeds, and place, skin side up, on the tray. Place the tray under the broiler about 3 inches from the heat. Broil until the skin blackens, about 4 minutes. Let cool. To speed the process, you can put the peppers into a paper bag and toss into the refrigerator for 5 to 10 minutes. Peel and chop the roasted peppers.

Shape the salmon medallions as directed in the accompanying box. Stick each with ¼ of the sliced garlic clove and sprinkle with lemon zest. Place a lettuce leaf on your work surface and lay a piece of fish on top. If the fish is larger than the lettuce leaf, place as many additional leaves underneath as necessary so the bottom of the fish is covered. Place another leaf on top and wrap over the fish to cover. If a single leaf is not enough, wrap as many additional leaves as necessary to cover the fish.

Empty the water you've been using for steaming and replace with fresh water, adding enough to reach the base of the steamer. Bring to a boil over medium-high heat. Add the wrapped salmon medallions, cover, and turn the heat down to medium-low. Steam until cooked through, about 10 minutes. Unwrap the lettuce, and remove the twine and skin from the salmon.

In a large mixing bowl, combine the oil, lemon juice, chives, and salt and pepper. Add the roasted peppers and steamed vegetables and toss well. Place a salmon medallion in the center of each plate and spoon the vegetables around it. Serve hot, at room temperature, or chilled.

Shape the medallions the day before.
- *Wrap tightly in plastic and refrigerate.*

Tender Ginger-Flavored Steamed Fish Fillets

SERVES 4

Crack enough cookbooks and you'll find that nearly every cuisine features recipes for fish steamed in lettuce leaves. The universal appeal of this ingenious method is easy to understand: The lettuce wrap makes the fish moist and sweet. This delectable version calls for Indian spices. Serve with rice (page 181).

TIME TO PREPARE (HANDS ON): *About 10 minutes*

TIME TO COOK: *About 10 minutes*

TOTAL TIME: *About 1 hour, including time to marinate*

¼ cup fresh lime juice
1 teaspoon salt
2 pounds monkfish, snapper, or haddock fillets
2 garlic cloves, crushed and minced
1 tablespoon grated peeled fresh ginger
¼ cup minced fresh cilantro
2 tablespoon minced fresh mint (see Note)
2 teaspoons ground cumin
1 medium tomato, peeled, seeded, and chopped
3 tablespoons dried unsweetened coconut flakes
12 soft (butterhead) lettuce leaves

Combine the lime juice and salt in a shallow dish, such as a pie plate. Add the fish and turn it to coat with the lime. Cover and set aside for 30 minutes. (If it's hot in the kitchen, refrigerate.)

In a blender or food processor, blend the garlic, ginger, cilantro, mint, cumin, tomato, and coconut into a paste.

Remove the fish from the marinade and lay on a flat work surface. Spread the paste on the fillets. Place a lettuce leaf on the work surface and lay a piece of fish on top. If the fish is larger than the lettuce leaf, place as many additional leaves underneath as necessary so the bottom of the fish is covered. Place another leaf on top and wrap over the fish to cover. If a single leaf is not enough, wrap as many additional leaves as necessary to cover the fish.

Fit a large pot with a steamer basket. Add enough water to come up to the base of the steamer. Place the fish bundles in the steamer, cover, and bring the water to a simmer over medium-high heat. Turn the heat down to medium-low and steam until the fish is cooked through, about 10 minutes, depending on thickness. (You'll have to poke a knife through the lettuce to check for doneness—*that's your portion!*)

NOTE: If you can't find fresh mint, leave it out—don't use dried *no matter what!*

• *You can't make these ahead. Prepare just before serving.*

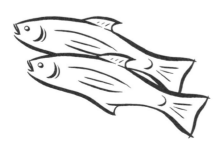

Seafood Stew with Spinach and Saffron

SERVES 4

We're told to beware false prophets and we'd be just as wise to avoid anyone claiming to make authentic bouillabaisse, the heady Provençal fish stew.* As for Paella (page 142) and other legendary dishes, claims to authenticity must be treated with suspicion, if only because they can't be verified. In fact, in the 1970s restaurateurs in Marseilles agreed to sign a pact to protect and defend the original recipe, but found they could not agree on what that recipe was. Here's a dish that owes a lot to bouillabaisse—the flavors of garlic and saffron, and the style in which it's served. Spoon out the soup for the first course, then serve the seafood immediately after, spooned into a mound of lemon risotto, if you'd like.

TIME TO PREPARE (HANDS ON): *About 25 minutes*

TIME TO COOK: *About 30 minutes*

TOTAL TIME: *About 1 hour*

1 tablespoon extra virgin olive oil
1 large onion, thinly sliced
1 large fennel bulb, trimmed and thinly sliced
2 leeks, white part plus 1 inch of green, cleaned and thinly sliced
2 garlic cloves, crushed
½ cup dry white wine
4 cups Vegetable Broth (page 286)
1 pound tiny new potatoes, scrubbed
1 pound cleaned calamari, sliced into rings

* (Psst: That's a pun—fish heads are thrown into traditional bouillabaisse for flavoring and for the thickening effect of the gelatin they release when boiled.)

½ teaspoon powdered saffron

1 pound fresh spinach, washed

½ pound medium shrimp, peeled

1 pound swordfish, cubed

4 thick slices French bread

Extra virgin olive oil

½ cup reduced-fat sour cream

Coarse salt and freshly ground black pepper

1 garlic clove, cut in half

1 recipe Lemon Risotto (page 74) or 5 cups cooked rice (page 181)

Heat the olive oil in a large deep skillet over medium-high heat. When hot, add the onion, fennel, leeks, and garlic. Turn the heat down to medium-low and sauté until the vegetables are soft, about 10 minutes. Add the wine, turn up the heat to medium-high, and stir until some of the wine has evaporated, about 2 minutes.

Add the vegetable broth, potatoes, squid, saffron, and spinach, and stir well. Cover and cook until the potatoes are cooked through, about 20 minutes.

Add the shrimp and cook, uncovered, until they turn pink, about 2 minutes.

Add the swordfish and cook, stirring often, until just cooked through, about 4 minutes.

Meanwhile, toast the bread. Pour a little olive oil into a wide shallow bowl and have a pastry brush handy.

Remove the fish stew from the heat and stir in the sour cream to blend thoroughly. Season with salt and pepper.

Carefully strain the soup into serving bowls. Cover the seafood with foil to keep warm.

Rub each piece of toast with the open end of the garlic clove and brush lightly with olive oil. Place on top of the soup, and serve. (Encourage your guests—by example—to dunk the toast into their soup, where it will get mushy and break up, seasoning and thickening the soup.)

When ready to serve the fish, place a mound of risotto or rice in the center of each plate. Use the back of a spoon to make a well. Fill with seafood and serve.

- *Seal leftovers in a container and refrigerate up to 3 days. To reheat, transfer to a heavy saucepan and stir over medium heat until warmed through. Or transfer to a microwavable bowl and microwave at full power, turning the bowl at 2-minute intervals, until warmed through.*

Tonnato Sauce

This is strictly for summer! Serve this refreshing sauce over cold poached chicken breast or cold roast turkey. Or make a salad, tossing this sauce with romaine lettuce, tomatoes, cucumbers, and chunks of bread . . . plus steamed sugar snap peas, fresh corn kernels, thinly sliced mushrooms . . .

TIME TO PREPARE (HANDS ON): *About 5 minutes*

TIME TO COOK: *None*

TOTAL TIME: *About 5 minutes, plus time to chill*

1 large anchovy fillet, rinsed and patted dry
One 6-ounce can tuna packed in water, drained
2 tablespoons mayonnaise
¼ cup nonfat plain yogurt
1 tablespoon extra virgin olive oil
2 teaspoons Dijon mustard
1 tablespoon capers, rinsed
2 tablespoons fresh lemon juice
¼ cup minced fresh chives
1 garlic clove, crushed and minced

In the work bowl of a food processor or blender, place the anchovy, tuna, mayonnaise, yogurt, olive oil, mustard, capers, lemon juice, chives, and garlic. Process until smooth, about 5 seconds.

Transfer to a glass bowl, cover, and refrigerate until chilled through, about 3 hours.

Make up to 3 days ahead.
- *Wrap or cover tightly, preferably in a glass container, and refrigerate. Serve cold.*

CHICKEN AND TURKEY

For reasons of principle, health, and general paranoia about the food supply, it's getting harder to please everyone with any single entrée. But if you've ascertained that chicken is cool with all concerned, you have lots of leeway. Chicken can be made simply (roast it as here), or elaborately (see the Vegetable-Filled Chicken Breasts, page 162).

Choosing Chicken

If candidates today were to run, as the GOP did in 1928, on the platform "A chicken in every pot," they'd have to get a lot more specific than that. Are they talking free-range chicken? Organic? "All-natural?" Or factory-farmed, hormone-enhanced and colorized?

When choosing a chicken, it's strictly "let the buyer beware." You have to set your priorities and know the wily ways of poultry marketers. Legal definitions for "organic," "free-range," and "all-natural" are in flux, and don't necessarily mean what the terms imply.

If You Can't Trust the Labels, What Can You Trust?

Your poultry person: If possible, buy your chicken at a poultry counter, not prepackaged. The person at the counter should be able to tell you something about the source of the chickens they carry, and offer you what's fresh.

Your eyes: Whole chickens and parts with the skin attached should be pinkish white, with no brownish blotches. Skinned meat should be glossy, pink, and springy. If you're determined to buy organic poultry, and all that's available is something small and scrawny, save it for yourself or use it in a casserole. Your guests may share your commitment to organic foods, but they're also entitled to the ample meal your invitation implies.

Roast Chicken

Serves 2 to 4

There's nothing better for the first-time host, or for anyone entertaining the homesick. For the former it's nearly guaranteed success, and for the latter, it offers unparalleled warmth and welcome.

TIME TO PREPARE (HANDS ON): *About 10 minutes*

TIME TO COOK: *Just under 1 hour, less if you roast at a higher temperature (see below)*

TOTAL TIME: *About 1 hour*

Buy a 3½- to 4-pound roaster—a plump white chicken with a pink hue. If it's wrapped, check the date. If it's over the counter, ask when it arrived. Check for dry patches and yellow/brown splotches. Smell—it should have no odor at all.

Heat the oven to 425° F. (see Note).

To prepare the chicken for cooking, reach into the cavity and pull out the packet of giblets. You can save them (minus the liver) to use in broth (if not within 2 days of purchase, then freeze them). Rinse the chicken and pat it dry with paper towels.

Use a shallow pan. If you line the pan with foil, you'll be grateful for your foresight when it's time to clean up.

If the pan comes with a roasting rack, grease the rack lightly with vegetable oil and place it inside the pan. If you don't have one just for roasting, use a cooling rack that fits in your pan. And if you don't have a rack of any kind, you can let the chicken sit right in the pan, but you'll have to drain the grease once or twice while it roasts.

Rub the skin of the chicken with any of the seasonings listed below. Be sure to rub some under the skin, too.

Place the chicken in the oven and set the timer for 50 minutes.

To check for doneness, pierce the chicken in the thickest part of the drumstick. If the juices that flow out are clear, the chicken is done. If they are still pink, give the bird another 10 minutes and test again.

It helps to have an instant-read thermometer. Stick the thermometer in the thigh. If the temperature reaches 170° F., the chicken is done.

Remove from the oven and let it sit for 10 minutes before carving.

NOTE: For crispier skin (and, alas, a much smokier kitchen), set the heat to 475° F. The meat will be moister, but your kitchen may smell a bit smoky for a day or two. If you decide to roast at the higher temperature, test for doneness after 40 minutes, then every 5 minutes after that if necessary.

- *Refrigerate leftovers, tightly wrapped. Use for chicken salad or sandwiches.*

Seasonings for Roast Chicken

Apricot, Fresh Rosemary, and Lemon
Heat $\frac{1}{4}$ to $\frac{1}{3}$ cup apricot preserves in a small saucepan until liquid. Brush over the skin, then rub 2 tablespoons minced fresh rosemary and 1 tablespoon grated lemon zest over the skin and underneath. Be careful not to tear the skin. Put a sprig of rosemary and a few slices of lemon into the chicken cavity

Garlic, Parsley, and Lemon
Rub the skin well with minced fresh parsley (about $\frac{1}{4}$ cup), and tuck whole unpeeled garlic cloves (about 6 for a medium chicken) and 2 tablespoons grated lemon zest underneath the skin. Put a sprig of parsley, another unpeeled whole garlic clove, and a few slices of lemon into the chicken cavity.

Garlic, Sage, Tarragon, and Thyme
Rub the skin well with minced fresh or crumbled dried sage, tarragon, and thyme (about 2 tablespoons for a medium chicken). Tuck whole unpeeled garlic cloves underneath the skin (about 6 for a medium chicken). Put a sprig of thyme, an unpeeled whole garlic clove, and a few slices of lemon into the chicken cavity.

From Frozen?
Having a chicken in the freezer won't be much help if you've got last-minute guests. It takes so long to defrost a frozen chicken, you'll have to run out for one that's fresh if you're going to serve it for supper rather than breakfast. But if you want to keep chicken in the freezer as a contingency, it will take from 12 hours (overnight) to 1 day to thaw in the refrigerator.

If you'd like to speed things along, don't leave the chicken at room temperature. You can fill a bowl with cold water and place the chicken in to thaw. But be sure to change the water every hour, or you may be bathing the chicken in bacteria. It will take between 4 and 8 hours for a chicken to defrost this way.

Chicken Breasts
Chicken breast meat is lean, which means given the opportunity, it will dry out. You can keep it moist in the following ways:

1. Cook chicken breasts with the skin on, then strip off the skin before serving. The skin keeps the meat moist. And studies have found that no significant amount of fat seeps from the skin to the sauce when you cook chicken this way.
2. Wrap boneless, skinless breasts in parchment before baking (see below).
3. Wrap boneless, skinless breasts in lettuce before steaming (see below).
4. Slice boneless, skinless chicken breasts into very thin strips and use in a stir-fry.
5. Place boneless, skinless chicken breasts between 2 pieces of wax paper and pound them. Poach, chill, and use for salads.

Chicken Baked in Parchment

PER POUND OF BONELESS CHICKEN

Heat the oven to 425°F.

Place a boneless, skinless chicken breast or thigh in the center of a piece of parchment paper. Top with a heaping spoonful of Minced Ratatouille (page 207), Artichokes in Lemon Sauce (page 196), or Tomato Sauce (page 337).

Wrap the paper over the chicken, sealing it by bringing the ends up and folding them down a few times, and place in a shallow baking dish or a pie plate. Bake until tender and cooked through, 10 to 15 minutes for breasts, 15 to 20 minutes for thighs.

Poached Chicken Breasts

PER 2 POUNDS OF BONELESS CHICKEN

Fill a deep skillet with broth or water. Add a chopped onion, 2 crushed garlic cloves, a chopped carrot, and some celery or parsley leaves. Bring to a simmer over medium-high heat, cover, and let simmer for 30 minutes. Add the boneless, skinless chicken breasts and simmer gently until just cooked through, 10 to 15 minutes.

For an Asian flavor, replace the onion, carrot, and celery with 3 chopped scallions, several tablespoons minced cilantro, and 4 thin slices fresh ginger. Use an additional crushed garlic clove, for a total of 3, and a dash of soy sauce. Simmer for 30 minutes before poaching the chicken for 10 to 15 minutes.

Chicken Breasts Steamed in Lettuce

PER POUND OF BONELESS CHICKEN

In a mixing bowl, combine 1 tablespoon soy sauce, 1 grated garlic clove, 2 teaspoons grated peeled fresh ginger, and 1 tablespoon sherry, rice wine, or rice vinegar. Marinate strips of skinned, boneless chicken for 30 minutes to 1 hour (see Note).

Remove the chicken from the marinade. Place a lettuce leaf on your work surface and lay a piece of chicken on top. If the chicken is larger than the lettuce leaf, place as many additional leaves underneath as necessary so the bottom of the meat is covered. Place another leaf on top and wrap over the chicken to cover. If a single leaf is not enough, wrap as many additional leaves as necessary to cover the piece.

Fit a large pot with a steamer basket. Add enough water to come up to the base of the steamer. Place the wrapped chicken in a single layer in the steamer, cover, and bring the water to a simmer over medium-high heat. Turn the heat down to medium-low and steam until the chicken has cooked through, 5 to 10 minutes.

NOTE: You can also use this marinade for fish (see page 153).

Chicken in Wine

SERVES 4

Guests are coming in an hour and a half, and all of your sincere intentions to prepare in advance have either proven impractical or, as if proof be needed, that you're not very well organized. Face it: You've always suspected that organization is overrated. And this dish suggests you may be right; with five minutes of hands-on time, garlic, onion, chicken, and wine, you'll make something that couldn't be better if you'd spent all day at it.

TIME TO PREPARE (HANDS ON): *About 5 minutes*

TIME TO COOK: *About 35 minutes*

TOTAL TIME: *About 1 hour, 40 minutes, including time to marinate*

1 cup red wine
1 onion, sliced
2 garlic cloves, minced
1 tablespoon crumbled dried oregano
1 bay leaf
2 teaspoons crumbled dried sage
2 teaspoons crumbled dried thyme
2 pounds skinless chicken breasts (with the bone)
$\frac{1}{2}$ cup dried porcini
2 cups fresh or canned peeled, seeded, and chopped tomatoes
Coarse salt and freshly ground black pepper

Heat the oven to 425°F.

In an ovenproof casserole, combine the wine, onion, garlic, oregano, bay leaf, sage, and thyme. Add the chicken, toss to combine, cover, and refrigerate at least 1 hour and up to 8.

Put the porcini in a bowl and add warm water to cover by an inch. Let soak until very soft, about 30 minutes. Drain the liquid and strain it.

Remove the cover from the chicken mixture and bring to a simmer on top of the stove. Let simmer until about $\frac{1}{3}$ of the wine has evaporated, about 5 minutes. Add the tomatoes, porcini, and $\frac{1}{2}$ the reserved soaking liquid. Season with salt and pepper.

Cover and place the casserole in the oven. Bake until the meat falls easily from the bone, about 35 minutes. Serve hot, or let cool to room temperature. Or chill and serve cold.

• *Wrap the leftovers in foil or plastic, or store in zip-lock bags, pressing out the air before you seal. Refrigerate. Serve cold or reheat in a baking dish covered with foil at 350°F. until warmed through.*

Chicken Sformata

SERVES 4

"Ground chicken" doesn't sound very fancy, but shaped as follows, placed on a modest mound of mashed potatoes and served with a vibrant sauce, it more than passes as an elegant entrée.

NOTE: If you have a powerful food processor, buy a skinless boneless chicken breast and grind it yourself to ensure that the meat is handled safely, in sanitary conditions.

TIME TO PREPARE (HANDS ON): *About 5 minutes*

TIME TO COOK: *About 25 minutes*

TOTAL TIME: *About 30 minutes, plus about 30 minutes to make the sauce*

1 cup soft breadcrumbs

¼ cup milk

2 pounds ground chicken breast

2 shallots, minced

½ garlic clove, crushed and minced

½ cup minced fresh parsley

1 large egg

1 tablespoon dried thyme

2 teaspoons crumbled dried oregano

Coarse salt and freshly ground black pepper

TO SERVE

Hot Mashed Potatoes (page 191)

Hot Tomato and Fennel Sauce (page 128)

Thyme sprigs (optional)

Heat the oven to 425° F.

In a small bowl, soak the breadcrumbs in the milk until the milk is absorbed, about 10 minutes. Drain any remaining liquid.

In a large mixing bowl, use your hands to combine the breadcrumbs, chicken, shallots, garlic, parsley, egg, thyme, and oregano. Season with salt and pepper.

Divide equally among 4 ramekins, packing it in lightly. Place in a large baking dish. Add water to the baking dish until it comes halfway up the side of the ramekins. Bake until firm and the meat is no longer pink, about 25 minutes.

Invert the terrines on a platter. Fill each ramekin halfway with mashed potatoes, and pat down. Invert the potato rounds onto each serving plate. Place a chicken terrine on top. Drizzle each with tomato and fennel sauce, and top each with a sprig of thyme, if you've got some.

Make the sauce up to 3 days ahead.
* *Seal in a tightly covered container and refrigerate.*
Wrap the leftovers in a dish covered with plastic. Refrigerate. Take out of the refrigerator 2 hours ahead, and serve at room temperature. If you'd like to reheat, put the sauce alone in a microwavable bowl and zap at medium strength, stirring each time, until heated through. Pour over the chicken and let sit for several minutes to warm it.

Vegetable-Filled Chicken Breasts

SERVES 4

In entertaining, as in politics, you can enhance your standing through a ploy known as "diminished expectations." Tell your guests ahead of time "we're only having chicken." Then present them with this: tender envelopes of chicken breast, filled with vegetables and coated with a light, creamy sauce.

TIME TO PREPARE (HANDS ON): *About 30 minutes*

TIME TO COOK: *About 20 minutes*

TOTAL TIME: *About 50 minutes*

1 tablespoon extra virgin olive oil
1 leek, white part plus 1 inch of green, cleaned and thinly sliced
2 carrots, peeled and thinly sliced
1 celery stalk, thinly sliced
1 medium turnip, peeled and diced
1 medium zucchini or summer squash, chopped
$\frac{1}{2}$ cup dry white wine, divided
2 cups shredded radicchio
4 boneless, skinless chicken breast halves
2 cups Chicken Broth (page 285) or Vegetable Broth (page 286)
$\frac{1}{4}$ cup half-and-half or reduced-fat sour cream
$\frac{1}{2}$ cup diced fontina cheese
Coarse salt and freshly ground black pepper

Heat the oil in a large nonstick skillet over medium-high heat. When hot, add the leek, carrots, celery, turnip, and squash. Turn the heat down to medium-low and sauté until the vegetables have softened, about 15 minutes. Add half of the wine, turn up the heat to medium, and continue cooking, stirring constantly, until most the wine has evaporated, about 3 minutes. Add the radicchio and continue stirring until it wilts, about 3 minutes. Transfer to a bowl and let cool. Do not rinse out the skillet.

Pound each chicken breast very thin (about $\frac{1}{4}$ inch). Spread 2 halves each with half the filling, or as much as will fit. Top with the other halves. Tie well with kitchen twine. Pour the broth into the skillet along with the remaining wine. Bring to a simmer. Add the chicken, cover, and cook until cooked though, about 15 minutes. Using a slotted spoon or spatula, transfer the chicken to a cutting board. Cut off the twine and slice each stuffed breast into 4 pieces. Place on a platter and cover loosely with foil to keep warm.

Bring the broth in the skillet to a boil and cook to reduce by about $\frac{1}{3}$, about 3 minutes. Turn down the heat to medium-low, and stir in the half-and-half and fontina cheese. Stir constantly to melt the cheese. Return the chicken to the pan to coat with the sauce. Season with salt and pepper. Serve immediately.

Wrap the leftovers in a dish covered with plastic. Refrigerate.
- *To reheat, replace the plastic wrap with foil and place in a 350° F. oven until warmed through. Or microwave individual portions at medium heat, rotating every minute, until heated through.*

Menu

SPINACH AND RICE SOUP (PAGE 57)

VEGETABLE-FILLED CHICKEN BREASTS

ORANGE-APRICOT CRANBERRY SAUCE (PAGE 179)

STEAMED BROCCOLI RABE

Chicken with Apricots and Pine Nuts

SERVES 6

It's hard to overstate the appeal of fruit and nuts in savory dishes, especially (but not only!) when there are children at the table.

TIME TO PREPARE (HANDS ON): *About 25 minutes*

TIME TO COOK: *About 20 minutes*

TOTAL TIME: *About 45 minutes*

2 tablespoons extra virgin olive oil

1 onion, chopped

4 garlic cloves, crushed and minced

1 green bell pepper, cored, seeded, and
   sliced

1 bay leaf

1 tablespoon ground cinnamon

1 tablespoon ground cumin

1 teaspoon ground allspice

1 teaspoon ground coriander

2 pounds boneless, skinless chicken breasts,
   cut into bite-sized pieces

2 tablespoons dry white wine

1 cup fresh or canned peeled, seeded and
   chopped tomatoes

10 dried apricots

$1/4$ cup raisins

1 tablespoon pine nuts, toasted

2 cups Vegetable Broth (page 286)

Salt and freshly ground black pepper

6 cups cooked bulgur wheat, brown rice, or
   white rice (from $1 1/2$ cups dry)

Heat the olive oil in a large skillet over medium-high heat. When hot, add the onion, garlic, green pepper, bay leaf, cinnamon, cumin, allspice, and coriander. Turn the heat down to medium-low and sauté until the onion and pepper are soft, about 8 minutes.

Add the chicken, turn up the heat to medium-high, and stir quickly to brown. Remove the chicken with a slotted spoon and set aside.

Add the wine and stir until most of it has evaporated, about 2 minutes. Add the tomatoes, apricots, raisins, and pine nuts, and stir well to combine. Add the broth and let it simmer until it reduces by about $1/4$, about 5 minutes. Add the chicken back to the pan, turn the heat down to medium-low, cover, and simmer until the chicken has cooked through, 15 to 20 minutes. Season with salt and pepper. Serve hot with bulgur or rice.

Make up to 2 days ahead.

* *Seal in a tightly covered container and refrigerate. To reheat, transfer to a baking dish and cover with foil. Place in a 350° F. oven until warmed through. Or place in a large microwavable bowl and zap at medium strength, rotating every 2 minutes, until heated through. Treat leftovers the same way, or serve cold.*

Grilled Spiced Ground Chicken

SERVES 4

Good intentions to reduce fat and cholesterol will not make a lean alternative to ground beef—ground chicken—palatably moist. Ground chicken will dry out on the grill unless you add something to tenderize it. Yogurt and lemon juice do the trick here, and the results are delicious.

TIME TO PREPARE (HANDS ON): *About 10 minutes*

TIME TO COOK: *About 10 minutes*

TOTAL TIME: *About 30 minutes*

1 pound ground chicken
1 tablespoon minced fresh cilantro
¼ cup minced red onion
1 tablespoon grated peeled fresh ginger
1 garlic clove, crushed and minced
½ teaspoon ground turmeric
½ teaspoon ground cumin
1 tablespoon nonfat plain yogurt
2 tablespoons fresh lemon juice
Coarse salt and freshly ground black pepper

FOR SERVING
Pita bread, homemade (page 224) or store-bought
Shredded lettuce
Diced tomatoes

In a large mixing bowl, combine the chicken, cilantro, onion, ginger, garlic, turmeric, cumin, yogurt, and lemon juice. Season with salt and pepper.

Heat the grill.

Using 2 tablespoons of the mixture at a time, roll into cigars 4 inches long and ¼ inch in diameter.

When the grill is hot, grill until cooked through, about 10 minutes, turning after 6 minutes.

Serve in pita pockets with lettuce and tomato.

- *Wrap the leftovers in a dish covered with plastic. Refrigerate. Serve at room temperature. Or, to reheat, replace the plastic wrap with foil and place in a 350°F. oven until warmed through. Do not microwave (they will dry out).*

Grilled Chicken in Yogurt Marinade

SERVES 4

The yogurt marinade seasons and tenderizes chicken for grilling. Serve these kabobs with steamed rice and pita or lavash.

TIME TO PREPARE (HANDS ON): *About 5 minutes*

TIME TO COOK: *About 10 minutes*

TOTAL TIME: *2 to 14 hours, depending on how long you choose to marinate the chicken*

---

1 cup nonfat plain yogurt
Juice of 1 lemon
Juice of 1 lime
1 Vidalia onion, finely chopped
2 garlic cloves, grated
3 tablespoons grated peeled fresh ginger
1 tablespoon ground cumin
2 teaspoons ground coriander
$\frac{1}{4}$ teaspoon ground cinnamon
$\frac{1}{4}$ cup minced fresh cilantro
1 teaspoon coarse salt
$\frac{1}{4}$ teaspoon paprika
2 pounds boneless, skinless chicken breasts, cut into 2-inch pieces
Vegetable oil
4 cups cooked white rice (1 cup dry)
Pita bread (homemade, page 224, or store-bought) or Lavash (page 228)

In a large mixing bowl, combine the yogurt, lemon juice, lime juice, onion, garlic, ginger, cumin, coriander, cinnamon, cilantro, salt, and paprika. Stir well to blend thoroughly. Add the chicken and mix well. Cover with plastic wrap and refrigerate at least 2 and up to 14 hours before grilling.

To grill the chicken, lightly grease the grill grate with vegetable oil. Heat the coals or gas grill to high heat. Meanwhile, put the chicken on skewers. If using wooden skewers, make sure to soak them in water for at least $\frac{1}{2}$ hour before grilling.

When the heat is high, place the chicken on the grill and cook until it's tender, about 7 to 10 minutes, turning once after 4 minutes.

Serve with rice and pita or lavash.

You can make the marinade up to 3 days ahead.
- *Seal in a tightly covered container and refrigerate.*
- *You can marinate the chicken overnight. Wrap in a deep dish covered with plastic. Refrigerate.*
- *Wrap the leftovers in plastic or store individual portions in zip-lock bags, pressing out the air before you seal. Refrigerate. Serve cold.*

Borscht with Chicken Dumplings

SERVES 6

Served for Sunday supper, this one-dish dinner will soothe all assembled through those melancholy last hours of the weekend. The prune and nut–stuffed meatballs won't seem unusual to anyone familiar with Middle Eastern foods. Leave them out, and you'll have a vegetarian first course.

TIME TO PREPARE (HANDS ON): *About 20 minutes*

TIME TO COOK: *About 40 minutes, less with a pressure cooker*

TOTAL TIME: *About 1 hour*

DUMPLINGS

1 cup fine bulgur wheat
4 large pitted prunes
$\frac{1}{4}$ cup chopped walnuts
$\frac{1}{2}$ pound ground chicken breast
1 shallot, minced
$\frac{1}{2}$ teaspoon ground cumin
2 tablespoons minced cilantro
$\frac{1}{2}$ teaspoon ground ginger

BORSCHT

1 tablespoon extra virgin olive oil
2 onions, chopped
2 garlic cloves, crushed and minced
2 tablespoons minced fresh mint (do not substitute dried)
2 tablespoons minced fresh oregano or 2 teaspoons crumbled dried
2 tablespoons minced fresh basil or 2 teaspoons crumbled dried
2 tablespoons minced fresh dill or 2 teaspoons crumbled dried

2 medium potatoes, preferably Yukon gold, peeled and diced
4 medium beets, peeled and chopped
4 cups Vegetable Broth (page 286)
$\frac{1}{2}$ cup reduced-fat sour cream
Coarse salt and freshly ground black pepper

Start the dumplings. In a medium saucepan, bring $1\frac{1}{2}$ cups water to a boil. Stir in the bulgur wheat, cover the pan, and let sit until soft, about 30 minutes. Drain off the excess water.

In a separate small saucepan, bring $\frac{1}{2}$ cup water to a boil. Pour over the prunes in a small bowl and let sit until soft, about 20 minutes. Drain and chop.

Meanwhile, make the borscht. Heat the olive oil in a heavy saucepan or pressure cooker over medium-high heat. When hot, add the onions, garlic, mint, oregano, basil, and dill. Turn the heat down to medium-low, and sauté until the onions are soft, about 7 minutes.

Stir in the potatoes and beets. Add the vegetable broth and bring to a gentle boil over medium-high heat. If using a saucepan, cover, turn the heat down to medium-low, and simmer until the potatoes and beets are cooked through, about 25 minutes. Remove from the heat.

If using a pressure cooker, lock on the lid and bring to full pressure. Cook at full pressure for 15 minutes. Remove from the heat. Let the pressure come down on its own. Tilt the cooker away from you when you unlock the lid.

If you're serving the borscht without the dumplings, you may want to puree it, in a food processor or blender, or using an immersion blender right in the pot. If adding the dumplings, leave it chunky.

To make the dumplings, in a small mixing bowl, combine the prunes and walnuts.

In a large mixing bowl, combine the bulgur, chicken, shallot, cumin, cilantro, and ginger. Working with about 3 tablespoons of the chicken mixture at a time, shape the dumplings. Poke a substantial hole in each, and place about 2 teaspoons of the prune and walnut mixture inside. Smooth over the hole to enclose the filling.

To finish the soup, bring the borscht (without the sour cream) to a simmer. Add the dumplings and simmer until cooked through, about 7 minutes. Stir in the sour cream, and season with salt and pepper. Serve hot.

Make up to 3 days ahead.
- *Seal in a tightly covered container and refrigerate.*
- *To reheat, transfer to a heavy saucepan and stir over medium heat until warmed through. Or transfer to a microwavable bowl and microwave at full power, turning the bowl at 2-minute intervals, until heated through.*

Freeze the dumplings and broth separately up to 6 months, well wrapped in a glass or firm plastic container.
- *The night before, move from the freezer to the refrigerator. Then combine in a saucepan or microwavable bowl and reheat as directed above.*

Menu

ORANGE-INFUSED BABA GHANOUJ (PAGE 27)

BORSCHT WITH CHICKEN DUMPLINGS

OR

BORSCHT AND CHEESE-FILLED RISOTTO RING (PAGE 184)

FENNEL, ORANGE, AND FIG SALAD (PAGE 175)

Roast Turkey

SERVINGS DEPEND ON TURKEY SIZE
(ALLOW 1 POUND PER SERVING)

Good turkey begins with a good turkey. As soon as you know how many guests you'll be serving, order a fresh bird to pick up the day before the dinner. Do not even consider a "self-basting" turkey, which is shot through with vegetable oil to keep it moist. You'll do far better following the simple guidelines below, roasting at low temperature under a broth-soaked cheesecloth.

TIME TO PREPARE (HANDS ON): *About 20 minutes*

TIME TO COOK: *Depends on the size of the turkey: 12 to 15 minutes per pound (see below)*

TOTAL TIME: *See Time to Cook*

4 to 8 cups Chicken Broth (page 285) or Vegetable Broth (page 286), depending on the size of the turkey
$\frac{1}{4}$ cup maple syrup
1 turkey (allow 1 pound per serving)
Pumpkin and Mushroom Risotto (see page 75)
Coarse salt and freshly ground black pepper to taste

Pour the broth into a large saucepan. Add the maple syrup and bring to a simmer over medium-high heat. Stir well to combine.

Heat the oven to 325°F.

Wipe down the turkey with wet paper towels, or rinse under the sink and pat dry. Line your work surface with heavy paper (grocery bags are good for this). Stuff the turkey cavity with the

▶

risotto and place the bird on the paper, breast side up. Bind the bird with kitchen twine, wrapping the twine underneath the tail and over the drumsticks. Turn the bird over, wrapping the twine around the body, then bind the wings. Once everything is held in tight, tie the twine.

Sprinkle generously all over with salt and pepper.

Cut a piece of cheesecloth, double thickness, large enough to drape over the turkey.

Fit a deep roasting pan with a rack (you can use a special V-shaped roasting rack available at kitchenware and most hardware stores). Place the bird on the rack, breast side up. Drench the cheesecloth in the broth mixture and drape over the turkey.

If the turkey is 16 pounds or less, roast 15 minutes per pound.

If the turkey is 17 pounds or more, roast for 12 minutes per pound.

After the first 45 minutes, soak the cheesecloth with additional broth. Repeat every 15 to 20 minutes. When enough moisture has accumulated in the pan, baste with the pan drippings, too.

The turkey is done when a meat thermometer registers 170°F. in the breast and 185°F. in the thigh.

Transfer to a serving platter and discard the cheesecloth. Scoop the stuffing into a serving dish and cover with foil to keep warm. Let the turkey sit for 10 to 20 minutes before carving.

See page 321 for a Thanksgiving menu.

Turkey Roulade

SERVES 6

Here's a twist on stuffed turkey: a whole breast pounded thin and rolled to enclose a colorful filling of bell peppers and ricotta cheese. You might want to consider this if you're preparing Thanksgiving dinner for four or fewer. It's not quite traditional, but it looks festive, and makes a more manageable amount of leftovers. You can ask your butcher to prepare the turkey breast for rolling.

NOTE: You can use the filling below to make the rice roulade on page 80, and have a vegetarian first course or entrée.

TIME TO PREPARE (HANDS ON):	*About 20 minutes*
TIME TO COOK:	*About 45 minutes*
TOTAL TIME:	*A little over 1 hour*

1 turkey breast (about 2 pounds), boned and pounded very thin
1 1/2 cups part-skim ricotta cheese
2/3 cup dry breadcrumbs
1/3 cup grated Asiago cheese
1 large egg
1/4 cup minced fresh parsely
2 red bell peppers, roasted, cored, seeded, peeled, and thinly sliced (see page 302)
2 yellow bell peppers, roasted cored, seeded, peeled, and thinly sliced (see page 302)
1/2 cup dry white wine
1 tablespoon extra virgin olive oil
4 ripe tomatoes, peeled and chopped
2 tablespoons minced fresh basil or 1 tablespoon crumbled dried

Heat the oven to 425°F.

Place the turkey on a flat surface.

In a large mixing bowl, combine the ricotta, breadcrumbs, Asiago cheese, egg, and parsley. Spread on the turkey, leaving a ½-inch margin. Distribute half of the red peppers and half of the yellow peppers evenly on top.

Roll up the turkey to enclose the filling. Tie with kitchen twine to secure. Wrap loosely in a large sheet of parchment paper.

Grease a roasting pan lightly with vegetable oil or squirt it with nonstick spray. Bake the turkey for 30 minutes. Add the wine to the pan, then continue baking for 10 more minutes.

In a medium saucepan, briskly stir together the olive oil, tomatoes, basil, and remaining bell peppers. Heat gently just to warm through.

Unwrap the turkey, cut off the twine, and slice. Serve the slices topped with the tomato mixture.

Wrap the leftovers in plastic or store individual portions in zip-lock bags, pressing out the air before you seal. Refrigerate.
- *To reheat, wrap in foil and place on a baking sheet in a 350°F oven until warmed through.*

Salads & Side Dishes

Elementary Theory of
Side-Dish Selection

They Only Look *Fancy*

▶ Salads

Abracadabra, Salad!
Chopped Mango, Tomato, and Avocado
   Salad
Avocado and Apple Salad
Fennel, Orange, and Fig Salad
Panzanella (Bread Salad)
Fresh Mozzarella Salad with Croutons,
   Tomato, and Leek
Cucumber Raita
Beet and Radish Salad
Beets and Sour Cream
Orange-Apricot Cranberry Sauce
Peach Buttermilk Dressing
Orange-Sesame Dressing

▶ Grains

"Perfect Rice Every Time"
Brown Rice with Cheddar
Couscous
Sweet and Nutty Bulgur Salad
Buttermilk Spoon Bread
Cheese-Filled Risotto Ring
Souffléed Sweet Potato Polenta
Barley with Apples
Baked Gnocchi with Cheese
Rice-Filled Baby Eggplant

▶ All Kinds of Vegetables

Yellow Turnips with Potatoes and
   Cheese
Potato Ring with Bell Peppers and Sage
Mashed Potatoes
Mashed Sweet Potatoes
Chickpeas with Onions, Spinach, and
   Raisins
Chickpeas with Coconut
Leeks Filled with Potato
Baked Ricotta with Leeks
Braised Fennel with Tomato
Artichokes in Lemon Sauce
Chard Filled with Artichokes
Asparagus Packets
Onions Filled with Cauliflower Soufflé
Cauliflower Broiled with Cheese
Curry Spiced Spinach and Potatoes
Sauces for Curry
Summer Squash and Tomato Melt
Golden Baked Eggplant Custard
Mushroom and Eggplant Layered with
   Cheese
Stuffed Baby Pumpkins
Spicy Eggplant Puree
Minced Ratatouille

Elementary Theory of Side-Dish Selection

IF I WERE TO TELL YOU THAT choosing a side dish to make involves considering flavor, color, and texture in relation to the rest of the meal, you might throw up your hands and call off your dinner.

But it's actually not complicated and boils down to this:

SIMPLE ENTRÉE? FANCY OR SIMPLE SIDE DISH

Roast Chicken with Rosemary (page 158)
Rice-Filled Baby Eggplant (page 188)

———

Fish Baked in Parchment (page 123)
Cauliflower Broiled with Cheese (page 199)

FANCY ENTRÉE? SIMPLE SIDE DISH(ES)

Sole and Salmon Terrines with Spinach (page 148)
Rice (page 181)
Sliced Tomatoes with Vinaigrette (page 299)

LOTS OF VEGETABLES IN THE ENTRÉE? GRAINS ON THE SIDE

All Kinds of Chili (page 106)
Brown Rice with Cheddar (page 182)

———

All Kinds of Curry (page 108)
Rice (page 181)

LOTS OF RED IN THE MAIN DISH? GREEN AND/OR YELLOW AND WHITE ON THE SIDE (AND VICE VERSA)

Sole with Fresh Tomatoes (page 150)
Baked Gnocchi (page 88) and Steamed Broccoli Rabe

———

Leek-Wrapped Salmon Stuffed with Shrimp (page 145)
Summer Squash and Tomato Melt (page 202)

For more, check the menus throughout the book and in the back.

They Only Look Fancy: Simple ways to make vegetables look elegant on the side

USE A VEGETABLE PEELER AND paring knife to shape root vegetables, such as potatoes, beets, carrots and turnips, into "torpedoes."

1. Peel the vegetable.
2. Holding the vegetable firmly in one hand, use the paring knife to taper the ends and trim the sides.
3. Steam according to the basic recipe below, checking often to avoid overcooking, which would make them mushy. It may be hard to tell if they're done without destroying one. So prepare an extra as the tester. After the time given below, insert the tip of the paring knife in the center. If it pierces smoothly, it's done. If it hits a solid center or scrapes against the inside, let it steam for 5 minutes more.

Basic Steaming Instructions

Fit a large pot with a steamer basket. Add enough water to come up to the base of the steamer. Place the vegetable in the steamer, cover, and bring the water to a simmer over medium-high heat. Turn the heat down to medium-low and steam until tender (potatoes, sweet potatoes, beets, turnips, for example) or until cooked through and still crisp (broccoli, cauliflower, asparagus, and so on).

Matchstick Bundles

Use 2 or 3 long vegetables, such as asparagus, carrots, and zucchini. Cut the carrots and zucchini lengthwise into thin sticks, then trim to about 3 inches (if you're using asparagus, trim them so you're using the top 3 inches, including the tip). Steam according to the directions above. Tie 6 together in a bundle, using a long chive. If your chives aren't pliable enough to tie, immerse them in boiling water for 10 to 15 seconds. Rinse the chives immediately with cold water, or they will become mushy.

Melon Ball Scoops

Use a medium-sized melon ball scoop to scoop out raw root vegetables such as beets, potatoes, and turnips (yellow and white). Steam as directed above and serve scattered over the plate.

Grains (Rice, Barley, Couscous)

Lightly grease as many ramekins or small custard cups or cups of a muffin tin as you'll need. (Ordinarily a serving is ¾ cup of cooked rice.) Press the rice or barley into the cups and smooth the tops. Turn the ramekins or custard cups out onto individual serving plates. Turn the muffin tin out onto a countertop covered with a sheet of wax or parchment paper. Lift each mound of rice or barley carefully with a wide spatula and place on serving plates.

Or hollow out large cherry tomatoes or plum tomatoes and fill with cooked grains. (Slice off the bottom of roma tomatoes so they will stand upright on the plate.)

Salads

A well-composed salad doesn't need a garnish. It contains enough color and varied texture from the ingredients. Arrange dark-colored greens at the bottom and layer lighter greens on top.

SALADS

Abracadabra, Salad!

Stumped for salad? Try these:

Fresh Corn and . . .

Fresh cooked corn kernels
Steamed sugar snap peas
Plus
Diced steamed beets or diced roasted bell
   peppers
Vinaigrette (page 299)

String Bean or Asparagus

Steamed French green beans or slender
   asparagus
Diced roasted red or yellow bell peppers
Garlic Vinaigrette (page 299)

Spinach and Almond

Baby spinach
Slivered almonds
Orange-Sesame Dressing (page 180) or
   Vinaigrette (page 299) with 1 tablespoon
   orange juice replacing 1 tablespoon
   balsamic vinegar

Just Plain Tomato

Thinly sliced fresh tomato
Any dressing (pages 299 and 300)

Chopped Mango, Tomato, and Avocado Salad

SERVES 6

This is sweet, zesty, and mercifully simple, just what you want when you're going to be grilling.

TIME TO PREPARE (HANDS ON): *About 5 minutes*	
TIME TO COOK: *None*	
TOTAL TIME: *About 5 minutes*	

2 large ripe mangoes
3 to 4 large ripe tomatoes, cored and chopped
1 ripe avocado, peeled and chopped
1 Vidalia onion, chopped
2 tablespoons minced fresh chives
$1/4$ cup fresh orange juice
2 tablespoons fresh lemon or lime juice
Salt and freshly ground black pepper

Peel the mangoes and chop them, making sure to catch all of the juice. Put them in a mixing bowl, and add the tomatoes, avocado, onion, and chives. Toss well. Add the orange juice and lemon juice and toss again. Season with salt and pepper.

Make up to 2 days ahead.
• *Seal in a tightly covered container and refrigerate.*

Avocado and Apple Salad

SERVES 4 TO 6

Why is it that when Caesar Cardini created a salad, he got to put his name on it, but when Oscar Tschirky invented his, it was named after the hotel that employed him (the Waldorf)? The divergent fates of their salads are a bit easier to understand. Calling for mayonnaise, nuts, iceberg lettuce, celery, and apple, Oscar's salad was sweet and rich, too much frivolity and confection to survive these days of serious salad. Still, he was on to something, which survives in this wholesome version.

TIME TO PREPARE (HANDS ON): *About 5 minutes*	
TIME TO COOK: *About 15 minutes*	
TOTAL TIME: *About 20 minutes*	

$1/4$ cup raisins
1 Granny Smith apple, peeled and chopped
1 ripe avocado, peeled and chopped
$1/4$ cup fresh lemon juice
3 tablespoons mayonnaise
6 tablespoons nonfat plain yogurt
2 teaspoons Dijon mustard
1 tablespoon honey
1 tablespoon red wine vinegar
Salt and freshly ground black pepper
3 cups chopped escarole or romaine lettuce

Bring $1/2$ cup of water to a boil. Add the raisins and remove from the heat. Let sit until the raisins are plump and soft, about 15 minutes. Drain off any remaining water.

Meanwhile, put the apple and avocado in a large bowl and toss with the lemon juice.

In a separate bowl, combine the mayonnaise,

yogurt, mustard, honey, and vinegar. Season with salt and pepper.

Toss with the apple and avocado, raisins, and lettuce, and serve.

Variation with Chicken and Possibly Walnuts

Add 2 cups chopped or shredded poached chicken breast (page 159) or leftover boiled or roasted chicken, plus $\frac{1}{3}$ cup chopped walnuts to the mayonnaise mixture.

Variation with Tuna

Add one 6-ounce can water-packed tuna, drained, to the mayonnaise mixture, along with $\frac{1}{4}$ cup chopped celery. Blend well.

- *You can't make this ahead. Prepare it shortly before serving.*

Fennel, Orange, and Fig Salad

SERVES 4

Fresh figs are not in season very long. When you see them, grab them for this salad.

TIME TO PREPARE (HANDS ON): *About 10 minutes*

TIME TO COOK: *None (unless you're soaking dried figs: about 30 minutes)*

TOTAL TIME: *About 10 minutes*

2 small fennel bulbs, thinly sliced

2 seedless oranges, peeled and separated into sections

4 fresh figs, quartered, or 8 dried Mission figs, soaked in hot water to cover until soft, about 30 minutes, drained, then quartered

$\frac{1}{4}$ cup chopped oil-cured black olives

2 tablespoons extra virgin olive oil

Juice of 1 lime

2 teaspoons whole fennel seeds

Salt and freshly ground black pepper to taste

Cut the sliced fennel into 1-inch pieces.

Cut the orange sections into thirds.

Arrange an equal number of fennel and orange slices on each serving plate. Arrange the figs on top and sprinkle with an even amount of olives (1 tablespoon per serving).

In a blender or food processor, or using an immersion blender, beat together the olive oil and lime juice to make a thick emulsion. Add the fennel seeds and salt and pepper, and stir well. Spoon an even amount over each serving.

- *You can't make this ahead. Prepare it shortly before serving.*

Panzanella
(Bread Salad)

SERVES 4

New life for old bread, and a wonderful salad for you!

TIME TO PREPARE (HANDS ON): *About 10 minutes*

TIME TO COOK: *None*

TOTAL TIME: *About 40 minutes, including time for the bread
to soak*

- 2 tablespoons balsamic vinegar, divided
- 8 slices bread, crusts removed and torn to
  small pieces, or 3 to 4 cups chunks of
  bread
- 2 cucumbers, peeled
- 1 red onion, chopped
- ¼ cup shredded fresh basil
- 2 large ripe tomatoes, chopped
- 1 bunch arugula, chopped
- 2 tablespoons extra virgin olive oil
- Salt and freshly ground black pepper

In a large mixing bowl, combine 1 tablespoon of
the vinegar with ½ cup water. Add the bread and
stir with your hands to make sure it gets thoroughly soaked. Cover with plastic wrap and let
sit for 30 minutes.

Meanwhile, slice the cucumbers in quarters
lengthwise. Run a paring knife under the seeds to
remove them. Dice the cucumber and put into a
large salad bowl. Add the onion, basil, tomatoes,
and arugula.

Squeeze the moisture out of the bread and
crumble it well. Add it to the salad bowl and toss.
In a small bowl, vigorously whisk together the
olive oil and remaining vinegar. Pour over the

salad and toss thoroughly. Season with salt and
pepper, and toss again.

- You can make this salad up to 1 day ahead. Refrigerate, covered, and toss well before serving.

Fresh Mozzarella Salad with Croutons, Tomato, and Leek

SERVES 6

*It can be hard to find mozzarella that's truly fresh and not
just labeled as such. Taste before you buy it to be sure it's
creamy and sweet, and not likely to hit the ceiling if you
drop it on the floor.*

TIME TO PREPARE (HANDS ON): *About 10 minutes*

TIME TO COOK: *None. Well, oven toasting the bread—about
5 minutes*

TOTAL TIME: *About 10 minutes*

- 6 thick slices bread, crusts removed
- 1 cucumber
- 3 ripe tomatoes, diced
- 6 ounces fresh mozzarella, cut into small
  cubes
- 1 leek, white part only, thinly sliced
- ¼ cup shredded fresh basil
- ½ small garlic clove, crushed and minced
- 3 tablespoons extra virgin olive oil
- 1 tablespoon balsamic vinegar
- Coarse salt and freshly ground black pepper

Heat the oven to 350°F.

Cut the bread into cubes and place on a non-stick baking sheet. Put in the oven until golden, about 3 minutes. Turn over and toast the other side, about 1 minute.

Meanwhile, slice the cucumber in quarters lengthwise. Run a paring knife under the seeds to remove them. Dice the cucumber and put into a large salad bowl along with the tomatoes, mozzarella, leek, basil, and toasted croutons.

Using a blender, immersion blender, or food processor, combine the garlic, olive oil, and vinegar and blend well. Season with salt and pepper. Pour over the salad and toss well.

• *You can't make this ahead. Prepare it right before serving.*

Cucumber Raita

SERVES 8

This is a cooling, crunchy accompaniment to curries and grilled foods.

TIME TO PREPARE (HANDS ON): *About 10 minutes*

TIME TO COOK: *None*

TOTAL TIME: *About 3 hours, including time to chill*

3 large cucumbers, peeled
1 Vidalia onion, chopped
2 1/2 cups nonfat plain yogurt
3 tablespoons minced fresh mint
3 tablespoons minced fresh dill
2 tablespoons minced fresh cilantro
1/2 teaspoon salt, or to taste

Cut the cucumbers lengthwise into quarters.

Run a paring knife down the center of each quarter to remove as many seeds as possible. Chop and place in a large mixing bowl. Add the onion, yogurt, mint, dill, cilantro, and salt.

Cover and refrigerate at least 3 hours before serving.

Variation with Beets

Add 2 cooked diced beets with the cucumbers.

To cook the beets, heat the oven to 450°F. Wrap each beet in foil and place on a baking sheet. Bake until tender, about 40 minutes. Unwrap. When cool enough to handle, strip off the peel and chop coarsely. To speed chilling, you can transfer the beets to a pie plate or shallow bowl, and put in the refrigerator for several minutes.

Variation with Potatoes

Add 2 to 4 small (2- to 3-inch) steamed and chopped red or white potatoes with the cucumber and/or beets.

To cook the potatoes, fit a large pot with a steamer basket. Add enough water to come up to the base of the steamer. Place the potatoes in the steamer, cover, and bring the water to a simmer over medium-high heat. Turn the heat down to medium-low and steam the until tender, 15 to 20 minutes, depending on size. When cool enough to handle, strip off the peel and chop coarsely. To speed chilling, you can put the potatoes on a plate and into the refrigerator for several minutes.

Make up to 3 days ahead.
• *Seal in a tightly covered container and refrigerate. Serve cold.*

Beet and Radish Salad

SERVES 4

This is one of those self-garnishing salads. The colors are spectacular, especially on deep green or dark blue plates.

TIME TO PREPARE (HANDS ON): *About 5 minutes*

TIME TO COOK: *40 minutes*

TOTAL TIME: *Under 1 hour*

6 medium beets, scrubbed
1 small red onion, thinly sliced
1 small garlic clove, crushed
1 small yellow or red bell pepper, cored,
    seeded, and thinly sliced
2 tablespoons minced fresh chives
2 tablespoons minced fresh thyme or
    1 tablespoon crumbled dried
Generous pinch coarse salt
2 tablespoons extra virgin olive oil, divided
$\frac{1}{2}$ tablespoon red wine vinegar
1 head soft lettuce, such as Boston
6 small radishes, thinly sliced

Heat the oven to 450°F.

Wrap each beet in foil and place on a baking sheet. Bake until tender, about 40 minutes. Unwrap. When cool enough to handle, strip off the peel and chop coarsely. To speed chilling, you can transfer the beets to a pie plate or shallow bowl, and put in the refrigerator for several minutes.

Meanwhile, in a large mixing bowl, combine the onion, garlic, bell pepper, chives, thyme, and salt. Add 1 tablespoon of the olive oil and stir well. Cover with plastic wrap and refrigerate for 30 minutes.

In a separate bowl, combine the beets, remaining olive oil, and the vinegar.

Put the lettuce in a salad bowl. Add the radishes and beets. Stir the refrigerated mixture well and toss into the salad bowl. Toss well and serve right away.

Bake the beets up to 3 days ahead.
• *Wrap tightly and refrigerate.*

Beets and Sour Cream

SERVES 4 TO 6

This is fast and refreshing. Don't be tempted to buy big beets, which tend to be tough and tasteless. And try to get organic root vegetables whenever you can. Because they're grown in smaller quantities, they're shipped to market faster and spend less time in storage gathering the starch that makes them bland.

TIME TO PREPARE (HANDS ON): *About 10 minutes*

TIME TO COOK: *About 40 minutes*

TOTAL TIME: *Just over 1 hour, including time to chill*

6 medium beets, scrubbed
$\frac{1}{3}$ cup reduced-fat sour cream
Juice of 1 lime
2 tablespoons fresh lemon juice
2 tablespoons fresh orange juice
Pinch ground cumin
$\frac{1}{2}$ cup diced sweet onion, such as Vidalia,
    Maui, or Texas
Coarse salt

Heat the oven to 450°F.

Wrap each beet in foil and place on a baking sheet. Bake until tender, about 40 minutes. Unwrap. When cool enough to handle, strip off the peel and chop coarsely. To speed chilling, you can transfer the beets to a pie plate or shallow bowl, and put in the refrigerator for several minutes.

Peel the beets and dice them.

In a large mixing bowl, combine the sour cream, lime juice, lemon juice, orange juice, and cumin. Stir well, then add the onion and beets. Toss well to blend. Season with salt. Refrigerate for several hours and serve chilled.

Make up to 3 days ahead.
- *Seal in a tightly covered container and refrigerate.*

Orange-Apricot Cranberry Sauce

SERVES 6

Cranberries have always enjoyed brief celebrity at Thanksgiving, but now they're chic, enjoyed yearlong in baked goods, chutneys, and salsas. Here's a sauce that calls for cranberries for their own sake, to be served alongside turkey, of course, but also with grilled or roasted vegetables, or fish.

TIME TO PREPARE (HANDS ON): *About 5 minutes*

TIME TO COOK: *About 30 minutes*

TOTAL TIME: *About 3½ hours, including time to chill*

1 cup fresh orange juice
⅓ cup dried apricots
1 cup sugar
1 pound fresh or frozen cranberries, rinsed
2 tablespoons fresh lime juice

Place the orange juice in a heavy saucepan and add the apricots. Bring to a simmer over medium-high heat. Cover and turn off the heat. (If you're using an electric stove, remove the pot from the burner.) Let sit until the apricots are soft and plump, about 20 minutes. Add the sugar and cranberries, and bring the mixture back to a simmer over medium-high heat. Cook, stirring often, until the cranberries "pop," about 10 minutes.

Remove from the heat and stir in the lime juice. Transfer to a glass or ceramic bowl, and chill thoroughly, at least 3 hours.

Make up to 3 days ahead.
- *Seal in a tightly covered container and refrigerate.*

Peach Buttermilk Dressing

MAKES ABOUT 1 CUP

This is terrific tossed with crisp romaine and assorted steamed vegetables, such as beets, potatoes, cauliflower, broccoli, and sugar snap peas.

TIME TO PREPARE (HANDS ON): *About 10 minutes*

TIME TO COOK: *Included in the preparation time*

TOTAL TIME: *About 10 minutes*

> 1 ripe peach
> 1 cup low-fat ricotta cheese
> ¼ cup buttermilk
> 1 teaspoon Dijon mustard
> 2 teaspoons honey
> 2 tablespoons minced fresh chives
> Salt and freshly ground black pepper

Fill a saucepan with water and bring it to a boil. Add the peach and let simmer about 45 seconds. Drain and set the peach aside to cool.

Put the ricotta, buttermilk, mustard, honey, and chives in the work bowl of a blender or food processor. Process until smooth.

Peel the peach, chop the pulp, and add to the mixture in the processor. Process in short pulses to blend. Season with salt and pepper.

Make up to 3 days ahead.
• *Seal in a tightly covered container and refrigerate.*

Orange-Sesame Dressing

MAKES 1 CUP

Serve this sweet and pungent dressing over steamed vegetables as well as salad greens. It's particularly good with cooked fresh spinach.

TIME TO PREPARE (HANDS ON): *About 5 minutes*

TIME TO COOK: *About 5 minutes*

TOTAL TIME: *About 10 minutes*

> 1 cup fresh orange juice
> 2 teaspoons cornstarch
> 2 tablespoons fresh lemon or lime juice (optional)
> 1 tablespoon honey
> 2 teaspoons Dijon mustard
> 1 scallion, white and green parts, minced
> 1 tablespoon sesame seeds
> ¼ cup plus 2 tablespoons buttermilk
> Salt

Combine 3 tablespoons orange juice with the cornstarch to make a paste. Heat the remaining orange juice to a simmer over medium-high heat or in a microwave. Stir in the cornstarch mixture and continue cooking over low heat—or microwave for 2 minutes—until thickened.

Stir in the lemon or lime juice, if using, honey, mustard, scallion, sesame seeds, and buttermilk. Season with salt.

Make up to 3 days ahead.
• *Seal in a tightly covered container and refrigerate.*

GRAINS

"Perfect Rice Every Time"

SERVES 4 TO 6

As noted elsewhere, people who claim to know the definitive way to cook anything are not to be taken seriously. There are often several ways to get very good results, and if you're able to cook rice well by strapping the pot to the hood of your car and driving steadily at 60 for an hour, then go for it.

Here are two methods for making perfect rice.

TIME TO PREPARE (HANDS ON): *Less than 1 minute*

TIME TO COOK: *See guidelines below*

TOTAL TIME: *See guidelines below*

LONG-GRAIN WHITE RICE

   1 cup rice
   1 $\frac{1}{2}$ cups water or broth
   15 minutes

SHORT-GRAIN WHITE RICE

   1 cup rice
   1 $\frac{1}{4}$ cups water or broth
   10 minutes

LONG-GRAIN BROWN RICE

   1 cup rice
   2 cups water or broth
   40 minutes

SHORT-GRAIN BROWN RICE

   1 cup rice
   1 $\frac{2}{3}$ cups water or broth
   40 minutes

Heat the oven to 325°F.

Put the rice and water or broth in an oven-proof saucepan and bring to a simmer over medium-high heat.

Cover and place in the oven.

Bake until all of the water has been absorbed, 10 to 40 minutes. Fluff with a fork before serving.

In a Pressure Cooker

LONG-GRAIN WHITE RICE

   1 cup rice
   1 $\frac{1}{2}$ cups water or broth
   7 minutes

SHORT-GRAIN WHITE RICE

   1 cup rice
   1 $\frac{1}{4}$ cups water or broth
   5 minutes

LONG-GRAIN BROWN RICE

   1 cup rice
   1 $\frac{1}{2}$ cups water or broth
   10 minutes

SHORT-GRAIN BROWN RICE

   1 cup rice
   1 $\frac{1}{2}$ cups water or broth
   10 minutes

Put the rice and water in the pressure cooker. Bring to moderate pressure. On an electric stove, move to a separate burner on low heat when it reaches moderate pressure. On a gas stove, turn the heat down to cook steadily at moderate pressure. For cooking times, consult your owner's manual, or use the times above as a guide.

- *To reheat rice, place in a heat-resistant dish or bowl. Cover loosely with foil and place inside a large baking dish. Add water to the outer dish until it comes halfway up the one inside. Heat for 20 minutes, stirring occasionally and adding water as necessary to maintain the level.*

Brown Rice with Cheddar

Serve with All Kinds of Chili (page 106).

TIME TO PREPARE (HANDS ON): *3 minutes*

TIME TO COOK: *None*

TOTAL TIME: *3 minutes*

1 recipe brown rice, cooked as above with
  Vegetable Broth (page 286) or water
$\frac{1}{4}$ cup reduced-fat sour cream
$\frac{1}{4}$ to $\frac{1}{3}$ cup shredded cheddar cheese
Salt and freshly ground black pepper

While the rice is still hot, toss with the sour cream and cheese. Season with salt and pepper.

Couscous

Couscous is a wheat that, like bulgur, requires reconstituting, but no cooking.

TIME TO PREPARE (HANDS ON): *2 minutes*

TIME TO COOK: *10 minutes*

TOTAL TIME: *12 minutes*

1 $\frac{1}{2}$ cups water
1 cup couscous
Salt

In a medium saucepan, bring the water to a boil. Stir in the couscous, cover the pan, remove from the heat, and let sit until soft, about 10 minutes. Transfer to a serving dish, fluff with a fork, and season with salt. Serve on the side of something with sauce, or stir Tahini Sauce (page 110) into it, or substitute it for bulgur in the Sweet and Nutty Bulgur Salad (below).

Sweet and Nutty Bulgur Salad

SERVES 4 TO 6

While it cooks much faster than barley, bulgur shares that grain's stubborn refusal to submit easily to seasoning. Here's one way to give it great flavor.

TIME TO PREPARE (HANDS ON): *About 10 minutes*

TIME TO COOK: *About 30 minutes*

TOTAL TIME: *About 3 hours, 40 minutes, including time to chill*

1 cup bulgur wheat
1 tablespoon extra virgin olive oil
1 large Vidalia onion, chopped
2 teaspoons ground cumin
2 teaspoons ground cinnamon
$\frac{1}{2}$ teaspoon ground allspice
$\frac{1}{2}$ cup chopped dried apricots
$\frac{1}{4}$ cup currants

2 tablespoons minced fresh mint

2 tablespoons pine nuts, toasted

1/4 cup fresh orange juice

Salt and freshly ground black pepper

In a medium saucepan, bring 1 1/4 cups water to a boil. Stir in the bulgur wheat, bring back to a boil, cover, and remove from the heat. Let sit 30 minutes.

Meanwhile, heat the oil in a small nonstick skillet over medium-high heat. When hot, add the onion, cumin, cinnamon, and allspice. Reduce the heat to medium-low and sauté, stirring often, until the onion is soft and limp, about 10 minutes.

Transfer the bulgur to a large glass or ceramic mixing bowl. Add the onion mixture, apricots, currants, mint, pine nuts, and orange juice. Toss thoroughly. Season with salt and pepper.

Chill for at least 3 hours before serving.

Make up to 3 days ahead.

- *Seal in a tightly covered container and refrigerate. Serve cold.*

Buttermilk Spoon Bread

SERVES 6

A soothing side dish for a modest supper. Serve it with All Kinds of Chili (page 106) or your choice of soup.

TIME TO PREPARE (HANDS ON): *About 20 minutes*

TIME TO COOK: *About 40 minutes*

TOTAL TIME: *About 1 hour*

2 1/2 cups buttermilk

1 cup yellow cornmeal, preferably stone-ground

Generous pinch salt

1/3 cup shredded sharp cheddar cheese, or cheddar cheese with jalapeño peppers (optional)

5 large eggs

Heat the oven to 400°F.

Lightly grease a 2-quart baking dish with unsalted butter or vegetable oil, or squirt it with nonstick spray.

Pour the buttermilk into a heavy nonreactive saucepan. Stir in the cornmeal and salt with a whisk and place over medium heat. Bring the mixture to just below the boiling point (don't let it boil). It's ready when the surface is very smooth and it seems as if it may puff up in the center. Stir constantly until it thickens to the consistency of porridge, about 15 minutes. Remove from the heat, stir in the cheese, if using, and let cool. You can speed the cooling by putting ice in a large bowl, transferring the mixture to a separate bowl, and putting the bowl into the ice, then into the refrigerator. Stir often until no longer hot.

Meanwhile, separate the eggs. Beat the yolks together and stir into the cornmeal mixture. Whip the whites until stiff peaks form and fold into the cornmeal 1/6 at a time.

Spoon into the prepared baking dish and bake until puffy and golden, about 40 minutes. If the top seems to be browning too fast, cover loosely with foil.

- *You can't make this ahead. Prepare it just before serving.*

Cheese-Filled Risotto Ring

SERVES 6

VEGETARIAN ENTRÉE!
Serve with Artichoke and Spinach Soup
(page 58) and Real Bread (page 212).

*Serving risotto plopped onto serving plates is fine among
family and intimate friends, and really ought to do for
anybody else concerned. But for the host who feels self-
conscious about such crude presentation, here is risotto layered with cheese and baked in a circular mold, baked in a
water bath to keep the rice tender.*

TIME TO PREPARE (HANDS ON): *About 40 minutes*

TIME TO COOK: *About 25 minutes*

TOTAL TIME: *A little over 1 hour, including time to set*

> 4 cups Chicken Broth (page 285) or
>   Vegetable Broth (page 286)
> 1 tablespoon extra virgin olive oil
> 2 shallots, minced
> 1 1/2 cups arborio rice
> 1/4 cup dry white wine
> 1/2 teaspoon powdered saffron
> Salt and freshly ground black pepper
> 1/4 cup shredded fontina cheese

Bring the broth to a simmer in a saucepan. Heat
the olive oil in another heavy saucepan. When
hot, add the shallots, lower the heat to medium,
and sauté until softened, about 5 minutes. Add
the rice and stir to coat with the shallot. Add the
wine and stir until it evaporates, about 3 minutes.
Add the saffron and enough broth to cover the

rice by an inch. Stir until it has been absorbed.
Add 1/3 cup more broth and continue stirring.
Add broth 1/3 cup at a time, and stir until the rice
is plump and cooked through (the core should be
clear, not hard white) and the mixture is creamy.
Season with salt and pepper.

To make it in a pressure cooker, heat the
olive oil in the pressure cooker and proceed as directed above up to the point where you begin
adding broth. (If you're using an electric stove,
turn on a separate burner at low.) Add 2 cups of
broth and bring to a boil. Lock on the lid and
bring to moderate pressure. Maintain the pressure for 7 minutes; if you're using a gas stove, you
can do this by turning the heat down as far as it
will go. If you're using an electric stove, transfer
the cooker to the preheated burner. After 7 minutes, turn off the heat. If you're using an electric
stove, take the cooker off the stove.

When the pressure comes all the way down,
tilt the cooker away from yourself and remove
the lid. (If there's any liquid left, return the
cooker to the stove and turn the heat to low, stirring until it is absorbed and the rice is creamy.)

Lightly grease a 10-inch circular mold. Spread
half of the risotto evenly into the mold. Sprinkle
the fontina cheese over the risotto and cover
with the rest of the rice. Place in a larger baking
pan, fill the outer pan with water so it comes
halfway up the sides of the mold, cover loosely
with foil, and bake at 350°F for 25 minutes. Remove and let cool on a rack for 10 minutes. Turn
out carefully, slice, and serve.

To reheat, place the mold in a water bath and
cover loosely with foil. Place in a 350°F. oven
until heated through, about 20 minutes.

Make up to 1 days ahead.

- *Leave in the mold and cover with plastic wrap. To re-heat, place the mold inside a large baking dish and cover loosely with foil. Add water to the outer dish until it comes halfway up the side of the mold. Heat in a pre-heated 350° F. oven until warmed through, about 20 minutes, adding water as necessary to maintain the level.*

▶

Souffléed Sweet Potato Polenta

SERVES 6

Did you feel duped by cotton candy when you were a kid? Betrayed by the first bite as it dissolved into a sandy coat of sugar on your tongue? Soufflés can turn on you in the same way, being nothing more than a magnificent puff of air. Here's one with substance and flavor.

TIME TO PREPARE (HANDS ON): *20 minutes*

TIME TO COOK: *About 30 minutes*

TOTAL TIME: *About 1¼ hours, including time for the polenta to cool*

3 medium sweet potatoes, peeled and quartered

2½ cups nonfat milk

2 cups yellow cornmeal, preferably stone-ground

1 tablespoon molasses

2 tablespoons brown sugar

1 teaspoon ground ginger

½ teaspoon ground nutmeg

1 teaspoon ground cinnamon

2 large egg whites

1 large egg yolk

Pinch salt

Fit a large pot with a steamer basket. Add enough water to come up to the base of the steamer. Place the sweet potatoes in the steamer, cover, and bring the water to a simmer over medium-high heat. Turn the heat down to medium-low and steam until the potatoes are soft enough to puree, 15 to 20 minutes. Remove from the heat and let the potatoes cool.

Meanwhile, heat the milk in a heavy saucepan over medium heat. Bring to a simmer, taking care not to boil.

Sprinkle the cornmeal into the milk, whisking constantly. Continue to whisk until the mixture becomes thick, like a dense porridge.

Remove from the heat and let cool for 15 minutes, stirring occasionally.

Meanwhile, heat the oven to 450° F.

Peel and mash the sweet potatoes in a large bowl. Add the molasses, brown sugar, ginger, nutmeg, and cinnamon, and stir well to blend. Stir into the cornmeal mixture. Beat the egg whites until stiff.

Stir the egg yolk into the potato mixture, then fold in the whites. Add the salt.

Transfer to a lightly greased 4- to 6-cup baking dish. Place inside a large baking dish. Add water to the outer dish until it comes halfway up the side of the terrine. Bake until puffed and golden brown, about 30 minutes, checking occasionally and adding water as necessary to maintain the level. Serve hot from the oven.

- *You can't make this ahead. Prepare it just before serving.*

Barley with Apples

SERVES 4

There is an annual event called the culinary Olympics, at which perfectly respectable chefs are called upon to do spectacularly silly things, such as build topiaries out of cruciferous vegetables. Anyone who's worked with barley knows that the true test of a superior cook is an ability to make it taste really good.

TIME TO PREPARE (HANDS ON): *About 10 minutes*

TIME TO COOK: *About 50 minutes*

TOTAL TIME: *About 1 1/4 hours, including time to rest*

---

    1 tablespoon extra virgin olive oil
    1 onion, chopped
    1 cup barley
    1/4 cup chopped dried apple
    1 fresh apple, such as Granny Smith or
        Rome, peeled, cored, and diced
    2 tablespoons cider vinegar
    2 cups Vegetable Broth (page 286)
    1/2 cup shredded cheddar cheese
    Salt and freshly ground black pepper

Heat the olive oil in a heavy saucepan or pressure cooker. When hot, add the onion and sauté until soft, about 7 minutes. Add the barley, dried apple, and fresh apple, and stir to coat with the onion. Add the vinegar, turn up the heat to medium-high, and stir until most of the vinegar has evaporated, about 1 minute. Stir in the vegetable broth and bring to a gentle boil. If you're using a saucepan, cover, turn the heat down to low, and let steam until the broth has been absorbed and the barley is soft and chewy, about 50 minutes. Remove from the heat, stir in the cheese, cover, and let sit 15 minutes before serving. Season with salt and pepper.

If you're using a pressure cooker, lock on the lid and bring to full pressure. Cook at full pressure for 10 minutes. Remove from the heat and let the pressure come down on its own. Tilt the cooker away from you as you unlock the lid. Stir in the cheese. Let sit about 15 minutes before serving.

Make up to 3 days ahead.
- *Seal in a tightly covered container and refrigerate. Take out of the refrigerator 2 hours ahead, and serve at room temperature.*
- *To reheat, place the barley in a heat-resistant dish or bowl. Cover loosely with foil and place inside a large baking dish. Add water to the outer dish until it comes halfway up the side of the one with the barley. Heat in a preheated 325° F. oven for 20 minutes, stirring occasionally and adding water as necessary to maintain the level.*
- *Or reheat with caution in a microwave in short spurts at medium strength.*

Baked Gnocchi with Cheese

SERVES 6

VEGETARIAN ENTRÉE!
Serve topped with Tomato and Fennel Sauce (page 128) and Sweet Bell Pepper Soup with Rice (page 56) to start.

In another context, gnocchi were described as dumplings made from potatoes or flour and cheese, boiled, then served under sauce as a first course. So what's with these? That definition was incomplete. Gnocchi are also made with semolina (hard-grain wheat), with bread (page 59), and occasionally polenta. Made this way, they're best as a side dish for something with sauce—such as Sole with Fresh Tomatoes (page 150). The gnocchi will soak up the runoff.

TIME TO PREPARE (HANDS ON): *About 30 minutes*

TIME TO COOK: *Included in the preparation time*

TOTAL TIME: *About 1 hour, including time to chill*

---

3 cups 1% or 2% milk
1 cup semolina flour
2 egg yolks
¾ cup grated Parmesan cheese, divided
Salt and freshly ground black pepper
Pinch ground nutmeg
Extra virgin olive oil or unsalted butter

In a large nonreactive saucepan, heat the milk until it starts to boil. Pour in the semolina, letting it fall in a thin stream, stirring constantly with a whisk so it won't clump. Continue stirring over medium heat until thick, about 15 minutes. Remove from the heat.

In a small bowl, beat together the egg yolks until combined. Beat them into the semolina mixture along with ½ cup of the cheese. Season with salt and pepper and nutmeg.

Spread the mixture onto a nonstick baking sheet to a thickness of about ½ inch. Cover with a kitchen towel or wax paper, and refrigerate until chilled through.

Lightly grease a 10-inch baking dish or a pie plate with olive oil or butter. Heat the broiler.

With a small round or diamond-shaped cookie cutter, cut the gnocchi into shapes. Place them in the baking dish, sprinkle with the remaining cheese, and broil until hot and bubbly, about 2 minutes.

Make the gnocchi and cut them out up to 3 days ahead.
- *Grease a baking dish as directed and cover with plastic wrap. Refrigerate. When you're ready to bake, proceed with the recipe.*

Rice-Filled Baby Eggplant

SERVES 4

You can recognize the Middle Eastern origins of this dish in the combination of cinnamon, cumin, and currants. And you'll enjoy it warm, room temperature, or chilled.

TIME TO PREPARE (HANDS ON): *About 15 minutes*

TIME TO COOK: *About 40 minutes*

TOTAL TIME: *A little over 1 hour, including time to rest*

2 long Japanese eggplant
1 tablespoon extra virgin olive oil
1 onion, chopped
$\frac{1}{4}$ cup minced fresh parsley
1 teaspoon ground cumin
1 teaspoon ground cinnamon
1 tablespoon currants
$\frac{1}{4}$ cup long-grain white rice
1 cup peeled, seeded, and chopped fresh or canned tomato
1 cup Vegetable Broth (page 286)

Cut the eggplant in half across the width. Use a paring knife to hollow out each half, leaving a $\frac{1}{2}$- to $\frac{3}{4}$-inch thickness all around, making a cup. Discard what you've scooped out. Stuff paper towels inside the cups to absorb bitter juices and set aside.

Meanwhile, heat the oil in a nonstick skillet over medium-high heat. When hot, add the onion, parsley, cumin, and cinnamon. Reduce the heat to medium-low and sauté, stirring often, until the onion is soft and limp, about 10 minutes. Remove from the heat and stir in the currants and rice. Mix thoroughly.

Take the paper towels out of the eggplant cups. Using a teaspoon, fill each cup halfway with the rice mixture.

Place the tomato and vegetable broth in a shallow baking dish. Lay the eggplant cups in a row on top. Cover the dish with foil and bake until the rice expands and cooks through, about 40 minutes. Remove from the oven, take the foil off the dish, and let sit 10 minutes before serving.

Make up to 3 days ahead.

• *Seal in a tightly covered container and refrigerate. Take out of the refrigerator 2 hours ahead and serve at room temperature. Or serve cold. (Yes!) Do not reheat.*

ALL KINDS OF VEGETABLES

Yellow Turnips with Potatoes and Cheese

SERVES 8

Thank goodness someone with some marketing sense has taken charge of peddling the root vegetable formerly known as the rutabaga. "Rutabaga" just doesn't sound like something you'd want to put in your stomach. Now that it's being sold as yellow turnip in most places, the sweet, dense root vegetable may finally draw the following it deserves.

TIME TO PREPARE (HANDS ON): *About 10 minutes*

TIME TO COOK: *About 40 minutes*

TOTAL TIME: *About 1 hour*

6 medium firm-fleshed potatoes, such as
    Yukon Gold, peeled and sliced
2 medium yellow turnips (rutabagas), peeled
    and sliced
1 Granny Smith apple, peeled and sliced
½ cup low-fat cottage cheese
½ cup buttermilk
½ cup shredded cheddar cheese
Coarse salt and freshly ground black pepper

Place the potatoes, rutabagas, and apple in a large basket steamer. Place the steamer in a pot large enough to hold it, and add water until it nearly touches the base of the steamer. Cover and bring the water to a boil. Lower the heat and simmer until the vegetables are soft, about 20 minutes.

Meanwhile, using a food processor or blender, combine the cottage cheese and buttermilk until smooth.

Heat the oven to 425° F.

Transfer the steamed vegetables to a large bowl. Add the cheddar cheese and the cottage cheese mixture. Mash together with a wooden spoon or potato masher. Season with salt and pepper. Spread the mixture into a lightly greased 9-inch square baking pan.

Bake until golden brown on top, about 20 minutes.

Refrigerate the leftovers in a deep dish covered with plastic. Take out of the refrigerator 2 hours ahead and serve at room temperature.

- *To reheat, replace the plastic wrap with foil and place inside a large baking dish. Add water to the outer dish until it comes halfway up the side of the mold. Heat in an oven set at 450° F. until warmed through, about 20 minutes, adding water as necessary to maintain the level.*
- *Or soak a paper towel in water. Wring out as much moisture as possible and drape over the potatoes. Microwave at medium strength, rotating 180 degrees every 2 minutes until warmed through.*

Potato Ring with Bell Peppers and Sage

SERVES 6

There may be times when you feel obligated to serve something fancy, and all you really want is mashed potatoes. Here's how you can reconcile your highfalutin dinner plans with your own down-home desires.

TIME TO PREPARE (HANDS ON): *About 20 minutes*

TIME TO COOK: *About 1 hour*

TOTAL TIME: *About 1½ hours*

2 pounds firm-fleshed potatoes, such as Yukon Gold, peeled and quartered
⅓ cup buttermilk
½ cup dry breadcrumbs
2 tablespoons minced fresh chives
2 tablespoons minced fresh parsley
⅓ cup grated Parmesan cheese
Pinch salt
1 tablespoon extra virgin olive oil
1 red bell pepper, seeded, cored, and sliced
1 green bell pepper, seeded, cored, and sliced
2 garlic cloves, crushed and minced
2 tablespoons minced fresh rosemary
3 tablespoons dry white wine
Unsalted butter or vegetable oil
6 fresh sage leaves

Place a steamer basket inside a large pot. Add enough water to touch the bottom of the steamer. Place the potatoes in the steamer, cover the pot, and bring the water to a boil over medium-high heat. Turn the heat down to medium-low so the water stays at a simmer. Steam the potatoes until soft, about 30 minutes, depending on size. Check the water level halfway through, adding more if necessary.

When cooked through, set aside to cool slightly. Coarsely chop the potatoes. Add the buttermilk and mash into the potatoes with a spoon or potato masher, along with the breadcrumbs, chives, parsley, cheese, and salt. Set aside.

Heat the oil in a medium nonstick skillet over medium-high heat. When hot, turn the heat down to medium-low, add the bell peppers, garlic, and rosemary, and sauté until the peppers are soft and limp, about 15 minutes. Add the wine, turn the heat up to medium-high, and continue stirring until most of it evaporates, about 2 minutes.

Heat the oven to 400°F. Lightly grease a 10-inch circular mold with butter or vegetable oil.

Lay the sage leaves into the mold, ends toward the center and the outer rim, spacing them evenly around the mold. Spoon the potato mixture into the mold. Bake until firm, about 15 minutes. Let sit for 10 minutes to set.

Turn the potato mold out onto a large serving platter. Turn out the pepper mixture into the center. To serve, cut into wedges and include a spoonful of peppers with each portion.

- *Refrigerate the leftovers in a deep dish covered with plastic wrap. Take out of the refrigerator 2 hours ahead and serve at room temperature.*
- *To reheat, replace the plastic wrap with foil and place inside a large baking dish. Add water to the outer dish until it comes halfway up the side of the mold. Heat in an oven set at 450° F. until warmed through, about 20 minutes, adding water as necessary to maintain the level.*
- *Or soak a paper towel in water. Wring out as much moisture as possible and drape over the potatoes. Microwave at medium strength, rotating 180 degrees every 2 minutes until warmed through.*

Mashed Potatoes

S E R V E S 6

"Mashed potatoes" used to refer to plain old spuds, milk, and a little butter smushed together and served with a shovel. That was before those celebrity chefs put on their thinking toques and starting pummeling "heirloom" potatoes with everything from sun-dried tomatoes to garlic and leeks. They'll get over it. Meanwhile, here's a simple, soothing version, something more like the original.

TIME TO PREPARE (HANDS ON): *About 5 minutes*

TIME TO COOK: *About 50 minutes*

TOTAL TIME: *About 1 hour*

6 large potatoes, such as russet or Yukon Gold
$1/3$ cup low-fat cottage cheese
$2/3$ cup buttermilk
Coarse salt and freshly ground black pepper
3 tablespoons minced fresh chives (optional)

Heat the oven to 450° F.

Wrap each potato in foil and bake until tender, about 50 minutes. Unwrap the potatoes.

When cool enough to handle but still warm, strip off the skin. Place in a large mixing bowl and mash with the back of a large spoon or a potato masher.

Place the cottage cheese in the work bowl of a food processor or blender. Process until smooth. Add the buttermilk and process briefly to blend. (Don't overdo it or it will be too liquid.)

Pour the mixture into the potatoes and mash again to blend. Season with salt and pepper. Stir in the chives, if desired.

- *Refrigerate the leftovers in a tightly sealed container. To reheat, transfer to a baking dish, cover loosely with foil, and place inside a large baking dish. Add water to the outer dish until it comes halfway up the side of the mold. Heat in an oven set at 450° F. until warmed through, about 20 minutes, adding water as necessary to maintain the level. Or microwave at medium strength, rotating the bowl 180 degrees every 2 minutes until warmed through.*

Mashed Sweet Potatoes

SERVES 6

Baked in foil, sweet potatoes have a sweeter, more intense flavor than boiled or steamed. Vanilla powder makes them even more special.

TIME TO PREPARE (HANDS ON): *About 5 minutes*

TIME TO COOK: *About 35 minutes*

TOTAL TIME: *About 45 minutes*

> 4 medium sweet potatoes
> 2 teaspoons brown sugar or 1 tablespoon maple syrup
> 1 teaspoon unsalted butter
> Pinch vanilla powder (see Sources, page 347) (optional)
> Salt

Heat the oven to 450° F. Line a baking sheet with foil.

Scrub each potato lightly with a vegetable brush and wrap each in foil.

Bake until very soft, about 40 minutes.

Unwrap and let cool. Strip away the peel and mash with the brown sugar or maple syrup, butter, and vanilla powder, if using. Season with salt.

• *Refrigerate the leftovers in a tightly sealed container. To reheat, transfer to a baking dish, cover loosely with foil, and place inside a large baking dish. Add water to the outer dish until it comes halfway up the side of the mold. Heat in an oven set at 450° F. until warmed through, about 20 minutes, adding water as necessary to maintain the level. Or microwave at medium strength, rotating the bowl 180 degrees every 2 minutes until warmed through.*

Chickpeas with Onions, Spinach, and Raisins

SERVES 6

VEGETARIAN ENTRÉE!
Serve with Hummus (page 28), Lentil Soup with Pumpkin (page 61), and Pita Bread (page 224).

These chickpeas, seasoned with cinnamon and raisins, are the closest thing to candy you can serve at supper. Spinach is there to lend credibility to the dish, which might otherwise seem inappropriately sweet at this point in the meal. If you serve it with any chicken or fish dish, it can be the entrée for the vegetarians at your table.

TIME TO PREPARE (HANDS ON): *About 30 minutes*

TIME TO COOK: *Included in the preparation time*

TOTAL TIME: *About 30 minutes*

> 1 tablespoon extra virgin olive oil
> 1 large onion, chopped
> 1 teaspoon ground cinnamon
> 2 medium fresh or canned tomatoes, peeled, seeded, and chopped
> 2 cups fresh baby spinach leaves, washed
> 2 cups cooked chickpeas
> 1/4 cup raisins
> Salt and freshly ground black pepper

Heat the oil in a nonstick skillet over medium-high heat. When hot, add the onion and cinnamon, reduce the heat to medium-low, and sauté, stirring often, until the onion is soft and limp, about 10 minutes.

Add the tomatoes and continue cooking until they break down into a thick sauce, about 5 minutes. Stir in the spinach, chickpeas, and raisins. Continue stirring until the spinach wilts and turns bright green, about 3 minutes. Season with salt and pepper.

Make up to 3 days ahead.
* *Seal in a tightly covered container and refrigerate. Take out of the refrigerator 2 hours ahead and serve at room temperature. Or serve cold.*

Chickpeas with Coconut

SERVES 6

VEGETARIAN ENTRÉE!
Serve with Crepes with Ricotta and Spices (page 100), Curry Spiced Spinach and Potatoes (page 202), Naan (page 226), Cucumber Raita (page 177), and rice (page 181).

The only way you can go wrong with this dish is to fail to make enough of it. There's an addictive quality to this combination, and those denied a second helping cannot be held accountable for their actions.

TIME TO PREPARE (HANDS ON): *About 15 minutes*

TIME TO COOK: *Included in the preparation time*

TOTAL TIME: *About 15 minutes*

1 tablespoon safflower or canola oil
1 large Vidalia onion, chopped
3 garlic cloves, crushed and minced
1 tablespoon ground cumin
1 tablespoon ground coriander
1 teaspoon turmeric
2 cups cooked chickpeas
3 tablespoon fresh lemon juice
$\frac{1}{4}$ cup dried shredded unsweetened coconut
$\frac{1}{4}$ cup raisins
Salt

Heat the oil in a medium nonstick skillet over medium-high heat. When hot, add the onion, garlic, cumin, coriander, and turmeric. Turn the heat down to medium-low and sauté until the onion is soft, about 7 minutes.

Add the chickpeas, lemon juice, coconut, and raisins, and stir well to combine.

Transfer to a serving bowl, season with salt, and stir well. Serve at room temperature or chilled.

Make up to 3 days ahead.
* *Seal in a tightly covered container and refrigerate.*

Leeks Filled with Potato

SERVES 4

The facts are lost to history, but it's certain that the person who first put leeks and potatoes together was amply rewarded for the inspiration—if by nothing other than the opportunity to be first to enjoy the brilliant match!

TIME TO PREPARE (HANDS ON): *About 10 minutes*

TIME TO COOK: *About 20 minutes*

TOTAL TIME: *About 30 minutes*

4 large leeks, ends trimmed, cleaned
2 medium potatoes, such as Yukon Gold,
    peeled and diced
1 cup Vegetable Broth (page 286)
Salt and freshly ground black pepper
Minced fresh chives, for garnish

Fit a large pot with a steamer basket. Add enough water to come up to the base of the steamer. Place the leeks in the steamer, cover, and bring the water to a simmer over medium-high heat. Turn the heat down to medium-low and steam the leeks until they're soft but not mushy, about 7 minutes. Remove from the heat. Once they've cooled enough to handle, slice through the outer layer of each leek without cutting through the leek. Slip off the outer layer of each, trying to keep it in one piece. If the layer is very thin and fragile, slip off the layer under it, too. They have to be strong and supple because you'll be using them as a wrapping.

Chop the remaining leeks, using the white and light green parts only, and put them in a medium saucepan with the potatoes and vegetable broth. Bring to a simmer over medium-high heat. Cover and turn the heat down to medium-low. Simmer until the potatoes are cooked through, about 10 minutes. Drain any excess liquid. Mash the potatoes and leeks together. Season with salt and pepper.

Spread an equal amount of potato mixture on each leek and roll up the leek. Cut into thirds and sprinkle with chives before serving.

• *You can't make this ahead. Prepare it just before serving.*

Baked Ricotta with Leeks

SERVES 6

Leeks so often share the sauté pan with such other aromatic vegetables as onions and garlic, it's nice to have a chance like this to taste them on their own.

TIME TO PREPARE (HANDS ON): *About 15 minutes*

TIME TO COOK: *About 40 minutes*

TOTAL TIME: *Just under 1 hour*

2 teaspoons unsalted butter
2 leeks, white part only, cleaned and thinly
    sliced
2 cups whole milk or part-skim ricotta
    cheese
2 large eggs
$\frac{1}{3}$ cup unbleached all-purpose flour
2 tablespoons grated Parmesan cheese
$\frac{1}{2}$ cup shredded mozzarella cheese

Melt the butter in a nonstick skillet. Add the leeks and sauté, stirring often until soft, about 7 minutes.

In a food processor or blender, combine the ricotta, eggs, flour, and Parmesan and mozzarella cheeses. Process until well combined.

Transfer to a mixing bowl and stir in the leeks.

Lightly grease a 3-cup soufflé dish or six $\frac{1}{2}$-cup ramekins or custard cups. Spoon the mixture into the dish(es). Place inside a larger baking dish. Add water to the outer dish so it comes halfway up the soufflé dish or ramekins. Bake until set, about 40 minutes. Let cool on a rack about 5 minutes before serving.

- *Make up to 2 days ahead. Refrigerate, covered. To reheat, place inside a baking dish. Add water to the outer dish so it comes halfway up the soufflé dish or ramekins. Cover loosely with foil and heat at 350° F. until warmed through, about 20 minutes.*

Braised Fennel with Tomato

SERVES 4 TO 6

Fennel is so often used as a seasoning, it's possible to forget it's a vegetable. Here's a delicious reminder. Serve with something simple, such as Parchment Baked Fish or Chicken (pages 123 and 159) or the Spinach and Rice Soup (page 57), so you can appreciate its subtle flavor.

TIME TO PREPARE (HANDS ON): *About 10 minutes*

TIME TO COOK: *Just under 1 hour*

TOTAL TIME: *A little over 1 hour*

2 teaspoons extra virgin olive oil

3 medium potatoes, peeled and sliced $\frac{1}{2}$ inch thick

2 medium fennel bulbs, sliced lengthwise, almost 1 inch thick

1 cup tomato puree

1 garlic clove, grated

$\frac{1}{2}$ tablespoon fennel seeds

$\frac{1}{2}$ cup Vegetable Broth (page 286)

Coarse salt and freshly ground black pepper

Heat the oven to 450° F.

Generously grease a deep 9-inch square baking pan with the olive oil. Line the bottom with half of the potatoes. Lay all of the fennel on top.

In a mixing bowl, combine the tomato puree, garlic, and fennel seeds. Stir in the broth, season with salt and pepper, and pour over the fennel. Top with the remaining potatoes.

Cover with foil and bake until tender, about 40 minutes. Remove the foil, turn up the heat to 475° F., and continue baking until the potatoes turn golden, about 15 minutes more.

Make up to 3 days ahead.
- *Refrigerate in a tightly sealed container. Take out of the refrigerator 2 hours ahead and serve at room temperature.*
- *To reheat, transfer to a baking dish, cover loosely with foil, and place in a 350° F. oven until warmed through.*
- *Or place in a microwavable dish and zap at medium strength, rotating the bowl 180 degrees every 2 minutes until warmed through.*

Artichokes in Lemon Sauce

SERVES 4 TO 6

VEGETARIAN ENTRÉE!
Double the portion and serve with
Carrot-Ginger Soup (page 63).

*This dish conforms with the law of ample incentive, which
states that for every unpleasant task, there must be a darned
nice treat at the end of it. Paring artichokes down to the
edible part isn't pleasant, but you can look forward to
artichoke hearts in a lemony cream sauce.*

*You can make the lemon sauce without the artichokes
and serve it over Poached Eggs Benedict–Style (page 249).*

TIME TO PREPARE (HANDS ON): *About 40 minutes*

TIME TO COOK: *About 10 minutes*

TOTAL TIME: *Just under 1 hour*

> 6 large artichokes
> 1 tablespoon unsalted butter
> 1 medium onion, chopped
> 1 garlic clove, crushed and minced
> 1/2 cup minced fresh parsley, divided
> 1 cup whole or nonfat milk
> 2 large egg yolks
> 1/4 cup fresh lemon juice

To prepare the artichokes, cut away the stem and
snap off the tough outer leaves. (This will
amount, alas, to more than half the artichoke.)
Once you're down to the light green, tender
leaves, cut the artichoke in half lengthwise. With
a melon scoop, paring knife, or teaspoon, scoop
out the fuzz at the center. Finally, cut the artichoke into quarters lengthwise, then cut each
quarter in half lengthwise again.

Fit a large pot with a steamer basket. Add
enough water to come up to the base of the
steamer. Place the artichokes in the steamer,
cover, and bring the water to a simmer over
medium-high heat. Turn the heat down to
medium-low and steam the until the artichokes
are tender enough to pierce with the tip of a paring knife, 6 to 8 minutes.

Melt the butter in a medium nonstick skillet
over medium-high heat.

Add the onion, garlic, and half of the parsley,
and sauté until the onion is soft, about 7 minutes.
Turn the heat to low.

In a large mixing bowl, stir together the milk,
egg yolks, and lemon juice. Slowly pour into the
skillet, stirring constantly to make a thick sauce,
about 10 minutes.

Add the artichokes and stir to coat with the
sauce.

- *Wrap the leftovers in a dish covered with plastic. Refrigerate. Take out of the refrigerator 2 hours ahead and
  serve at room temperature, or serve cold. Do not reheat.*

LOVE THOSE LEFTOVERS!
Make pasta: Toss room-temperature leftover
Artichokes in Lemon Sauce with hot pasta and
grated Parmesan cheese. Serve right away. Or
spoon over hot brown rice.

Chard Filled with Artichokes

SERVES 8

Whenever you entertain, it's nice to treat your guests to something they wouldn't ordinarily make for themselves.

TIME TO PREPARE (HANDS ON): *About 40 minutes*

TIME TO COOK: *About 20 minutes*

TOTAL TIME: *About 1 hour*

6 artichokes
16 large Swiss chard leaves
1 tablespoon unsalted butter
2 shallots, minced
$\frac{1}{4}$ cup minced fresh parsley
$\frac{1}{4}$ cup minced fresh chives
2 tablespoons dry white wine
$\frac{1}{4}$ cup grated Parmesan cheese
2 large eggs
1 tablespoon fresh lemon juice
Coarse salt and freshly ground black pepper

To prepare the artichokes, cut away the stem and snap off the tough outer leaves. (This will amount to more than half the artichoke.) Once you're down to the light green, tender leaves, cut the artichoke in half lengthwise. With a melon scoop, paring knife, or teaspoon, scoop out the fuzz at the center. Finally, cut the artichoke into quarters lengthwise, then cut each quarter in half lengthwise again.

Fit a large pot with a steamer basket. Add enough water to come up to the base of the steamer. Place the artichokes in the steamer, cover, and bring the water to a simmer over medium-high heat. Simmer until the artichokes are very tender, about 12 minutes. Remove them from the steamer and set aside.

Check the water level in the steamer, adding more if necessary. Place the chard leaves in the basket, cover, and bring the water to a simmer. By the time the water reaches a simmer, the leaves should be soft and pliable. If they are, lift out the steamer and set the leaves aside to cool. If not, let them steam for 1 minute longer before you take them off the heat.

Melt the butter in a medium skillet over medium-high heat. Reduce the heat to medium and add the shallots, parsley, and chives. Sauté until the shallots turn translucent, about 4 minutes. Add the artichokes and stir to coat with the herbs. Add the wine, turn up the heat to medium-high, and stir until it evaporates, about 2 minutes. Remove from the heat. Transfer the artichoke mixture to a food processor. Add the cheese and the eggs and process in short pulses just to blend, about 3 pulses.

Lay 2 chard leaves on your work surface one on top of the other. Place $\frac{1}{8}$ of the artichoke mixture in the center and roll up the leaves to enclose it, tucking the sides in before the final roll to seal it.

Return the filled leaves to the steamer basket and place inside the large pot. Cover and steam over simmering water for 5 minutes. Drizzle with lemon juice and season with salt and pepper. Serve hot.

You can steam the artichokes up to 3 days ahead.
• *Seal in a tightly covered container and refrigerate.*

Asparagus Packets

This isn't as much a recipe as assembly instructions. What you're serving is steamed asparagus and carrots with olive oil and lemon. But tie them into a bundle with chives, and you're presenting something special.

TIME TO PREPARE (HANDS ON): *About 10 minutes*

TIME TO COOK: *About 5 minutes*

TOTAL TIME: *About 30 minutes, including time to cool*

12 slender asparagus spears, firm, not wispy
1 carrot
4 long, supple chives for tying (if the chives you have aren't supple enough, dunk them in boiling water for several seconds, then pat dry), plus 1 tablespoon minced fresh chives
1 tablespoon extra virgin olive oil
1 tablespoon fresh lemon juice
Salt to taste

Trim off the bottom of each asparagus spear and cut the spear into pieces 3 inches long.

Slice the carrot into 3-inch matchsticks.

Fit a medium pot with a steamer basket. Add enough water to come up to the base of the steamer. Place the carrots in the steamer, top with the asparagus, cover, and bring the water to a simmer over medium-high heat. Turn the heat down to medium-low and steam until the asparagus turns bright green, about 2 minutes. Remove immediately, transfer to a plate, and put into the refrigerator. Continue steaming the carrots until they are tender but not mushy, 3 to 5 minutes more. Transfer to the refrigerator to cool.

When the vegetables are cool enough to handle, make 4 bundles, using an equal amount of asparagus and carrots and the chives. If the bundles are too fat to be tied with the chives, thin them out until they fit.

Tie the bundles with the chives.

Whisk together the oil, lemon juice, salt, and minced chives, and drizzle over the bundles before serving.

• *You can't make this ahead. Prepare it just before serving.*

Onions Filled with Cauliflower Soufflé

SERVES 4

Always good for a "Wow!" these onions with a creamy, light filling of cauliflower and cheddar cheese are a lot easier to prepare than you'd guess from a glance at them. They'll dress up any simple entrée.

TIME TO PREPARE (HANDS ON): *About 10 minutes*

TIME TO COOK: *About 50 minutes*

TOTAL TIME: *About 1 hour*

$\frac{1}{2}$ pound cauliflower, separated into florets
2 turnips, peeled and quartered
1 medium potato, peeled and quartered
4 medium onions, peeled and left whole
1 large egg, separated
$\frac{1}{3}$ cup shredded cheddar cheese
$\frac{1}{2}$ teaspoon ground ginger
2 teaspoons extra virgin olive oil
1 cup Vegetable Broth (page 286)

Fit a large pot with a steamer basket. Add enough water to come up to the base of the steamer. Place the cauliflower, turnips, and potato in the steamer. Cover and bring the water to a simmer over medium-high heat. Turn the heat down to medium-low and steam until the vegetables are soft enough to puree, about 20 minutes.

Fill a large pot with water and bring it to a boil. Boil the onions until the layers separate easily but don't fall apart, about 5 minutes. Let them drain and cool in a colander.

Heat the oven to 375°F.

In a food processor or blender, puree the cauliflower, turnips and potato with the egg yolk, cheese, and ginger.

Beat the egg white until stiff and fold into the cauliflower mixture.

Scoop out enough of each onion to fill them with an equal portion of cauliflower. Lightly rub the inside of each onion with olive oil. Fill with the cauliflower puree. Place the filled onions in a baking dish large enough to hold them and add enough vegetable broth to come up 1 inch on the sides. Bake for 30 minutes.

- *You can't make this ahead. Prepare it shortly before serving.*

Cauliflower Broiled with Cheese

SERVES 4

It's hard to believe anything so easy could be even half as good. All you need is fresh, snowy cauliflower and grated hard cheese.

TIME TO PREPARE (HANDS ON): *About 5 minutes*

TIME TO COOK: *About 10 minutes*

TOTAL TIME: *About 15 minutes*

1 large head cauliflower, cut in half
$1/3$ to $1/2$ cup grated Parmesan or shredded cheddar cheese

Fill a large pot with water and bring it to a boil.

Add the cauliflower and boil gently until it has cooked through, about 7 minutes. Drain in a colander.

Heat the broiler. Lightly grease a shallow flameproof baking dish with extra virgin olive oil or squirt it with nonstick spray.

Place the cauliflower inside, cut side down, and sprinkle evenly with the cheese.

Broil 2 inches from the heat until bubbly, about 3 minutes.

- *You can't make this ahead. Prepare it just before serving.*

Curry Spiced Spinach and Potatoes

Calling something "curry spiced" is really a cheat because "curry" means nothing more specific than "stew," and stew could be seasoned with just about anything. But since the stews commonly referred to as curry are Indian in origin and the spices used in this dish are frequently used to season them, the description is more or less apt. Like most dishes featuring these spices, this is best made a day or two ahead.

TIME TO PREPARE (HANDS ON): *About 30 minutes*

TIME TO COOK: *Included in the preparation time*

TOTAL TIME: *About 1 hour, including time to chill*

---

 1 tablespoon safflower oil or canola oil
 1 medium onion, chopped
 1 tablespoon grated peeled fresh ginger
 1 clove garlic, crushed and minced
 1/2 teaspoon mustard seeds
 1 teaspoon ground fenugreek
 1/2 pound fresh or canned peeled chopped tomatoes
 4 medium potatoes, peeled and cut into bite-sized pieces
 10 ounces fresh or defrosted frozen spinach, chopped
 2 tablespoons fresh lemon juice
 1 teaspoon garam masala (optional) (see Note)
 Salt and freshly ground black pepper

Heat the oil in a medium skillet. When hot, add the onion, ginger, garlic, mustard seeds, and fenugreek. Sauté until the onion has softened, about 7 minutes.

Add the tomatoes and stir well until the juice has nearly evaporated, about 2 minutes.

Add the potatoes, spinach, and enough water to keep the mixture from sticking to the pan. Cover and simmer over very low heat until the potatoes are cooked through, about 18 minutes.

Stir in the lemon juice and garam masala. Season with salt and pepper. Serve warm or at room temperature.

NOTE: Garam masala is a spice blend available at stores with a good selection of seasonings and at Indian specialty shops.

Make up to 3 days ahead.
- *Seal in a tightly covered container and refrigerate. Take out of the refrigerator 2 hours ahead and serve at room temperature. Or cover with foil and place in a 350° F. oven until warmed through. Or place in a microwavable bowl and zap at medium strength, rotating the bowl 180 degrees every 2 minutes until warmed through.*

Sauces for Curry

Use either (or both!) of these sauces to compound the flavor of any kind of curry, or serve the sauce alone over rice for a simple lunch or supper. Like most things curried, these taste best the day after they're made.

TIME TO PREPARE (HANDS ON): *About 10 minutes*

TIME TO COOK: *Included in the preparation time*

TOTAL TIME: *About 10 minutes*

Spinach Sauce

10 ounces fresh spinach or one 10-ounce
    package frozen spinach, thawed and
    squeezed dry
1 green bell pepper, cored, seeded, and
    chopped
1 tablespoon peanut oil
1 shallot, minced
1 garlic clove, crushed and minced
1 tablespoon grated peeled fresh ginger
2 tablespoons minced fresh cilantro
1 teaspoon mustard seeds
1 teaspoon ground coriander
1 teaspoon ground cumin
1 tablespoon fresh lemon juice
1/2 cup buttermilk or Vegetable Broth
    (page 286)
Coarse salt

Place the spinach and the chopped bell pepper in a saucepan, and add water to cover. Bring to a simmer over medium heat, cover, turn the heat down to medium-low, and cook until the pepper is soft enough to puree, about 5 minutes.

Using a slotted spoon, transfer the spinach and pepper to a food processor or blender, reserving the water that remains. Puree and set aside.

Heat the oil in a medium skillet. When hot, add the shallot, garlic, ginger, cilantro, mustard seeds, coriander, and cumin. Sauté on low heat until the shallot has softened, about 3 minutes.

Stir in the spinach mixture, along with the lemon juice and buttermilk or vegetable broth. If the sauce seems too dense, add as much of the reserved cooking water or additional vegetable broth as you'd like to thin it. Season with salt.

Make up to 3 days ahead.
- *Seal in a tightly covered container and refrigerate.*
- *To reheat, transfer to a heavy saucepan and stir over medium heat until warmed through. Or transfer to a microwavable bowl and microwave at full power, turning the bowl at 2-minute intervals, until heated through.*

Sweet Potato Sauce for Curry

SERVES 6

TIME TO PREPARE (HANDS ON): *About 20 minutes*

TIME TO COOK: *About 15 minutes*

TOTAL TIME: *About 45 minutes, including time to cool*

4 medium sweet potatoes, peeled and halved
1 onion, chopped, divided
2 tablespoons grated peeled fresh ginger
1 tablespoon safflower oil or canola oil
1 teaspoon ground cumin
1/2 teaspoon ground fenugreek
1 cup fresh or canned peeled chopped
    tomatoes
1/2 cup nonfat plain yogurt
Salt

In a large saucepan, place the sweet potatoes, half the onion, the ginger, and water to cover. Bring to a gentle boil over medium-high heat, cover, reduce the heat to medium, and let simmer until the sweet potatoes are cooked through, about 15 minutes. Drain the cooking water. In a food processor or using an immersion blender, puree until smooth.

Transfer to a large mixing bowl and set aside to cool.

Heat the oil in a skillet. When hot, add the remaining onion, along with the cumin and fenugreek. Sauté until the onion is soft, about 7 minutes. Add the tomatoes and continue cooking until most of the juice has evaporated, about 5 minutes.

Stir into the sweet potato mixture and let cool for 15 minutes. Stir in the yogurt and salt to taste.

Make up to 3 days ahead.
- *Seal in a tightly covered container and refrigerate.*
- *To reheat, transfer to a heavy saucepan and stir over medium heat until warmed through. Or transfer to a microwavable bowl and microwave at full power, turning the bowl at 2-minute intervals, until heated through.*

Summer Squash and Tomato Melt

Serves 4

Summer squash and zucchini get soggy when steamed. Baked, as here, they're at their best.

TIME TO PREPARE (HANDS ON): *About 10 minutes*

TIME TO COOK: *About 20 minutes*

TOTAL TIME: *About 30 minutes*

Extra virgin olive oil
$\frac{1}{2}$ cup fine breadcrumbs
$\frac{1}{3}$ cup grated Parmesan cheese
$\frac{1}{4}$ cup minced fresh basil or 1 tablespoon crumbled dried
2 medium summer squash, thinly sliced lengthwise

1 large ripe tomato, thinly sliced
2 medium zucchini, thinly sliced lengthwise

Heat the oven to 450° F.

Cut 2 pieces of parchment paper to fit a small (8-inch) baking dish or a pie plate. Place one piece inside the dish and put the other aside.

Pour several droplets of olive oil onto the paper and spread them to grease it.

In a mixing bowl, combine the breadcrumbs, Parmesan cheese, and basil.

Lay the summer squash on top of the paper and sprinkle evenly with $\frac{1}{3}$ of the breadcrumb mixture. Lay the tomato slices in a single layer on top. Sprinkle evenly with $\frac{1}{3}$ of the breadcrumb mixture. Finish with a layer of zucchini and the remaining breadcrumb mixture.

Grease the reserved sheet of parchment paper with olive oil and lay it, oiled side down, on top.

Bake until the vegetables are just cooked and the cheese has melted, about 15 minutes. Peel the parchment back carefully, scraping any cheese that sticks to it back onto the vegetables. Serve right away.

- *You can't make this ahead. Prepare it just before serving.*

Golden Baked Eggplant Custard

SERVES 6 AS A SIDE DISH

VEGETARIAN ENTRÉE!
Serve with Borscht (page 166).

If you've never had a savory bread pudding, you may well wonder what good could come of stale bread, milk, and eggs. Lots! See here!

TIME TO PREPARE (HANDS ON): *About 5 minutes*

TIME TO COOK: *About 1 hour, 10 minutes*

TOTAL TIME: *About 1 1/2 hours, including time to rest*

1 large eggplant
Extra virgin olive oil
1 large red bell pepper
4 large eggs, lightly beaten
1/2 cup milk
2/3 cup grated Parmesan cheese
1/4 cup minced fresh basil or 2 tablespoons
    crumbled dried
Salt and freshly ground black pepper to
    taste
3 cups bread chunks, crusts removed

Heat the oven to 450°F.

Slice the eggplant in half. Lightly grease a sheet of foil with olive oil, and lay the eggplant, skin side up, on the foil. Slice the bell pepper, and pull out the core and seeds. Place it, skin side up, next to the eggplant. Bake until the eggplant buckles and feels tender throughout, about 40 minutes, and the skin on the peppers chars, about 20 minutes. Remove the peppers from the oven while the eggplant finishes cooking. Set aside to cool. Turn the oven temperature down to 375°F.

Meanwhile, combine the eggs, milk, cheese, basil, and salt and pepper in a large mixing bowl. Add the bread and dunk the bread to soak it thoroughly with the egg and milk mixture.

Carefully scoop the pulp out of the eggplant, discarding as many seeds as you can and leaving the shell intact. Chop the pulp and stir into the bread mixture. Peel the pepper and chop it very fine. Add to the bread mixture and stir well to blend.

Slice the eggplant skin into lengthwise strips roughly 1/2 inch wide. Lightly grease an 8-inch round baking dish. Lay the eggplant strips in a lattice pattern on the bottom of the dish. Pour the bread mixture on top.

Bake until puffy and golden, about 40 minutes.

Let cool on a rack for 10 minutes. Using a metal spatula to loosen the edges, turn it out onto a serving plate. Slice it to serve.

Make up to 3 days ahead.
- *Wrap tightly and refrigerate. Take out of the refrigerator 2 hours ahead and serve at room temperature. Or reheat, wrapped in foil in a 350°F. oven, until warmed through. Do not microwave.*

Mushroom and Eggplant Layered with Cheese

SERVES 4

Here's a treat: eggplant and mushrooms, baked until chewy, seasoned with basil and layered with mozzarella cheese.

TIME TO PREPARE (HANDS ON): *About 10 minutes*

TIME TO COOK: *About 25 minutes*

TOTAL TIME: *About 45 minutes, including time to cool*

1 large eggplant, thinly sliced
Salt
4 large portobello mushroom caps
1 tablespoon plus 2 teaspoons extra virgin olive oil, divided
1 garlic clove, thinly sliced
2 tablespoons minced fresh basil
1 cup shredded whole milk mozzarella

Slice the eggplant into rounds $\frac{1}{4}$ inch thick. If there are lots of seeds, place the slices in a single layer on paper towels and sprinkle both sides with salt. Let sit for 30 minutes. Quickly rinse off the salt and dab off the moisture with fresh paper towels.

Heat the oven to 425°F.

Slice the mushroom caps into 4 slices each.

Lightly grease a baking sheet with olive oil. Place the eggplant and mushroom slices on the sheet and bake until they soften and start to brown, about 15 minutes. Check often and remove those pieces that are done before the others.

Meanwhile, lightly grease 4 custard cups with olive oil.

In a small nonstick skillet, heat 1 tablespoon of the oil over medium-high heat. Add the garlic. Turn the heat down to low and swish the garlic through the oil until the garlic starts to color, about 1 $\frac{1}{2}$ minutes. Strain out the garlic.

Put $\frac{1}{2}$ teaspoon of the oil into each custard cup. Place an eggplant slice on top. Top with 2 tablespoons of mozzarella and a pinch of basil. Place 2 slices of mushroom on top. Top with eggplant, then make an identical layer, ending with a slice of eggplant.

Place the custard cups in the oven and bake for about 10 minutes, to set. Transfer to a cooling rack for 10 minutes. Using a pot holder, invert the cups onto serving plates. Serve warm.

- *You can't make these ahead. Prepare just before serving.*

Stuffed Baby Pumpkins

SERVES 4

Just once during the very short season for baby pumpkins, you must make this for someone you love.

TIME TO PREPARE (HANDS ON): *About 20 minutes*

TIME TO COOK: *About 20 minutes*

TOTAL TIME: *About 40 minutes*

4 miniature pumpkins
1 tablespoon extra virgin olive oil
1 onion, chopped
2 garlic cloves, crushed and minced
$\frac{1}{4}$ cup minced fresh parsley
1 tablespoon minced fresh sage
10 ounces fresh button mushrooms, cleaned
    and chopped
$\frac{1}{2}$ cup dry breadcrumbs
$\frac{1}{4}$ teaspoon ground nutmeg
Salt and freshly ground black pepper
$\frac{1}{2}$ cup Vegetable Broth (page 286)

Heat the oven to 450°F.

Wrap each pumpkin in foil and place on a baking sheet. Bake until softened, about 20 minutes.

Unwrap the pumpkins and set aside to cool.

Meanwhile, heat the oil in a nonstick skillet over medium-high heat. When hot, add the onion, garlic, parsley, and sage. Reduce the heat to medium-low and sauté, stirring often, until the onion is soft and limp, about 7 minutes. Add the mushrooms and continue to sauté until they are soft and dark, about 7 minutes more. Remove from the heat.

Carefully slice off the top of each pumpkin and scoop out the center. Separate the seeds from the flesh, chop the flesh, and stir it into the mushroom mixture along with the breadcrumbs and nutmeg. Season with salt and pepper.

Pour the vegetable broth into a shallow baking dish and place the pumpkins inside. Cover loosely with foil and bake to heat through, about 20 minutes.

Make up to 3 days ahead.
- *Seal in a tightly covered container and refrigerate.*
- *To reheat, place on a baking sheet, cover with foil, and place in a 350°F. oven until warmed through.*

Spicy Eggplant Puree

SERVES 6

Travel where you will, and you'll find eggplant as a vehicle for the signature seasonings of wherever you happen to be eating it. In the Mediterranean you'll have it prepared with garlic and olives; in parts of China, with sesame, ginger, and spring onions; and in southern India, the spices used here.

TIME TO PREPARE (HANDS ON): *About 15 minutes*

TIME TO COOK: *About 20 minutes*

TOTAL TIME: *About 45 minutes*

2 medium eggplants, peeled and halved
1 tablespoon vegetable oil, such as canola or safflower
1 onion, chopped
6 garlic cloves, crushed and minced
2 tablespoons grated peeled fresh ginger
1 small green bell pepper, cored, seeded, and chopped
2 tablespoons mustard seeds
2 teaspoons ground cinnamon
2 teaspoons ground coriander
2 teaspoons ground cumin
1 teaspoon turmeric
3 tablespoons reduced-fat sour cream

Fit a large pot with a steamer basket. Add enough water to come up to the base of the steamer. Place the eggplants in the steamer, cover, and bring the water to a simmer over medium-high heat. Turn the heat down to medium-low and steam until the eggplants are soft enough to mash with a fork, about 20 minutes. Transfer the eggplant to a bowl to cool.

Meanwhile, heat the oil in a nonstick skillet over medium-high heat. When hot, add the onion, garlic, ginger, green pepper, and mustard seeds. Lower the heat to medium-low and sauté, stirring often, until the onion and pepper are soft and limp, about 7 minutes. Add the cinnamon, coriander, cumin, and turmeric, and stir well to blend. Turn the heat down to low.

Mash the eggplant with a fork or the back of a spoon. Drain any excess liquid. Stir the eggplant into the skillet. Add the sour cream and continue to stir until everything's well blended. Bring to a simmer over medium heat until it thickens slightly, about 5 minutes.

Make up to 3 days ahead.
• *Seal in a tightly covered container and refrigerate. Take out of the refrigerator 2 hours ahead and serve at room temperature. Or serve cold.*

Minced Ratatouille

SERVES 4

A fast, summer side dish or a filling for vegetarian Corona di Riso (page 114). Be sure the eggplant is very fresh (firm, smooth, and evenly colored), or it will be bitter. Add the chickpeas and feta for a lunch dish, with Pita Bread (page 224) and rice (page 181).

TIME TO PREPARE (HANDS ON): *About 30 minutes*

TIME TO COOK: *Included in the preparation time*

TOTAL TIME: *About 30 minutes*

- 1 tablespoon extra virgin olive oil
- 1 onion, chopped
- 2 garlic cloves, crushed and minced
- ¼ cup minced fresh basil or 1 tablespoon crumbled dried
- 2 baby eggplant, diced
- 2 slender zucchini, diced
- 2 slender summer squash, diced
- 2 tablespoons minced oil-cured black olives (optional, but encouraged!)
- 2 tablespoons balsamic vinegar
- 2 medium tomatoes, peeled, seeded, and chopped
- 1½ cups cooked chickpeas, rinsed and drained (optional)
- Coarse salt and freshly ground black pepper

FOR SERVING
- Grated Parmesan or Asiago cheese or crumbled feta cheese

Heat the oil in a nonstick skillet over medium-high heat. When hot, add the onion and garlic. Reduce the heat to medium-low and sauté, stirring often, until soft and limp, about 7 minutes. Add the basil, eggplant, zucchini, squash, and olives, if using. Sauté over medium-high heat, stirring, until the vegetables cook through, about 3 minutes. Add the balsamic vinegar, turn up the heat, and stir rapidly until most of it evaporates, about 1 minute.

Add the tomatoes, turn down the heat, and stir until they break down, about 2 minutes.

If you'd like to make a more substantial dish, add the chickpeas just after the tomatoes cook down, and stir to heat through. Season with salt and pepper. Pass the grated cheese at the table.

Make up to 3 days ahead.
- *Seal in a tightly covered container and refrigerate.*

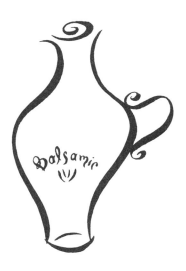

Breads

The Truth About Bread

The Truth About Bread

EVEN IF YOU BUY ALL OF THE food you serve with it, make your own bread and you have made the meal.

When you've got good bread, you have Food; everything else is just something to eat. And this is not a modern baker's homily. It's a sentiment toward bread that goes back to ancient times, when the Greeks referred to two food groups: bread and all-the-things-that-aren't-bread. Each time you pull a fully risen loaf from the oven, fragrant and golden brown, you see this makes perfect sense.

That's the romance of bread baking; here's the reality. You need time. But if it's true that how we spend our time reveals our values, you will prove yourself a person of unassailable character when you devote several hours to something that gives others such pleasure.

You need good flour. Since it's virtually the only ingredient, it's implausible to imagine you could make decent bread out of poor flour. (You wouldn't think of making jam with a batch of bad berries.)

Good flour is fresh; shop at stores with rapid turnover in the baking goods department. Or order it directly from the mill or distributor. Good bread flour is high in gluten, the protein that reacts with yeast to build a thriving, pliant dough. Low-gluten flours make a sticky wad that won't rise much, yielding a tough, heavy loaf in the end. Most whole wheat flour has insufficient gluten to make good bread without some white flour in the mix. (King Arthur brand whole wheat is an exception. It is has an uncommonly high gluten content, and makes fine bread on its own. See page 347.)

NO TIME TO BAKE? ASK THE EXPERT: HOW TO BUY BREAD

Peter Reinhart, founder of Brother Juniper's Bakery in Santa Rosa, California, and author of the inspiring and rewarding *Brother Juniper's Bread Book*, among others, gave my then-fiancé and me our first engagement gift. We had gotten engaged in Sonoma, California, and left for Santa Rosa the next day. I had met Peter at a book signing in L.A. a week before, and promised I'd stop by if I ever made it up to his neighborhood. I had no idea it would be so soon, the trip to Sonoma and the engagement being entirely impulsive. We found him at his bakery, told him our news, watched him vanish, then reappear with a fresh "stromboli," a heavily herbed, pizza-style bread that was a house special. Making bread is for Peter, as for all true bakers, a way of sharing the things that sustain us—food, warmth, and love.

Peter offers this advice to those in search of Real Bread:

- Look for a bakery that calls itself "artisan," "village," or "European style," one of the new breed of bakeries in this country devoted to real bread. A true artisan bakery is distinguished by beautiful, crusty breads, usually baked on a stone or brick hearth and made with care, not speed. The best ferment their dough overnight, or at least 4 to 6 hours.
- Once you tear open or slice a loaf you'll discover how well the bread has been made. Fermented dough will taste creamy and fresh, and will have large irregular holes rather than the uniform holes you find in

machine-made bread. Sandwich-style loaves should have a richer color and creamier crumb than what you'd find elsewhere.

How you can tell if a loaf is fresh before you buy it? If you buy plastic-wrapped bread at a bakery within a supermarket, read the "pull by" dates on the tags (the date the supermarket should remove the bread from the shelves), or learn the code for the color tags that indicate the "pull by" day of the week (green Monday, blue Tuesday, etc.). Often stores put the oldest bread at the front to encourage you to take it. Reach behind it to check whether those in back are fresher. If you buy paper-wrapped bread that's delivered to your store from a bakery, find out what days they make the deliveries and buy the bread on those days only—usually it's only two days out of the week.

How can you tell if a bread will be good? Read the label. Ingredients are listed from largest quantity to smallest, which should give you some indication of the dominant flavor. Also, if you find a number of chemical names or ingredients labeled "conditioner," the bread is made for endurance, not enjoyment.

Try to smell it (plastic wrap can make this difficult). A good bread will smell fresh and wheaty, or have the pleasant aroma of whatever special ingredients are involved (such as sesame seeds, cinnamon, or black olives). And if a hearth-style bread retains an attractive, crackly crust, it is a sign that it will taste good.

How to Store Bread at Home

Under three days: Keep the bread covered, in a cool, dark place, such as a bread box, not the refrigerator, where it will dry out.

More than three days: Freeze the bread, wrapped well in aluminum foil. Defrost it on the countertop, still wrapped. Heating it, unwrapped, for a few minutes in a preheated 350° to 400° F. oven will help bring out its optimal flavor and texture, and recrisp the crust. You may also heat it wrapped in foil while it is still completely or partially frozen, until it is warm throughout, then unwrap it at the end so the crust gets crisp.

Breads That Keep Best

The less fat in the bread, the sooner it goes stale. Butter, eggs, whole milk, and other sources of fat help breads stay moist. Since most French bread and sourdough contain nothing but flour, water, and salt, you can't expect to keep them long, so buy that type of bread the day you plan to eat it. If the bread's good enough, you won't have to worry how long the leftovers will keep.

You need good salt to bring out the flavor in the flour. Bread made without salt is hopelessly bland. You'll get more flavor with less sodium if you use sea salt, which is "saltier" than plain table salt.

It's nice (but not necessary) to have a baking stone or clay tiles. The stone absorbs moisture from the bread, so the crust turns crisp.

For loaves that are beautifully split on the top, have a razor blade handy.

About Yeast

Active dry yeast: This is the most common form of commercial yeast, although instant yeast (see below) is easier to use. Before you proceed with a bread recipe, you have to "proof" active dry yeast, i.e., dissolve it in warm water, sometimes along with sugar, and wait for it to get creamy and for small bubbles to form. The bubbles are the "proof" that the yeast is alive and breathing. If you see no such proof, try again with a fresh packet.

Instant yeast: "Instant" does *not* refer to the time it takes the bread to rise. Rather, it means you can mix the yeast with the flour and water, without first dissolving it and waiting for it to "proof." Instant yeast is potent, so use less per recipe than active dry. But without the proofing stage you will have to trust that the yeast is active. With either kind of yeast, be sure to check the expiration date on the package.

Rapid-rise yeast: If you want your bread to rise faster, you can try rapid-rise yeast. Read the instructions on the packet and follow them as you proceed with any bread recipe. Be aware that breads made with rapid-rise may taste of raw yeast. Consequently, you may want to use it only in dough or batter for things full of other flavors, such as calzone, and yeast-raised waffles that will be covered with syrup or a sauce.

▶

Real Bread

MAKES ABOUT 20 SUBSTANTIAL SLICES

It's been proven that you can make a perfectly fine human being in a test tube, but baking good bread in a machine is another matter.

As far as anyone can tell, in vitro babies aren't adversely affected by the sterile nature of their conception. But yeast and flour coldly thrust into a chamber to incubate don't thrive as they do when kneaded in the open air by the nurturing hands of someone who cares. Since sales of machines and special mixes continue apace, it's clear that many people are happy enough with the bread they make in them. But there are others who have given it every chance, only to affirm what they've always believed: The best bread comes from the hands and heart working as one. It requires time and tranquillity, rare commodities, to be sure; but it's bread you're making, and you'll enjoy not only sustenance but a triumphant sense of self-sufficiency in the end.

TIME TO PREPARE (HANDS ON): *About 20 minutes, with a food processor*

TIME TO BAKE: *About 35 minutes*

TOTAL TIME: *About 20 hours, including time for the sponge to ferment*

---

1 teaspoon active dry yeast
1 cup warm water (98° to 115°F.)
1 cup bread flour or unbleached all-purpose flour

In a large mixing bowl, stir the yeast, water, and flour together until smooth.

Cover with plastic wrap and set aside for 4 to 24 hours. (If you're leaving it for more than 6 hours, put it in the refrigerator.)

All of the sponge from above
$\frac{1}{2}$ teaspoon active dry yeast
1 $\frac{1}{2}$ teaspoons coarse salt
Approximately 3 cups bread flour or unbleached all-purpose flour

In a food processor or heavy-duty mixer fitted with a dough hook (or a large mixing bowl), put the sponge, active dry yeast, $\frac{1}{2}$ cup water, salt, and 3 cups of flour.

Run the processor or mixer, or stir by hand,

until the ingredients form a dough that's soft but not sticky. This will take about 90 seconds in the processor, 5 to 7 minutes in the mixer, and up to 15 minutes by hand.

Turn the dough out onto a lightly floured surface. Knead until it's smooth and springy, about 5 minutes. You'll have to add some flour to keep it from sticking to your hands. Add as little as possible. (You may also use an electric mixer with a dough hook.)

Shape the dough into a ball and place it in a large mixing bowl. Cover with plastic wrap and set aside in a warm, draft-free place for 2 hours, until doubled in size.

Press the air out of the dough. Cover it with plastic wrap again and let it rise for 45 minutes to 1 hour.

Press the air out of the dough again and divide it into 2 pieces. Working with one piece at a time, flatten it into a rectangle about 10 inches long (horizontal) and 6 inches wide (vertical). Fold the upper right-hand corner to the center. Fold the lower left-hand corner up to meet it. Now fold the dough in half diagonally, bringing the upper portion down and making a seam along the bottom. Put it seam side down on a baking sheet *or* seam side up on a floured towel inside a French loaf pan. Cover with a towel and let rise for 40 minutes.

Meanwhile, heat the oven to 450°F.

When you're ready to bake the bread, make a few diagonal slashes with a razor blade or very sharp knife on the loaves on the baking sheet, put them in the oven, and, using a plant spritzer or your hand and a bowl of water, lightly splash some water onto the oven floor to make steam. Or carefully turn the loaves from the towels onto a baking sheet or baking stone, slash them, then put them in the oven, spritzing or splashing water onto the oven floor. Close the oven door. After 1 minute, spritz or splash more water onto the oven floor.

Bake until golden and you get a hollow sound when you tap on the bottom of the bread, about 25 minutes. If the top of the bread is browning too quickly, cover it loosely with foil until it's done.

Let the bread cool on a rack for 20 minutes before you slice it.

NOTE: What do you do with a burnt crust? Run a cheese grater over the blackened parts and scrape it away.

Freeze the dough up to 1 week. Wrap in plastic and seal in a zip-lock bag. Leave at room temperature to thaw and use as soon as it's thawed. Do not refreeze or refrigerate.

- *Slice the bread before freezing so you can toast individual pieces. Store the slices in zip-lock bags, pressing out the air before you seal. Do not defrost before toasting.*

- *To defrost and reheat without toasting, wrap in foil, place on a baking sheet or stone, and place in a 350°F. oven until heated through. To defrost in a hurry, soak a paper towel in water. Wring out as much moisture as possible and wrap around the bread. Microwave at full power for 45 seconds to 1 minute. Let rest for 30 seconds, then feel if it's warm inside. If it's still frozen, return to the microwave and zap at 20-second intervals until heated through. Eat right away or it will be impossibly tough.*

Bagels

MAKES 8

Wherever you may live, chances are you can go out your door, head for several blocks in either direction, and buy a dozen bagels. Why, then, would you bother making them from scratch?

Most of the purported bagels sold today are nothing but rolls with a hole in the center. When you bite into a genuine bagel, it should yield just short of chipping your teeth; it should be very dense and chewy, and a bit sweet. Eating a good bagel ought to occupy the better part of a morning, making it perhaps the best part of the morning!

What distinguishes a genuine bagel from the rest is (1) High-gluten bread flour. This flour makes the bread chewy instead of pasty. Most packaged commercial bagels use little, if any, high-gluten flour, which is why they're so uninteresting. You can find it at supermarkets that carry a good variety of baking ingredients, or you can get it by mail (see page 347).

(2) Before baking they are briefly boiled in water and barley malt syrup. This makes the crust shiny and sweet, and keeps the bagels from rising too much when they're baking. Many large commercial bakeries brush their dough with malt syrup and water, which makes them shine but does not make them bagels.

TIME TO PREPARE (HANDS ON): *About 20 minutes, in a food processor*

TIME TO COOK: *About 30 minutes*

TOTAL TIME: *Under 4 hours, including time for the dough to rise*

---

2 teaspoons active dry yeast *or* 1 teaspoon
  instant yeast
1 tablespoon brown sugar

Approximately 1 $\frac{1}{4}$ cups warm water (98° to
  115° F.)
3 $\frac{1}{4}$ cups high-gluten bread flour (see
  Sources, page 347)
2 teaspoons salt
Vegetable oil, for greasing pan
2 tablespoons malt syrup

If you're using active dry yeast, dissolve the yeast and sugar in $\frac{1}{4}$ cup of warm water, and let sit until creamy and bubbly, 3 to 5 minutes.

Place the flour and salt in the work bowl of a food processor or Mixmaster fitted with a dough hook. Process in short pulses to combine. With the machine running, add the yeast mixture and remaining 1 cup of water, processing until a dough forms.

If you're using instant yeast, place the yeast, sugar, 3 $\frac{1}{4}$ cups flour, and salt in the work bowl of a food processor or Mixmaster fitted with a dough hook. Process in short pulses to combine. With the machine running, add 1 $\frac{1}{4}$ cups of the warm water, processing until a dough forms.

Let the food processor run for about 90 seconds. Let the Mixmaster run for about 10 to 12 minutes. Feel the dough after $\frac{1}{2}$ the time: If it seems dry and crumbly, add 2 tablespoons of water and resume processing. If it's too sticky to handle, add 2 tablespoons to $\frac{1}{4}$ cup flour, and process again until you're able to shape the dough into a ball that's soft and pliant but won't stick to your hands.

Shape the dough into a ball and place in a large ceramic bowl. Cover with plastic wrap and refrigerate for 1 hour. The dough will be puffy but not doubled.

Place a sheet of parchment paper over a baking sheet. (I strongly recommend a Cushionaire sheet for this. See About Those Appliances . . . , page 340.) Grease the paper lightly with vegetable oil.

Press down the dough and turn it out onto a lightly floured flat work surface. (If you're using a marble countertop or slab, you may not need to flour it.) Divide the dough into 6 even-sized pieces. Cover 4 of the pieces while you work with 2.

Roll one piece of dough into a cigar shape about 4 inches long. Set it aside to rest while you do the same with the other piece. Going back and forth between pieces, stretch each piece to a wide strand of about 8 inches. (The reason for working with 2 pieces at a time, going back and forth between them, is to let the gluten in each rest so the dough won't spring back at you as you stretch and shape it.)

Finally, wrap the strand of dough around the 4 fingers of your hand, overlapping the ends of the strand by 1 inch over your palm. Press the ends together, then put your hand flat on your work surface and roll the dough under your palm to seal the circle. Pull your hand out so that the bagel lies flat. Carefully transfer it to the parchment-lined baking sheet and cover loosely with plastic wrap. Your first bagel may be lopsided—fat on one side, then narrow near the seal. But with practice you'll manage to even things out. Repeat until you've shaped all of the bagels.

Heat the oven to 425°F.

Fill a stockpot with water. Bring to a boil and add the malt syrup. Stir well. Carefully pick up a bagel and place it in the boiling water. Add 2 more, boiling 3 at a time. Boil on one side for 1½

minutes, then gently turn over with tongs or a slotted spoon and boil the other side for 1½ minutes. Using a slotted spoon, remove the bagels, one at a time. As you lift each out, hold a paper towel folded to double or triple thickness under the spoon so the bagel can drain. Gently slide each onto the parchment.

Bake until the bagels are golden brown and crusty, about 20 minutes. Turn them over after the first 10 minutes of baking to ensure even browning. Cool on a wire rack, and serve warm or at room temperature.

DO TRY THIS AT HOME:
Try this dough in place of conventional calzone dough. Make one of the fillings for calzone (see page 230). Once you have divided the dough into 6 pieces, working with one at a time, roll it out into an oblong about 7 inches long and 5 inches across. Place ⅙ of the filling just below the center and fold the top over to encase it. Seal the edges with a fork. Bring the water to a boil as directed above, add the malt syrup, and proceed from there, boiling and baking as for the bagels.

Freeze up to 6 months. Store in zip-lock bags, pressing out the air before you seal.

- *To defrost, soak a paper towel in water. Wring out as much moisture as possible and wrap around the bagel. Microwave at full power for 30 seconds. Split and toast.*
- *Or wrap in foil and place in a 350°F. oven until thawed enough to split and toast.*

Pretzels

MAKES 6

Not tooth-cracking, thirst-making, salt-sprinkled snacks, but soft rolls that are best served warm, especially with soup. The origins are obscure, but it's said that the shape is meant to represent arms at prayer, suggesting that twisted pretzels (like Champagne!) were created by monks. The best soft pretzels are boiled in a baking soda solution before they're baked, for a crispy crust and chewy center.

TIME TO PREPARE (HANDS ON): *About 20 minutes, in a food processor*

TIME TO COOK: *About 30 minutes*

TOTAL TIME: *Under 4 hours, including time for the dough to rise*

> 1 tablespoon active dry yeast or 2 teaspoons instant yeast
> 1 tablespoon brown sugar
> Approximately ½ cup warm water (98° to 115°F.)
> Approximately 3½ cups bread flour or unbleached all-purpose flour
> 2 teaspoons coarse salt
> 1 cup room-temperature buttermilk
> Vegetable oil, for greasing pan
> 1 tablespoon baking soda
> Coarse salt (optional)

If you're using active dry yeast, dissolve the yeast and sugar in ¼ cup warm water, and let sit until creamy with small bubbles, 3 to 5 minutes.

Place the flour and salt in the work bowl of a food processor or Mixmaster fitted with a dough hook. Process in short pulses to combine. With the machine running, add the yeast mixture, but-termilk, and remaining water, processing until a dough forms.

If you're using instant yeast, place the yeast, sugar, flour, and salt in the work bowl of a food processor or Mixmaster fitted with a dough hook. Process in short pulses to combine. With the machine running, add the buttermilk and water, processing until a dough forms.

Let the food processor run for about 90 seconds. Let the Mixmaster run for about 10 to 12 minutes. Feel the dough about halfway through the mixing time. If it seems dry and crumbly, add 2 tablespoons of water and resume processing. If it's too sticky to handle, add 2 tablespoons to ¼ cup flour, and process again until you're able to shape the dough into a ball that's soft and pliant but won't stick to your hands.

Shape the dough into a ball and place in a large ceramic bowl. Cover with plastic wrap and refrigerate for 1 hour.

Place a sheet of parchment paper over a baking sheet. (I strongly recommend a Cushionaire sheet for this. See About Those Appliances . . . , page 340.) Grease the paper lightly with vegetable oil.

Press down the dough and turn it out onto a lightly floured flat work surface. (If you're using a marble countertop or slab, you may not need to flour it.) Divide the dough into 6 even-sized pieces. Cover 4 of the pieces while you work with 2.

Roll one piece of dough into a cigar shape about 4 inches long. Set it aside to rest while you do the same with the other piece. Going back and forth between pieces, stretch each piece to a wide strand of about 8 inches. (The reason for working with 2 pieces at a time, going back and forth between them, is to let the gluten in each rest, so the dough won't spring back at you as you stretch and shape.) Twist into a pretzel shape.

Repeat until you've shaped all of the pretzels. Heat the oven to 425°F.

Fill a stockpot with water. Bring to a boil and add the baking soda. Stir well. Carefully pick up a pretzel and place it in the boiling water. Add another, boiling 2 at a time. Boil on one side for 1½ minutes, then gently turn over with tongs or a slotted spoon and boil the other side for 1½ minutes. Using a slotted spoon, remove the pretzels, one at a time. As you lift each out, hold a paper towel folded to double or triple thickness under the spoon so it can drain. Gently slide each onto the parchment. Sprinkle with coarse salt, if you'd like.

Bake until the pretzels are golden brown and crusty, about 20 minutes. Cool on a wire rack and serve warm or at room temperature.

Freeze up to 6 months. Store in zip-lock bags, pressing out the air before you seal.

- *To reheat, wrap in foil and place in a 350°F. oven until soft and warm.*

Cinnamon Raisin Bread

The aroma will tempt you to eat it straight from the oven, but if you can manage the restraint to save a loaf overnight, you will enjoy perhaps the best toast you've ever had.

TIME TO PREPARE (HANDS ON): *About 20 minutes, with a food processor*

TIME TO BAKE: *About 35 minutes*

TOTAL TIME: *Just under 4 hours, including time for dough to rise*

1 cup raisins
2 tablespoons active dry yeast or
　1 tablespoon instant yeast
½ cup brown sugar
4 cups bread flour or unbleached all-
　purpose flour
2 cups whole wheat flour
1 tablespoon ground cinnamon
1 tablespoon coarse salt
⅔ cup buttermilk

Put 1 cup of water in a small saucepan. Bring to a boil. Add the raisins and simmer 1 minute. Remove from the heat and let sit until soft and plump, about 5 minutes. Strain, reserving the warm water and the raisins.

If you're using active dry yeast, dissolve the yeast and 1 tablespoon of the sugar in ¼ cup of the warm raisin water, and let sit until creamy with small bubbles, about 5 minutes.

Place the bread flour, whole wheat flour, remaining sugar, cinnamon, and salt in the work bowl of a food processor or Mixmaster fitted with a dough hook. Process in short pulses to combine. With the machine running, add the yeast mixture, remaining raisin water, buttermilk, and raisins, processing until a dough forms, about 90 seconds for a food processor, 5 to 7 minutes for a mixer.

Or mix the ingredients by hand in a large bowl, adding them in the same order given. Stir until you have a dough that is soft, but firm enough to handle.

If you're using instant yeast, place the yeast, sugar, bread flour, whole wheat flour, cinnamon, and salt in the work bowl of a food processor or Mixmaster fitted with a dough hook. Process in short pulses to combine. With the machine running, add the warm raisin water, buttermilk, and raisins, processing until a dough forms, about 90 seconds for a food processor, 5 to 7 minutes for a mixer.

Or mix the ingredients by hand in a large bowl, adding them in the same order given. Stir until you have a dough that is soft, but firm enough to handle.

Continue kneading with the machine until the dough is smooth and springy. Or, to enjoy the pleasure of kneading, turn the dough out onto a lightly floured surface and do it yourself, about 10 minutes. (You'll have to add some flour to keep it from sticking to your hands. Add as little as possible.)

Shape the dough into a ball and place in a large ceramic bowl. Cover with plastic wrap or a light towel. Let rise in a warm, draft-free place until doubled in bulk, about 2 hours. Meanwhile, lightly grease three 9-inch loaf pans.

Press the air out of the dough. Divide the dough into 3 equal-sized pieces. Shape each piece of dough to fit a loaf pan by rolling or pressing it into a rectangle about 10 inches long and 6 inches wide. Roll it up lengthwise, making a seam along the bottom. Tuck the ends under toward the seam and pinch to seal. Gently roll the loaf back and forth to smooth the seal at the seams. Place seam side down in the loaf pan and cover with a light towel. Let rest until the dough rises above the sides of the pan, about 40 minutes.

Bake for 30 to 35 minutes. Tilt the pans to remove the breads. Tap the bottoms; if the loaves sound hollow, place on a wire rack to cool. (Or stick each loaf with an instant-read thermometer. If the gauge hits 200° F., it's done.) If neither sign indicates they are done, return to the oven on a baking sheet or stone, testing every 5 minutes until they're baked. If the top seems about to burn, cover loosely with foil.

- *Slice before freezing in zip-lock bags so you can toast individual pieces.*
- *Do not defrost before toasting.*

Cinnamon Raisin Bagels

Once the dough has risen for the second time, divide it into 10 pieces. Shape, boil, and bake according to the instructions on pages 214–215, adding the 2 tablespoons barley malt syrup to the boiling water.

Chocolate Bread

SERVES 8

Not cake, but real bread, honest and true, and perfect for toast, buttered, with orange marmalade or raspberry jam. For the richest flavor, use the darkest cocoa you can find (see page 347).

TIME TO PREPARE (HANDS ON): *About 15 minutes*

TIME TO COOK: *About 35 minutes*

TOTAL TIME: *About 3½ hours, including time for the dough to rise*

1 tablespoon active dry yeast or 2 teaspoons instant yeast

¼ cup sugar

1¼ cups warm water (98° to 115°F.)

Approximately 3¼ cups bread flour or unbleached all-purpose flour

1 teaspoon salt

½ cup unsweetened cocoa powder

1 large egg yolk

1¼ cups buttermilk

If you're using active dry yeast, dissolve the yeast and 1 tablespoon of the sugar in ¼ cup warm water, and let sit until creamy with small bubbles, about 5 minutes.

Place the flour, salt, cocoa powder, egg yolk, and buttermilk in the work bowl of a food processor or Mixmaster fitted with a dough hook. Process in short pulses to combine. With the machine running, add the yeast mixture and remaining 1 cup of warm water, processing until a dough forms, about 90 seconds for a food processor, 5 to 7 minutes for a mixer.

Or mix the ingredients by hand in a large bowl, adding them in the same order given. Stir until you have a dough that is soft, but firm enough to handle.

If you're using instant yeast, place the yeast, sugar, flour, salt, cocoa powder, egg yolk, and buttermilk in the work bowl of a food processor or Mixmaster fitted with a dough hook. Process in short pulses to combine. With the machine running, add 1¼ cups of warm water, processing until a dough forms, about 90 seconds for a food processor, 5 to 7 minutes for a mixer.

Or mix the ingredients by hand in a large bowl, adding them in the same order given. Stir until you have a dough that is soft, but firm enough to handle.

Continue kneading with the machine until the dough is smooth and springy. Or turn the dough out onto a lightly floured surface and do it yourself, about 10 minutes. (You'll have to add some flour to keep it from sticking to your hands. Add as little as possible.)

Shape the dough into a ball and place in a large ceramic bowl. Cover with plastic wrap or a light towel. Let rise in a warm, draft-free place until doubled in bulk, about 2 hours. Meanwhile, lightly grease a 9-inch loaf pan.

Press the air out of the dough. Shape the dough to fit the loaf pan by rolling or pressing it into a rectangle about 10 inches long and 6 inches wide. Roll it up lengthwise, making a seam along the bottom. Tuck the ends under toward the seam and pinch to seal. Gently roll the loaf back and forth to smooth the seal at the seams. Place the loaf seam side down in the loaf pan and cover with a light towel. Let rest until the dough rises above the sides of the pan, about 40 minutes.

▶

Bake for 30 to 35 minutes. Tilt the pan to remove the bread. Tap the bottom; if the loaf sounds hollow, place on a wire rack to cool. (Or stick the loaf with an instant-read thermometer. If the gauge hits 200°F., it's done.) If neither sign indicates it's done, return to the oven on a baking sheet or stone, testing every 5 minutes until it's baked. If the top seems about to burn, cover loosely with foil.

- *You can refrigerate the dough up to 1 day. Wrap in wax paper, then plastic or a zip-lock bag. Shape into a loaf straight from the refrigerator. (It will take longer to rise in the pan, but that's okay.)*
- *You can freeze the dough up to 1 month. Wrap in wax paper, then plastic or a zip-lock bag. Leave at room temperature to thaw and use as soon as it's thawed.*
- *Slice before freezing so you can toast individual pieces. Store the slices in zip-lock bags, pressing out the air before you seal. Do not defrost before toasting.*

Peanut Butter Bread

MAKES 10 SLICES

The obvious point of this bread is to cut it into shapes with cookie cutters and top with jelly as a pass at providing something nourishing before the cake at children's birthday parties. The surprise is that you'll like it, too, especially toasted and spread with honey.

TIME TO PREPARE (HANDS ON): *About 15 minutes, with a food processor*

TIME TO COOK: *About 35 minutes*

TOTAL TIME: *Just under 4 hours, including time for the dough to rise*

1 tablespoon active dry yeast or 2 teaspoons instant yeast

$1/4$ cup brown sugar

Approximately $1 1/4$ cups warm water (98° to 115°F.)

$3 1/2$ cups bread flour or unbleached all-purpose flour

6 tablespoons unsalted smooth peanut butter

1 teaspoon salt

If you're using active dry yeast, dissolve the yeast and 1 tablespoon of the sugar in $1/4$ cup warm water, and let sit until creamy with small bubbles, about 5 minutes.

Place the flour, remaining sugar, peanut butter, and salt in the work bowl of a food processor or Mixmaster fitted with a dough hook. Process in short pulses to combine. With the machine running, add the yeast mixture and remaining 1 cup of warm water, processing until a dough forms, about 90 seconds for a food processor, 5 to 7 minutes for a mixer.

If you're using instant yeast, place the yeast, sugar, flour, peanut butter, and salt in the work bowl of a food processor or Mixmaster fitted with a dough hook. Process in short pulses to combine. With the machine running, add 1¼ cups of water, processing until a dough forms, about 90 seconds for a food processor, 5 to 7 minutes for a mixer.

Continue kneading with the machine until the dough is smooth and springy. Or, to enjoy the pleasure of kneading, turn the dough out onto a lightly floured surface and do it yourself, about 10 minutes. (You'll have to add some flour to keep it from sticking to your hands. Add as little as possible.)

Shape the dough into a ball and place in a large ceramic bowl. Cover with plastic wrap or a light towel. Let rise in a warm, draft-free place until doubled in bulk, about 2 hours.

Press the air out of the dough. Lightly grease a 9-inch loaf pan. Shape the dough to fit the loaf pan by rolling or pressing it into a rectangle about 10 inches long and 6 inches wide. Roll it up lengthwise, making a seam along the bottom. Tuck the ends under toward the seam and pinch to seal. Gently roll the loaf back and forth to smooth the seal at the seams. Place seam side down in the loaf pan and cover with a light towel. Let rest in a warm, draft-free place until the dough rises above the sides of the pan, about 40 minutes.

Bake for 30 to 35 minutes. Tilt the pan to remove the bread. Tap the bottom; if the loaf sounds hollow, place it on a wire rack to cool. (Or stick the loaf with an instant-read thermometer. If the gauge hits 200°F., it's done.) If neither sign indicates it's done, return to the oven on a baking sheet or stone, testing every 5 minutes until it's baked. If the top seems about to burn, cover loosely with foil.

- *You can refrigerate the dough up to 1 day. Wrap in wax paper, then plastic or a zip-lock bag. Shape into a loaf straight from the refrigerator. (It will take longer to rise in the pan, but that's okay.)*
- *You can freeze the dough up to 1 month. Wrap in wax paper, then plastic or a zip-lock bag. Leave at room temperature to thaw and use as soon as it's thawed.*
- *Slice before freezing, so you can toast individual pieces. Store the slices in zip-lock bags, pressing out the air before you seal. Do not defrost before toasting.*

Fruit Bread

MAKES ABOUT 20 SLICES

Like the Chocolate Bread on page 219 this is not cake or even close, but a real bread to serve with salads, egg dishes, or cheese. When cherries are in season, it's worth the pain of pitting them to make a loaf or two. The fruit bursts during baking, spreading flavor and moisture throughout the loaf.

TIME TO PREPARE (HANDS ON): *About 20 minutes, with a food processor*

TIME TO COOK: *About 40 minutes*

TOTAL TIME: *About 21 hours, including time for the sponge to ferment*

---

1 recipe **Real Bread** (page 212), made through the first rising
2 to 3 cups seedless grapes (see Note) or pitted cherries

Push the air out of the dough and cut into 2 pieces. Roll each out on a lightly floured surface to a disk about 8 inches in diameter. Alternate rolling between one and the other, giving the gluten a chance to rest so it will roll out more easily each time you return to it.

Spread the fruit evenly over one of the disks. Place the other disk on top, pinch the edges to seal them, and roll the rolling pin lightly over the top to press the fruit into the dough. If you're using a baking stone, place the loaf on a well-floured baker's peel to rise. Otherwise, place it on a nonstick baking sheet. Cover with a light-weight towel. Let it rise in a warm, draft-free place until puffy, about 40 minutes.

About 30 minutes before baking, heat the oven to 450° F.

Bake until golden brown and hollow sounding when you tap it on the bottom, about 30 to 40 minutes. If it seems to be browning too fast, cover loosely with foil.

Let cool on a rack at least 20 minutes before slicing and serving.

NOTE: Taste them to make sure they're very sweet. Concord grapes are wonderful in this, although you'll probably have to seed them yourself.

- *Slice the bread before freezing so you can toast individual pieces. Store the slices in zip-lock bags, pressing out the air before you seal. Do not defrost before toasting.*
- *To defrost and reheat without toasting, wrap in foil, place on a baking sheet or stone, and place in a 350° F. oven until heated through. To defrost in a hurry, soak a paper towel in water. Wring out as much moisture as possible and wrap around the bread. Microwave at full power for 45 seconds to 1 minute. Let rest for 30 seconds, then feel if it's warm inside. If it's still frozen, return to the microwave and zap at 20-second intervals until heated through. Eat right away or it will be impossibly tough.*

Pane al Latte

MAKES ABOUT 30 SLICES

It's odd that in Italy at least this bread is so popular at Easter: One bite, and you know you're sinning. Light and sweet, it has that melting quality that has only one source on this earth: butter.

TIME TO PREPARE (HANDS ON): *About 20 minutes, with a food processor*

TIME TO BAKE: *About 40 minutes*

TOTAL TIME: *Just under 4 hours, including time for dough to rise*

1 tablespoon active dry yeast or 2 teaspoons instant yeast

$\frac{1}{3}$ cup sugar

1$\frac{1}{2}$ cups nonfat milk, warmed to 98° to 115°F.

4 cups unbleached all-purpose flour

1 large egg

$\frac{1}{4}$ cup ($\frac{1}{2}$ stick) unsalted butter, cut into chunks

1 teaspoon salt

FOR THE GLAZE

1 large egg

$\frac{1}{4}$ cup nonfat milk

If you're using active dry yeast, dissolve the yeast and 1 tablespoon of sugar in $\frac{1}{4}$ cup of the warm milk, and let sit until creamy with tiny bubbles, about 5 minutes.

Place the flour, remaining sugar, egg, butter, and salt in the work bowl of a food processor or Mixmaster fitted with a dough hook. Process in short pulses to combine. With the machine running, add the yeast mixture and the remaining milk, processing until a dough forms, about 90 seconds for a food processor, 5 to 7 minutes for a mixer.

Or mix the ingredients by hand in a large bowl, adding them in the same order given. Stir until you have a dough that is soft, but firm enough to handle.

If you're using instant yeast, place the yeast, flour, sugar, egg, butter, and salt in the work bowl of a food processor or Mixmaster fitted with a dough hook. Process in short pulses to combine. With the machine running, add the milk, processing until a dough forms, about 90 seconds for a food processor, 5 to 7 minutes for a mixer.

Or mix the ingredients by hand in a large bowl, adding them in the same order given. Stir until you have a dough that is soft, but firm enough to handle.

Continue kneading with the machine until the dough is smooth and springy. Or, to enjoy the pleasure of kneading, turn the dough out onto a lightly floured surface and do it yourself, about 10 minutes. (You'll have to add some flour to keep it from sticking to your hands. Add as little as possible.)

Shape the dough into a ball and place in a large ceramic bowl. Cover with plastic wrap or a light towel. Let rise in a warm, draft-free place until doubled in bulk, about 1$\frac{1}{2}$ hours.

Press the air out of the dough and knead lightly by hand until smooth, about 5 minutes. Divide the dough into 2 pieces of equal size. Working with one piece at a time, use your hands to roll the dough into 2 long fat strands about 12 inches long and 3 inches wide. Twist them to-

▶

gether, overlapping the strands at the top and coiling them around each other, pinching the dough to seal at both ends. Place on a well-floured baking sheet and cover with a light towel.

Using a fork, beat together the egg and milk. Brush over the loaf and bake until golden, about 30 to 40 minutes. Remove the loaf from the baking sheet and let cool on a wire rack.

- *Slice the bread before freezing so you can toast individual pieces. Store the slices in zip-lock bags, pressing out the air before you seal. Do not defrost before toasting.*
- *To defrost and reheat without toasting, wrap in foil, place on a baking sheet or stone, and place in a 350° F. oven until heated through. To defrost in a hurry, soak a paper towel in water. Wring out as much moisture as possible and wrap around the bread. Microwave at full power for 45 seconds to 1 minute. Let rest for 30 seconds, then feel if it's warm inside. If it's still frozen, return to the microwave and zap at 20-second intervals until heated through. Eat right away or it will be impossibly tough.*

Pita Bread

MAKES 8

"Pita bread," "pocket bread," call it what you will, you will also appreciate finding that it can be far more than a bland receptacle for sandwich fillings. A small amount of protein-rich soy flour enhances the gluten, making soft dough and supple bread with distinctive flavor. Made of ground soybeans, soy flour is available wherever there's a good selection of flours (see Sources, page 347).

TIME TO PREPARE (HANDS ON): *About 20 minutes, with a food processor*

TIME TO COOK: *About 6 minutes each*

TOTAL TIME: *Just under 4 hours, including time for the dough to rise*

> 2 teaspoons active dry yeast or 1 teaspoon instant yeast
> 1 teaspoon brown sugar
> Approximately $\frac{1}{2}$ cup warm water (98° to 115° F.)
> Approximately 3$\frac{1}{4}$ cups unbleached all-purpose flour
> 2 tablespoons soy flour
> 2 teaspoons coarse salt
> $\frac{3}{4}$ cup room-temperature buttermilk or nonfat yogurt (stir yogurt well to thin it before adding)
> Vegetable oil, for greasing pan

If you're using active dry yeast, dissolve the yeast and sugar in $\frac{1}{4}$ cup warm water, and let sit until creamy with small bubbles, about 5 minutes.

Place the all-purpose flour, soy flour, and salt in the work bowl of a food processor or Mixmaster fitted with a dough hook. Process in short pulses to combine. With the machine running, add the yeast mixture, the remaining water, and the buttermilk, processing until a dough forms, about 90 seconds for a food processor, 5 to 7 minutes for a mixer.

Or mix the ingredients by hand in a large bowl, adding them in the same order given. Stir until you have a dough that is soft, but firm enough to handle.

If you're using instant yeast, place the yeast, sugar, all-purpose flour, soy flour, and salt in the work bowl of a food processor or Mixmaster fitted with a dough hook. Process in short pulses to combine. With the machine running, add the buttermilk and warm water, processing until a dough forms, about 90 seconds for a food processor, 5 to 7 minutes for a mixer.

Or mix the ingredients by hand in a large bowl, adding them in the same order given. Stir until you have a dough that is soft, but firm enough to handle.

Continue kneading with the machine until the dough is smooth and springy. Or, to enjoy the pleasure of kneading, turn the dough out onto a lightly floured surface, and do it yourself, about 10 minutes. (You'll have to add some flour to keep it from sticking to your hands. Add as little as possible.)

Shape the dough into a ball and place in a large ceramic or glass bowl. Cover with plastic wrap or a light towel, and let rest 3 hours in a warm, draft-free place. Or refrigerate and leave up to 8 hours.

Divide the dough into 8 pieces. Roll each into a ball. Cover with plastic wrap or a light towel, and let rest 20 minutes.

Heat the oven to 450°F. If you're using a baking stone, place it on a shelf in the lower third of your oven. If you're not using a baking stone, grease a baking sheet with vegetable oil (even a nonstick baking sheet).

Roll each piece of dough into a round about 6 inches in diameter. Cover each with a towel as you finish. Immediately place the loaves in the oven, either directly on the baking stone or on the baking sheet. (If your oven isn't big enough to bake all 8 at once, make 4 at a time.)

Bake until puffy (a pocket will have formed) and golden, about 6 minutes. Remove and wrap in a large piece of parchment paper or a large kitchen towel. Repeat with the remaining dough and serve right away, or later that day at room temperature. Or wrap the parchment or towel in foil to keep warm for up to 1 hour.

- *You can refrigerate the dough for up to 3 days. Wrap in wax paper, then in plastic.*
- *Freeze the dough for up to 1 week. Wrap in wax paper, then plastic. Thaw at room temperature and use right away. Do not refreeze or refrigerate.*
- *Freeze leftover pita up to 1 month, wrapped in foil.*
- *To reheat, place the foil-wrapped pita in a 350°F. oven until soft and warm. Do not defrost before reheating.*

Naan

MAKES 8

Over a bowl of curry, it's interesting to contemplate: Does a culture customize its bread to complement the native cuisine or does a cuisine develop to suit a favored bread? This springy, pocketless sort of pita goes so well with curries, who can say which was made for which?

TIME TO PREPARE (HANDS ON): *About 30 minutes*

TIME TO COOK: *About 5 minutes each*

TOTAL TIME: *Just under 3 hours, including time for the dough to rise*

- 1 teaspoon active dry yeast or $\frac{1}{2}$ teaspoon instant yeast
- 2 tablespoons warm water (98° to 115° F.)
- 1 teaspoon sugar
- $\frac{1}{2}$ cup nonfat plain yogurt
- $\frac{1}{2}$ cup buttermilk
- 3 to 3$\frac{1}{2}$ cups unbleached all-purpose flour
- 1 teaspoon salt

If you're using active dry yeast, dissolve it in the warm water along with the sugar. Let sit until creamy with small bubbles, 5 minutes.

In a mixing bowl, combine the yogurt and buttermilk, stirring until smooth.

Place the flour and salt in the work bowl of a food processor or Mixmaster fitted with a dough hook. Process in short pulses to combine. With the machine running, add the yeast mixture and yogurt mixture, processing until a dough forms, about 90 seconds for a food processor, 5 to 7 minutes for a mixer.

If you're using instant yeast, place the instant yeast, sugar, salt, and flour in the work bowl of a food processor or Mixmaster fitted with a dough hook, or in a large mixing bowl.

With the motor of either machine running, add the yogurt and buttermilk mixture. Or stir in the wet ingredients by hand.

Process or stir to make a soft dough, 2 minutes by machine, 5 by hand.

Remove the dough from the machine or mixing bowl if necessary and knead on a lightly floured surface until it is soft and springy, about 7 minutes. Place in a clean ceramic or glass bowl, cover with plastic wrap or a light towel, and let rest in a warm, draft-free place until doubled, about 2 hours.

Heat the oven to 500° F. If you have a baking stone, insert it now.

Turn out the dough, press it down, and divide it into 8 to 10 pieces. Roll each piece into a ball. For each naan, flatten a ball of dough with your hand, and roll into an 8-inch-long oval with a rolling pin. Cover loosely with plastic wrap while you complete the batch, layering plastic wrap between the pieces of dough.

Generously flour a baker's peel or a cookie sheet with one rimless side. Place 3 or 4 naan on the peel or sheet and slide onto the baking stone, or put the baking sheet in the oven. Bake until they puff up and turn golden brown on top, about 5 minutes. Remove with the peel or take off the baking sheet and repeat with the remaining naan. If you're not serving them immediately, transfer the baked naan to a damp kitchen towel (one that you've rinsed and wrung as dry as you can), stacking them on top of one another. Fold the towel over the naan, then wrap the works in aluminum foil. They should stay warm and pliant for about an hour. If they get cold, reheat by unwrapping the foil and towel, dampening the towel again, wrapping as before, and heating in a low oven, about 200°F., for 10 minutes.

- *You can refrigerate the dough for up to 3 days. Wrap in wax paper, then in plastic.*
- *Freeze the dough for up to 1 month. Wrap in wax paper, then plastic. Thaw at room temperature and use right away. Do not refreeze or refrigerate.*
- *Freeze leftovers, wrapped in foil, up to 3 months.*
- *To reheat, place the foil-wrapped naan in a 350°F. oven until soft and warm. Do not defrost before reheating.*

Potato Focaccia

SERVES 6

Maybe you've made focaccia (pizza-like bread with additional ingredients pressed or kneaded into the dough rather than placed on top), and it's turned out just great. Or maybe you've found it a bit dry, a little bland, and a bit tougher than you'd like. Nothing can foil your focaccia that potatoes won't cure. A time-honored dough conditioner, potato makes flavorful bread that's chewy and moist.

TIME TO PREPARE (HANDS ON): *About 20 minutes, with a food processor*

TIME TO BAKE: *About 1 hour*

TOTAL TIME: *About 4 hours, including time for the dough to rise*

1 medium firm-fleshed potato (such as russet or Yukon Gold)
2 teaspoons active dry yeast or 1 teaspoon instant yeast
$\frac{1}{2}$ cup warm water (98° to 115°F.)

2 cups bread flour or unbleached all-purpose flour
$\frac{1}{2}$ teaspoon coarse salt
1 tablespoon extra virgin olive oil
Coarse sea salt

OPTIONAL TOPPINGS
Minced fresh rosemary
Diced sun-dried tomatoes and diced mozzarella cheese
Minced fresh basil and finely grated garlic (Dare ya!)
Crushed red pepper and shredded fontina cheese
Chopped spinach and crumbled feta cheese

Bake the potato in a preheated 400°F. oven until it's soft, about 45 minutes. Let cool, then peel and mash with a fork.

If you're using dry active yeast, dissolve the yeast in $\frac{1}{4}$ cup warm water and let sit until creamy with small bubbles, about 5 minutes.

Place the flour and salt in the work bowl of a food processor or Mixmaster fitted with a dough hook. Process in short pulses to combine. With the machine running, add the yeast mixture, the potato, and the remaining warm water, processing until a dough forms, about 90 seconds for a food processor, 5 to 7 minutes for a mixer.

Or mix the ingredients by hand in a large bowl, adding them in the same order given. Stir until you have a dough that is soft, but firm enough to handle.

If you're using instant yeast, place the yeast, potato, flour, and salt in the work bowl of a food processor or Mixmaster fitted with a dough hook.

Process in short pulses to combine. With the machine running, add the warm water, processing until a dough forms, about 90 seconds for a food processor, 5 to 7 minutes for a mixer.

Or mix the ingredients by hand in a large bowl, adding them in the same order given. Stir until you have a dough that is soft, but firm enough to handle.

Continue kneading with the machine until the dough is smooth and springy. Or, to enjoy the pleasure of kneading, turn the dough out onto a lightly floured surface and do it yourself, about 10 minutes. (You'll have to add some flour to keep it from sticking to your hands. Add as little as possible.)

Shape the dough into a ball and place in a ceramic or glass bowl. Cover with plastic wrap or a light towel, and let rise in a warm, draft-free place until doubled in bulk, about 1 hour.

Press the air out of the dough and turn out onto a lightly floured work surface. Pat into a round about 6 inches in diameter and 2 inches thick and transfer to a greased baking sheet. Or grease an 8-inch round or square cake pan and pat the dough into the pan.

Cover the dough with a light towel and let rest until puffy, about 40 minutes.

Use your fingertips to dimple the top of the dough. Brush with the olive oil and sprinkle with salt. Distribute the topping of your choice over the top. Bake until golden brown, about 25 minutes. Serve warm or at room temperature.

- *Freeze pieces, wrapped in foil, up to 3 months. To reheat, place the foil-wrapped focaccia on a baking sheet in a 450° F. oven until warmed through. Do not defrost before heating.*

Lavash

MAKES 8

The *bread to use for wraps.*

If you love lavash and want to make it often, consider buying a tortilla press (page 347) for that purpose.

TIME TO PREPARE (HANDS ON): *About 20 minutes*

TIME TO COOK: *About 3 minutes each*

TOTAL TIME: *Just under 4 hours, including time for the dough to rise*

---

1 teaspoon active dry yeast or $^1/_2$ teaspoon instant yeast
1 teaspoon brown sugar
1$^1/_4$ cups warm water (98° to 115° F.)
3 cups unbleached all-purpose flour
1 cup whole wheat flour
1 teaspoon coarse salt
Vegetable oil

If you're using dry active yeast, dissolve the yeast and sugar in $^1/_4$ cup warm water, and let sit until creamy with small bubbles, about 5 minutes.

Place the all-purpose and whole wheat flours along with the salt in the work bowl of a food processor or Mixmaster fitted with a dough hook. Process in short pulses to combine. With the machine running, add the yeast mixture and remaining water, processing until a dough forms, about 90 seconds for a food processor, 5 to 7 minutes for a mixer.

Or mix the ingredients by hand in a large bowl, adding them in the same order given. Stir until you have a dough that is soft, but firm enough to handle.

If you're using instant yeast, place the yeast, sugar, all-purpose and whole wheat flours, and salt in the work bowl of a food processor or Mix-master fitted with a dough hook. Process in short pulses to combine. With the machine running, add the warm water, processing until a dough forms, about 90 seconds for a food processor, 5 to 7 minutes for a mixer.

Or mix the ingredients by hand in a large bowl, adding them in the same order given. Stir until you have a dough that is soft, but firm enough to handle.

Continue kneading with the machine until the dough is smooth and springy. Or, to enjoy the pleasure of kneading, turn the dough out onto a lightly floured surface and do it yourself, about 10 minutes. (You'll have to add some flour to keep it from sticking to your hands. Add as little as possible.)

Shape the dough into a ball and place in a large ceramic or glass bowl. Cover with plastic wrap or a light towel, and let rest 3 hours in a warm, draft-free place. Or refrigerate and leave up to 8 hours.

Divide the dough into 8 pieces. Roll each into a ball. Cover the balls with plastic wrap or a light towel, and let rest 20 minutes.

Heat the oven to 500°F. If you're using a baking stone, place it on a shelf in the lower third of your oven. If you're not using a baking stone, grease a baking sheet with vegetable oil (even a nonstick baking sheet).

Roll one piece of dough into a round about 4 inches in diameter. Set it aside while you do the same with another piece. Return to the first piece and roll it thinner, to a diameter of about 6 inches. Now return to the second piece and do the same, alternating until you have 2 thin disks about 8 inches across. (The reason for rolling 2 at a time with a rest in between is to let the gluten relax so the dough won't spring back at you.) Immediately place the disks in the oven, either directly on the baking stone or on the baking sheet. Bake until just golden, about 3 minutes. Remove and wrap in a large piece of parchment paper or a large kitchen towel. Repeat with the remaining dough and serve right away. Or wrap the parchment or towel in foil to keep warm for up to 1 hour. Lavash is best eaten within an hour of baking.

- *You can refrigerate the dough for up to 3 days. Wrap in wax paper, then in plastic.*
- *Freeze the dough for up to 1 month. Wrap in wax paper, then plastic. Thaw at room temperature and use right away. Do not refreeze or refrigerate.*
- *Freeze the leftovers, wrapped in foil, up to 3 months.*
- *To reheat, place the foil-wrapped lavash in a 350°F. oven until soft and warm. Do not defrost before reheating.*

To Use a Tortilla Maker

Roll each round out to a fat disk 4 inches in diameter. Place on the tortilla maker, and press the lid down firmly and swiftly to flatten. Turn the dough over and press the lid down again to flatten some more. Turn the dough over and bake on the baking stone or baking sheet until golden and slightly puffy, about 2 minutes. Follow the directions above for keeping until serving.

Calzone and Bread Bowls

MAKES 4 CALZONE OR
6 BREAD BOWLS

It's hard to reconcile what's required of this dough in one recipe: It shouldn't get soggy when you fill it with soup or sauce and cheese. Yet it must be soft enough to allow you to bite into it. Semolina, the hard-grain flour typically used for pasta, combined with all-purpose flour makes a dough that is sturdy and soft, thus perfect for both purposes.

TIME TO PREPARE (HANDS ON): *About 20 minutes, with a food processor*

TIME TO COOK: *About 25 minutes for bread bowls and small calzone, 40 for large calzone*

TOTAL TIME: *Under 3 hours, including time for the dough to rise*

---

1 tablespoon active dry yeast or 2 teaspoons
   instant yeast

1 teaspoon sugar

1 1/4 cups warm water (98° to 115°F.)

3 cups unbleached all-purpose flour

2/3 cup semolina flour

2 teaspoons coarse salt

FOR FILLING CALZONE

1 recipe filling for Frittata Crepes (page
   112) or Sformata di Frittata (page 251)

FOR BREAD BOWLS

Unsalted butter or vegetable oil, for
   greasing the bowls

1 egg, lightly beaten

1/4 cup milk

If you're using active dry yeast, dissolve the yeast and sugar in 1/4 cup warm water, and let sit until creamy with small bubbles, about 5 minutes.

Place the all-purpose and semolina flours and salt in the work bowl of a food processor or Mixmaster fitted with a dough hook. Process in short pulses to combine. With the machine running, add the yeast mixture and remaining warm water, processing until a dough forms, about 90 seconds for a food processor, 5 to 7 minutes for a mixer.

Or mix the ingredients by hand in a large bowl, adding them in the same order given. Stir until you have a dough that is soft, but firm enough to handle.

If you're using instant yeast, place the yeast, sugar, all-purpose and semolina flours, and salt in the work bowl of a food processor or Mixmaster fitted with a dough hook. Process in short pulses to combine. With the machine running, add the warm water, processing until a dough forms, about 90 seconds for a food processor, 5 to 7 minutes for a mixer.

Or mix the ingredients by hand in a large bowl, adding them in the same order given. Stir until you have a dough that is soft, but firm enough to handle.

Continue kneading with the machine until the dough is smooth and springy. Or, to enjoy the pleasure of kneading, turn the dough out onto a lightly floured surface and do it yourself, about 10 minutes. (You'll have to add some flour to keep it from sticking to your hands. Add as little as possible.)

Shape the dough into a ball and place it in a large mixing bowl. Cover with plastic wrap and set aside in a warm, draft-free place for 1 hour.

Heat the oven to 425°F. If you are using a baking stone, place it on a shelf in the lower third of your oven. If not, grease a baking sheet with vegetable oil (even a nonstick baking sheet).

To make 4 individual calzone, press the air out of the dough and divide it into 4 pieces. Working with one piece at a time, roll it out to a round approximately 7 inches in diameter. Place a quarter of the filling in the center and press it down lightly to spread it, making sure to leave a margin of at least an inch from the edge. Fold the top over the filling and press the edges together with the tines of a fork to seal it. Use the fork to poke air holes in the top as well. Place on a floured baking sheet or peel, cover with a light towel, and let rest 15 minutes.

Slide the calzone from the baking sheet or peel onto the baking stone. Or place the baking sheet in the center of the oven. Bake until golden brown, about 25 minutes.

To make 1 large spiral calzone, press the air out of the dough and roll it out into a rectangle about 12 inches long and 8 to 10 inches wide. Spread the filling on the dough, leaving a margin of at least 1½ inches around the edges. Roll up the dough lengthwise, tucking the ends in at the bottom to seal. Place seam side down on a prepared baking sheet, cover with a light towel, and let rest 15 minutes.

Slide the calzone from the baking sheet or peel onto the baking stone. Or place the baking sheet in the center of the oven. Bake until golden brown, about 40 minutes.

To make bread bowls, grease the outside of six 8-ounce (approximately) ovenproof soup or cereal bowls with butter or oil.

Press the air out of the dough and divide it into 6 pieces. Working with one piece at a time, roll it out in a round so that it will wrap all the way around the soup bowl. Place the bowl in the center, then mold the dough around it. Place upside down on a baking sheet. Repeat with the remaining pieces of dough.

Beat together the egg and milk in a small bowl. Brush the outside of each bowl, reserving the remaining egg mixture. Bake the bread bowls until the dough is firm, about 15 minutes.

Remove from the oven and carefully separate the soup bowls from the bread. Brush the inside of the bread bowls with the egg mixture. Return to the oven and continue baking until the bowls are golden brown inside and out, about 10 minutes more. Let cool on a rack before filling with soup or salad, such as Spinach and Rice Soup (page 57) and Corn and Sweet Potato Chowder (page 66), or All Kinds of Caesar-Style Salad (page 105).

You can make the dough up to 1 day ahead.
- *Wrap in wax paper, then plastic, and refrigerate.*
- *Freeze the dough, wrapped in wax paper, then plastic, up to 1 month. Defrost at room temperature and use right away. Do not refreeze or refrigerate.*
- *Freeze the calzone up to 6 months wrapped in foil. To reheat, place the foil-wrapped calzone on a baking sheet in a 450° F. oven until warmed through. Do not defrost before heating.*
- *Do not freeze bread bowls.*

Steamed Buns

MAKES ABOUT 12

For the serious bread eater, having a Chinese meal, even a very good one, can be an unsatisfying experience. Rice may suffice for most of the people in the world. But demographic statistics will not persuade a person hankering for bread to enjoy a meal without it. Fortunately for those who'd like to offer bread but don't want dissonant baguettes at their Chinese-style dinner, steamed buns such as these are perfectly consistent with the cuisine.

TIME TO PREPARE (HANDS ON): *About 20 minutes*

TIME TO COOK: *About 15 minutes per batch*

TOTAL TIME: *Just under 4 hours, including time for the dough to rise*

2 teaspoons active dry yeast or 1 teaspoon instant yeast

2 teaspoons brown sugar

1 1/4 cups warm water (98° to 115°F.)

3 1/2 cups unbleached all-purpose flour

1 teaspoon coarse salt

If you're using active dry yeast, dissolve the yeast and sugar in 1/4 cup warm water and let sit until creamy with small bubbles, about 5 minutes.

Place the flour and salt in the work bowl of a food processor or Mixmaster fitted with a dough hook. Process in short pulses to combine. With the machine running, add the yeast mixture and 1 cup of water, processing until a dough forms, about 90 seconds for a food processor, 5 to 7 minutes for a mixer.

Or mix the ingredients by hand in a large bowl, adding them in the same order given. Stir until you have a dough that is soft, but firm enough to handle.

If you're using instant yeast, place the yeast, sugar, flour, and salt in the work bowl of a food processor or Mixmaster fitted with a dough hook. Process in short pulses to combine. With the machine running, add the warm water, processing until a dough forms, about 90 seconds for a food processor, 5 to 7 minutes for a mixer.

Or mix the ingredients by hand in a large bowl, adding them in the same order given. Stir until you have a dough that is soft, but firm enough to handle.

Continue kneading with the machine until the dough is smooth and springy. Or, to enjoy the pleasure of kneading, turn the dough out onto a lightly floured surface and do it yourself. (You'll have to add some flour to keep it from sticking to your hands. Add as little as possible.)

Shape the dough into a ball and place in a large ceramic or glass bowl. Cover with plastic wrap or a light towel and let rise in a warm, draft-free place for 2 hours, until doubled in size.

Press the air out of the dough and knead lightly by hand on a lightly floured surface until smooth, about 5 minutes. Cut the dough into 12 pieces, roll each into a ball, and place on a baking sheet lined with parchment or greased lightly with vegetable oil. Cover loosely with plastic wrap or a light towel, and let rest 45 minutes, until they get puffy. (Don't flour the baking sheet, or the buns may be gummy.)

Meanwhile, lightly grease the bottom and 4 inches up the sides of a large steamer basket. Place in a large stockpot and add water up to the base of the steamer. Bring to a simmer over medium-high heat.

Place half of the buns in the steamer and the others in the refrigerator. Cover the steamer and reduce the heat to medium-low, keeping the water at a simmer. Steam the buns for 15 minutes. Remove from the heat. Repeat with the remaining buns. Let the buns cool on a rack for at least 10 minutes before serving, slightly warm or at room temperature.

• *Wrap the leftovers in plastic or store individual portions in zip-lock bags, pressing out the air before you seal. Freeze. To reheat, set up the steamer as directed in the recipe and bring the water to a boil. Place the frozen buns in the steamer and steam, covered, until heated through. Do not defrost before steaming.*

Breakfast & Brunch

▶ Breakfast and Brunch

Oatmeal Soufflé
Cherry Vanilla Muesli
Sweet Brunch Roulade
Apple Cinnamon Bread Pudding
Breakfast Cobbler
Jam Burst Muffins
Lemon Blueberry Muffins
Pumpkin Corn Muffins
Individual Baked Blueberry Pancakes
Fresh Corn Pancakes with Blueberries
Filled French Toast
Yeast-Risen Waffles
Popovers 'n Eggs ('n jelly!)
Poached Eggs Benedict–Style
Eggs Valentine (or Vice Versa)
Frittata Roll-Ups
Sformata di Frittata

▶ Beverages

Coffee
Iced Coffee
Tea
Iced Tea
Fruit Drinks
Fruit Fizz
"Tropical"
"Vitality"

Entertaining at Breakfast and Brunch

ENTERTAINING AT BREAKFAST IS NOT all that oxymoronic. A time may come when you have no choice. You may, for instance, have houseguests.

Many people who have houseguests say they don't do breakfast. This must suit a lot of people fine, or the hosts who don't serve breakfast wouldn't have any guests to not serve breakfast to. But it just may be that those very guests who assure you that they're "fine" without breakfast would be finer still if it were offered to them.

Even if you're planning to let your guests fend for themselves in the morning, be prepared. Ask ahead: Coffee? Decaf? Tea? Orange juice? Grapefruit? Tomato? Cereal? Toast? Yogurt? Fruit?

Set everything out the night before, including cups, plates, and silverware, and point out the milk in the fridge, so they won't need help from you finding that they want.

You might plan a morning meal for friends you can't see at any other time. If it's been impossible to meet for lunch, dinner, or afternoon tea, you might be able to clear an hour in the morning to catch up and enjoy some fresh muffins.

There are even advantages in having people early:

1. You can prepare most breakfast foods ahead of time.
2. Like you, your guests will have other things to do, so they, like you, will appreciate the time together, then swiftly get on with the day.

A Word to the Wise: Mixes

There are a number of very good muffin, pancake, and waffle batter mixes available. To choose the best brand, read the labels. The better brands have the fewest ingredients, each of them something simple and natural, including flour, sugar, and baking soda. If you want to be able to pass them off as your own, you can add your own fresh or dried fruit to the muffins or pancakes.

Brighten up the Breakfast Table

Cereal, toast, and muffins are varying shades of neutral, beige, and brown, so even a bountiful breakfast table can look blah. In late spring and summer, you can use a variety of fresh fruit for color. But in autumn and winter, you must be more resourceful.

- Buy oversized martini glasses with colored stems and use them for orange juice.
- If you're serving pancakes, waffles, or French toast, put jam, butter, maple syrup, and sour cream in bright-colored ramekins and place on a matching plate in the center of the table.
- To garnish with sliced strawberry "hearts," remove the stems from the strawberries and slice the berries lengthwise. Cut a piece from the top, making a V-shaped indentation to make "hearts."
- Flowers are always nice. If you don't have time to get them for yourself, suggest them to any guest who asks, "What can I bring?"

BREAKFAST AND BRUNCH

Oatmeal Soufflé

S E R V E S 4

So, your friends are too sophisticated for hot cereal. Guess again!

TIME TO PREPARE (HANDS ON): *About 10 minutes*

TIME TO COOK: *About 25 minutes*

TOTAL TIME: *About 35 minutes*

1 cup oat flour (see page 347)

2 cups milk

2 tablespoons brown sugar

Pinch ground cinnamon

4 large egg whites

$\frac{1}{4}$ cup confectioners' sugar

T O S E R V E

$\frac{1}{4}$ cup plus 2 tablespoons maple syrup

Preheat the oven to 425°F.

In a heavy saucepan, combine the oat flour, milk, brown sugar, and cinnamon. Bring to a simmer over medium-high heat, stirring constantly, until thick and smooth, about 5 minutes. Remove from the heat. Transfer to a large bowl to cool. To speed chilling, plug the sink and fill $\frac{1}{3}$ with cold water and as many ice cubes as you can spare. Put the bowl in the sink, watching that to water gets into the bowl, and stir until it stops steaming.

In a separate bowl or in an electric mixer, whip the egg whites until frothy. Sprinkle the confectioners' sugar over them, and resume whipping until firm and glossy but not dry.

Fold the whites into the oatmeal mixture, about $\frac{1}{6}$ of the whites at a time, until they are all incorporated.

Spoon into 4 ramekins or soufflé dishes.

Place the dishes inside a large baking dish. Add water to the outer dish until it comes halfway up the sides of the ramekins. Bake for 20 minutes, checking occasionally, adding water as necessary to maintain the level.

Five minutes before the soufflés are done, put the maple syrup in a small nonreactive saucepan. Place over low heat until hot. Keep warm until serving.

The soufflés are done when they have puffed up and the tops are golden brown, firm, and dry to the touch.

Serve right away, with the warm maple syrup spooned into the center, using a teaspoon to create a small indentation. Serve the ramekins in the middle of small plates.

Cherry Vanilla Muesli

SERVES 4

With fresh or dried cherries, this is delicious. Serve it in goblets, if you can . . . it's that special. Dried fruit is available at health and specialty stores, and many supermarkets. Also see Sources, page 347.

TIME TO PREPARE (HANDS ON): *About 10 minutes*

TIME TO COOK: *None*

TOTAL TIME: *About 8 hours, including time to soak in the refrigerator*

1 $1/2$ cups old-fashioned (not instant) rolled oats
$1/2$ cup chopped dried apples
$1/2$ cup chopped dried prunes
$1/2$ cup raisins
1 cup pitted fresh cherries or $1/2$ cup dried cherries
$1/4$ cup plus 2 tablespoons chopped toasted almonds (optional)
2 tablespoons fresh lemon juice
3 tablespoons maple syrup
1 teaspoon vanilla extract or vanilla powder (see Sources, page 347)

FOR SERVING
Milk
Brown sugar

In a large mixing bowl, combine the oats, apples, prunes, raisins, cherries, and almonds, if you're using them. In a measuring cup, combine 1 $1/2$ cups of water, the lemon juice, maple syrup, and vanilla extract. (If you're using vanilla powder, stir it in with the oat and fruit mixture.) Stir and add the wet ingredients to the dry, mixing well.

Cover with plastic wrap and refrigerate for at least 8 hours.

Distribute the muesli among 4 serving bowls. Pass the milk and brown sugar at the table.

Make up to 1 day ahead.
- *Seal in a tightly covered container and refrigerate.*

Sweet Brunch Roulade

1 cup soft fresh breadcrumbs
$1/3$ cup half-and-half or reduced-fat sour cream
6 large eggs, separated
Approximately $1/2$ cup confectioners' sugar, plus extra for serving

FRUIT FILLING
$2/3$ cup part-skim or nonfat ricotta cheese
2 tablespoons reduced-fat cream cheese (Neufchâtel cheese)
$1/2$ cup fruit preserves of your choice

Heat the oven to 400° F. Line a jelly roll pan with parchment paper.

In a mixing bowl, combine the breadcrumbs, half-and-half or sour cream, and egg yolks. Beat well to blend.

In a separate bowl, whip the egg whites until stiff with an electric mixer or a whisk. Fold them into the yolk mixture until evenly incorporated. Gently spread it over the parchment paper in an even layer. Bake until set, 10 to 15 minutes.

Wet a clean, lightweight dish towel and wring

it out. (Sniff the towel first to make sure it doesn't have residue from laundry detergent.) Lay the towel over the omelet while it cools.

Meanwhile, drain the ricotta in a mesh strainer lined with paper towels to remove excess moisture, about 5 minutes. Combine the ricotta, Neufchâtel cheese, and preserves for the filling.

Dust another clean kitchen towel with the additional confectioners' sugar to make a fine layer. Take the damp cloth off the eggs and turn them out onto the prepared towel. Spread the filling on the center of the omelet, leaving a ½-inch margin all around. Carefully roll up the omelet, using the towel as a guide (but being sure not to roll the end of the towel into the omelet!). Once you've rolled it fully, put it on a cutting board, seam side down.

Trim the edges and cut into slices 2 inches thick. Lay on serving plates to display the swirls. Sprinkle the edges of the plate with confectioners' sugar just before serving.

Apple Cinnamon Bread Pudding

SERVES 4

Soak the bread the night before and pop it in the oven before you hit the shower. You'll emerge from the steam to a most appetizing aroma. (Use Cinnamon Raisin Bread, page 217, for intensified flavor.)

TIME TO PREPARE (HANDS ON): *About 5 minutes*

TIME TO COOK: *About 20 minutes*

TOTAL TIME: *Under 30 minutes*

¼ cup raisins
1 cup nonfat milk
¼ cup apple butter
2 tablespoons brown sugar
2 eggs, lightly beaten
1 teaspoon ground cinnamon
2 cups 1½-inch bread chunks, crust removed

FOR SERVING
½ cup reduced-fat sour cream
1 tablespoon brown sugar

Put the raisins in a small saucepan and add water to cover by an inch. Bring to a simmer over medium-high heat. Remove from the heat and let sit until the raisins are plump, about 5 minutes.

Meanwhile, in a large mixing bowl, combine the milk, apple butter, brown sugar, eggs, and cinnamon. Mix well with a whisk. Add the bread and press it into the mixture to soak it thoroughly. Drain the raisins and add to the mixture.

Heat the oven to 375°F.

Lightly grease an 8-inch deep baking dish with vegetable oil or squirt it with nonstick spray. Add the bread mixture and bake until crusty on top and set throughout, about 20 minutes. (If the top starts to darken too fast, cover loosely with foil.)

Stir together the sour cream and brown sugar, and spoon over each serving.

● *You can made this up to 2 days ahead. Refrigerate well wrapped. If making ahead, serve cold or at room temperature; do not reheat.*

Breakfast Cobbler

SERVES 4

A treat for all seasons. Don't wait for guests; this one's for you!

TIME TO PREPARE (HANDS ON): *About 10 minutes*

TIME TO COOK: *About 40 minutes*

TOTAL TIME: *Just under 1 hour*

TOPPING

⅓ cup unbleached all-purpose flour
⅓ cup oat flour (see page 347)
⅓ cup oat bran
⅓ cup brown sugar
2 teaspoons baking powder
1 teaspoon baking soda
¾ cup buttermilk

Filling of your choice (see below)

Heat the oven to 375°F.

In a large mixing bowl, combine the all-purpose flour, oat flour, oat bran, brown sugar, baking powder, and baking soda. Stir with a whisk or long-tined fork to blend. Add the buttermilk, stirring just enough to blend.

Lightly grease a deep 8-inch baking dish with vegetable oil or squirt it with nonstick spray. Place the filling inside and spread the batter on top.

Bake until golden brown and bubbly, about 40 minutes. If the top starts to brown too fast, cover loosely with foil and turn the heat down to 350°F.

APPLE FILLING

3 tablespoons brown sugar
1 tablespoon maple syrup
2 teaspoons ground cinnamon
1 teaspoon vanilla extract
4 medium baking apples (such as Granny Smith, Rome, or Stayman), peeled, cored, and thinly sliced

In a large mixing bowl, combine the brown sugar, maple syrup, cinnamon, and vanilla. Add the apples and toss well to coat.

BLUEBERRY OR CHERRY FILLING

2 tablespoons sugar
1 tablespoon cornstarch
2 cups fresh blueberries or pitted cherries, or frozen and not defrosted
1 tablespoon fresh lemon juice

In a large mixing bowl, combine the sugar and cornstarch.

In a separate bowl, combine the berries or cherries and lemon juice. Stir into the sugar mixture.

PEACH FILLING

4 large fresh peaches
1 tablespoon fresh lemon juice
2 tablespoons brown sugar
1 teaspoon ground cinnamon
Pinch ground ginger

Fill a large pot with water and bring it to a boil. Add the peaches and let return to a boil. Boil for 10 minutes. Drain.

Peel the peaches and chop them. Put in a bowl and toss with the lemon juice.

In a large mixing bowl, combine the brown sugar, cinnamon, and ginger. Stir in the peaches.

• *Make any of the fillings up to 3 days ahead. Refrigerate, covered, until ready to use.*

Jam Burst Muffins

MAKES 6

Since you use preserves rather than fresh fruit, you can make these muffins any flavor at any time of year. If you crave blueberry muffins in the middle of March, use good blueberry jam and you won't have to spring for imported off-season produce.

TIME TO PREPARE (HANDS ON): *About 10 minutes*

TIME TO BAKE: *About 20 minutes*

TOTAL TIME: *About 40 minutes, including time to cool*

   1 cup unbleached all-purpose flour
   1 cup whole wheat flour or oat flour (see page 347) or oat bran
   ½ cup brown or granulated sugar
   2 teaspoons baking powder
   1 cup buttermilk
   2 large egg whites
   ¼ cup plus 2 tablespoons fruit preserves of your choice

Heat the oven to 500° F. Lightly grease the cups of a 6-muffin tin with vegetable oil or squirt with nonstick spray.

In a large mixing bowl, combine the all-purpose flour, whole wheat flour, sugar, and baking powder. Stir with a whisk or long-tined fork to blend.

In a separate bowl, combine the buttermilk and egg whites. Stir well to blend.

Add the buttermilk mixture to the dry ingredients, stirring just until everything's moist—don't make a smooth batter or the muffins will be tough.

Spoon enough batter into each muffin cup to fill it by ⅓. Top with a tablespoon of preserves. Cover each with an even amount of the remaining batter.

Put in the oven and reduce the heat to 400° F. Bake until golden brown, about 20 minutes.

Let cool, in the tin, on a rack at least 15 minutes before serving.

Freeze the leftovers up to 6 months.

• *To reheat, wrap in foil and place in a 350° F. oven until warmed through. Or soak a paper towel in water. Wring out as much moisture as possible, wrap around the muffin, and microwave at full strength for 50 seconds to 1 minute. Let rest another minute before serving.*

Lemon Blueberry Muffins

MAKES 6

Breakfast may not be everyone's favorite meal, but when blueberry muffins are baking, they tend to summon even the bleariest-eyed guests to the table. Lemon not only lends its own flavor to this version, but also enhances the flavor of the berries.

TIME TO PREPARE (HANDS ON): *About 10 minutes*

TIME TO BAKE: *About 20 minutes*

TOTAL TIME: *About 40 minutes, including time to cool*

1 $\frac{1}{2}$ cups unbleached all-purpose flour
$\frac{1}{2}$ cup oat flour (see page 347) or
    additional all-purpose flour
$\frac{1}{2}$ cup sugar
2 teaspoons baking powder
$\frac{3}{4}$ cup buttermilk
2 tablespoons fresh lemon juice
1 egg white
1 tablespoon grated lemon zest
1 $\frac{1}{2}$ cups fresh blueberries, rinsed or frozen

Heat the oven to 500°F. Lightly grease the cups of a 6-muffin tin with vegetable oil or squirt with nonstick spray.

In a large mixing bowl, combine the all-purpose flour, oat flour, sugar, and baking powder. Stir with a whisk or long-tined fork to blend.

In a separate bowl, combine the buttermilk and lemon juice. Let sit about 2 minutes, stir again, then add the egg white and lemon zest. Stir well to blend.

Add the buttermilk mixture to the dry ingredients, stirring just until everything's moist—don't make a smooth batter or the muffins will be tough. Fold in the blueberries.

Spoon an even amount of batter into each cup of the prepared tin.

Put in the oven and reduce the heat to 400°F. Bake until golden brown and a toothpick inserted in the middle comes out clean, about 20 minutes.

Let cool, in the tin, on a rack at least 15 minutes before serving.

Freeze the leftovers up to 6 months.
• *To reheat, wrap in foil and place in a 350°F. oven until warmed through. Or soak a paper towel in water. Wring out as much moisture as possible, wrap around the muffin, and microwave at full strength for 50 seconds to 1 minute. Let rest another minute before serving.*

ONE STEP FURTHER
Sprinkle each muffin with poppy seeds just before baking.

Pumpkin Corn Muffins

S ERVES 6

Whoever discovered the affinity between cornmeal and pumpkin puree has my respect; together they make the perfect morning meal in late autumn, as here in these hearty, flavorful muffins.

TIME TO PREPARE (HANDS ON): *About 10 minutes*

TIME TO COOK: *About 30 minutes*

TOTAL TIME: *About 40 minutes*

---

1 cup whole wheat flour

$\frac{1}{2}$ cup wheat bran

$\frac{1}{4}$ cup yellow cornmeal, preferably stone-
   ground

2 teaspoons baking powder

$\frac{1}{3}$ cup brown sugar

1 teaspoon pumpkin pie spice or
   $\frac{1}{2}$ teaspoon ground cinnamon and
   $\frac{1}{2}$ teaspoon ground ginger

2 egg whites

1 cup buttermilk

$\frac{1}{2}$ cup canned or fresh pumpkin puree

$\frac{1}{4}$ cup molasses

Heat the oven to 500°F. Lightly grease the cups of a 6-muffin tin with vegetable oil or squirt with nonstick spray.

In a large mixing bowl, combine the flour, bran, cornmeal, baking powder, brown sugar, and pumpkin pie spice. Stir with a whisk or long-tined fork to blend.

In a separate bowl, combine the egg whites, buttermilk, pumpkin, and molasses. Stir well to blend.

Add the buttermilk mixture to the dry ingredients, stirring just until everything is moist—don't make a smooth batter or the mufffins will be tough.

Spoon the batter evenly into the muffin cups. Put in the oven and lower the heat to 400°F. Bake until golden brown and a toothpick inserted in the center comes out clean, about 20 minutes.

Let cool, in the tin, on a rack at least 5 minutes before serving.

Freeze the leftovers, individually wrapped in zip-lock bags, up to 6 months.
- *To reheat, wrap in foil and place in a 350°F. oven until warmed through. Or soak a paper towel in water. Wring out as much moisture as possible, wrap around the muffin, and microwave at full strength for 50 seconds to 1 minute. Let rest another minute before serving.*

Individual Baked Blueberry Pancakes

Serves 6

You can fix this dense, custardy dish at any time of the year with frozen blueberries or dried cherries.

TIME TO PREPARE (HANDS ON): *About 5 minutes*

TIME TO COOK: *About 30 minutes*

TOTAL TIME: *About 35 minutes, plus at least 30 minutes to let the batter rest*

1 ½ cups whole wheat pastry flour or unbleached all-purpose flour
2 tablespoons brown sugar
1 ½ cups buttermilk
5 large eggs
3 cups washed blueberries or pitted cherries, or 2 cups dried cherries

To Serve
Confectioners' sugar, maple syrup, or additional brown sugar

In a large mixing bowl, whisk together the flour and sugar. In a separate bowl, whisk together the buttermilk and eggs. Add the wet ingredients to the dry and whisk until smooth. Cover with plastic wrap and refrigerate 30 minutes to overnight.

Heat the oven to 425°F.

Generously grease 6 custard cups or individual soufflé dishes with unsalted butter or vegetable oil, or spray with nonstick spray. Distribute the berries or cherries equally among the dishes. Whisk the batter well and pour an even amount over the fruit in each dish.

Bake until puffy and lightly browned, about 35 minutes.

Serve warm, with confectioner's sugar, maple syrup, or additional brown sugar on top, if you'd like. Or let them cool, refrigerate, and serve chilled.

You can mix the batter the night before.
- *Seal in a tightly covered container and refrigerate. Stir well before baking.*

Fresh Corn Pancakes with Blueberries

S ERVES 4

A seasonal treat. Serve with just a little maple syrup and some additional fresh berries. Sift confectioners' sugar on top.

TIME TO PREPARE (HANDS ON): *About 20 minutes*

TIME TO COOK: *Included in the preparation time*

TOTAL TIME: *About 15 minutes*

1 $\frac{1}{2}$ cups unbleached all-purpose flour
$\frac{1}{2}$ cup yellow cornmeal, preferably stone-
   ground
1 tablespoon sugar
1 teaspoon baking soda
4 large egg whites
2 cups buttermilk
1 cup fresh corn kernels (scraped from
   1 large ear of corn)
1 cup blueberries, fresh or frozen

F OR S ERVING
Maple syrup and/or blueberry jam

In a large mixing bowl, combine the flour, corn-meal, sugar, and baking soda. Stir with a whisk or long-tined fork to blend.

In a separate bowl, combine the egg whites and buttermilk. Add to the flour mixture and stir well to blend. Gently stir in the corn kernels and blueberries.

Lightly grease a nonstick skillet or griddle with unsalted butter or vegetable oil, or squirt with nonstick spray. Place over medium heat until hot. You can test the heat by letting a few drops of water fall on the surface. If they sizzle and "dance," the skillet is ready.

Using a $\frac{1}{4}$-cup measuring cup, drop the batter onto the griddle, leaving room between pancakes for each to spread. Cook over medium heat until bubbles appear all over the surface, about 3 to 4 minutes. Carefully turn over with a wide spatula. Cook until the bottom is set, about 2 minutes.

Transfer to a serving plate and keep warm while you complete the batch. Serve with maple syrup and/or blueberry jam.

You can make the batter the night before.
- *Seal in a tightly covered container and refrigerate, Stir well before cooking.*

- *Freeze the leftovers, individually wrapped in plastic and sealed in zip-lock bags, up to 1 month. To reheat, place a cooling rack on a baking sheet. Heat the oven to 350°F. and put the pancakes in a single layer on the rack in the oven. Heat until warmed through. (Laying the pancakes directly on the baking sheets will make them soggy.)*

Filled French Toast

SERVES 4

Here's a venerable breakfast treat done one better: golden French toast with a sweet, fruity filling.

TIME TO PREPARE (HANDS ON): *About 10 minutes*

TIME TO COOK: *About 15 minutes*

TOTAL TIME: *About 30 minutes*

FRENCH TOAST

2 large eggs, lightly beaten

¾ cup nonfat milk

2 tablespoons brown sugar

1 teaspoon ground cinnamon

½ teaspoon vanilla extract

8 slices white or whole wheat bread

FILLING

4 tablespoons reduced-fat or fat-free cream
cheese

⅔ cup part-skim or nonfat ricotta cheese

¼ cup confectioners' sugar

2 tablespoons fruit preserves of your choice

FOR SERVING

Maple syrup

Additional confectioners' sugar

Heat the oven to 375°F.

Lightly grease a cookie sheet with unsalted butter or vegetable oil, or squirt with nonstick spray.

In a large mixing bowl, combine the eggs, milk, brown sugar, cinnamon, and vanilla.

In a separate bowl, combine the cream cheese, ricotta, and confectioners' sugar. Stir thoroughly by hand or with an electric hand mixer to blend. Stir in the preserves.

Dunk 4 pieces of bread into the milk mixture to soak. Lay each on the cookie sheet. Spread with an even amount of filling.

Dunk the remaining pieces of bread in the milk mixture and place on top, sandwiching the filling. Bake until the bottom has toasted, about 7 minutes. Turn and bake until golden brown, about 12 minutes. Serve right away, drizzled with maple syrup and dusted with additional confectioners' sugar. To dust the sugar, hold a sieve over each portion. Pour some sugar into the sieve and push it through with your finger so it snows onto the toast.

Make the filling the night before.
* *Seal in a tightly covered container and refrigerate.*

Yeast-Risen Waffles

SERVES 4

Light and crisp, and easy to make. Mix the batter the night before and stir well before baking. Serve doused with maple syrup.

TIME TO PREPARE (HANDS ON): *About 10 minutes*

TIME TO COOK: *About 10 minutes each*

TOTAL TIME: *About 20 minutes, plus overnight to let the batter rise*

- 1 teaspoon instant yeast or 2 teaspoons
   active dry yeast
- 1 cup buttermilk
- 2 large eggs, lightly beaten
- 1 cup whole wheat flour
- ¼ cup soy flour (see Note) *plus*
   ¼ cup unbleached all-purpose flour, *or*
   ½ cup unbleached all-purpose flour
- 1 tablespoon sugar

In a medium mixing bowl, combine the yeast, buttermilk, and eggs.

In a separate large mixing bowl, whisk together the whole wheat flour, soy and all-purpose flours, and sugar, or the whole wheat flour, all-purpose flour, and sugar.

Stir the wet ingredients into the dry until smooth. Cover with plastic wrap and refrigerate overnight.

In the morning, remove from the refrigerator and stir gently.

Heat a waffle iron according to the manufacturer's directions. Pour the recommended amount (this will vary according to the size of your waffle maker) onto the prepared waffle iron, and bake until crisp and golden brown, about 4 minutes, again depending on the appliance.

NOTE: Available in most stores with a good stock of health foods. The protein in the flour makes the batter light. Don't be alarmed by the odor—in small amounts it doesn't affect the flavor of the dish.

Make the batter the night before.
- *Seal in a tightly covered container and refrigerate. Stir well before cooking.*
- *Freeze the leftovers, individually wrapped in plastic and sealed in zip-lock bags, up to 1 month. To reheat, place a cooling rack on a baking sheet. Heat the oven to 350° F. and put the waffles in a single layer on the rack in the oven. Heat until warmed through. (Laying the waffles directly on the baking sheet will make them soggy.)*

Popovers 'n Eggs ('n jelly!)

S E R V E S   6

Popovers beckon something to fill them. Scrambled eggs and jam seem just right to me!

TIME TO PREPARE (HANDS ON): *About 10 minutes*

TIME TO COOK: *About 40 minutes*

TOTAL TIME: *About 1 hour, 20 minutes, including time for the batter to rest*

POPOVERS

3 large eggs, lightly beaten
1 cup 1% or 2% milk
1 cup unbleached all-purpose flour
¼ teaspoon salt

FILLING

6 large eggs
½ cup cottage cheese
Salt and freshly ground black pepper
About ¼ cup fruit preserves of your choice

Lightly grease the cups of a 6-cup nonstick popover tin with vegetable oil or unsalted butter, or squirt with nonstick spray.

In a large mixing bowl, combine the eggs and milk, beating with a whisk until frothy. Add the flour and salt, and continue stirring until you have a smooth batter. Set aside for 30 minutes.

Heat the oven to 400°F.

Beat the batter again, then pour into the tin, filling the cups halfway. Put into the oven and bake for 40 minutes, until they've billowed and turned golden brown.

Remove from the oven and prick each on top with a fork to let the steam out before you split them. Keep warm while you finish the eggs.

Just before the popovers are done, lightly grease an 8-inch nonstick skillet with vegetable oil or squirt with nonstick spray. In a bowl, beat the eggs with the cottage cheese. Heat the skillet over medium-high heat. When hot, add the eggs, lower the heat to medium, and let the eggs cook until the bottom starts to set, about 1 minute. With a gentle pushing motion, stir the eggs, taking care not to scramble them so roughly they crumble.

When the eggs are entirely set, remove from the heat. Season with salt and pepper.

Slice the top off each popover. Spread the hollow inside with jam, then fill with egg. Serve immediately.

You can mix the batter the night before.
* *Cover and refrigerate.*
* *Stir well before baking.*

Poached Eggs
Benedict–Style

FOR EACH SERVING

The problem with genuine eggs Benedict, made with a slab of ham or Canadian bacon and super-rich hollandaise, is that it's so heavy it pins you to your seat for the rest of the day. This version, delicious in its own right, allows you to move when you're done.

TIME TO PREPARE (HANDS ON): *About 5 minutes, not including the optional sauce*

TIME TO COOK: *About 5 minutes*

TOTAL TIME: *About 10 minutes*

FOR EACH SERVING

- 1 large egg
- 1 English muffin or bagel, split
- 1 tablespoon reduced-fat cream cheese, plain or with chives
- 1 or 2 slices smoked salmon, preferably Nova Scotia (unless you like heavy smoked flavor)
- Lemon Sauce (from Artichokes in Lemon Sauce, page 196)

Fill a small skillet with water and bring it to a simmer.

Crack the egg and drop it into the water. As soon as the water returns to a simmer, cover the skillet and remove from the heat. Let sit, covered, for 3 minutes. If the egg hasn't set, uncover and cook over medium heat for about 1 minute more, tilting the pan so the hot water washes over the yolk.

Toast the English muffin or bagel, and spread with the cream cheese. Top with a slice of salmon.

Using a slotted spatula and draining off as much water as possible, place the egg on top of one half. Serve the other half alongside it.

Drizzle with lemon sauce.

You can make the sauce up to 3 days ahead.
- *Seal in a tightly covered container and refrigerate.*

Eggs Valentine
(or Vice Versa)

SERVES 2

Serve when appropriate, with chocolate toast (page 219) and raspberry jam.

TIME TO PREPARE (HANDS ON): *About 5 minutes*

TIME TO COOK: *About 5 minutes*

TOTAL TIME: *About 10 minutes*

- $\frac{1}{2}$ teaspoon unsalted butter or vegetable oil
- 4 large eggs
- 4 slices toast

Lightly grease a nonstick skillet with the butter or vegetable oil, and place over medium heat until hot. You can test the heat by letting a few drops of water fall on the surface. If they sizzle and "dance," the skillet is ready.

Place two heart-shaped cookie cutters on the surface of the skillet. Crack 2 of the eggs and drop each into a cookie cutter. When the white has nearly set, add 1 tablespoon of water to the skillet. Cover loosely and continue cooking until the white is entirely set and the yolk is covered with a thin opaque veil, about 1 minute.

Lift off the cookie cutter and use a wide spatula to transfer the eggs to serving plate. Repeat with the remaining butter or oil and the eggs. Serve with toast.

- *You can't make these ahead. Prepare them just before serving.*

NEAT TRICK
You can cut the bread with a heart-shaped cookie cutter, too.

Frittata Roll-Ups

SERVES 4

A fluffy omelet is rolled around savory salmon or sweet pine-apple spread . . . easier than it looks, but every bit as good.

TIME TO PREPARE (HANDS ON): *About 30 minutes*

TIME TO COOK: *Included in the preparation time*

TOTAL TIME: *About 30 minutes*

8 large eggs
Pinch salt
1 recipe Smoked Salmon Spread (page 30)
    or Cream Cheese and Pineapple Spread
    (page 31)
Chopped fresh chives for garnish

ABOUT ORGANIC FREE-RANGE EGGS

Organic free-range egg farms produce fewer eggs than conventional egg farms. This has two consequences. First, the eggs cost up to twice as much. But more important, they get to the market faster and fresher than conventional eggs, and are likely to taste better as a result, as long as you use them right away. I buy organic eggs for dishes that feature eggs as a main ingredient, such as this, and use conventional eggs for most other purposes.

Heat the oven to 450°F.

In a large mixing bowl, beat the eggs and salt with a whisk until the yolks and whites are thoroughly blended. Grease an 8-inch nonstick oven-proof skillet or omelet pan with unsalted butter or squirt with nonstick spray. Heat the pan over medium heat. When hot, add $\frac{1}{3}$ of the egg mixture. Cook over medium heat until the bottom sets. Place the pan in the oven and continue cooking until the top is dry and the frittata is springy, about 2 minutes. Gently slide a spatula underneath to loosen it and turn the frittata out onto a large plate. Repeat twice to make 3.

Spread each frittata with a thin layer of one of the spreads. Roll each up tightly and trim off the ends. Slice the rolled frittatas into segments just short of 2 inches long. You should have 12 rolls. Place spiral up on serving plates and sprinkle with chives. Allow 3 rolls per serving.

- *You can't make these ahead. Prepare them just before serving.*

Sformata di Frittata

SERVES 6 TO 8

Despite what you may have heard, indecision has its merits. When you're planning brunch, for instance, you may feel you have to decide where to place the accent, on the "Br" or on the "unch." But you'll do fine being noncommittal, with a savory egg dish, such as this "Sformata,"* three layers of frittata filled with pepper and cheese.

TIME TO PREPARE (HANDS ON): *About 30 minutes*

TIME TO COOK: *40 minutes*

TOTAL TIME: *About 1 hour, 10 minutes*

---

8 large eggs
2 cups part-skim ricotta cheese
2 red bell peppers, cored, seeded, and sliced
¼ cup minced fresh basil
½ cup shredded cheddar cheese

GARNISH
Minced red bell pepper
Minced fresh basil

Heat the oven to 375°F.

In a large mixing bowl, beat the eggs with a whisk until the yolks and whites are thoroughly blended. Squirt an 8-inch nonstick ovenproof skillet or omelet pan with nonstick spray. Heat the pan over medium heat. When hot, add ¼ of the egg mixture. Cook over medium heat until the bottom sets. Place the pan in the oven and continue cooking until the top is dry and the frittata is springy. Gently slide a spatula underneath to loosen it and turn the frittata out onto a large plate. Repeat 3 times, to make 4 frittatas.

In a separate mixing bowl, combine the ricotta, bell peppers, basil, and cheddar cheese. Fit a piece of parchment paper into the bottom of a 9-inch round cake pan. Grease it lightly with vegetable oil or squirt it with nonstick spray. Lay 1 frittata over the paper. Spread with ⅓ of the ricotta-pepper mixture. Lay another frittata over it and spread with another third of the ricotta-pepper mixture. Repeat, ending with a frittata.

Cover loosely with foil and bake until set, 30 to 40 minutes. Let cool for 15 minutes before turning out onto a serving plate. Garnish with the minced red pepper and basil.

- *Wrap in plastic or store in zip-lock bags, pressing out the air before you seal. Refrigerate. Do not reheat; serve cold or at room temperature.*

---

* There is no succinct, appetizing English translation for sformata, any dish that's made in a mold. Literally, it would be "molded thing," which has unappetizing connotations.

BEVERAGES

Coffee

COFFEE LOVERS, LIKE THOSE WITH a passion for wine and cheese, tend toward fanaticism. But coffee fanatics are different from oenophiles and cheese connoisseurs in one critical respect: They are addicts. So it is important when cultivating a taste for good coffee to avoid the slippery slope from enthusiasm to snobbery, not only because others find that attitude distasteful, but because there are likely to be times when you cannot get a good cup of coffee, and driven by addiction, you will have to settle for something more like sludge.

What's the Attraction?
The Germans have a word to express the appeal of coffee: *Genussmittel,* meaning things that are consumed for pleasure. We call them stimulants, but that is a narrow description of something that both tastes good and dings your brain.

Coffee is as temperamental as its devotees. So much can go wrong throughout the long process involved in bringing it from bush to cup that it probably wouldn't be as popular if it weren't addictive. Foul weather can damage beans; the beans can be roasted poorly, then stored so they spoil, then ground improperly, then badly brewed. In fact, it's so easy to see how you can come to get a bad cup of coffee that it seems like a miracle to get a good one. Here's how you can up the odds of making yours the best:

How to Buy Coffee

- Shop where there is rapid turnover. Like food of any kind, coffee that's been sitting around goes stale. It shows its age in weak, bitter taste.

- Shop where the clerks know the stock. Although coffee shops look more sophisticated than ever, not all of them provide training for their personnel (see box). You're as likely to get stale, poorly ground coffee in many of them as from your local supermarket (where you shouldn't let those clear plastic canisters of coffee beans trick you into thinking the stock is fresh. Unless it's delivered regularly, it's probably worse than what's sold in vacuum packs on the shelves.)

- You may get the best coffee from a specialty food shop, where the manager acts as a purveyor, choosing among the many coffees available. They are also likely to order smaller amounts of everything, and have fresher stock on hand than chains that order what the company offers and reorder only as necessary.

However, each chain has different standards and procedures, and you may find that you can get superb coffee at an outlet near you.

- Ask to smell the beans. Aroma is the best indication of how the coffee will taste. Light-colored beans will not smell as strong as dark, and the flavor will be milder, too.
- Fail to be impressed by fancy exotic names. If the coffee is bitter and bores a hole in your gut, who cares if it comes from Kathmandu? In fact, the origin of the beans matters less than the way they're roasted and how soon after roasting they get to your grinder.
- Have it ground! Grinding the beans yourself doesn't make a whole lot of difference when you're starting with freshly roasted beans. Just be sure to store the beans in an airtight, moisture-resistant container in the freezer, and take out just what you need each time, replenishing frequently (once a week, if you're serious).

How to Brew It

- Start with cold water. If you plan to use tap water, smell it first. If you smell anything, switch to bottled or filtered water.
- Follow the instructions that come with your coffee maker to the letter. If the coffee is too strong, dilute it when you serve it by offering lots of hot milk. If it's too weak, it's too late for that batch, but increase the amount of coffee by a single scoop next time. Continue to adjust until you've got it just right. Most authorities recommend 2 tablespoons for each cup. But once you find your own strength, you'll be able to measure by eye.
- Serve it promptly. Brewed coffee is not at its best after 45 minutes; it becomes bitter, but fast.
- Nice touch: Serve with unrefined sugar cubes and a small pitcher of warmed milk

Iced Coffee

Brew a double batch of coffee. Freeze one batch in an ice cube tray. Before you freeze it, add sugar and/or milk or cream, if you'd like. Chill the remaining batch. Serve together.

ONE STEP FURTHER:
Combine the coffee and frozen coffee cubes in a blender. Add coffee or vanilla ice cream or frozen yogurt and blend until frothy. Drink straight or add sparkling water, for a soda effect. (Psst . . . you can add Kahlúa for *another* effect.)

Tea

YOU JUST HAVE TO CONSIDER the ratio of tea-rooms to coffeehouses in this country to realize we are not tea sort of people. Iced with lemon and mint, sure. But steeped, strained, and sipped daintily from china? Lovely . . . yet unlikely. On the whole we like our stimulants strong; we want to be jolted, not gently jostled.

Yet tea drinkers have been clamoring (nicely!) to be heard above the whoosh of espresso machines. Tea is tranquillity. It takes time and attention to prepare, and more time to savor. Tea drinkers do not want to blast off; they want to settle into the here and now. They want you to try it, too, if only to encourage you to calm down a second and give them a break.

In fact, the very reasons some reject tea make it ideal for entertaining. It allows you to dawdle; it insists you do. Finally, delicate foods taste far better with tea than with coffee, which overwhelms them.

The problem is finding good tea and preparing it properly. Tea bags are easy and widely available but, with few exceptions, not very good. Loose tea is real tea, and making it well takes some practice, but not much skill.

How to Buy Tea

- Shop where there is fast turnover. Like coffee, tea has a limited shelf life. Old tea tastes stale and bitter.
- Buy your tea from someone who cares about it and is happy to help you with your selection.
- Smell the tea, if samples are available. The aroma will indicate the flavor and potency of the brew.
- Buy tea in small amounts so that what you have is fresh.

How to Brew It

- You will need a dedicated teapot, an infuser, and a kettle.
- Bring cold water to a boil in the kettle. If you're using tap water, smell it first. If it has an odor, switch to bottled or filtered water.
- Meanwhile, warm the teapot by filling it with warm water and swirling it around.
- Put the tea in the infuser. Start with 1 level teaspoon for each cup. If you decide you'd like stronger tea, use more next time. Put the infuser in the pot, then add the boiling water. Cover the teapot and let the tea steep for about 3 to 6 minutes, depending on how strong you like it. Remove the infuser and serve the tea at once.
- Nice touch: Serve with seeded lemon wedges, unrefined sugar cubes, a pot of pale honey, and a small pitcher of warmed milk. (My grandfather used to stir strawberry or raspberry preserves into his tea, as I now do.)

Infusers come in many sizes and shapes, some practically useless. Make sure the holes are large enough to expose the tea to the water but not so large they let it out into the pot.

There are spoon-shaped infusers for brewing a single cup, and some work very well. Again, look for holes of a sensible size.

As for the bags you can fill with tea, they are no less trouble than brewing with an infuser and the tea is a lot less satisfying.

Iced Tea

Brew a double batch of tea. Freeze one batch in an ice cube tray. Put minced mint leaves, sugar cubes, or even whole raspberries in the trays, letting the tea freeze over them, if you'd like. Chill the remaining batch. Serve together. You can sweeten iced tea with extra fine granulated sugar or raspberry syrup.

Fruit Drinks

Fruit Fizz

FOR EACH SERVING

¼ cup fresh pineapple juice
1 fresh kiwi, peeled and chopped
¼ cup apple juice (not from concentrate)
¼ cup sliced fresh strawberries
1 tablespoon nonfat plain yogurt
¼ cup dry Champagne or ginger ale

In a blender, combine the pineapple juice, kiwi, apple juice, strawberries, and yogurt. Pour into a tall glass and stir in the Champagne or ginger ale. Serve right away.

"Tropical"

FOR EACH SERVING

⅓ cup fresh pineapple juice
⅓ cup fresh orange juice
1 tablespoon fresh lemon juice
1 tablespoon coconut juice (available at most health food stores, sold in glass bottles on the shelf, not refrigerated)

In a blender, combine the pineapple, orange, lemon, and coconut juices. Serve right away.

"Vitality"

FOR EACH SERVING

⅓ cup carrot juice
⅓ cup orange juice
¼ cup strawberry juice (available at most health food stores)
1 tablespoons fresh lime juice
1 tablespoon sparkling water
Ice

Stir together the carrot juice, orange juice, strawberry juice, and lime juice in a glass. Add the sparkling water and ice.

Desserts

A True Epicurean Theory of Desserts

Ingredients

Cake Decorating: Ask an Expert

▶ Cakes and Frostings

Chocolate Cake
Layered Cream Cake with Fruit
Steamed Apple Cake
Pumpkin Cheesecake
Pumpkin Pudding Cake
Raspberry Jelly Roll
Spice Bars
Brownies
Chocolate Bavarian Cream Filling
Fruit Cream Filling
Jelly Dumplings
Cream Cheese Icings
Sugar Glaze for Cakes
Birthday Cake

▶ Puddings and Such

Apple-Ginger Custard
Autumn and Winter Fruit Clafouti
Charlotte
Two Soufflés
Fresh Fruit and Sour Cream
Chocolate Ricotta Pudding
Summer Pudding
Semolina Pudding

▶ Frozen Desserts

Glacé
Sorbet

If the adage is correct and "The end crowns the work," there could be big trouble for those of us who take pride in poaching salmon, but take flight when asked to bake a cake. The motto implies that a poor dessert could foil every wonderful thing that came before it. We could buy something, but then there's the awful possibility that our meal would not be crowned, but trumped by some miracle of butter and flour brought in for the occasion.

People are more prickly about dessert than any other course. I have a friend who maintains with utter conviction that dessert is chocolate by definition. There are others who insist that the only proper place for fruit at the end of the meal is in a pastry crust, or maybe in a bowl as a centerpiece.

Then there are those of us who consider dessert part of the meal. If the dishes you've served feature fresh, clean flavors, ending with a triple-decker Black Forest cake would throw the entire thing wildly off-key, so keep balance in mind.

A True Epicurean Theory of Desserts

EPICURUS HAS BECOME ASSOCIATED WITH gluttony when, in fact, he was against it. True, he believed that pleasure was the object of life. But nothing was pleasurable to him if it was ultimately harmful . . . regardless how much fun it was in the meantime. Among other things, this ruled out overindulging in rich foods.

And so, despite the modish backlash against low-fat cooking, I remain unapologetically unreconstructed in that regard. Whether the Professional Arbiters of Taste like it or not, many people worry about eating too much. If the host

is meant to put everyone at ease, there's no better way than serving something all can savor with peace of mind on that score.

Finally, there are times when an elaborate dessert seems a means of compensating for the shortcomings of preceding courses. The desserts that follow assume that everyone has eaten well indeed, and would enjoy something sweetly, simply good for that crowning touch.

Ingredients

THE FOLLOWING GIVE MOISTURE AND substance to low-fat desserts.

Agar flakes (also called agar-agar): Used to thicken and gel liquids. Agar flakes are dried seaweed, a vegetarian alternative to gelatin, which is made from animal marrow. They're available at health food stores, with instructions for use on the package.

Oat Flour: Used in combination with all-purpose flour or pastry flour, makes moist, rich-tasting baked goods. Oat flour gives baked goods a sweet, buttery flavor. It is available at most health food stores and by mail (see Sources, page 347). The brand most widely available is Arrowhead Mills. Since oat flour is nothing but pulverized oats, you can make it yourself by processing old-fashioned rolled oats (not instant) in a food processor until it is a fine powder.

Prune Puree: Sunsweet Brand or Just Like Shortnin' in the baking supplies section of your supermarket, or Lekvar, sold with the jellies and jams. Or you can make your own (page 267). Used to replace some or all of the fat in fruity cakes and bar cookies, and chocolate desserts.

Fat-Free Sweetened Condensed Milk: Virtually indistinguishable from the full-fat version, this ingredient is irreplaceable in frozen desserts (page 279) and in a flan-style pudding (page 278).

Fat-Free Ricotta Cheese: Choose a brand that isn't runny. If you can't find one, use part-skim ricotta instead. Or line a strainer with a piece of cheese-cloth and pour the ricotta into it. Let it drain for about 30 minutes.

Reduced-Fat Sour Cream: Few brands of nonfat sour cream taste good enough. Buy the purest brand you can find (additive-free; without artificial sweeteners).

Fat-Free Cream Cheese: When combined with flavoring such as vanilla, cocoa powder, or lemon zest, and beaten with confectioners' sugar, it makes a full-bodied replacement for the real thing. Again, buy the purest brand you can find (additive-free; without artificial sweeteners).

Buttermilk: Low-fat or nonfat buttermilk makes moist, light baked goods and rich-tasting frozen desserts. Fat-free buttermilk is not a contradiction in terms; buttermilk is a misnomer—once it was a by-product of butter making. Now, like yogurt, it is cultured skim milk.

Cake Decorating: Ask an Expert

CAKE MAKERS ARE BORN NOT made, and any day now we'll hear that some lab has isolated the gene for squeezing buttercream through pastry bags. They might draw their sample from Dede Wilson, author of the magnificent and practical(!) *Wedding Cakes.* A professional pastry chef, Dede remains uncommonly sympathetic to home cooks, offering these simple, effective suggestions:

- Buy an icing spatula. This expert would not attempt to ice a cake without one.

- Before you ice the entire cake, put a thin coat of icing over it to seal in the crumbs. Chill it, then apply the final layers. The icing will go on more smoothly than it would on a cake with loose crumbs.

- Dip the icing spatula in hot water and run it over the final coat to make it ultra smooth.

- Center a round layer cake on a turntable or lazy Susan, rotating it to smooth the icing.

- To decorate, cut out stencils from heavy paper, or buy them. Place them on a cake that has been smoothly frosted and chilled. Sift cocoa or confectioners' sugar, or sprinkle sprinkles into the stencil, then lift carefully to reveal the design. You can also use cookie cutters, pressing them into the cake lightly to leave an impression, then brushing in the impression with melted chocolate or fruit glaze.

- You can decorate with sliced fresh fruit or whole berries. Sprinkle raspberries on top or arrange overlapping sliced fresh peaches in concentric circles. Heat fruit preserves in a saucepan until runny, then brush over the peaches, if you'd like.

- Layer a cake with fruit preserves instead of icing. Brush the layers with jam, then ice the outside. Try apricot jam or orange marmalade with chocolate or yellow cake, raspberry with any kind of cake.

- If, despite your best efforts, the cake doesn't look as lovely as you'd like, cut it in the kitchen and place individual servings on plates. Sift confectioners' sugar over each serving and garnish with berries, or drizzle the cake and plate with a bit of melted chocolate. Your guests will feel as if they're being served dessert in a fancy restaurant.

CAKES AND FROSTINGS

Chocolate Cake

SERVES 8

If you are going to win the heart of any child, loved one, or mother-in-law, you must be able to make a good chocolate cake. (Some may favor you more if you make it fat-free.)

TIME TO PREPARE (HANDS ON): *About 10 minutes*

TIME TO COOK: *About 30 minutes*

TOTAL TIME: *About 40 minutes*

1 $\frac{1}{2}$ cups unbleached all-purpose flour
$\frac{1}{2}$ cup oat flour (see page 258)
1 $\frac{1}{2}$ cups sugar
$\frac{1}{2}$ cup unsweetened cocoa powder
2 teaspoons baking soda
1 $\frac{3}{4}$ cups buttermilk
1 large egg white
2 teaspoons vanilla extract

FOR SERVING (OPTIONAL)
Confectioners' sugar
Vanilla Cream Cheese Icing (page 269) or
   Chocolate Glaze (page 270)
Chocolate Bavarian Cream Filling (page
   267)

Heat the oven to 350°F. Lightly grease a 9 × 13-inch cake pan with vegetable oil or squirt with nonstick spray.

In a large mixing bowl, combine the all-purpose flour, oat flour, sugar, cocoa powder, and baking soda. Stir with a whisk or a long-tined fork to blend.

In a separate bowl, combine the buttermilk, egg white, and vanilla, blending well. Stir into the flour mixture until smooth.

Bake until a knife inserted in the center comes out clean, about 30 minutes.

To serve simply, turn the cake out onto a serving plate, and turn it over again onto a cooling rack. When cool, slide it onto a serving plate, using your hands to keep it right side up. Place a doily or a cookie cutter (without a handle) on top and sprinkle with confectioners' sugar. Lift the doily or cookie cutter carefully.

To serve as a layer cake, let the cake cool on a rack. Turn out onto a flat work surface and carefully slice in half horizontally to make 2 layers. Spread the top of one slice with Chocolate Bavarian Cream Filling. Sandwich with the other layer. Spread the Vanilla Cream Cheese Icing over the cake in a thin layer. Decorate as desired (see tips on page 259).

Make up to 3 days ahead.
* *Wrap tightly in plastic and refrigerate. Let come to room temperature before serving, or wrap in foil and heat in a 350°F. oven until warmed through.*
* *Freeze up to 3 months, well wrapped. To defrost, leave at room temperature for several hours. Or wrap in foil and heat in a 350°F. oven until warmed through. Do not microwave, or it will be tough.*

Layered Cream Cake with Fruit

S E R V E S   6

You look at the ingredients, the steps, the clock. You furrow your brow and you think, "This had better be good." It is.

TIME TO PREPARE (HANDS ON): *About 40 minutes*

TIME TO COOK: *Included in the preparation time*

TOTAL TIME: *About 6 hours, 40 minutes, including time to chill*

1 pound cherries, pitted and chopped
1 very ripe mango, peeled and chopped
$\frac{1}{4}$ cup sugar
1$\frac{1}{2}$ cups nonfat milk, divided
1 package gelatin or 1 tablespoon agar-agar
  (see Sources, page 347)
1 whole egg
1 egg yolk
$\frac{1}{2}$ cup sugar
3 tablespoons rice flour (see Note)
2 teaspoons finely grated lemon zest

1 recipe Just Plain Cake (page 304) or
  1 6-ounce package ladyfingers

In a large mixing bowl, combine the cherries, mango, and $\frac{1}{4}$ cup sugar. Cover with plastic wrap and refrigerate.

In another bowl, pour $\frac{1}{2}$ cup of milk. Sprinkle the gelatin or agar flakes on top and stir.

In a medium saucepan, beat together the egg, egg yolk, and $\frac{1}{2}$ cup sugar. Add the rice flour, stir in the remaining milk, and cook over low heat, stirring constantly until you've got a dense cream, about 10 minutes. Using a wire whisk, stir the cream thoroughly into the gelatin mixture along with the lemon zest. Set aside to cool.

Strain the fruit, reserving the juice. Soak the cake or ladyfingers in the juice. Line a loaf pan with plastic wrap. Place $\frac{1}{3}$ of the cake or ladyfingers in the bottom of the pan. Distribute half of the fruit and half of the cream on top. Repeat and finish with the last $\frac{1}{3}$ of the cake. Cover tightly with plastic wrap and refrigerate for at least 6 hours before serving.

To serve, remove the plastic and run a dull-edged knife around the rim. Invert onto a serving plate, slice, and serve chilled.

NOTE: Rice flour, available at most health food stores and by mail (see Sources, page 347), is ground rice and works like wheat flour to thicken sauces and custards. I prefer rice flour for thickening because it is less likely than wheat flour to turn gummy. The brand most widely available nationwide is Arrowhead Mills.

You can make this cake up to 2 days ahead.
• *Wrap and refrigerate. Serve cold.*

Steamed Apple Cake

Can you wait to taste this? Serve with sour cream and brown sugar, or lightly sweetened whipped cream. Or glaze with Lemon Glaze (page 270).

TIME TO PREPARE (HANDS ON): *About 10 minutes*

TIME TO COOK: *About 2 hours*

TOTAL TIME: *About 2½ hours*

Unsalted butter or vegetable oil
3 cups unbleached all-purpose flour (see
    Note)
⅔ cup granulated brown sugar
2 teaspoons baking powder
1 teaspoon baking soda
2 teaspoons ground ginger
1 teaspoon ground cinnamon
½ teaspoon ground cloves
1 cup nonfat or low-fat buttermilk
4 large egg whites
1 cup apple butter
1 cup grated fresh apple, such as Granny
    Smith or Rome

TO SERVE

Whipped cream, vanilla ice cream, or
    Eggnog Glacé (page 281)

Lightly grease the inside of a 6-cup pudding mold or 10-inch springform pan with butter or vegetable oil.

In a large mixing bowl, combine the flour, brown sugar, baking powder, baking soda, ginger, cinnamon, and cloves. Whisk well to blend.

In a separate bowl, combine the buttermilk, egg whites, apple butter, and grated apple. Stir into the dry ingredients until thoroughly combined.

Spoon the mixture into the prepared pan. If you're using a pudding mold, snap on the lid. If you're using a springform pan, wrap it well in several pieces of aluminum foil, being sure to enclose the entire pan, leaving no space for water to seep through.

Place a cake rack on the bottom of a large stockpot (if you don't have a rack that fits, use a small heatproof flat-bottomed bowl, such as stainless steel or Pyrex, turned upside down). Add 3 cups of water and place the pudding pan on the rack, making sure the water doesn't come above the bottom of the mold or pan. Cover and bring the water to a simmer. Allow to simmer for 2 hours, adding water as necessary to maintain the level you started with.

Remove the pan from the water and let it cool for 10 minutes before taking off the lid or unwrapping.

Use a pressure cooker (30 minutes vs. 2 hours). Place a rack in a pressure cooker and add 3 cups of water as directed for the stockpot above. Put the lid on the pressure cooker and bring to full pressure. Maintain at full pressure for 30 minutes. Remove from the heat and let the pressure come down naturally.

Remove the pan from the water and let it cool before taking off the lid or unwrapping.

Serve warm, at room temperature, or chilled, with whipped cream, vanilla ice cream, or Eggnog Glacé.

NOTE: If you like, you may substitute whole wheat flour for up to half of the all-purpose flour.

Make up to 3 days ahead.

- *Wrap tightly in plastic and refrigerate. Let come to room temperature before serving, or wrap in foil and heat in a 350° F. oven until warmed through.*

- *Freeze up to 3 months, well wrapped. To defrost, leave at room temperature for several hours. Or wrap in foil and heat in a 350° F. oven until warmed through. Do not microwave, or it will be tough.*

Pumpkin Cheesecake

SERVES 8

What if everyone finally acknowledged that pumpkin pie is sort of silly? Crust is entirely superfluous (and often soggy) in the presence of good pumpkin custard.

TIME TO PREPARE (HANDS ON): *About 5 minutes*

TIME TO COOK: *About 1 hour*

TOTAL TIME: *About 4 hours, including time to chill*

---

2 large eggs

2 large egg whites

$2\frac{1}{2}$ cups nonfat or reduced-fat ricotta cheese

1 cup brown sugar

2 tablespoons molasses

$\frac{1}{2}$ cup reduced-fat sour cream

$\frac{1}{2}$ cup canned or fresh pumpkin puree

$\frac{1}{2}$ cup unbleached all-purpose flour

1 teaspoon ground cinnamon

1 teaspoon ground ginger

$\frac{1}{4}$ teaspoon ground cloves

$\frac{1}{4}$ teaspoon ground nutmeg

TO SERVE (OPTIONAL)

Whipped cream, vanilla ice cream, or Eggnog Glacé (page 281)

Heat the oven to 425° F. Lightly grease a 10-inch springform pan.

In the work bowl of a food processor, place the eggs, egg whites, ricotta cheese, brown sugar, molasses, sour cream, pumpkin, flour, cinnamon, ginger, cloves, and nutmeg. Process until smooth and well combined.

Pour the batter into the springform pan. Fill a baking dish with water and place on the bottom rack of the oven. Put the cake pan on the center rack and cover loosely with foil.

Bake until almost firm, about 30 minutes and until a knife inserted in the center comes out clean. Remove the foil, and continue baking until firm and golden brown on top, about 20 minutes more. Chill thoroughly before serving.

Serve plain or with whipped cream, vanilla ice cream, or Eggnog Glacé.

You can made this cake up to 2 days ahead.

- *Wrap and refrigerate. Serve cold.*

Pumpkin Pudding Cake

(A Last-Minute Dessert)

SERVES 4 TO 6

There is much to be admired in the work of a classically trained pastry chef and given enough time, butter, and marble counter space, you, too, could do pretty well. But let's say you have 5 minutes, and not much more than a can of pumpkin . . .

TIME TO PREPARE (HANDS ON): *About 5 minutes*

TIME TO COOK: *About 40 minutes*

TOTAL TIME: *About 45 minutes*

---

1 cup unbleached all-purpose flour
2 teaspoons baking powder
1 teaspoon ground cinnamon
1 teaspoon ground ginger
$\frac{1}{4}$ teaspoon ground cloves
$\frac{1}{4}$ teaspoon ground nutmeg
1 $\frac{1}{4}$ cups brown sugar
1 cup buttermilk
1 cup canned or fresh pumpkin puree

To Serve

**Whipped cream, vanilla ice cream, or
Eggnog Glacé (page 281)**

Heat the oven to 350°F. Lightly grease a 10-inch cake pan.

In a large mixing bowl, whisk together the flour, baking powder, cinnamon, ginger, cloves, and nutmeg. In a separate bowl, combine the brown sugar and buttermilk, stirring until smooth. Add the pumpkin and stir well to blend.

Pour the wet ingredients into the dry ingredients and stir to blend thoroughly. Pour into the prepared pan and bake until set, about 40 minutes. The cake should be soft but not runny. Serve warm, cold, or at room temperature, with whipped cream, vanilla ice cream, or Eggnog Glacé.

You can make this up to 3 days ahead.

- *Refrigerate, covered. Served chilled or at room temperature. Do not reheat.*

Raspberry Jelly Roll

SERVES 6

Everyone loves jelly rolls, and anyone who's made one knows it's hard to roll up the cake without having it crack. Perhaps a school of divination could come out of this — just as the Romans used to determine the fate of armies by watching which direction their chickens moved as they ate, you could assign meaning to the various types and locations of cracks and consult the jelly roll when you're trying to decide, for instance, whether to get married.

Auguries aside, how can you keep the cake from cracking?

Don't bake it too long—if it dries out in the oven, it will be brittle. Take it out as soon as it's firm and springy. Turn it out onto a sugar-sprinkled towel immediately and roll it up. Leave it wrapped in the towel to cool completely before you unroll it, fill it, and roll up again.

What can you do if the cake cracks anyway? Serve it sliced, and everyone will be too enthralled by the beautiful raspberry swirl in the center to notice.

TIME TO PREPARE (HANDS ON): *About 20 minutes*

TIME TO COOK: *About 10 minutes*

TOTAL TIME: *About 2½ hours, including time to rest*

CAKE

5 large eggs, separated

½ cup granulated sugar

½ cup confectioners' sugar, plus additional for rolling the cake

1 cup cake flour or unbleached all-purpose flour

1 teaspoon baking powder

1 tablespoon grated lemon zest

1 teaspoon vanilla powder or extract

FILLING

2 cups part-skim or nonfat ricotta cheese

½ cup confectioners' sugar

1 tablespoon grated lemon zest

6 tablespoons raspberry preserves

Any of the icings or glazes on pages 269 to 270

Heat the oven to 350°F. Line the bottom of two 9-inch round cake pans with parchment paper.

With an electric mixer, beat the egg whites until soft peaks form. Beat in the granulated sugar and continue beating until stiff, but not dry, peaks form.

In a separate mixing bowl, beat the egg yolks with the confectioners' sugar until light and fluffy. In another bowl, use a whisk or a long-tined fork to combine the flour and baking powder. Blend the flour mixture, the lemon zest, and vanilla into the egg yolks. Fold that mixture into the egg whites just until combined.

Line a jelly roll pan with parchment paper and lightly dust the paper with confectioners' sugar. Spread the batter onto the paper and bake for 12 minutes, until springy.

When the cake is done, remove it from the oven. Immediately dust the surface of the cake with confectioners' sugar. Sprinkle a clean dish towel heavily with additional confectioners' sugar. Turn the cake onto it and peel the parchment paper off the bottom. Carefully roll up the cake and let it sit until thoroughly cool, about 2 hours.

Meanwhile, make the filling. Put the ricotta, confectioners' sugar, lemon zest, and raspberry preserves in the work bowl of a food processor or blender, and process until smooth.

Unroll the cake, remove the towel, and spread the filling inside. Carefully roll up again. Ice or glaze with the desired icing, or sift additional confectioners' sugar over the top.

Make up to 3 days ahead.
- *Wrap tightly in plastic and refrigerate. Let come to room temperature before serving, or wrap in foil and heat in a 350°F. oven until warmed through.*

Freeze up to 3 months, well wrapped.
- *To defrost, leave at room temperature for several hours. Or wrap in foil and heat in a 350°F. oven until warmed through. Do not microwave, or it will be tough.*

Spice Bars

You have to have these at holiday time. They are also a great tea snack all winter long. Glaze with Orange Glaze (page 270).

TIME TO PREPARE (HANDS ON): *About 10 minutes*

TIME TO COOK: *About 15 minutes*

TOTAL TIME: *Just under 1 hour, including time to cool*

- ¼ cup apple butter
- 2 tablespoons buttermilk
- ½ cup brown sugar
- 3 large egg whites
- ½ cup molasses
- 2 cups unbleached all-purpose flour
- 1 teaspoon baking soda
- 1 teaspoon ground cinnamon
- ½ teaspoon ground cloves
- ½ teaspoon ground nutmeg
- ¼ cup currants

Heat the oven to 350°F. Lightly grease a 9 × 13-inch cake pan with unsalted butter or squirt it with nonstick spray.

In a mixing bowl, combine the apple butter, buttermilk, brown sugar, egg whites, and molasses. Stir well to blend.

In a separate large mixing bowl, combine the flour, baking soda, cinnamon, cloves, and nutmeg. Stir well with a whisk to blend. Switch to a spoon and stir in the currants.

Pour the wet ingredients into the flour mixture and stir well to blend. Pour into the prepared pan, and bake until firm and golden, about 20 minutes.

Let cool thoroughly on a rack before slicing and serving.

Make up to 3 days ahead.
- *Seal in a tightly covered container at room temperature. Freeze up to 6 months, well wrapped in plastic. Defrost at room temperature.*

Brownies

SERVES 6

Walnuts are the only source of fat in these brownies, making them particularly good for when girlfriends gather. You'll need organic powdered milk, which doesn't have a plastic aftertaste like conventional brands. It's available at most health-oriented stores, some supermarkets, and by mail (see Sources, page 347). You will also need a fruit puree, which you can purchase or make yourself.

TIME TO PREPARE (HANDS ON): *About 5 minutes*

TIME TO COOK: *About 30 minutes*

TOTAL TIME: *About 45 minutes, including time to cool*

- ½ cup prune puree (Sunsweet Brand, "Just Like Shortenin'," or see recipe below)
- ¾ cup sugar
- 3 egg whites
- 1 teaspoon vanilla extract
- ½ cup unbleached all-purpose flour
- ½ cup unsweetened cocoa powder
- 3 tablespoons organic nonfat dry milk (available at most health food stores or by mail; see Sources, page 347)
- ½ cup chopped walnuts

Heat the oven to 325°F.

Lightly grease an 8-inch cake pan with unsalted butter or squirt it with nonstick spray.

In a large mixing bowl, combine the prune puree, sugar, egg whites, and vanilla.

In a separate bowl, combine the flour, cocoa powder, dry milk, and nuts. Stir into the wet ingredients until well combined.

Pour into the prepared baking dish. Bake until set and firm, about 25 minutes. Watch closely to make sure the top doesn't burn.

Cool on a rack before slicing and serving.

Prune Puree

1 $\frac{1}{3}$ cups pitted prunes
Prune juice or water to cover

Place the prunes in a small saucepan. Add the prune juice or water, cover, and bring to a simmer. Remove from the heat and let rest until the prunes are plump and soft, about 15 minutes.

Drain off the liquid and reserve. Place the prunes in a blender or food processor, along with $\frac{1}{4}$ cup plus 2 tablespoons of the liquid. Process to puree.

Make up to 3 days ahead.
* *Seal in a tightly covered container at room temperature. Freeze up to 6 months, well wrapped in plastic. Defrost at room temperature, or wrap in foil and place in a 350°F. oven until thawed through.*

Chocolate Bavarian Cream Filling

FILLS ONE 8-INCH LAYER CAKE

Spread this filling between layers of plain or chocolate cake, or serve it chilled as a pudding . . . with whipped cream and raspberries.

TIME TO PREPARE (HANDS ON): *About 10 minutes*

TIME TO COOK: *None!*

TOTAL TIME: *About 6 hours, including, time to set*

1 cup nonfat milk, divided
1 tablespoon agar flakes (see page 258) or
   1 envelope gelatin
3 tablespoons unsweetened cocoa powder
One 15-ounce container part-skim or nonfat
   ricotta cheese
$\frac{1}{2}$ cup sugar
1 teaspoon vanilla extract

Pour $\frac{1}{2}$ cup of the milk into a small saucepan over medium heat and bring to a simmer.

Meanwhile, pour the remaining $\frac{1}{2}$ cup milk into the work bowl of a food processor or blender. Sprinkle the agar flakes or gelatin over it. Let stand 2 minutes.

Add the hot milk and cocoa powder. Process until dissolved. Add the ricotta cheese, sugar, and vanilla, and process again until smooth.

Transfer to a large bowl, cover, and chill until set, about 6 hours.

Make up to 2 days ahead.
* *Seal in a tightly covered container and refrigerate.*

Fruit Cream Filling

FILLS ONE 8-INCH LAYER CAKE

Spread the filling between layers of plain or chocolate cake, or spoon it into the center of an angel food cake and serve a dollop with each slice.

TIME TO PREPARE (HANDS ON): *About 10 minutes*

TIME TO COOK: *None!*

TOTAL TIME: *About 6 hours, including time to set*

    1 cup nonfat milk, divided
    1 tablespoon agar flakes (see page 258) or
        1 envelope gelatin
    $\frac{1}{2}$ cup sugar
    2 cups fresh or defrosted frozen raspberries
        or strawberries
    One 15-ounce container part-skim or nonfat
        ricotta cheese
    1 teaspoon vanilla extract

Pour $\frac{1}{2}$ cup of the milk into a small saucepan over medium heat and bring to a simmer.

Meanwhile, pour the remaining $\frac{1}{2}$ cup milk into the work bowl of a food processor or blender. Sprinkle the agar flakes or gelatin over it. Let stand 2 minutes.

Add the hot milk and sugar. Process until the sugar and agar have dissolved. Add the fruit and process to puree. Add the ricotta cheese and vanilla and process again until smooth.

Transfer to a large bowl and chill until set, about 6 hours.

Make up to 2 days ahead.
• *Seal in a tightly covered container and refrigerate.*

Jelly Dumplings

SERVES 6

You may not be able to say you're having potatoes for dessert and get much enthusiasm in return. To be fair, you can't expect people to know that potato makes an excellent chewy pastry, a perfect casing for fruit preserves . . . until they taste this.

TIME TO PREPARE (HANDS ON): *About 40 minutes*

TIME TO COOK: *About 15 minutes*

TOTAL TIME: *About 1½ hours, including time to chill the dough*

    1 pound red or white potatoes, peeled and
        quartered
    3 large eggs
    2 large egg yolks
    1 cup unbleached all-purpose flour
    1 teaspoon vanilla extract
    $\frac{1}{2}$ cup confectioners' sugar, plus additional
        for finishing
    1 cup strawberry preserves, divided
    1 tablespoon granulated sugar

Fit a large pot with a steamer basket. Add enough water to come up to the base of the steamer. Place the potatoes in the steamer, cover, and bring the water to a simmer over medium-high heat. Turn the heat down to medium-low and steam until the potatoes are tender all the way through, about 12 minutes. Transfer to a large bowl and let them cool.

When cool enough to handle, peel the potatoes and mash them well by hand. Any electric appliance will overdo it.

In a separate bowl, combine the eggs, egg

yolks, flour, vanilla, and confectioners' sugar. Stir into the potatoes, making a soft dough.

Divide the dough into 12 pieces and flatten each into a disk. Place a dollop of fruit preserves (about 1 1/2 teaspoons) in the center and fold the dough over, pressing along the edges to form a dumpling. Refrigerate for about 20 minutes.

Heat the oven to 400°F.

Place some confectioners' sugar on a plate or in a shallow bowl. Bring water to boil in a large pot. Add the granulated sugar. Carefully add the dumplings and boil gently until they rise to the surface. Line a baking sheet with parchment paper. Roll each dumpling in confectioners' sugar and bake for 10 minutes, until golden.

Meanwhile, put the remaining fruit preserves in a small nonreactive saucepan, and heat until liquid. Drizzle over the dumplings before serving.

- *Wrap the leftovers in wax paper, then seal in zip-lock bags. Refrigerate. Serve cold for breakfast(!)*

▶

Cream Cheese Icings

FOR ONE 8-INCH LAYER CAKE

Rich-tasting icings for special-occasion cakes. You can double or triple the amounts when the events call for a Really Big dessert. If you're wary of raw eggs, or if you are feeding guests who are pregnant or suffer with low immunity, this is not for you. Use a sugar or fruit glaze instead.

TIME TO PREPARE (HANDS ON): *About 5 minutes*

TIME TO COOK: *None*

TOTAL TIME: *About 5 minutes*

VANILLA CREAM CHEESE ICING

    1 cup reduced-fat cream cheese
    1 1/2 cups confectioners' sugar
    1 large egg white
    1/2 teaspoon vanilla extract or generous pinch ground vanilla (see Sources, page 347)

In a large mixing bowl, combine the cream cheese, confectioners' sugar, egg white, and vanilla. Using a heavy rubber spatula or an electric beater set on low, blend to make a smooth frosting.

Or place the ingredients in the work bowl of a mixer and blend, using low power, until smooth.

(Don't use a food processor for this, or it may be too thin.)

Chocolate

Substitute chocolate confectioners' sugar (see Note) for the confectioners' sugar, or replace 1/4 cup of the confectioners' sugar with unsweetened cocoa powder.

Lemon

Substitute lemon-flavored confectioners' sugar (see Note) for the confectioners' sugar, or add 1 tablespoon grated lemon zest, adding it with the vanilla.

NOTE: Chocolate and lemon confectioners' sugar are manufactured by Domino sugar and available in supermarkets nationwide.

Make up to 1 day ahead.
- *Seal in a tightly covered container and refrigerate.*

Sugar Glaze for Cakes

FOR ONE 8-INCH CAKE

These are simple icings for all kinds of cake.

TIME TO PREPARE (HANDS ON): *About 10 minutes*

TIME TO COOK: *Included in the preparation time*

TOTAL TIME: *About 10 minutes*

Chocolate Glaze

Try it on Angel Food Loaf (page 303) or Chocolate Cake (page 260).

> 1 $\frac{1}{2}$ cups chocolate confectioners' sugar, or
> 1 $\frac{1}{4}$ cups confectioners' sugar plus 3
> tablespoons unsweetened cocoa powder
> 3 tablespoons nonfat milk, warmed, or warm
> coffee
> 1 teaspoon vanilla extract

In a small saucepan, combine the confectioners' sugar, cocoa powder, if using, milk or coffee, and vanilla. Place over medium heat and stir constantly until the sugar has dissolved and the mixture is smooth. Drizzle over the cake and let it rest until it hardens.

Orange Glaze

This is great on Spice Bars (page 266) and Sponge Cake (page 304).

> 3 tablespoons fresh orange juice, warmed
> 2 $\frac{1}{2}$ cups confectioners' sugar

In a large mixing bowl, combine the orange juice and confectioners' sugar. Stir until smooth. Drizzle the glaze onto the cooled cake, where it will harden.

Lemon Glaze

This is great on Angel Food Loaf (page 303) or Raspberry Jelly Roll (page 264).

> 3 tablespoon fresh lemon juice, warmed
> 1 tablespoon grated lemon zest
> 2 $\frac{1}{2}$ cups confectioners' sugar

In a large mixing bowl, combine the lemon juice, lemon zest, and confectioners' sugar. Stir until smooth. Drizzle the glaze onto the cooled cake, where it will harden.

Fruit Glaze

Brush onto cake or pie crust.

> 1 $\frac{1}{2}$ cups fruit preserves

Place the preserves in a small nonreactive saucepan. Heat gently until liquid. If the preserves are chunky, try to brush so the chunks are distributed evenly.

- *You can't make these glazes ahead. Prepare just before using.*

Birthday Cake

SERVES 8 TO 10

There is no truer display of love (or lunacy) than making a birthday cake. Since it is destined to be the centerpiece of the party, the pressure's on you to make it perfect. To double the amount, make two batches of each part and combine them in a single bowl. Do not double the recipes.

TIME TO PREPARE (HANDS ON): *About 1½ hours, including chocolate layer, plain layer, and icings*

TIME TO COOK: *Up to 1 hour, if you bake the chocolate and plain cakes separately*

TOTAL TIME: *About 6 hours, including time to set*

1 recipe Just Plain Cake (page 304)
1 recipe Chocolate Cake (page 260)
1 recipe Chocolate Bavarian Cream Filling (page 267)
One 10-ounce jar raspberry preserves
1 recipe Chocolate Cream Cheese Icing (page 269)
Decorations of your choice (see tips on page 259)

Using kitchen shears, a pizza cutter, or a paring knife, cut the Just Plain Cake into a circle to fit between the layers of the Chocolate Cake. (Save the scraps for Summer Pudding [page 277] or Charlotte [page 274].) Spread the Bavarian Cream over a layer of Chocolate Cake. Place the layer of Just Plain Cake on top of that.

In a small saucepan, heat the preserves until liquid. Brush the preserves over the layer of Just Plain Cake, and top with the remaining layer of Chocolate Cake. You will now have 3 layers.

Using an icing spatula, spread a thin layer of cream cheese icing over the entire cake. Chill for at least 1 hour.

Remove the cake from the refrigerator and apply another coat of icing.

Decorate as desired.

You can make the Chocolate Cake or Just Plain Cake up to 3 days ahead.
• *Wrap well in plastic and refrigerate.*
Make the Bavarian Cream up to 2 days ahead.
• *Refrigerate, covered.*
Assemble and decorate the cake no more than several hours before serving.

PUDDINGS AND SUCH

Apple-Ginger Custard

SERVES 6

If it's the perfect apple dessert you're after, consider this a contender. You can serve it warm or cold, with vanilla ice cream or not.

TIME TO PREPARE (HANDS ON): *About 15 minutes*

TIME TO COOK: *About 1 hour*

TOTAL TIME: *About 1¾ hours, including time to rest*

6 Granny Smith apples, peeled, cored, and sliced
¾ cup sugar, divided
1 teaspoon ground ginger
1 teaspoon ground cinnamon
½ cup reduced-fat sour cream
¼ cup unbleached all-purpose flour
1 large egg, lightly beaten
1 teaspoon vanilla extract

Place the apples and ½ cup sugar in a heavy saucepan. Cook, covered, until the apples are soft, about 25 minutes. Uncover and turn up the heat until most of the juice has evaporated. Remove from the heat and let cool for about 15 minutes, stirring occasionally. Meanwhile, heat the oven to 425°F.

Combine the apples with the remaining ¼ cup sugar, ginger, cinnamon, sour cream, flour, egg, and vanilla. Pour the mixture into 6 ramekins or a 6-cup pudding mold. Place inside a large baking dish and pour in water until it comes halfway up the side of the pudding molds or ramekins. Bake until firm, covering the puddings with foil if the tops brown too quickly. Remove the puddings from the water bath to cool. Let rest about 20 minutes before serving.

Make up to 3 days ahead.
* *Seal in a tightly covered container and refrigerate. Serve cold.*

Autumn and Winter Fruit Clafouti

SERVES 6

Part pudding, part pancake, all delicious.

TIME TO PREPARE (HANDS ON): *About 5 minutes*

TIME TO COOK: *About 40 minutes*

TOTAL TIME: *About 1½ hours, including time for the batter to rest*

½ cup part-skim or nonfat ricotta cheese
1½ cups buttermilk
1 cup unbleached all-purpose flour
2 tablespoons sugar
4 large eggs, lightly beaten
2 teaspoons grated lemon zest
1 teaspoon vanilla extract
Prepared fruits (see choices below)

Place the ricotta in the work bowl of a food processor or blender. Process until smooth. Add the buttermilk and process again to blend. Add the flour, sugar, eggs, lemon zest, and vanilla.

Process to make a smooth batter. Transfer to a large bowl, cover with plastic wrap, and set aside for 30 minutes.

Lightly grease an 8-inch baking dish or 6 individual ramekins with unsalted butter or vegetable oil, or squirt with nonstick spray. Place the prepared fruits at the bottom of the dish and pour the batter evenly on top.

Place the dish(es) inside a large baking dish. Add water to the outer dish until it comes halfway up the side of the clafouti. Bake until puffy and golden, about 40 minutes, checking occasionally, adding water as necessary to maintain the level. If the top starts browning too quickly, cover loosely with foil. Serve right away, at room temperature, or chilled.

Pears

2 ripe fresh pears, peeled and thinly sliced

Sprinkle with ¼ cup brown sugar and 2 tablespoons fresh lemon juice before putting in the baking dish.

Figs

8 tender ripe figs, stem removed, and sliced

Sprinkle with ¼ cup brown sugar before putting them into the baking dish.

Apples

2 large apples, peeled, cored, and thinly sliced

Drizzle with 3 tablespoons maple syrup and 2 tablespoons fresh lemon juice before putting into the baking dish.

Dried Bing Cherries

Spread a layer, roughly ½ cup, over the bottom of the baking dish. (They plump up in the batter, so you don't have to soak them first.)

Prunes

½ cup dried prunes
½ cup prune juice
1 cinnamon stick
2 tablespoons fresh orange juice

Put the prunes, prune juice, cinnamon stick, orange juice, and enough water to cover in a small saucepan, and bring to a simmer over medium-high heat. Let simmer, uncovered, 5 minutes. Remove from the heat, cover, and let sit until the prunes are plump, about 15 minutes. Drain, chop the prunes, and spread evenly on the bottom of the baking dish.

Make up to 3 days ahead.
* *Cover with plastic wrap and refrigerate. Serve cold.*

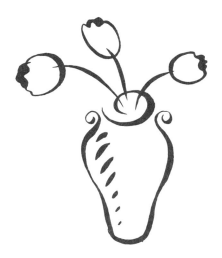

Charlotte

SERVES 8

While the name of poor King George III become synony-mous with tyrant, his wife's didn't make out so badly. Her name, Charlotte, was attached to this excellent (and easy!) dessert: apple custard baked in a shell of buttered bread or sponge cake.

TIME TO PREPARE (HANDS ON): *About 10 minutes, once you've made or bought the cake or bread*

TIME TO COOK: *About 50 minutes*

TOTAL TIME: *About 1½ hours*

Unsalted butter
1 recipe Sponge Cake (page 304) or 1
   store-bought cake, or 1 loaf Cinnamon
   Raisin Bread (page 217), crusts removed
1 recipe Apple-Ginger Custard, unbaked
   (page 272)

Heat the oven to 350°F.

Grease a charlotte mold or 6-cup soufflé dish heavily with butter. Line the bottom and sides with 1-inch-thick pieces of sponge cake or raisin bread, cutting the pieces to fit as evenly as possible inside the mold.

Fill with apple custard. Cover loosely with foil. Bake until the custard has set, about 50 minutes.

Let cool on a rack at least 20 minutes. Place a large plate on top and turn the charlotte over. Lift off the mold. Serve warm.

Make up to 3 days ahead.
• *Wrap and refrigerate.*

Two Soufflés

SERVES 4

TIME TO PREPARE (HANDS ON): *About 15 minutes*

TIME TO COOK: *About 1 hour for sweet potato and 30 minutes for banana*

TOTAL TIME: *About 1¼ hours*

Sweet Potato

1 medium sweet potato
¼ cup fat-free or low-fat sweetened
   condensed milk
1 teaspoon ground cinnamon
½ teaspoon ground ginger or 1½ teaspoons
   pumpkin pie spice
4 large egg whites
¼ cup confectioners' sugar
¼ cup plus 2 tablespoons orange marmalade

Heat the oven to 450°F.

Wrap the sweet potato in foil and place on a baking sheet. Bake until tender but not mushy, about 40 minutes. Turn the oven down to 425°F. Unwrap the potato. When cool enough to handle, strip off the peel, and chop the potato coarsely. To speed chilling, you can put it in the refrigerator for several minutes.

In a large mixing bowl, mash the potato. Add the condensed milk, cinnamon, and ginger, and stir well to blend.

In a separate bowl or in an electric mixer, whip the egg whites until frothy. Sprinkle the confectioners' sugar over them, and resume whipping until firm and glossy.

Fold the whites into the sweet potato mixture, about ⅙ of the whites at a time.

Spoon into 4 individual ramekins or soufflé dishes, or one 4-cup soufflé dish.

Place the dish(es) inside a large baking dish. Add water to the outer dish until it comes halfway up the sides of the ramekins. Bake for 20 minutes, 30 minutes for one larger dish, until puffy and golden, checking occasionally, adding water as necessary to maintain the level.

Five minutes before the soufflés are done, put the marmalade in a small nonreactive saucepan. Place over low heat until liquid. Keep warm until serving.

Serve right away, with the warm marmalade spooned into the center.

Banana

- 2 ripe bananas
- ¼ cup fat-free or low-fat sweetened condensed milk
- 1 teaspoon vanilla powder or vanilla extract
- 4 large egg whites
- ¼ cup confectioners' sugar
- ¼ cup plus 2 tablespoons chocolate sauce

Heat the oven to 425°F.

In a large mixing bowl, mash the bananas. Add the condensed milk and vanilla, and stir well to blend, making it as smooth as possible.

In a separate bowl or in an electric mixer, whip the egg whites until frothy. Sprinkle the confectioners' sugar over them, and resume whipping until firm and glossy.

Fold the whites into the banana mixture, about ⅙ of the whites at a time.

Spoon into 4 individual ramekins or soufflé dishes, or one 4-cup soufflé dish.

Place the dish(es) inside a large baking dish. Add water to the outer dish until it comes halfway up the sides of the ramekins. Bake for 20 minutes, 30 minutes for one larger dish, puffy and golden, checking occasionally, adding water as necessary to maintain the level.

Five minutes before the soufflés are done, put the chocolate sauce in a small nonreactive saucepan. Place over low heat until runny. Keep warm until serving.

Serve right away, with the warm chocolate sauce spooned into the center.

You can make the sweet potato mixture (but not the banana) up to a day ahead.

- *Seal in a tightly covered container and refrigerate.*

Fresh Fruit and Sour Cream

SERVES 4

The word "dessert" is from the French (of course) desservir, meaning to remove what has been served. In other words, at its essence dessert refers to anything offered once the main course and salad have been cleared away. This is very broad, and suggests we're thinking too narrowly if we consider only pie, cake, and fancy pudding— type things. This here's dessert by any reckoning.

TIME TO PREPARE (HANDS ON): *About 5 minutes*

TIME TO COOK: *None*

TOTAL TIME: *About 5 minutes*

1 cup nonfat plain yogurt
$1/4$ cup reduced-fat sour cream
3 tablespoons brown sugar
2 to 3 cups rinsed fresh blueberries, grapes, or pitted cherries

In a mixing bowl, combine the yogurt, sour cream and brown sugar. Stir well to blend.

Add the fruit, stir, and serve in goblets or pretty individual bowls.

• *You can't make this ahead. Prepare it just before serving.*

Chocolate Ricotta Pudding

SERVES 4

Poor John Hannon learned the literal meaning of "chocolate to die for." The founder of America's first commercial chocolate factory, in Milton, Massachusetts, Hannon disappeared on a voyage to buy cocoa beans in the West Indies.

Throughout its colorful history, chocolate has had many uses: currency, stimulant, and aid to amorousness. It's especially nice to have in pudding.

TIME TO PREPARE (HANDS ON): *About 10 minutes*

TIME TO COOK: *About 45 minutes*

TOTAL TIME: *About 1 hour*

2 large eggs
2 cups nonfat, low-fat, or whole milk ricotta cheese
$1/2$ cup buttermilk
$2/3$ cup sugar
$1/4$ cup unsweetened cocoa powder
1 teaspoon vanilla extract
$1/2$ cup unbleached all-purpose flour

TO SERVE
Whipped cream, vanilla ice cream, or vanilla frozen yogurt

OPTIONAL GARNISH
Mint leaves

Heat the oven to 425°F. Grease six 3-inch ramekins or custard cups.

In a food processor, combine the eggs, ricotta, buttermilk, sugar, cocoa powder, vanilla, and flour until blended.

Pour the mixture into the custard cups or ramekins. Place in a large baking dish. Add water to the baking dish until it comes halfway up the sides of the custard cups. Cover the baking dish loosely with foil. Bake until the puddings are set, about 35 minutes. Remove the foil and continue baking until the tops are firm, about 10 minutes more. Let cool to room temperature if serving shortly, or refrigerate right away.

To serve, invert each pudding on a serving plate. Top with whipped cream, ice cream, or frozen yogurt. Garnish with mint leaves, if you'd like.

You can make up to 3 days ahead.
- *Wrap and refrigerate. Serve cold.*

Summer Pudding

SERVES 6 TO 8

You'd recognize this as "pudding" only if you use the word, as the English do, to refer to desserts in general. It's just as well they have a word for it, since nothing at our disposal describes this unique preparation. It's great picnic food because it tastes best when it's soggy.

TIME TO PREPARE (HANDS ON): *About 10 minutes*

TIME TO COOK: *Included in the preparation time*

TOTAL TIME: *Overnight (to soak)*

4 cups strawberries or raspberries, or blueberries (although don't use blueberries with chocolate bread)
1 cup superfine sugar
1 loaf good-quality (store-bought or Real Bread, page 212) or Chocolate Bread (page 219), sliced, and crusts removed, or 1 recipe Just Plain Cake (page 304)

In a large saucepan, combine the berries and the sugar. Heat gently over medium heat, stirring often, until the fruit breaks down into a sauce, about 5 minutes.

Line a 9-inch loaf pan or 8-inch baking dish with about ⅔ of the slices of bread or cake, reserving the rest to lay on top.

Pour the fruit mixture into the pan. Lay the remaining slices of bread on top, then press a piece of plastic wrap over it. Lay something heavy on top of the plastic to weight it down. (If you're worried the fruit will spill over the sides, put a large plate underneath before you add the weight.)

Refrigerate for at least 6 hours, or overnight.

To serve, remove the weight and plastic wrap. Place a serving plate over the loaf pan, and holding the plate over the pan, turn both over, so the pudding slips out onto the serving plate. Slice and serve with ice cream, whipped cream, sour cream and brown sugar, or frozen yogurt.

You have to make a day ahead.
- *Wrap and refrigerate. Keeps only 2 days.*

Semolina Pudding

SERVES 4

Although it was a massive best-seller for years after it was written, Dale Carnegie's How to Win Friends and Influence People *had one critical shortcoming: He left out the dessert chapter.*

This is the kind of dish that people love so much, you need do little more than serve it to make friends for life. Semolina flour (sold mostly for making pasta) is finely ground durum wheat, and widely available in supermarkets as well as by mail (see Sources, page 347).

TIME TO PREPARE (HANDS ON): *About 15 minutes*

TIME TO COOK: *About 40 minutes*

TOTAL TIME: *About 4 hours, including time to chill*

$\frac{1}{3}$ cup semolina flour

1 cup nonfat milk

1 cup nonfat or reduced-fat ricotta cheese

$\frac{1}{2}$ cup nonfat sweetened condensed milk

3 large eggs

1 teaspoon vanilla extract

TO SERVE (OPTIONAL)

Fruit syrup or sliced fresh fruit

Heat the oven to 375°F.

Put the semolina and milk in a saucepan, and heat over medium heat, stirring constantly with a whisk, until the mixture is thick, like porridge, about 7 minutes. Remove from the heat and let cool until no longer steaming.

Put the ricotta, condensed milk, eggs, and vanilla in the work bowl of a food processor. Process until smooth. Add the semolina mixture and process again until smooth.

Lightly butter a 3-cup soufflé dish or pudding mold or 4 individual 3-inch ramekins. Pour in the pudding mixture. Place the dish or ramekins in a large shallow baking dish. Add water to the outer dish until it comes halfway up the pudding dish(es). Cover loosely with foil and bake until the pudding is firm to the touch, about 40 minutes.

Remove from the heat and transfer the pudding to a cooling rack for 10 minutes. Refrigerate to chill through before serving, about 3 hours.

To serve, run a wet knife around the edge of the pudding and invert on a serving plate.

Serve plain, drizzled with fruit syrup, or topped with sliced fresh fruit such as strawberries, peaches, or bananas, or pitted cherries.

You can make up to 3 days ahead.
* *Wrap and refrigerate. Serve cold.*

FROZEN DESSERTS

Glacé
(Creamy Frozen Dessert)

SERVES 4 TO 6

After a good meal, ice cream can be too rich to be refreshing. To end on a note of sweetness and light, serve one of these cool, creamy (nonfat) iced desserts instead.

The amount of time it takes depends on your method for freezing the ingredients.

Also, these don't keep; encourage everyone to polish them off.

TIME TO PREPARE (HANDS ON): *About 3 minutes*

TIME TO COOK: *None*

TOTAL TIME: *Varies depending on ice cream maker*

Real Vanilla
- 2 cups buttermilk
- 1 cup part-skim or nonfat ricotta cheese
- 1 cup confectioners' sugar
- $\frac{1}{2}$ cup fat-free or low-fat sweetened condensed milk
- 1 teaspoon ground vanilla bean (see Sources, page 347) or 1 $\frac{1}{2}$ teaspoons vanilla powder

Place the buttermilk, ricotta, confectioners' sugar, condensed milk, and vanilla in the work bowl of a food processor or blender. Process until smooth. Pour into an ice cream maker and proceed according to the manufacturer's instructions.

NEAT TRICK
Put fruit jam in a small saucepan over low heat until syrupy. Pour over the glace before serving.

Chocolate or Coffee
- 2 cups buttermilk
- 1 cup part-skim or nonfat ricotta cheese
- 1 cup confectioners' sugar
- $\frac{1}{2}$ cup fat-free or low-fat sweetened condensed milk
- 3 tablespoons unsweetened cocoa powder or 2 tablespoons instant espresso powder
- 1 teaspoon vanilla extract

Place the buttermilk, ricotta, confectioners' sugar, condensed milk, cocoa or espresso powder, and vanilla in the work bowl of a food processor or blender. Process until smooth. Pour into an ice cream maker and proceed according to the manufacturer's instructions.

Lemon
- $\frac{1}{2}$ cup fresh lemon juice
- 1 tablespoon grated lemon zest
- 3 cups buttermilk
- 1 cup confectioners' sugar
- $\frac{1}{2}$ cup fat-free or low-fat sweetened condensed milk

Place the lemon juice, lemon zest, buttermilk, confectioners' sugar, and condensed milk in the work bowl of a food processor or blender. Process until smooth. Pour into an ice cream maker and proceed according to the manufacturer's instructions.

Strawberry or Raspberry

2 cups fresh or defrosted frozen strawberries, or 1 cup fresh or defrosted frozen raspberries

2 cups buttermilk

1 cup part-skim or nonfat ricotta cheese

1 cup confectioners' sugar

1/2 cup fat-free or low-fat sweetened condensed milk

1 teaspoon vanilla extract

Place the strawberries or raspberries, buttermilk, ricotta, confectioners' sugar, condensed milk, and vanilla in the work bowl of a food processor or blender. Process until smooth. Pour into an ice cream maker and proceed according to the manufacturer's instructions.

Pumpkin

1 cup fresh or canned pumpkin puree

1 1/2 cups buttermilk

1 cup part-skim or nonfat ricotta cheese

1/2 cup confectioners' sugar

1/2 cup fat-free or low-fat sweetened condensed milk

Generous pinch each: ground cinnamon, ground nutmeg, ground ginger

Place the pumpkin puree, buttermilk, ricotta, confectioners' sugar, condensed milk, cinnamon, nutmeg, and ginger in the work bowl of a food processor or blender. Process until smooth. Pour

into an ice cream maker and proceed according to the manufacturer's instructions.

Neat Trick
Put ginger marmalade in a small saucepan over low heat until syrupy. Pour over the glacé before serving.

Mango

1 large ripe mango (or 2 medium), peeled and chopped

1/4 cup confectioners' sugar

1/2 cup fat-free or low-fat sweetened condensed milk

2 cups nonfat plain yogurt

Juice of 1 lime

Place the mango, confectioners' sugar, condensed milk, yogurt, and lime juice in the work bowl of a food processor or blender. Process until smooth. Pour into an ice cream maker and proceed according to the manufacturer's instructions.

Coconut

1 cup light coconut milk

1 cup nonfat plain yogurt

1 cup nonfat ricotta cheese

1/2 cup confectioners' sugar

1 teaspoon vanilla extract or vanilla powder

Place the coconut milk, yogurt, ricotta, confectioners' sugar, and vanilla in the work bowl of a food processor or blender. Process until smooth. Pour into an ice cream maker and proceed according to the manufacturer's instructions.

Eggnog

1 cup commercial prepared eggnog (low-fat if desired)

1 cup nonfat ricotta cheese

¼ cup confectioners' sugar

1 teaspoon vanilla extract

Place the eggnog, ricotta, confectioners' sugar, and vanilla in the work bowl of a food processor or blender. Process until smooth. Pour into an ice cream maker and proceed according to the manufacturer's instructions.

- *You can't make these ahead. Prepare them just before serving.*

Sorbet

S E R V E S   4   T O   6

The secret to smooth, creamy sorbet is confectioners' sugar. The cornstarch gives it a fuller consistency and prevents ice crystals from forming. Eat the sorbet promptly; the texture doesn't hold up during lengthy freezing.

Strawberry

TIME TO PREPARE (HANDS ON): *About 5 minutes*

TIME TO COOK: *None*

TOTAL TIME: *Varies depending on your ice cream machine*

2 pints ripe fresh strawberries, hulled and sliced

Juice of 1 lemon

½ cup confectioners' sugar

¼ cup superfine sugar

Place the strawberries in the work bowl of a food processor or blender and process to puree. Add the lemon juice, confectioners' sugar, and superfine sugar. Process again to blend.

Transfer the mixture to an ice cream maker and process according to the manufacturer's instructions.

- *You can't make this ahead. Prepare it just before serving.*

Peach

TIME TO PREPARE (HANDS ON): *About 10 minutes*

TIME TO COOK: *Less than 1 minute*

TOTAL TIME: *Varies depending on your ice cream machine*

1 ½ pounds very ripe peaches

Juice of 1 lemon

½ cup confectioners' sugar

¼ cup superfine sugar

Bring a large saucepan of water to a boil. Add the peaches and allow to return to a boil. Boil for 40 seconds. Drain. Peel the peaches, remove the pit, and chop.

Place the peach pulp in the work bowl of a food processor or blender and process to puree. Add the lemon juice, confectioners' sugar, and superfine sugar. Process again to blend.

Transfer the mixture to an ice cream maker and process according to the manufacturer's instructions.

- *You can't make this ahead. Prepare it just before serving.*

Basics

"Nobody Cooks"

Broth
Chicken Broth
Vegetable Broth
Shrimp Broth
Lobster Broth

Tomato Sauces
Homemade Tomato Sauce (Uncooked)
Homemade Tomato Sauce (Cooked)
Béchamel Sauce

Dough
Bread Dough
Pizza Dough
Fresh Pasta
Dumpling Wrappers

Pastry Crusts
Pastry (Savory for Quiche and Savory Tortes)
Ricotta Pastry Crust (Sweet)
Crepes
Polenta
Potato Gnocchi

Salad Dressings
Vinaigrette
Creamy Vinaigrette
Herb Dressing
Modified Mayonnaise
Pesto
Roasted Bell Peppers

Cakes
Angel Food Loaf
Just Plain Cake
Sponge Cake

"Nobody Cooks"

THE IDEA THAT ANYONE HAS the time, energy, or presence of mind to make such things as pasta, gnocchi, and sponge cake from scratch is the cherished fantasy of food writers who continue to turn out recipes for them. Supermarkets are as likely to carry ready-made fresh pasta, for instance, as the ingredients to make it. In fact, you can find each of these "basics" at most well-stocked grocery stores in this country.

Of course there are advantages to making things yourself. You can choose the best ingredients and control how much salt, fat, and sugar go into your food. And what you make may taste fresher and better than what you'd buy off the shelf.

But if you have a choice between making part of a meal and not entertaining at all, make what you can and buy the rest; use select prepared foods to manage your time.

For example, if you buy ready-made sheets of fresh pasta, you'll save roughly ⅔ of the preparation time for a dish that calls for it, such as ravioli or lasagna. You can devote the time you have to making a sauce and to doing what you really need to do, like maybe putting your shoes away and sweeping the crumbs off the couch.

Broth

JUST WHEN YOU'RE READY TO tackle that really tempting recipe, you scan the ingredients and there it is: "Vegetable broth" or just "broth." Maybe you reach for a can of commercial, ready-made broth. Or perhaps, nagged by something you read somewhere about homemade being so much better than anything you can purchase frozen, canned, or in a cube, you get on with the tedious business of boiling a broth far better than money can buy. There is a difference between stubborn resistance to using canned foods and sensible adherence to the principles of good taste. The difference is broth.

Plan the day you'll make it. No other cooking is to occur at your stove on that day. Take out lunch and dinner. This is broth day. No arguments.

Clear the counter of everything but a chopping board. And keep clearing as you peel and chop. Peel the onion, chuck the skin, chop the onion, and put it in the pot. Peel the carrots, chuck the skin, chop the carrots, and put them in the pot. Peel the potatoes, and so on.

Get a pressure cooker; you'll make better broth and spend less time making it. The temperature inside a pressure cooker rises far beyond the normal boiling point, so the vegetables cook, infusing the water with flavor, much faster than when you boil them (roughly 20 minutes vs. 1½ hours). And by keeping all of the steam inside, the pressure cooker preserves flavor that might otherwise waft out of the pot and condense on your ceiling.

While the broth simmers, get some storage containers open and ready. When it's time to strain the broth, put a large bowl in the sink. Place a strainer over the bowl and pour the broth into it (slowly!). Use a ladle to transfer the broth into individual containers. Use containers of varying sizes (from ice cube trays to half-gallon cartons) so you can defrost only as much as you need for each recipe.

Label your broth, with the type and date, even if you're storing it in clear containers. You never know what else you may freeze that resembles it, and you don't want to wait until you're making risotto to discover that the liquid you're pouring into the pan is lemonade, not chicken broth.

Chicken Broth

MAKES ABOUT 2 QUARTS

Here's how to get in touch with your inner grandmother and make an essential ingredient for soups and risotto at the very same time. You also get a boiled chicken to use in salads (Avocado and Apple Salad, page 174, or Caesar, page 105), sandwiches, and under Tomato Sauce (page 156).

TIME TO PREPARE (HANDS ON): *About 15 minutes*

TIME TO COOK: *About 3 hours; about 40 minutes in a pressure cooker*

TOTAL TIME: *About 3¼ hours; about 1 hour with a pressure cooker*

1 chicken, 3½ to 5 pounds, or the same amount of chicken parts

2 large carrots, peeled and each cut into 4 pieces

1 onion, peeled and quartered

2 leeks, cleaned and chopped

2 large celery stalks, with leaves, each cut into 4 pieces, or 1 bulb fennel

Stems from 1 bunch parsley, chopped

4 whole black peppercorns

2 quarts water (if you plan to use tap water, smell it first. If there's a foul or chemical odor, switch to spring or filtered water)

Wash the chicken and pat it dry. If you're using a whole bird, bind it with kitchen twine so the wings and legs don't flare out.

Put it in a large stockpot with the carrots, onion, leeks, celery or fennel, parsley stems, peppercorns, and water. Bring the water to a simmer, cover, and cook until the meat is tender, about 1 hour.

Remove the chicken and set aside to cool.

Continue simmering the broth, covered, over medium or medium-low heat. When the chicken is cool enough to handle, strip and discard the skin, and transfer the meat to a bowl or storage container. Return the bones to the pot and simmer for another 2 hours.

Strain into a large bowl and refrigerate 8 hours, or overnight. Lift the fat off the surface the next day. Transfer to storage containers and store as directed on page 284.

Using a pressure cooker instead of a stockpot, follow the directions above through the point where you add the water. Lock on the lid and bring to full pressure. Adjust the heat on your stove to hold at full pressure for 45 minutes. Remove from the heat. Let the pressure come down on its own. Tilt the cooker away from you when you unlock the lid. Remove the chicken, and strain, chill, defat, and store the stock as directed on page 284. (There's no need to return the bones to the pot. Pressure cooking extracts ample flavor.)

- *Refrigerate or freeze in tightly sealed containers. Refrigerate up to 3 days. Freeze up to 6 months.*

Vegetable Broth

TIME TO PREPARE (HANDS ON): *About 15 minutes*

TIME TO COOK: *About 1½ hours; about 30 minutes with a pressure cooker*

TOTAL TIME: *About 1¾ hours; about 45 minutes with a pressure cooker*

2 large onions, peeled and quartered
2 large leeks, trimmed, cleaned, and
   chopped
4 carrots, peeled and chopped
1 large sweet potato, peeled and chopped
4 celery stalks, leaves included, chopped
Stems from 1 bunch parsley, coarsely
   chopped
3 quarts water (if you plan to use tap water,
   smell it first. If there's a foul or chemical
   odor, switch to spring or filtered water)

Place the onion, leeks, carrots, sweet potato, celery, parsley stems, and water in a large stockpot. Bring it to a boil, cover, and turn the heat down to medium-low. Simmer until the water is well infused with flavor, about 1½ hours. Strain and store as directed on page 284.

Or place the onions, leeks, carrots, sweet potato, celery, parsley stems, and water in a pressure cooker. Lock on the lid and bring to full pressure. Turn the heat down to medium-low to maintain pressure and cook for 20 minutes. Remove from the heat and let the pressure come down on its own. Strain and store as directed on page 284.

• *Refrigerate or freeze in tightly sealed containers. Refrigerate up to 4 days. Freeze up to 1 year.*

Shrimp Broth

Shrimp shells make a delicate, distinctive broth that's best as a base for dishes that include seafood of some kind. Make it in small batches because it doesn't keep as well as chicken or vegetable stock.

TIME TO PREPARE (HANDS ON): *About 10 minutes*

TIME TO COOK: *About 1 hour; about 20 minutes with a pressure cooker*

TOTAL TIME: *About 1 hour, 10 minutes; about 30 minutes with a pressure cooker*

Shells of 8 to 12 large shrimp
1 onion, peeled and quartered
1 carrot, peeled and cut into 4 pieces
1 celery stalk, with leaves, cut into 4 pieces
1 leek, cleaned and chopped
4 cups water (if you plan to use tap water,
   smell it first. If there's a foul or chemical
   odor, switch to spring or filtered water)

Put the shrimp shells, onion, carrot, celery, leek, and water in a large stockpot or pressure cooker. In a stockpot, bring to a simmer over medium-high heat. Cover and turn the heat down to medium-low. Simmer gently for 1 hour. Strain and store as directed on page 284.

Using a pressure cooker, lock on the lid and bring to full pressure. Adjust the heat on the stove to hold at full pressure for 10 minutes. Remove from the heat. Let the pressure come down on its own. Tilt the cooker away from you when you unlock the lid. Strain and store as directed on page 284.

- *Refrigerate or freeze in tightly sealed containers. Refrigerate up to 2 days. Freeze up to 3 months.*

Lobster Broth

M A K E S   6   C U P S

Who isn't troubled by too many lobster shells?

But seriously . . . lobster is so expensive, it's a shame to waste any part of it. And once you've taken the meat from the tail and claws, here's what you do with the empties: make a potent broth that adds a velvety, rich flavor to seafood dishes, stir-fries, and grains.

TIME TO PREPARE (HANDS ON): *About 10 minutes*

TIME TO COOK: *About 1 1/2 hours; about 30 minutes in a pressure cooker*

TOTAL TIME: *About 1 hour, 40 minutes; about 40 minutes in a pressure cooker*

Shells of two 1- to 1 1/2-pound lobsters, including the head
1 onion, peeled and quartered
2 carrots, peeled and cut into 4 pieces
1 celery stalk, with leaves, cut into 4 pieces
2 leeks, cleaned and chopped
6 cups water (if you plan to use tap water, smell it first. If there's a foul or chemical odor, switch to spring or filtered water)

Put the lobster shells, onion, carrot, celery, leeks, and water in a large stockpot or pressure cooker. In a stockpot, bring to a simmer over medium-high heat. Cover and turn the heat down to medium-low. Simmer gently for 1 1/2 hours. Strain and store as directed on page 284.

Using a pressure cooker, lock on the lid and bring to full pressure. Adjust the heat on your stove to hold at full pressure for 20 minutes. Remove from the heat. Let the pressure come down on its own. Tilt the cooker away from you when you unlock the lid. Strain and store as directed on page 284.

NOTE: You can "custom season" any broth for use in Asian dishes as follows:

2 cups strained broth (or canned broth)
1/2-inch slice peeled fresh ginger
1 garlic clove, crushed
1/4 cup chopped scallion greens
1 teaspoon miso (optional)

Combine all of the ingredients in a medium saucepan and simmer for 30 minutes. Strain and use in recipes for dishes calling for Asian seasonings, such as stir-fries or steamed fish (page 152).

- *Refrigerate or freeze in tightly sealed containers. Refrigerate up to 2 days. Freeze up to 4 months.*

Tomato Sauces

HERE'S THE difference a word can make: tomato sauce.

Not too inspiring, huh?

Homemade tomato sauce.

Now you're talking big bowls of pasta, steam rising through the richly colored sauce on top. You're catching the aroma of garlic and basil, and you are suddenly very hungry.

Homemade Tomato Sauce
(Uncooked)

MAKES ABOUT 2 CUPS

This light, multipurpose sauce is strictly seasonal because it must be made with ripe fresh tomatoes. The pale orange-pink off-season force-grown or imports are too mealy and bland. Fortunately this sauce freezes well, so you can put away a batch or two for when you want the taste of summer on your midwinter pasta or pizza.

TIME TO PREPARE (HANDS ON): *About 15 minutes*

TIME TO COOK: *Included in the preparation time*

TOTAL TIME: *About 15 minutes*

> 3 tablespoons extra virgin olive oil
> 2 large garlic cloves, thinly sliced lengthwise
> 10 to 12 large ripe tomatoes
> Coarse salt and freshly ground black pepper
> to taste
> ¼ to ½ cup minced fresh basil and/or
> oregano

Heat the oil in a nonstick skillet over medium-high heat. When hot, add the garlic, reduce the heat to medium-low, and sauté, stirring often, until the garlic turns golden, about 2 minutes. Remove from the heat and discard the garlic. Reserve the oil.

Fill a large pot with water and bring it to a boil. Add the tomatoes and bring to a boil again. Let boil for 30 seconds. Drain the water. When the tomatoes are cool enough to handle, peel them and cut into quarters. Squeeze out as many seeds as possible, and put the tomatoes in the work bowl of a blender or food processor. Or, if you have an immersion blender, put them into a mixing bowl. Blend on low, or process in short pulses to chop. Add the olive oil, salt and pepper, and herbs and process again gently to combine.

Make up to 3 days ahead.
- *Seal in a tightly covered container and refrigerate.*
- *To reheat, transfer to a heavy saucepan and stir over medium heat until warmed through. Or transfer to a microwavable bowl and microwave at full power, turning the bowl at 2-minute intervals, until heated through.*

Freeze up to 6 months, well wrapped in a glass or firm plastic container.
- *To defrost, follow directions for reheating above.*
- *To speed defrosting, put in a microwavable bowl (do not microwave in plastic), place a damp paper towel on top, and zap at medium strength, stirring each time, until heated through.*

Homemade Tomato Sauce

(Cooked)

MAKES 4 CUPS

TIME TO PREPARE (HANDS ON): *About 15 minutes*

TIME TO COOK: *Included in the preparation time*

TOTAL TIME: *About 15 minutes*

8 to 10 large ripe tomatoes or 6 cups
   canned whole or chopped tomatoes
3 tablespoons extra virgin olive oil
2 onions, chopped
2 garlic cloves, crushed and minced
2 anchovy fillets, minced (optional)
¼ cup dry white wine
¼ cup minced fresh basil or 2 tablespoons
   crumbled dried
¼ cup minced fresh oregano or
   2 tablespoons crumbled dried (optional)
Coarse salt and freshly ground black pepper

If using fresh tomatoes, fill a large pot with water and bring it to a boil. Add the tomatoes and bring to a boil again. Let boil for 30 seconds. Drain the water. When the tomatoes are cool enough to handle, peel them and cut into quarters. Squeeze out as many seeds as possible. If using canned whole tomatoes, chop them coarsely.

Heat the oil in a nonstick skillet over medium-high heat. When hot, add the onion, garlic, and the anchovy, if using. Reduce the heat to medium-low and sauté until the onion is soft and limp, about 7 minutes. Add the wine and stir until most of it evaporates, about 4 minutes.

Add the tomatoes, stirring until they cook down into a sauce, about 7 minutes. Transfer to a blender or food processor and gently puree, stopping before the sauce is liquefied, or use an immersion blender right in the skillet. Add the basil and oregano, if using. Season with salt and pepper.

NOTE: For additional fresh tomato sauce, see the recipe for Sole with Fresh Tomatoes (page 150).

Make up to 3 days ahead.
* *Seal in a tightly covered container and refrigerate.*
* *To reheat, transfer to a heavy saucepan and stir over medium heat until warmed through. Or transfer to a microwavable bowl and microwave at full power, turning the bowl at 2-minute intervals, until heated through.*

Freeze up to 6 months, well wrapped in a glass or firm plastic container.
* *To defrost, follow directions for reheating above.*
* *To speed defrosting, put in a microwavable bowl (do not microwave in plastic), place a damp paper towel on top, and zap at medium strength, stirring each time, until heated through.*

Béchamel Sauce

For decades, a "simple white sauce" was expected to be part of every home cook's repertoire. Now it's all but obsolete, partly because authentic béchamel recipes call for lots of butterfat, but mostly because the odds of making one that was silky, with a clean, fresh taste, were nothing against the likelihood that it would be lumpy and taste of singed flour.

It's time to bring it back in a version that is light and easy to make. Add béchamel to commercial tomato sauce, and you have something rich and elegant. Season it to taste (see below) and pour it over crepes. Use it to enhance the flavor of fillings for pastas or omelets.

TIME TO PREPARE (HANDS ON): *About 15 minutes*

TIME TO COOK: *Included in the preparation time*

TOTAL TIME: *About 15 minutes*

> 1 tablespoon unsalted butter or extra virgin olive oil
> 1 tablespoon unbleached all-purpose flour
> 1 $^1/_2$ cups low-fat milk or Vegetable Broth (page 286)
> Salt

Melt the butter or heat the oil in a small nonstick skillet or saucepan. Add the flour and stir constantly over medium heat to make a paste. As soon as the paste turns golden, after about 2 minutes, pour in the milk or broth. Using a whisk, continue to stir over medium-high heat until thickened, about 8 minutes. Season with salt. If it's too thick, add more milk or broth, or a dash of dry white wine. Serve promptly, while hot.

Cheese

While it's still hot, add to the thickened sauce 2 to 4 tablespoons grated Parmesan, Gruyère, or sharp cheddar cheese, stirring to melt. Serve promptly, whole hot.

Spinach

While it's still hot, add 1 tablespoon grated Parmesan or Gruyère cheese, 2 tablespoons finely chopped spinach, and a pinch ground nutmeg to the thickened sauce, and stir to blend well. Serve promptly, while hot.

- *Make up to 3 days ahead.*
- *Seal in a tightly covered container and refrigerate.*
- *To reheat, transfer to a saucepan and stir in 2 tablespoons dry white wine or additional vegetable broth. Stir constantly over medium-low heat until warmed through. If too viscous, add another tablespoon or two of wine or broth.*

Dough

THE READY-MADE dough sold in the refrigerator section of most supermarkets makes it easy to fill your house with the aroma of fresh bread—or have pizza that's not a bad compromise between frozen and homemade. But if you'd like to have a batch of your own basic dough, these are a cinch.

Bread Dough

M A K E S   2   L O A V E S / 8   R O L L S

TIME TO PREPARE (HANDS ON): *About 15 minutes (using a food processor)*

TIME TO COOK: *About 35 minutes*

TOTAL TIME: *About 3½ hours, including time for the dough to rise*

- 1½ tablespoons active dry yeast (about 1½ packages) or 1 tablespoon instant yeast
- 2 teaspoons brown sugar
- 2½ cups bread flour or unbleached all-purpose flour
- 3½ cups unbleached all-purpose flour or whole wheat flour
- 1 tablespoon sea salt
- About 2¼ cups water

If you're using active dry yeast, dissolve the yeast and sugar in 2 tablespoons warm water, and let sit until creamy with small bubbles, about 5 minutes.

Place the flour and salt in the work bowl of a food processor or Mixmaster. Process in short pulses to combine. With the machine running, add the yeast mixture and 1 cup of water, processing until a dough forms, about 90 seconds for a food processor, 5 to 7 minutes for a mixer.

If you're using instant yeast, put the flour, yeast, sugar, and salt in a food processor or electric mixer (or in a large mixing bowl).

Run the processor or mixer, or stir by hand, until the ingredients form a dough that's soft but not sticky. This will take about 90 seconds in the processor, 5 to 7 minutes in the mixer, and up to 15 minutes by hand.

Turn the dough out onto a lightly floured surface. Knead until it's smooth and springy. (You'll have to add some flour to keep it from sticking to your hands. Add as little as possible.)

Shape the dough into a ball and place it in a large mixing bowl. Cover with plastic wrap and set aside in a warm, draft-free place until doubled, about 1 hour, 40 minutes.

Press the air out of the dough. Cover it with plastic wrap again, and let it rise until doubled again, about 45 minutes.

Press the air out of the dough again and divide it into 2 pieces. Working with one piece at a time, flatten it on a lightly floured surface into a rectangle about 10 inches long and 6 inches wide. Fold the upper right-hand corner to the center. Fold the lower left-hand corner up to meet it. Now fold the dough in half diagonally, bringing the upper portion down and making a seam along the bottom. Put it seam side down on a baking sheet *or* seam side up on a floured towel inside a French loaf pan. Cover with a towel and let rise for 40 minutes.

To bake in 10-inch loaf pans, flatten each piece into a rectangle the length of the pans. Fold in half, then roll to form a fat cylinder and seal the seam. Place seam side down in the loaf pans. Cover with a towel and let rest until the dough has risen above the rim of the pans, about 40 minutes.

To make rolls, divide the dough into 8 to 12 pieces (depending on the size of the muffin cups). Shape each into a ball, rolling it with your palm on a flat surface to make it round and smooth. Place in the cup of a nonstick muffin tin. Cover with a towel and let rest in a warm, draft-free place until the dough has risen above the rim of the pans, about 30 minutes.

Meanwhile, heat the oven to 450°F.

When you're ready to bake the bread, use a razor or serrated knife to slash the loaves on the baking sheet lengthwise down the center. Or carefully turn the loaves from the towels onto a baking sheet or baking stone, slash them, then put them in the oven. Or put the loaf pans or muffin tins into the oven.

Bake until golden and until you get a hollow sound when you tap on the bottom of the bread, about 35 minutes for loaves, 25 to 30 minutes for rolls. If the top of the bread is browning too quickly, cover it loosely with foil until it's done.

Let the bread cool on a rack for at least 20 minutes before you slice it.

Freeze the dough up to 3 months. Wrap in plastic and seal in a zip-lock bag. Leave at room temperature to thaw, and use as soon as it's thawed.

- *Slice the bread before freezing, so you can toast individual pieces. Store the slices or rolls in zip-lock bags, pressing out the air before you seal. Do not defrost before toasting.*
- *To defrost and reheat without toasting, wrap in foil, place on a baking sheet or stone, and place in a 350°F oven until heated through. To defrost in a hurry, soak a paper towel in water. Wring out as much moisture as possible and wrap around the bread. Microwave at full power for 45 seconds to 1 minute. Let rest for 30 seconds, then feel if it's warm inside. If it's still frozen, return to the microwave and zap at 20-second intervals until heated through. Eat right away, or it will be impossibly tough.*

Pizza Dough

In Naples, birthplace of pizza as we know it, there is a self-appointed regulator who has assumed responsibility for safeguarding the authenticity of the dish. Real pizza, he has decreed, comprises tomato sauce, mozzarella, and either oregano or basil (not both!), and a crust made of flour, water, and salt. Top this crust any way you'd like.

TIME TO PREPARE (HANDS ON):	*About 20 minutes*
TIME TO COOK:	*About 15 minutes*
TOTAL TIME:	*About 2 hours, 40 minutes, including time for the dough to rise*

1 tablespoon (1 package) active dry yeast or 2 teaspoons instant yeast
3$\frac{1}{2}$ cups bread flour or unbleached all-purpose flour
1 tablespoon coarse salt
About 1$\frac{1}{4}$ cups water
Cornmeal
Topping (pages 48 and 49)

If you're using active dry yeast, dissolve the yeast in 2 tablespoons warm water, and let sit until creamy with small bubbles, about 5 minutes.

Place the flour and salt in the work bowl of a food processor or Mixmaster. Process in short pulses to combine. With the machine running, add the yeast mixture and 1 cup of water, processing until a dough forms, about 90 seconds for a food processor, 5 to 7 minutes for a mixer. If the dough is too dry to cohere, add more water, 1 tablespoon at a time.

If you're using instant yeast, put the flour, yeast, and salt in a food processor or electric mixer (or in a large mixing bowl).

Run the processor or mixer, or stir by hand, adding the water until the ingredients form a dough that's soft but not sticky. This will take about 90 seconds in the processor, 5 to 7 minutes in the mixer, and up to 15 minutes by hand.

Shape the dough into a ball and place in a large bowl. Cover with plastic wrap and set in a warm place to rise until doubled, about 1½ hours.

Press the air out of the dough with your hands and divide into 2 pieces. Cover each loosely with a lightweight towel and let rest 30 minutes.

If you have a pizza stone, place it on the bottom rack of the oven. Heat the oven as high as it will go (500°F. ordinarily). On a lightly floured surface, roll out each piece of dough as thin as you'd like. Alternate between the 2 pieces as you go, so the gluten will have a chance to rest in each—this will allow you to stretch it thinner, without having it snap right back into place.

Put on a well-floured baker's peel (a flat, long-handled shovel designed for this purpose) or on a baking sheet lightly sprinkled with cornmeal, and spread with the toppings. Slide or place into the oven and bake until the crust has browned, 8 to 15 minutes, depending on how thick you've rolled it and how hot the oven is. (The oven may not be large enough to handle more than one at a time, so keep the other covered until you bake it.)

Wrap leftover pizza in foil and freeze up to 3 months.
- *To reheat, place on a baking sheet or stone in a 450°F. oven until warmed through.*

Freeze the dough up to 3 months. Wrap in plastic and seal in a zip-lock bag. Leave at room temperature to thaw, and use as soon as it's thawed.

Fresh Pasta

ENOUGH FOR 6 SERVINGS

If you take the trouble to make fresh pasta, you won't have to sweat over the filling or sauce. Fresh pasta is so good, there's no point making anything fancy that will obscure the flavor.

TIME TO PREPARE (HANDS ON): *About 30 minutes by hand; about 15 minutes with a food processor*

TIME TO COOK: *About 2 to 3 minutes*

TOTAL TIME: *About 1½ hours, including time for the dough to rest*

2 cups plus 2 tablespoons unbleached all-purpose flour
3 large eggs
2 teaspoons finely grated lemon zest

To make it by hand, on a clean, flat work surface, make a mound of flour with a well in the center. Drop the eggs and lemon zest into the well, and beat lightly with a fork. Gradually incorporate the flour, using your hand to guide it into the eggs as you beat them. Continue mixing until you have a firm, stiff dough. Knead the dough until it's smooth, 7 to 10 minutes. Wrap in plastic and set aside for 30 minutes.

To make it in a food processor, in a mixing bowl, beat the eggs together lightly.

Put the flour and lemon zest into a food processor, and pulse to combine. With the motor running, pour the eggs in slowly, allowing them to be incorporated into a stiff dough. Take the dough out of the food processor, and knead it by hand until it's smooth and supple, about 3 minutes. Shape it into a ball and place it in a glass or

▶

ceramic bowl. Cover with plastic wrap and let it rest for 20 to 30 minutes.

Divide the dough into 4 pieces. Take one piece and flatten it with your hands. Generously flour it on each side. Put it through a hand-cranked pasta maker at the widest setting. Fold the dough in half and pass it through again. Adjust the setting two notches down, and pass the dough through again. Fold it in half and pass through again. Adjust the setting one notch down, and repeat. The pasta should be very thin, but not translucent. If you accidentally overdo it and roll the pasta so thin it tears, ball it up and start again, stopping short of the fragile, superthin sheet. Cover the sheet of pasta with plastic wrap while you roll out the rest of the dough.

For ravioli, place the pasta on a lightly floured surface, and cut with a 3-inch biscuit cutter. Put a teaspoon of filling in the lower half of each circle. Fold the top over to enclose the filling. Dip a long-tined fork in water and press along the edges to seal. Transfer to wax paper and cover loosely with plastic while you complete the batch.

For lasagna, cut the dough to the desired length and width.

For noodles, crank the dough through the desired cutter on your pasta maker.

Cook according to your recipe. Remember, fresh pasta cooks much faster than dry, about 2 minutes for noodles and 3 for ravioli.

You can make the dough up to 3 days ahead.
- *Dust well with flour, wrap in wax paper, then plastic, and refrigerate or freeze.*

Freeze up to 3 months.
- *To defrost, transfer to the refrigerator until pliable. Do not allow to get soft, or it will tear when you use it.*

Dumpling Wrappers

MAKES ABOUT 40

The difference between making dumpling wrappers and fresh pasta for lasagna, ravioli, and the like is that you must roll dumpling wrappers much thinner. You can use a pasta machine, setting the rollers on the narrowest notch, or you can buy commercial wrappers, which tend to be very good.

TIME TO PREPARE (HANDS ON): *About 20 minutes*

TIME TO COOK: *Depends on whether steamed or boiled; check the recipe*

TOTAL TIME: *About 20 minutes (for the dough)*

2 cups unbleached all-purpose flour
$1/2$ to $2/3$ cup cold water

Put the flour in a mixing bowl and stir in the water gradually, using only as much as you need to bind the flour into a dough. Use your hands to work the mess into a smooth dough. Turn out onto a flat, flour-dusted work surface (or a marble slab), and continue kneading until the dough is very smooth, 7 to 10 minutes.

Shape into a ball and cover with a towel.

Divide the dough into 4 pieces, and roll each out as thin as possible using a rolling pin, or with a pasta machine, following the directions on page 293. Cut the rolled dough with round biscuit cutters. Fill, shape, and cook according to the recipe (page 40).

You can make the dough up to 3 days ahead.
- *Dust with flour or cornstarch. Wrap tightly in wax paper, then cover with plastic wrap. Refrigerate or freeze.*

Freeze up to 3 months.

- *To defrost, transfer to the refrigerator until pliable. Do not let the dough get soft, or it will tear when you fill it.*

Pastry Crusts

THERE ARE several reasons to know how to make pastry crust. First, you never know when you're going to come in to some really good cherries, blueberries, or tart green apples. Second, fresh pastry tastes so much better than frozen or refrigerated commercial pie crusts, it's worth the small effort to make it. And third, a pie shell is a great place for leftovers.

Taste in crust varies as much as preference for fillings. Just as you might choose peach over pecan, you might want a crust that tastes of butter, while someone else would prefer something not quite as rich. These are simple, modest crusts, working pastry that won't upstage your filling.

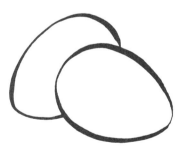

Pastry

(Savory for Quiche and Savory Tortes)

MAKES ONE 9-INCH SHELL

TIME TO PREPARE (HANDS ON): *About 10 minutes*

TIME TO COOK: *Depends on the pie recipe*

TOTAL TIME: *About 1 hour, 10 minutes, including time to chill the dough, but not the time to bake it*

---

1 $\frac{3}{4}$ cups unbleached all-purpose flour
4 tablespoons ($\frac{1}{2}$ stick) unsalted butter, cut
   into small pieces
1 large egg, lightly beaten
Pinch salt

In a mixing bowl using your fingers, or the work bowl of a food processor or mixer, combine the flour and butter until crumbly. Add the egg, salt, and enough cold water, 1 tablespoon at a time, to make a stiff, pliable dough. Shape into a ball, wrap in wax paper, and refrigerate at least 1 hour.

Roll, shape, and bake according to the recipe.

You can make the dough up to 3 days ahead.

- *Dust well with flour, wrap in wax paper, then plastic, and refrigerate.*

Freeze up to 3 months.

- *To defrost, transfer to the refrigerator until pliable. Do not allow to get soft or it will tear when you use it.*

Ricotta Pastry Crust

(Sweet)

MAKES ONE 9-INCH SHELL

TIME TO PREPARE (HANDS ON): *About 10 minutes*

TIME TO COOK: *Depends on the pie recipe*

TOTAL TIME: *About 1 hour, 10 minutes, including time to chill the
dough, but not the time to bake it*

1 ¾ cups unbleached all-purpose flour
½ cup sugar
2 tablespoons unsalted butter, cut into small
   pieces
¼ cup nonfat ricotta cheese
1 large egg, lightly beaten
2 tablespoons cold buttermilk

In a mixing bowl using your fingers, or the work
bowl of a food processor or mixer, combine the
flour, sugar, and butter until crumbly. Add the ricotta, egg, and buttermilk, and blend into a
smooth, pliable dough. Shape into a ball, wrap in
wax paper, and refrigerate at least 1 hour.

Roll, shape, and bake according to the recipe.

You can make the dough up to 3 days ahead.
- *Dust well with flour, wrap in wax paper, then plastic,
  and refrigerate.*

Freeze up to 3 months.
- *To defrost, transfer to the refrigerator until pliable. Do
  not allow to get soft, or it will tear when you use it.*

Crepes

MAKES ABOUT 20

*If you have the patience and skill to make a tissue-thin
pancake without burning it while you work up the nerve to
turn it over, or tearing it when you do, then go ahead and
make your own crepes. Otherwise, you might want to leave
it to the pros. There are several very good commercial
brands; buy them fresh and use them promptly, and you'll
save more than half the time involved in making dishes that
call for crepes.*

TIME TO PREPARE (HANDS ON): *About 20 minutes*

TIME TO COOK: *About 2 minutes each*

TOTAL TIME: *About 1 hour, including time for the batter to rest*

3 large eggs, lightly beaten
1 cup 1% milk
1 cup unbleached all-purpose flour
Pinch salt
Unsalted butter or vegetable oil

In a large mixing bowl, combine the eggs and
milk. Stir together the flour and salt, add it to the
liquids, and whisk together until smooth. Set
aside for 30 minutes.

Lightly grease an 8-inch nonstick pan with
butter or vegetable oil. Heat over medium heat.

Whisk the batter. Measure out 3 tablespoons
of batter (you can use a ¼ cup measuring cup,
and fill it ¾ full) and pour into the pan. Swirl the
pan quickly to coat the bottom evenly with batter. When the bottom has set, about 1 minute,
loosen the edge with a thin knife or spatula and
flip with your fingers. Cook for another 30 seconds to 1 minute. Transfer to a plate and repeat
until you've used all of the batter.

For Sweet Crepes

Before you add the flour to the eggs and milk, stir 1 tablespoon sugar into it with a whisk or a long-tined fork.

Make up to 3 days ahead.
- *Stack, wrap in plastic, and refrigerate. Let come to room temperature before filling.*

Freeze up to 6 months, well wrapped in plastic.
- *To defrost, leave at room temperature for several hours.*

Polenta

SERVES 6 TO 8

It was clear we'd reached a new age of culinary awareness when grocery stores began carrying ready-made polenta. Sold in sausage-shaped packages, commercial polenta can be sliced, topped with cheese, pesto, or olive oil and herbs, oven toasted, and served moments later . . . in much shorter time than it would take you to make it from scratch.

However, the flavor of any polenta depends on the quality of the cornmeal that goes into it, and you may prefer the taste you get when you make it yourself from fresh stone-ground cornmeal (available at most stores with a good selection of grains). Moreover, you can't serve the solid ready-made stuff as a soft, cereal-like side dish.

TIME TO PREPARE (HANDS ON): *About 20 minutes*

TIME TO COOK: *Included in the preparation time*

TOTAL TIME: *About 20 minutes*

**4 cups Chicken Broth (page 285) or
  Vegetable Broth (page 286)
1 cup cornmeal, preferably stone-ground**

Pour the broth into a large, heavy saucepan and bring to a boil over high heat. Gradually sprinkle in the cornmeal and stir until it becomes too thick to stir any longer, about 15 minutes.

You can spoon it straight from the pot onto serving plates, making a well in the center and filling it with sauce, or with unsalted butter or extra virgin olive oil and grated cheese. Or you can bake it, as follows:

Remove from the heat and let cool slightly. Meanwhile, line a baking sheet with a piece of parchment paper.

Spread the polenta on the paper and smooth into an even layer. Let cool completely. Top with anything you'd put on pizza, or brush lightly with extra virgin olive oil and sprinkle with minced fresh or crumbled dried herbs. Bake at 425° F. until golden brown, about 15 minutes. Cut into squares and serve hot.

For additional uses, see Crostini di Polenta (page 26).

Make up to 3 days ahead.
- *Spread onto a parchment lined baking sheet as directed above and let cool completely. Cut into squares, wrap in plastic, and refrigerate. To serve, unwrap, return to the baking sheet, and top and bake as directed.*

Potato Gnocchi

SERVES 4 TO 6

The literal translation from Italian is "lumps," but you may prefer to think of them as dumplings. ("Lumps" is not the only Italian food name of dubious appeal to the appetite. There is a pasta called strangolapreti, "priest stranglers.") Gnocchi make a comforting first course, especially in winter when they offer something warm and hearty to sink your teeth into. Treat them like pasta, tossing them with a fresh, hot sauce. Or put them in a lightly greased baking dish, top with sauce and cheese, and bake at 350° F. until the cheese browns and bubbles.

You can cut roughly ⅔ off the time involved in making a gnocchi dish if you buy prepared potato gnocchi. Look for it wherever you can buy fresh pasta, or check the frozen food case at your supermarket. Some commercial gnocchi is very good: chewy, light, and clean tasting. However, some are mealy or pasty, with a bitter aftertaste. Sample some before you serve them.

TIME TO PREPARE (HANDS ON): *About 20 minutes*

TIME TO COOK: *Under 30 minutes*

TOTAL TIME: *Under 1 hour*

2 pounds russet or Yukon Gold potatoes, peeled and quartered
1 large egg, lightly beaten
Approximately 1¾ cups unbleached all-purpose flour (you may need up to ½ cup more if the potatoes aren't starchy)
Unsalted butter or extra virgin olive oil
Coarse salt

Fit a large pot with a steamer basket. Add enough water to come up to the base of the steamer. Place the potatoes in the steamer, cover, and bring the water to a simmer over medium-high heat. Turn the heat down to medium-low and steam until the potatoes are cooked through, about 20 minutes.

Using a long-tined fork, mash together the egg and potatoes. Add the flour ½ cup at a time and use your hands to blend into a dough that is soft but firm. (Do not use a food processor or electric mixer for this, or the mixture will be too mushy to mold.) Place in a bowl, cover with plastic wrap, and refrigerate while you make the sauce.

Lightly flour a work surface.

Cut the dough into 6 pieces. Working with one piece at a time, roll each into a rope about 8 inches long and as thick as your thumb. Cut each rope into 1-inch-long pieces. Transfer to a well-floured dish or baking sheet. Place in the refrigerator while you lightly grease a baking dish with unsalted butter or extra virgin olive oil.

Fill a large pot with water and bring to a boil. Add salt, then add the gnocchi, about 8 at a time. When they rise to the surface, remove with a slotted spoon and transfer to the prepared baking dish. Serve as directed in the recipe.

Make up to 3 days ahead.
- *Wrap or cover tightly, preferably in a glass container, and refrigerate.*
- *Take out of the refrigerator about 2 hours before serving, transfer to a serving bowl, cover with plastic wrap, and let come to room temperature. Toss with warm sauce to heat through before serving.*

Freeze up to 6 months, well wrapped in a glass or firm plastic container.

- *To defrost, transfer to the refrigerator overnight. Then leave at room temperature several hours before serving, tossing with warm sauce to heat through.*
- *Or you can put the thawed gnocchi in a lightly greased baking dish, cover with sauce, sprinkle with cheese, and bake at 425° F. until the cheese is bubbly, about 10 minutes.*

Salad Dressings

THE WORD "salad" comes from "salt," which was used as dressing for greens in the days before such things were bottled and sold with profits for charity. But even when you have it in mind to make something simple, it's unlikely you'll want to go back to basics in quite that way.

Vinaigrette

SERVES 6

TIME TO PREPARE (HANDS ON): *Under 5 minutes*

TIME TO COOK: *None*

TOTAL TIME: *Under 5 minutes*

3 tablespoons extra virgin olive oil
1 tablespoon balsamic vinegar, red wine
   vinegar, or fresh lemon juice
$\frac{1}{2}$ teaspoon Dijon mustard
Pinch salt

In a blender or with an immersion blender, process the olive oil, vinegar or lemon juice, and mustard to blend. Season with salt. Use right away on salad greens or steamed vegetables, tossing well to coat.

Variations
- Add $\frac{1}{2}$ teaspoon grated fresh garlic
- Add $\frac{1}{2}$ teaspoon honey
- Add 1 tablespoon reduced-fat sour cream
- Add 1 tablespoon minced fresh chives
- Substitute 2 tablespoons walnut oil for the olive oil and orange juice for the lemon juice

Make up to 4 days ahead.
- *Seal tightly and refrigerate.*
- *Shake well before serving.*

Creamy Vinaigrette

SERVES 4

TIME TO PREPARE (HANDS ON): *About 5 minutes*

TIME TO COOK: *None*

TOTAL TIME: *About 5 minutes*

$\frac{1}{4}$ teaspoon grated fresh garlic
$\frac{1}{2}$ cup reduced-fat sour cream
$\frac{1}{2}$ cup cottage cheese
$\frac{1}{2}$ teaspoon Dijon mustard
1 tablespoon fresh lemon juice
$\frac{1}{2}$ tablespoon honey
1 teaspoon low-sodium soy sauce
$\frac{1}{4}$ cup minced fresh chives

Place the garlic, sour cream, cottage cheese, mustard, lemon juice, honey, and soy sauce in a food processor or blender, and process until smooth.

Transfer the mixture to a large mixing bowl and stir in the chives.

Make up to 3 days ahead.
• *Seal in a tightly covered container and refrigerate.*

Herb Dressing

SERVES 6

TIME TO PREPARE (HANDS ON): *Under 5 minutes*

TIME TO COOK: *None*

TOTAL TIME: *Under 5 minutes*

3 tablespoons extra virgin olive oil
1 egg yolk (see Note)
1 tablespoon capers, rinsed
3 tablespoons minced fresh parsley
3 tablespoon minced fresh chives
1 teaspoon Dijon mustard
Juice of 1 lemon
3 tablespoons minced fresh thyme
Salt

In a mixing bowl, blender, or with an immersion blender, combine the olive oil, egg yolk, capers, parsley, chives, mustard, lemon juice, and thyme. Whisk vigorously or blend to combine. Season with salt.

NOTE: Because of the albeit minimal risk of salmonella, do not serve anything containing raw eggs to young children or anyone who is pregnant, infirm, or suffering low immunity.

• ***Do not*** *make this dressing ahead of time. Because it contains raw egg, it won't keep well. (See note above.)*

Modified Mayonnaise

MAKES $^1/_2$ CUP

There are many things that defy good sense, but few more than fat-free mayonnaise. It's a product that means well, aspiring to give some of the pleasure of the real thing without the harmful consequences of fat and cholesterol. But gee whiz, can't you cut the fat from somewhere else? Mayonnaise is irreplaceable, and fortunately, a little goes a long way toward making simple foods delicious. You can dilute the fat and extend the flavor with a good brand of nonfat plain yogurt or reduced-fat sour cream. Because the mayonnaise flavor carries so well, diluted real mayonnaise tastes better than the reconfigured low-fat versions.

TIME TO PREPARE (HANDS ON): *About 5 minutes*

TIME TO COOK: *None, except roasted garlic, which takes about 40 minutes*

TOTAL TIME: *About 5 minutes*

$^1/_4$ cup mayonnaise
$^1/_4$ cup nonfat plain yogurt
Seasoning (choose one of the following combinations)

In a mixing bowl, combine the mayonnaise and yogurt. Stir well with a whisk to blend thoroughly. Then stir in any of the following:

FOR SHELLFISH
1 tablespoon minced sweet gherkins
1 tablespoon capers, drained
1 tablespoon minced fresh parsley

FOR BOILED POTATOES
1 cup loosely packed minced basil leaves
1 large ripe tomato, peeled and chopped

FOR FISH
1 tablespoon minced fresh sage
1 tablespoon minced fresh oregano
1 tablespoon minced fresh thyme
1 tablespoon minced fresh rosemary
1 tablespoon grated lemon zest

FOR COLD CHICKEN SANDWICHES
$^1/_2$ cup fresh spinach leaves
3 to 6 cloves from 1 head roasted garlic (see Note)

Place $^1/_4$ cup of water in a medium saucepan and bring it to a boil. Coarsely tear the spinach leaves and put them in the water. Cover and let simmer until the spinach is cooked, about 2 minutes. Remove with a slotted spoon and drain on paper towels. When cool, squeeze out the moisture with paper towels.

Peel 3 garlic cloves and place in a food processor along with the mayonnaise, yogurt, and spinach. Process in short pulses. Taste and add more garlic if you'd like.

NOTE: Roasted Garlic: Heat the oven to 450°F. Wrap the head of garlic in foil and place on a baking sheet. Roast until the cloves are soft enough to mash with your fingers, about 40 minutes. Unwrap and let cool.

Make up to 1 week ahead.
* *Seal in a tightly covered container and refrigerate.*
* *Do not freeze.*

Pesto

SERVES 6

*If you have pesto, you have a meal—or at least an appe-
tizer. A versatile spread with a flavor that's always welcome, it lets you make something of anything when you
have some on hand. Stir it into prepared tomato sauce and
toss with hot pasta, smear it on sliced bread and bake for a
minute or two until golden, or stir it into eggs (with some
roasted red bell peppers?), pour into an omelet pan, and
cook over medium heat until set.*

TIME TO PREPARE (HANDS ON): *About 10 minutes*

TIME TO COOK: *None*

TOTAL TIME: *About 10 minutes*

---

1 $\frac{1}{2}$ to 2 cups loosely packed basil leaves
2 tablespoons pine nuts
2 tablespoons grated Parmesan cheese (or
   half pecorino)
2 tablespoons ricotta cheese
1 garlic clove, crushed
2 tablespoons extra virgin olive oil
Salt and freshly ground black pepper

In a blender or a food processor fitted with a
small work bowl, place the basil, pine nuts,
Parmesan, ricotta, garlic, and olive oil. Process
into a paste. Season with salt and pepper.

Make up to 1 week ahead.
• *Seal in a tightly covered container and refrigerate.*

Freeze in small portions up to 9 months.
• *To defrost, transfer to the refrigerator overnight or leave
   at room temperature for a couple of hours.*

Roasted Bell Peppers

*Everyone should know at least one neat trick, some simple
way of making something from nothing, such as adding
roasted bell peppers to just about any savory thing. You
can buy roasted peppers or make them yourself, creating in
the process an aroma that will enhance the illusion that you
are preparing something far grander than pasta with
scrambled eggs (page 337) or a baked cheese sandwich
(page 336). You can also serve them as appetizers with feta
or goat cheese and cured olives.*

TIME TO PREPARE (HANDS ON): *About 5 minutes*

TIME TO COOK: *About 15 to 20 minutes*

TOTAL TIME: *About 30 minutes*

Heat the oven to 450°F.

   Slice as many bell peppers as you wish in half
lengthwise, and pull out the core and seeds. Place
skin side up on a baking sheet. Bake until the skin
chars, about 15 to 20 minutes. Transfer to a paper
bag and toss into the refrigerator for 5 to 10 minutes. Peel the skin, and slice or chop the peppers
as needed.

Make up to 4 days ahead.
• *Seal in a tightly covered container and refrigerate.*

Cakes

Angel Food Loaf

S E R V E S   8

TIME TO PREPARE (HANDS ON): *About 15 minutes*

TIME TO COOK: *About 40 minutes*

TOTAL TIME: *About 1 hour*

 1 cup white cake flour
 1 cup granulated sugar
 12 large egg whites
 ½ cup confectioners' sugar
 1 teaspoon vanilla powder or vanilla extract

Heat the oven to 325° F.

In a large mixing bowl, whisk together the flour and granulated sugar.

Put the egg whites in a separate large mixing bowl or work bowl of a heavy mixer and beat until frothy. Sprinkle with the confectioners' sugar. Continue beating until the egg whites form stiff peaks. Add vanilla. Using a rubber spatula, gradually fold in the flour mixture.

Spoon the batter into two 9-inch loaf pans or an angel food tube pan. Bake until golden brown and springy, about 40 minutes.

Let cool completely. (If you turn the pans upside down on a rack, you'll be able to free the cake more easily. If you're using a tube pan, you can cool it inverted, with the tube portion stuck in a bottle.)

To serve, loosen the cake by running a knife between the cake and the pan. Separate slices by inserting 2 forks into the cake and pulling apart.

Variations

Chocolate
Substitute ¼ cup unsweetened cocoa powder for ¼ cup cake flour.

Lemon or Orange
Add 1 tablespoon grated lemon zest or orange zest when you add the confectioners' sugar.

Ginger
Add 2 teaspoons ground ginger when you add the confectioners' sugar.

Make up to 3 days ahead.
* *Wrap tightly in plastic and refrigerate. Let come to room temperature before filling and frosting.*
Freeze up to 3 months, well wrapped.
* *To defrost, leave at room temperature for several hours.*

Just Plain Cake

These are simple, firm sheets you can serve plain with fruit, fill and layer for something fancier, or cut and shape for a custom-made birthday cake. You can also use it for Charlotte (page 274) and Summer Pudding (page 277).

TIME TO PREPARE (HANDS ON): *About 10 minutes*

TIME TO COOK: *About 15 minutes*

TOTAL TIME: *About 40 minutes*

Unsalted butter

1 $\frac{1}{2}$ cups cake flour or all-purpose flour, plus extra for dusting

1 cup sugar

4 eggs

1 teaspoon vanilla extract

Tear off 2 sheets of parchment paper the length of a jelly roll pan. Grease each lightly with unsalted butter and dust with flour. Shake off excess flour.

Heat the oven to 350°F.

With an electric mixer, beat together the sugar, eggs, and vanilla until light. Fold in the flour.

Spread the mixture on one prepared sheet of parchment paper, then cover with the other. Bake until firm and springy, about 12 minutes.

Turn onto a rack to cool, then peel away the parchment paper. Use as called for in the recipe.

Make up to 3 days ahead.

• *Wrap tightly in plastic and refrigerate. Let come to room temperature before filling and frosting.*

Freeze up to 3 months, well wrapped. To defrost, leave at room temperature for several hours.

Sponge Cake

SERVES 6 TO 8

TIME TO PREPARE (HANDS ON): *About 15 minutes*

TIME TO COOK: *About 1 hour*

TOTAL TIME: *About 1 $\frac{1}{4}$ hours, plus time to cool*

5 large eggs, separated

$\frac{1}{2}$ cup confectioners' sugar

$\frac{1}{2}$ cup granulated sugar

1 cup white pastry flour or unbleached all-purpose flour

1 teaspoon baking powder

1 tablespoon grated lemon zest

1 teaspoon vanilla powder or extract

Heat the oven to 350°F. Line the bottom of two 9-inch round cake pans with parchment paper.

With an electric mixer, beat the egg whites until soft peaks form. Beat in the confectioners' sugar and continue beating until stiff peaks form.

In a separate mixing bowl, beat the egg yolks with the granulated sugar until light and fluffy. In another bowl, use a whisk or a long-tined fork to combine the flour and baking powder. Blend the flour mixture, the lemon zest, and vanilla into the egg yolks. Fold that mixture into the egg whites.

Pour the batter evenly into the 2 pans. Bake until springy, about 1 hour. Let cool completely in the pan on a cooling rack before turning out and cutting.

Chocolate Sponge Cake

Replace ¼ cup of flour with ¼ cup unsweetened cocoa powder. Omit the lemon zest.

Make up to 3 days ahead.
- *Wrap tightly in plastic and refrigerate. Let come to room temperature before filling and frosting.*

Freeze up to 3 months, well wrapped. To defrost, leave at room temperature for several hours.

Occasions

A Good Basic Dinner
A Basic Nice Dinner
An Elegant Dinner
Backyard Barbecue
Picnics
Brunch
Sunday Supper
Housewarming
Entertaining Your Parents
Valentine's Day
You've Invited You-Know-Who to Dinner
You're Fixing up a Friend
Child's Birthday Party
When You're Hosting the Book Group (Investment
    Club . . .)
Happy Holidays!

A GOOD BASIC DINNER

The concept of Dinner has been declining in recent years, and seemed to reach rock bottom not long ago when a major news magazine illustrated a piece about eating trends with a photo of an affluent young couple sitting on their kitchen floor having breakfast cereal for supper.

Not that we'd like to return to meals as they were in the Renaissance when people with equal earning power ate roughly ten courses at a sitting, half of them meat of some kind. But to have come this far through the ages only to forsake the pleasures of food and the grace of the table is to have come for nothing.

When you invite people to "Dinner" you should serve, at minimum, this:

Main Dish
Ample Salad or (if the entrée is vegetarian) Grain Side Dish
Dessert

ADAPTABLE FOR ANYONE
All Kinds of Chili (page 106)
(Up to 3 days ahead)
Brown Rice with Cheddar (page 182)
Apple-Ginger Custard (page 272)
(Up to 2 days ahead)
Pale beer

CHICKEN
Chicken Sformata with Tomato and Fennel Sauce (page 161)
(Make the sauce up to 3 days ahead)
Mashed Potatoes (page 191)
Fresh Fruit and Sour Cream (page 276)
Medium fruity white wine

SEAFOOD
Shrimp with Corn and Bell Pepper (page 129)
Rice (page 181)
Chocolate Ricotta Pudding (page 276)
(Up to 2 days ahead)
Pale beer or medium fruity white wine

A BASIC NICE DINNER

This is a Good Basic Dinner, dressed up with a first course and a bottle of wine.

MENU
First Course
Main Course/Side Dish and/or Salad
Dessert
One wine or two

VEGETARIAN
Three-Vegetable Terrine (page 92)
(Up to 3 days ahead)
Potato Focaccia (page 227)
(Up to 2 weeks ahead. Freeze.)
Sweet Bell Pepper Soup with Rice (page 56)
(Up to 3 days in advance. Make pesto up to
1 month ahead. Freeze.)
Fresh Fruit and Sour Cream (page 276)

FISH
Vacherin
Lemon Risotto (page 74)
Seafood Stew with Spinach and Saffron (page 154)
Beets and Sour Cream (page 178)
Pumpkin Pudding Cake (page 264) with
Eggnog Glace (page 281)
Gavi de Gavi
or
Vino Nobile de Montepulciano

AN ELEGANT DINNER

Elegant isn't what it used to be . . . thank goodness. State dinners in ancient Athens could last for days, and include a hundred or so courses. In these menus, a substantial vegetarian side dish(*) can serve as an entrée for those who won't be eating poultry or fish.

MENU
Appetizers
First Course
Entrée/Side Dish/Salad
Dessert
Wines

FISH AND VEGETARIAN
Pumpkin and Mushroom Risotto* (page 75)
Simple Baked Fish in Foil (page 133)
Potato Ring with Bell Peppers and Sage (page 190)
Mixed salad greens with Vinaigrette (page 298)
Apple-Ginger Custard (page 272)
A Loire Valley Vouvray
or
A Côtes du Rhône Rouge

CHICKEN AND VEGETARIAN
Bell Pepper Spread with Olives and Feta (page 36)
Assorted sheep's milk cheeses
Grape Risotto* (page 73)
Chicken Baked in Parchment (page 159) with vegetables
Fresh Fig Clafouti (page 272)
A California Chardonnay
or
A Fleurie

BACKYARD BARBECUE

The way the Backyard Barbecue has been romanticized in our culture is fraudulent and cruel. It looks so easy: the lovely yard, the guests relaxed and happy with their ice-cold beer, the kids delighting everyone with their adorable antics, the dog loping merrily among the crowd. Then there's the host, standing over the grill, sipping from a highball glass, and flipping the food with a spatula. The grid marks are perfect.

But anyone who's ever had a cookout can tell you that before those guest arrived, there was a frantic mowing of the lawn, which meant not getting around to transferring the beer from shopping bag to refrigerator in time to chill. The sanitized version doesn't show those children ducking and diving around the dinner table, upending the bowl of potato salad—conveniently as far as the dog is concerned. And it does not show what you are drinking from that highball glass, but surely it's something to get your mind off the fact that you can't for the life of you flip the food with your spatula because it is stuck to the grid and turning black so fast it's not funny.

Rules to Party By

GRILL FOR good friends and family only. It's too risky for entertaining people you don't know very well because so much can go wrong.

Do everything except grill the food ahead of time. Have the appetizers, side dishes, beverages, and dessert completely finished. If everything else is ready to serve, you can devote yourself to building and tending the fire, then cooking the main course.

MENUS

Grilled Chicken in Yogurt Marinade (page 165)
Marinated Mixed Vegetables (Eggplant, Mushrooms,
Onions, and Beets)
Cucumber Raita (page 177)
Chopped Mango, Tomato, and Avocado Salad (page 174)
Rice (page 181)
Pita Bread (page 224), Lavash (page 228), or flour tortillas
Sorbet (page 281) or ice cream
Minted iced tea/Chablis/Pilsner

STRICTLY VEGETARIAN

Replace the chicken and marinated mixed vegetables with:
Grilled Vegetable Salad (page 116)
Tahini Sauce (page 110)

Timing Is Everything . . .

Up to Two Weeks Ahead: Make the lavash or pita bread (optional) and freeze it.

Two Days Ahead and/or the Day Before: Blanch the vegetables. Mix the marinades for the chicken and the vegetables. Mix the salad dressing. Make the cucumber salad. Make the mint ice cubes for the tea.

That Morning: Marinate the chicken and vegetables. Make the tea.

Two or Three Hours Ahead: Make the rice. When it's done fluff it once—quickly, then cover and leave it in the pot or steamer until you're ready to serve. Make sure the drinks are chilling. If the bread is frozen, take it out of the freezer and wrap it in foil.

One Hour Ahead: Light the fire. When the coals are covered with fine ash, glowing but no longer in flames, cook the chicken and vegetables according to the recipes.

Just Before Serving: Place the foil-wrapped stack of bread or tortillas on the grill to warm through, about 3 minutes, depending on how much heat remains.

PICNICS

Mrs. Isabella Beeton, the Mother of All Homemakers, knew that a picnic is no mere frolic in the grass. To do it properly, she wrote in her formidable *Book of Household Management* (1861), one must prepare beef two ways— boiled and roasted— lamb (ribs and shoulders) duck, ham, veal and ham pie, pigeon pie, lobster, and calf's head. Then there were multiple salads and desserts.

Here is what I recommend.

SEAFOOD

Cherry Fruit Bread (page 222)

Havarti Cheese

(Make the bread up to 1 month before. Freeze)

Swordfish Ceviche (page 98)

(That morning)

Shrimp Tabbouleh (page 130)

(The day before)

Scallop and Potato Salad (page 143)

(That morning)

Fresh Corn, and Steamed Sugar Snap Pea Salad (page 173)

(The day before)

Blueberries and sour cream (page 276)

Rosé

———————

or

Baked Falafel with Sweet Potato (page 110)

on

Pita Bread (page 224)

(Make the pita up to 1 month before. Freeze.
Make the falafel up to 3 days ahead.)

with tomatoes, sprouts, and Tahini Sauce (page 110)

(Tahini Sauce up to 4 days ahead)

Cucumber Raita (page 176)

(2 days ahead)

Summer Pudding (page 277) made with Sponge Cake

(page 304) and peaches or strawberries

(The night before)

Amber or pale beer or iced tea

Packing

WHEN YOU'RE planning a picnic within the cozy shelter of your home, it's easy to forget that the greatest threat to a good meal outdoors is not soggy sandwiches or limp pasta salad. It's insects. So when you go to shop for food, pick up a set of citronella candles and a bottle of insect repellent. Pack them first so you won't forget them.

If you're using reusable plastic containers, take a good sniff before you pack your food in them. You may find that they need a wash to eliminate odors and/or residue from previous contents.

Always wash new containers and dry them thoroughly. It's rare for any plastic product to come from the factory without an odor that will affect the flavor of your food.

Bring extra zip-lock bags for packing leftovers and lots of napkins. A handful of moist towelettes may be appreciated.

Tableware

There are two distinct attitudes toward serving a picnic and which is yours is a highly personal matter:

1. Anything you've taken the trouble to make merits real plates and silverware, tablecloth, and candles.

   And there is:

2. What in heaven's name is the *point* in a picnic if you're going to have to wash dishes afterward?

Take Inventory (In Writing!)

Forget to put out forks at home? No problem. In the woods or on the beach? Yes problem. Write down everything you're serving so you'll bring the right kind and amount of tableware.

What to Eat: Choose foods that won't get soggy or that benefit from being soggy, such as Tuna Spread (page 147) on Real Bread Rolls (page 212), Panzanella (page 176), Shrimp Tabbouleh (page 130), and Summer Pudding (page 277) . . . all of which get better sitting around soaking up juices from their own ingredients.

Pack the fillings and bread separately, and make the sandwiches (except Tuna Spread, which is best when it's soggy) when you're ready to eat. The same goes for some salads and dressings.

Pour iced tea, iced coffee, lemonade, or fruit juice into small individual plastic cartons. Freeze them overnight and carry them with other foods in the cooler.

Include foods that are naturally cooling, such as cucumbers, lettuces, and melons, so you won't have to worry about keeping them ice cold.

BRUNCH

Aside from "Sure, I'll volunteer for the bake sale" and "Marry me," "Come for brunch" may be the most regretted words in use today. It commits you not only to waking up early on Sunday to prepare, but to settling on something to serve.

If you don't like breakfast foods, it's easy: serve lunch. But if you're partial to pancakes and waffles, muffins and eggs, it's harder to make up your mind and menu. This one can go either way— sweet for breakfast, savory for lunch.

MENU

Omelet Roulade (Sweet or Savory) (page 119)
Souffléed Sweet Potato Polenta (with savory roulade) (page 185) or Oatmeal Soufflé (with sweet roulade) (page 237)
Fruit Bread (page 222)
(Up to 1 month ahead. Freeze [see Note, page 316.])
Fruit Fizz (page 255)

BIG SPRING BRUNCH

This menu, which includes a vegetarian entrée as well as chicken or poached salmon, makes an excellent buffet for any large spring or early summer celebration.

Frittata Crepes (page 112)
Avocado Salad with Chicken, Apples, and Walnuts (page 174)
or
Poached Salmon (page 124) with Modified Mayonnaise (page 301)
Sweet and Nutty Bulgur Salad (page 182)
Pane al Latte (page 223)
Lemon Angel Food Loaf (page 303) with fresh strawberries

Timing Is Everything . . .

Up to One Month Before: Bake the bread and freeze according to directions in the recipe. Bake the cake and freeze according to directions in the recipe. Make the tomato sauce and freeze according to directions in the recipe.

Three Days Before: Poach the chicken breasts or salmon. Make the spinach filling. Refrigerate. Clean the house.

The Day Before: Make the rice salad. Slice the strawberries, and toss with sugar and lemon juice. Make the crepes. Stack, wrap in plastic, and refrigerate. Set the table.

That Morning: Defrost the tomato sauce. Take the angel cake and bread out of the freezer. Reheat the bread according to directions in the recipe, 40 minutes before serving. Make the dressing for the chicken salad or the mayonnaise for the salmon. Toss the chicken and dressing. Layer the crepes and filling. Bake.

SUNDAY SUPPER

This is the time for good friends and close family, people who know you won't mind if they seem kind of melancholy when they arrive. After all, people tend to be sensitive on Sunday evenings, sometimes feeling anxious and alone. They can be soothed by good company and good simple food.

Sunday evening may also be the best time to entertain friends with young children. They'll want to keep it short—school night, you know—so you can have time to clean up after them and compose yourself for the week ahead.

ADAPTABLE FOR ANYONE

Any Kind of Chili (page 106)
(Up to 3 days ahead. Add the main ingredient according to the timing suggested in the recipe)
Brown Rice with Cheddar (page 182)
(Up to 2 days ahead)
Buttermilk Spoon Bread (page 183)
(Just before they come)
or
Lavash (page 228) or store-bought tortillas
(Make lavash up to 1 month ahead. Freeze [see Note].)
Chocolate Ricotta Pudding (page 276)
(Up to 3 days ahead)

NOTE: Don't forget to remove in time to defrost and reheat according to the instructions at the end of the recipe!

HOUSEWARMING

As soon as you move to a new home, fix a date for a housewarming and you'll be grateful for as long as you live in that place. Once you've invited everyone you know to storm the premises, you'll do all the pesky domestic things that need doing but you might otherwise postpone forever.

Not Sooo Fast: Give yourself enough time to get to know your house so you won't have any surprises during the party. You cannot be certain about plumbing, for one thing, until you've lived with it for a while.

APPETIZER BUFFET

Three-Vegetable Terrine (page 92)
(3 days ahead)
Salmon and Shrimp Terrine (page 91)
(2 days ahead)
Real Bread (page 212)
(Up to 1 month ahead. Freeze [see Note].)
Caponata (page 32)
(4 days ahead)
Hummus (page 28)
(4 days ahead)
Pita Bread (page 224)
(Up to 1 month ahead. Freeze [see Note].)
Ricotta-Filled Figs (page 51)
(day before)

Also try the brunch menu on page 313 as a buffet.

NOTE: Don't forget to remove in time to defrost and reheat according to the instructions at the end of the recipe!

ENTERTAINING YOUR PARENTS

The timeless trouble with meeting your parents socially is that sooner or later, everyone reverts to their customary roles. It's inevitable because, the fact is, you're programmed! You to act thirteen and they to behave like the stressed-out parents of a wild adolescent.

You can postpone, if not prevent, the relapse by serving Really Sophisticated Food and inviting friends to join you.

The In-Laws Are Coming!

COURTESY, GENEROSITY, AND GRACE. Bywords for those entertaining in-laws.

Every so often, we're told by well-meaning social commentators that it's time to bury the "myth" that in-laws—particularly mothers in-law—are the scourge of married life. Certainly in-laws are an asset to many families in many ways. But the stereotype will persist because, despite the efforts of the saints among us to reason it away, it's often apt.

Conflict may flare around meals if you're not careful to consider everything from their point of view.

No Fair

• Making a dish your mother in-law considers a specialty of hers.

• Failing to ask about preferences and aversions. *Hint:* Don't ask, "What do you like?" because they'll almost certainly say, "Oh, anything is fine." Ask, for example, "Do you like swordfish? How much garlic can you stand?"

• Accepting a compliment without offering two in return.

• Losing your sense of humor NO MATTER WHAT! (See Note.)

Item of Housekeeping

Check the family photos on display to make sure everyone's evenly represented.

NOTE: I know one desperate daughter in-law who lets her best friend know several days ahead whenever her in-laws are coming to dinner. At some point during the evening, her friend calls with a really good joke.

And you can always remember in-laws who were more difficult than yours, for example, Henry VIII or Lucretia Borgia.

MENUS

Assorted Fresh Cheeses
Real Bread (page 212)
(Up to 1 month ahead. Freeze [see Note].)
Blueberry Risotto (page 70) or Lemon Risotto (page 74)
Sole and Salmon Terrines with Spinach (page 148)
(Prepare the filling the day before)
Artichokes in Lemon Sauce (page 196)
(the day before)
Ginger Angel Food Loaf (page 303) with Real Vanilla Glacé
(page 279)
(Make the cake up to 2 weeks ahead. Freeze
[see Note].)

Savory Puff Pastry (page 50)

(Filling the day before)

Lentil Soup with Pumpkin (page 61)

(Up to 2 days ahead)

Rice Roulade with Spinach or Bell Peppers (page 80)

(Make the roulade up to 2 days ahead)

Cauliflower Broiled with Cheese (page 199)

Beet and Radish Salad (page 178)

(Make the dressing up to 3 days ahead)

Ginger Angel Food Loaf (page 303) with Real Vanilla Glacé
(page 279)

(Make the cake up to 2 weeks ahead. Freeze
[see Note].)

NOTE: Don't forget to remove in time to defrost
and reheat according to the instructions at the
end of the recipe!

VALENTINE'S DAY

Now you've done it.
   Once you've invited someone for Valentine's dinner, you've committed yourself to making something special. You can relieve some of the pressure by preparing most of the food in advance or by planning to make the meal together.

CHICKEN OR VEGETARIAN

Bell Pepper Spread with Olives and Feta (page 36)

(3 days ahead)

Assorted sheep's milk cheeses

Real Bread (page 212)

(Up to a month ahead. Freeze [see Note].)

Lemon Risotto (page 74)

*Chicken Sformata (page 161) on Mashed Potatoes (page
191) with Tomato and Fennel Sauce (page 128)*

or

*Omelet Roulade with Spinach Filling (page 119) and
Béchamel (page 290)*

(One of you can make and shape the sformatas or
make the roulade while the other makes the sauce.
Eat the appetizers while the entrée is cooking)

*Heart-Shaped Chocolate Cake (page 260) with Raspberry
Cream Filling (page 268)*

(Cake up to 2 weeks ahead. Freeze [see Note].)

NOTE: Don't forget to remove in time to defrost
and reheat according to the instructions at the
end of the recipe!

YOU'VE INVITED YOU-KNOW-WHO TO DINNER

I f it's going to go well, it's going to go well regardless what you serve. But nothing can ever
go so well that it wouldn't be a whole lot better
with:

VEGETARIAN

Three-Vegetable Terrine (page 92)
(Up to 3 days ahead)
Real Bread (page 212)
(Up to a month ahead. Freeze [see Note].)
Corn and Sweet Potato Chowder (page 66)
(Up to 2 days ahead)
*Rice Roulade with Bell Peppers (page 80) and
Béchamel (page 290)*
(that day)
*Steamed baby spinach with Orange-Sesame Dressing
(page 180)*
(Dressing up to 5 days ahead)
*Chocolate Angel Food Loaf (page 303) with Raspberry Glaze
(page 270)*
(Cake up to 2 days before. Glaze several hours
before serving.)

SHELLFISH

*Vacherin or Abondance
Real Bread (page 212)*
(Up to a month ahead. Freeze [see Note].)
Creamy Lobster and Potato Soup (page 69)
(the day before)
Sole with Fresh Tomatoes (page 150)
(Sauce up to 3 days ahead)

Baked Gnocchi with Cheese (page 187)
(the day before)
Salad greens with Vinaigrette (page 299)
(Just before serving)
*Chocolate Angel Food Loaf (page 303) with Orange Glaze
(page 270)*
(Cake up to 2 weeks ahead. Freeze [see Note].)

NOTE: Don't forget to remove in time to defrost
and reheat according to the instructions at the
end of the recipe!

From the Department of Fair Warnings
There was a respected English novelist who lived
at the Ritz Hotel in Paris, where she wrote a
monthly food column for a popular fashion magazine. She didn't have a kitchen, so she wrote
recipes without testing them—until the month
the magazine ran her Bourbon Cake column, calling for dousing batter with hard liquor before
baking it. Ovens exploded all over Europe . . .
who knows how many during an evening meant
to be like the one you're planning.

It would be nice to assure you that nothing
like this could occur today, but untested recipes
are still published, and even recipes that are thoroughly tested may be printed with typos. Play it
safe: Serve something you've made before. And
of course you want to make it look easy—but
you can only play it cool once you've sweated
over every detail.

YOU'RE FIXING UP A FRIEND

On most occasions, you want to make something that involves spending nearly no time away from the table. On an occasion like this, however, you want to excuse yourself for as long as possible, hoping that nobody turns up in the kitchen.

VEGETARIAN OR SHELLFISH

Bruschetta (page 28)

Mushroom Soup with Gnocchi (page 60)

(You have to boil the gnocchi in the soup just before serving)

Corona di Riso with Minced Ratatouille or Mussels

(page 114)

(You have to unmold the corona and fill it with the other ingredients)

Any flavor glacé (page 279)

(You have to process it in your ice cream maker and put it into serving dishes)

CHILD'S BIRTHDAY PARTY

It's only the cake that counts.

Be honest with yourself about who the party is for, then resolve that it's meant only for the children. Invite their parents for another occasion if entertaining them means that much to you. But if you're going to be planning an adult menu along with food and activities for the kids, you'll feel unduly stressed, and worse, you'll be shifting the focus from the birthday child.

MENU

Heart-shaped jelly sandwiches on
Peanut Butter Bread (page 220)
Mini pitas with tuna salad (page 147)
Birthday Cake (page 271)

Timing Is Everything . . .

Up to One Month Ahead: Bake the Peanut Butter Bread. Slice before freezing.

Up to Two Weeks Ahead: Bake the layers for the cake. Freeze.

Two Days Before: Make the tuna salad. Clean the house or do the lawn.

The Day Before: First thing in the morning, make the filling and icing for the cake. Decorate the house. That night, fill the cake and put the first rough layer of icing on it. Cover loosely with plastic wrap and refrigerate.

The Morning of: Take the Peanut Butter Bread out of the freezer. Spread with jelly and cut with cookie cutters. Place on a serving plate and cover with plastic wrap. Leave at room temperature. Fill the mini pitas with tuna salad and put on a serving plate. Cover with plastic wrap. Finish decorating the cake. Cover loosely with plastic and put out of harm's way.

WHEN YOU'RE HOSTING THE BOOK GROUP (INVESTMENT CLUB . . .)

Modesty is the best policy. You want everyone to enjoy the food without worrying about how they're going to match it when it's their turn. You can put out an assortment of store-bought dips and spreads, or offer any of the following:

Menu

Caponata (page 32)
(5 days ahead)
Ricotta-Filled Figs (page 51)
(the day before)
Hummus (page 28)
(5 days ahead)

———

Cheese Fondue (page 122)
with bread and vegetables for dipping
(Just before they arrive)

———

Brownies (page 266)
(Up to a month ahead. Freeze)
Fresh Fruit

HAPPY HOLIDAYS!

Every year it is reported without a touch of irony that holidays are a major source of depression. Count on it: The moment the Halloween pumpkins appear, so do the mental health experts warning us of imminent nervous breakdown. And no wonder. The very same programs that feature these experts devote subsequent segments to the million things you need to do and buy to have the perfect holiday. Anyone would go mad.

But you will not go mad this year. For one thing, you are going to make a sanity-saving decision. If you're going to host a Big Winter Holiday, you're going to choose which it will be: Thanksgiving or Christmas, or one night of Hanukkah or Kwanzaa (see Note). Choose. If you go ahead and plan to do both, you're on your own.

Historical Note: If you choose Thanksgiving and feel bad about not doing another big winter holiday as well, remember that one of the religious liberties the Pilgrims sought in the New World was the freedom *not* to celebrate Christmas, which was too close to its pagan roots and far too decadent for our puritanical predecessors.

NOTE: About Kwanzaa and Hanukkah: Kwanzaa is a recent invention, an evolving holiday with no established traditions. You're free to celebrate as you please, expressing the values assigned to the holiday in a way that feels most genuine to you. An appropriate menu for the occasion would include recipes handed down through your family and meals that evoke your heritage. Try the Vegetables Stewed in Peanut Sauce (page 118), for example, with Buttermilk Spoon Bread (page 183).

Hanukkah, while not an invention by any means, is not as significant in the Jewish calender as it has become just because it falls near Christmas. Celebrating over seven days could sap the holiday spirit from anyone. If you're going to do a big-deal dinner, I suggest you plan it for the last night, when you can celebrate with the full complement of candles.

Thanksgiving

MOST PEOPLE who are planning Thanksgiving dinner eventually reach a point where they would like to have a few words with Norman Rockwell . . . and not the kind of words his mawkish characters would likely coo to one another. Ever since Rockwell's fanciful depiction of Thanksgiving seized the public imagination, the holiday seems meant to test how close you can come to matching it.

Well, turkey feathers. It's *your* Thanksgiving, and if you're going to test anything this year, it's going to be whether your turkey (or Stuffed Baby Pumpkins, page 205) is done, and how much time, warmth, and good food you can share with your family and friends.

Thank goodness Abraham Lincoln had second thoughts. When he first declared the Thanksgiving Holiday, the date he chose was August 6. Perhaps it wasn't the idea of roasting a turkey at that time of year that made him change his mind, but it's just as well he did.

Caponata (page 32)

Corn and Sweet Potato Chowder (page 66)

Roast Turkey (page 167)

Stuffed Baby Pumpkins (page 205)

Cheese-Filled Risotto Ring (page 184)

Orange-Apricot Cranberry Sauce (page 179)

Real Bread (page 212) or Buttermilk Spoon Bread (page 183)

Pumpkin Cheesecake (page 263)

Timing Is Everything . . .

Early October: Check that you have the equipment you'll need, and that what you have is in working order. If you wait until November, you may face shortages and higher prices. You may need: an "Insta Read" thermometer, cheesecloth, roasting pan, and kitchen twine. Order special ingredients and/or utensils and baking equipment from King Arthur or Maid of Scandinavia (page 347). Make the broth for the soup, risotto, and stuffing and freeze.

First Week of November: Bake the bread for the table and the stuffing. Make the soup and freeze according to the directions in the recipe. Make the stuffing and freeze according to the directions in the recipe.

Second Week of November: Get your final guest count (or as close as practical). Order a fresh turkey (1 pound per person up to 12 pounds; ½ pound per person over 12 pounds). Take inventory of your ingredients and shop for whatever you need to complete the meal.

Four or Five Days Ahead: Make the caponata and refrigerate. Make the cranberry sauce and refrigerate.

Three Days Ahead: Make the Pumpkin Cheesecake and refrigerate. Clean the house.

The Day Before: Make the risotto ring. Pick up the turkey. Set the table.

Thanksgiving Day: Prepare and roast the turkey. Stuff and bake the pumpkins along with the turkey. Defrost and reheat all frozen and refrigerated food according to directions in the recipes.

Thanksgiving Dinner Modified for 2 to 4

One of the more pleasurable taboos in American life is the intimate Thanksgiving meal. Thanksgiving is by definition a communal holiday, so when it's celebrated by two, three, or four alone, it can feel quite (and quite lusciously) illicit.

If there will be only two, three, or four of you at your Thanksgiving table, meal planning may be a problem. Unless you have a large freezer and a high tolerance for turkey, roasting a whole bird may be impractical. You can roast a whole breast, or prepare the roulade on page 168. If you're all vegetarians, you have no problem at all if you make the Stuffed Baby Pumpkins (page 205).

Savory Puff Pastry (page 50)

(Make the filling up to 2 days ahead. Refrigerate.)

Corn and Sweet Potato Chowder (page 66)

(Up to 3 days ahead. Refrigerate.)

Turkey Roulade (page 168) or Stuffed Baby Pumpkins (page 205)

Orange-Apricot Cranberry Sauce (page 179)

(Up to 1 month ahead and freeze)

Rolls

(Up to 1 month ahead and freeze)

Pumpkin Cheesecake (page 263)

(Up to 3 days ahead. Refrigerate.)

The year we lived in Milan, I rashly invited a couple of American acquaintances and some Italian friends to Thanksgiving dinner at our place. This was before I had checked out the turkey situation. It happens that in Italy, they raise turkeys to sell them part by part. It's rare to find a whole one because the practice of breeding poultry with legs, thighs, and breasts ample enough to sell on their own produces birds so massive that butchers can't possibly display them. So it was with mounting panic that I raced in and out of poultry shops throughout our quarter of the city on the afternoon in question, finally finding a whole bird weighing less—although not much less—than thirty pounds. I brought it home to find that even at its relatively puny size, it was several inches too long and a bit too high to fit into my oven. I figured I could tuck it in here and there, then truss it to hold everything in place. As it roasted, it would shrink to fit. To truss it tightly, I had to hold it against my chest and bend over, steadying the bird with my chin while I secured the cord. As you might guess, the turkey slid out and went gliding along the floor. I rinsed it off, wrestled with it for a while longer, and finally wedged it into the roasting pan and then into the oven. With each basting, it seemed smaller, and the bird I took from the oven was the perfect size . . . for twenty. Since there were only six of us, none with freezers bigger than a shoe box, we toasted absent friends and ate for them, too.

On Tradition

NONCONFORMISTS LIKE to remind us that turkey isn't mentioned in accounts of the first Thanksgiving. It may well have been served, however, since the meal included native fowl of every other kind. In any event, it was eaten at the second, in 1623, along with cranberries and pumpkin pie.

Not that eating something other than turkey —or a vegetarian stand-in for it —is antisocial, unpatriotic, or symptomatic of a dangerous personality disorder, *but* the annual turkey dinner gives us a rare chance to enjoy a spell of national unity. There's something stirring about sitting down to a meal very much like the one being served at your neighbor's house, and the next, and so on clear across the land. And there's some inestimable value in being at one with the millions checking what temperature to set the oven, how long to set the timer, how often to baste it, and how to tell when it's done (see page 167).

Christmas

"At Christmas, play and make good cheer
For Christmas comes but once a year."
—1542 tract on domestic life

CHRISTMAS ISN'T complicated. You need a tree, good steamed pudding (page 262), some Santa-smitten children, and, above all, Philosophical Perspective.

Start by making a distinction between idealization and ideals. Idealization involves catch words like "Dickensian and Victorian." In fact, Christmas was dismal in the Dickens household, and soot, not snow, covered the rooftops in Victorian London. Of course, if you have the impulse, stamina, and artistic flare to deck your halls from wall to wall, hold an open house for your colleagues or neighbors, and organize a chorus of carolers, go for it. But if you find yourself burdened by the apparent expectations of the season, consider your fundamental ideals. Ideals can't be imposed from outside; they come from your values and your love for the people who'll be celebrating with you. They have little to do with the trappings of the season and everything to do with its abiding spirit. You may find that if you refuse to fuss so much about decor and other details, and devote your energy to simply being with your family and friends, everyone will enjoy the best holiday they've ever had.

Three Secrets of Highly Successful Holidays

1. Be realistic. Remember last year in detail. Remember bickering with your mother. Remember watching your brother's girlfriend ("Do you think they'll ever get married?") picking at her food. If this is your reality, you will enjoy the holiday much more if you don't expect your folks to arrive by wing—halos, harps, and all.

2. Be ready. Plan as far in advance as you can (see below). Get a calendar with Great Big Blocks to fill with detailed reminders for each day.

3. Be prudent. Let pride yield to practicality. If you realize you're not going to be able to do everything yourself, ask your guests to help, or buy yourself some slack—prepared foods, paper tablecloth, whatever is going to make it easier for you.

MENU

Roasted Bell Peppers (page 302) and assorted cheeses
Paella (page 139)
Chickpeas with Onions, Spinach, and Raisins (page 192)
Fennel, Orange, and Fig Salad (page 175)
Bread
Steamed Apple Cake (page 262)
with
Lemon Glacé (page 279) or Eggnog Glacé (page 281)

Timing Is Everything . . .

Mid-November: Order special ingredients and/or equipment and utensils.

The Week After Thanksgiving: Make the broth for the Paella and freeze according to directions at the end of the recipe. Bake the bread, if you're making your own. Freeze according to directions at the end of the recipe. Steam the pudding and freeze according to directions at the end of the recipe.

One Week Ahead: Order the seafood for the Paella. Arrange for pickup Christmas Eve.

Five Days Ahead: Make the bell pepper spread and refrigerate.

Three Days Ahead: Clean the house. Make the Chickpeas with Onions, Spinach, and Raisins.

Christmas Eve: Shop for cheese. Pick up seafood for the Paella.

Christmas Day: In the morning, make the base for the Paella, excluding the seafood. Make the glacé. Defrost or reheat frozen or refrigerated foods according to directions in the recipes. An hour before dinner, prepare the salad. Complete the Paella.

Passover

PASSOVER IS something like Thanksgiving with responsive reading and singing. What sets Passover apart from other big family holidays, aside from the odd reference to plagues and the smiting of oppressors, is that the food isn't supposed to be very good. The dietary restrictions, which differ depending on your heritage, are meant in part to inspire empathy for our forebears, who'd had to bolt across the desert too fast to fuss over food.

Needless to say, people have been tinkering with the empathy part of this tradition for a long time, trying to make Passover food palatable (often shamelessly—chocolate-covered matzos come to mind). I have to admit that while it's inspiring to participate in the ritual recounting of the flight from Pharaoh, when the meal is served, it feels as if we're being punished for having survived it.

So when it was time for us to host a seder, I took a highly unorthodox step away from my Ashkenazi Eastern European heritage—which allows little more than meat, potatoes, and vegetable oil—to prepare a menu from the more permissive Sephardic Far Eastern tradition. It was easy to rationalize taking a new identity for the occasion: All Jews started in the same place, so any one of them could have ended up anywhere. If my ancestors had turned one way instead of another, they would have been able to eat rice and legumes on Passover, too.

MENU

Curried Lentil Soup with Mango (page 62)
Date-Nut Charoseth (page 325)
All Kinds of Curry with Chicken and/or Chickpeas
(page 108)
Rice (page 181)
Spinach Sauce (page 201; see Note)
Matzos
Pureed frozen banana with pineapple and toasted almonds
Kosher wine from the Galil district

NOTE: Make with vegetable broth in place of the buttermilk.

Timing Is Everything . . .

Three Weeks Ahead: Clean the house. Housecleaning is critical to the observation of Passover, and ought to be thorough and complete by the time you start to cook.

Two Weeks Ahead: Make the broth for the soup, and freeze according to directions at the end of the recipe.

Five Days Ahead: Make sure you have enough haggadahs, candles, and yarmulkes. Check that you have the items for the ritual plate.

Four Days Ahead: Make the Charoseth. Make the Matzos.

Three Days Ahead: Make the Spinach Sauce and refrigerate. Make the curry sauce and refrigerate.

The Day Before: Set the table.

Passover: Defrost and reheat frozen and refrigerated foods. Finish cooking the curry according to which main ingredients you're using. Peel the bananas, wrap in foil, and freeze several hours before dessert will be served. Make the rice. Finish the soup just before serving.

Date-Nut Charoseth

SERVES 6 TO 8

There's a Passover story concerning a couple of Civil War soldiers holding a seder between battles. They had no food to use for the ritual, but found an ingenious stand-in for charoseth, the paste prepared with apples and nuts (or dates and nuts in Sephardic tradition) meant to represent the mortar used by the Jewish slaves to lay the bricks of the pyramids. They put a brick on the table between them, an unequivocal symbol of the same.

TIME TO PREPARE (HANDS ON): *About 20 minutes*

TIME TO COOK: *About 45 minutes*

TOTAL TIME: *About 3¼ hours, including time to rest*

---

3 cups pitted dates
½ cup coarsely chopped walnuts

Place the dates and water to cover in a heavy saucepan and bring to a simmer over medium-high heat. Cover the pan and remove from the heat.

Let sit for 2 hours, without stirring.

Line a colander with cheesecloth and place over a mixing bowl. Using a large ladle, transfer ¼ of the date mixture to the colander. Force through as much liquid as you can, picking up the cheesecloth, twisting it over the mixture, and squeezing with your hands. Scrape off the date residue to a separate bowl and repeat 3 times.

Return the drained syrup to the saucepan and bring to a simmer over medium-high heat. Continue simmering until very thick, about 30 minutes, skimming off any residue that rises to the surface in the process. Stir half of the syrup into the reserved boiled date mixture, along with the walnuts to make a rich paste. Save the remaining syrup for another use, such as a novel topping for pancakes or sweet potatoes.

- *You can make this up to 3 days ahead. Refrigerate, covered. Let come to room temperature before serving.*

Menus & Meal-Planning Tips

Do-It-Yourself Timetable

Perfect Timing: Three Principal Principles

- Choose your menu as soon as you know who's likely to be coming.
- Check the "Refrigerate up to" and "Freeze up to" notes at the end of each recipe, and plan your preparation schedule accordingly . . . in *writing* on a *calendar* in your *kitchen*. In print each step has imperative authority. You're more likely to do it when it's staring you in the face.
- Shop and cook on separate days (*mental health experts agree!*), unless you need to pick up last-minute perishables, such as fish, which can't be purchased further ahead of time.

Two-Week Plan

Two Weeks Ahead: Choose your menu, take inventory, and shop. Bake bread and/or cake, if you're planning to do it. Freeze according to directions at the end of the recipe.

Anytime up to a Week Ahead: Make any sauce and/or soup you plan to serve. Freeze it according to directions at the end of the recipe.

Three Days Ahead: Make anything that can be refrigerated (see the ends of recipes).

Day Before: Clean the house. Get fresh flowers. Buy any ingredients you will need for the Day Of cooking.

The Day Of: Cook anything you haven't prepared ahead. Defrost or reheat frozen or refrigerated food according to directions at the end of each recipe.

Five-Day Plan

Five Days Ahead: Choose the menu. Take inventory and make a shopping list. In addition to food, include cleaning equipment and utensils in your inventory and shopping list.

Four Days Ahead: Shop.

Three Days Ahead: Prepare anything that can be refrigerated or frozen ahead.

Two Days Ahead: Prepare more food. Clean the house.

Day Before: Buy any ingredients you will need for Day Of cooking.

Day Of: Buy fresh flowers (you can have them delivered to avoid rushing out). Make hot appetizers, if you're serving them. Defrost frozen food and/or heat refrigerated foods according to directions given at the end of the recipe.

Three-Day Plan

Three Days Ahead: Plan the menu, take inventory, and shop.

Day Before: Prepare two dishes that can be made ahead. Clean the house. Buy any ingredients you need for Day Of cooking.

Day Of: Prepare one more dish. Heat refrigerated foods according to directions at the end of the recipe.

Two-Day Plan

Day Before: Plan menu, take inventory, and shop. Include prepared foods, such as spreads, marinated artichoke hearts, sun-dried tomatoes, and olives for appetizers and sorbet or ice cream and crepes or angel food cake for dessert. Don't forget good bread (see page 210).

Day Of: Make one of the Guests at Short Notice menus (page 331). Clean the house while dinner is cooking.

One-Day Plan

- Take inventory, then choose what to make from the Guests at Short Notice menus (page 331), according to whatever will involve the shortest time shopping.
- Bring home prepared foods for appetizers

along with the dinner ingredients, and purchase anything that allows you to avoid preparing it yourself (see Two-Day Plan).
- Clean the house and put out the appetizers.
- Cook dinner while your guests enjoy the appetizers.

Menus

FISH

Vacherin
Lemon Risotto (page 74)
Seafood Stew with Spinach and Saffron (page 154)
Beets and Sour Cream (page 178)
Pumpkin Pudding Cake (page 264) with Eggnog Glacé
(page 281)
Gavi de Gavi
or
Vino Nobile de Montepulciano

VEGETARIAN

Chickpeas with Coconut (page 193)
Crepes with Ricotta and Spices (page 100)
Vegetables Stewed in Peanut Sauce (page 118)
Steamed Rice (page 181)
Naan (page 226)
Mango Glacé (page 280)
German Riesling
or
Spanish Rioja

ADAPTABLE FOR ANYONE

All Kinds of Curry with Chicken, Fish, or
Cauliflower (page 108)
Spinach Sauce for Curry/Sweet Potato Sauce for Curry
(page 201)
Cucumber Raita (page 176)
Steamed Rice (page 181)
Naan (page 226)
Lemon Glacé (page 279)
Chenin Blanc
or
Pomerol

CHICKEN

Bruschetta (page 28)
Sweet Bell Pepper Soup with Rice (page 56)
Chicken Sformata (page 161) on Mashed Potatoes
(page 191)
with Tomato and Fennel Sauce (page 128)
Fresh Pear Clafouti (page 272)
Italian Trebbiano
or
Rosso di Montalcino

CHICKEN

Roast Chicken with Rosemary (page 157)
Sweet and Nutty Bulgur Salad (page 182)
Orange-Apricot Cranberry Sauce (page 179)
Yellow Turnips with Potatoes and Cheese (page 189)
Chocolate Ricotta Pudding (page 276)
Rhone Valley Viognier
or
California Zinfandel

VEGETARIAN

Lentil Soup with Pumpkin (page 61)
Stuffed Grape Leaves (page 44)
Orange-Infused Baba Ghanouj (page 27)
Pita Bread (page 224)
Chickpeas in Tomato Sauce with
Feta and Wine (page 111)
Beet Raita (page 177)
Semolina Pudding (page 278)
California Sauvignon Blanc
or
American Pinot Noir

FISH AND VEGETARIAN

Pumpkin and Mushroom Risotto (page 75)*
Potato Ring with Bell Peppers and Sage (page 192)
Simple Baked Fish in Foil (page 133)
Mixed salad greens with Vinaigrette (page 299)
Apple Cobbler (page 240) with Ricotta Pastry (page 296)
Loire Valley Vouvray
or
Côtes du Rhône Rouge

CHICKEN AND VEGETARIAN

Bell Pepper Spread with Olives and Feta (page 36)
Assorted sheep's milk cheeses
Grape Risotto (page 73)*
Chicken Baked in Parchment (page 159) with vegetables
Fresh Fig Clafouti (page 272)
California Chardonnay
or
Fleurie

FISH

Bell Pepper Spread with Olives and Feta (page 36)
Blueberry Risotto (page 70)
Sole and Salmon Terrines with Spinach (page 148)
Layered Cream Cake with Fruit (page 261)
Bandol Rosé

Cherry Vanilla Muesli (page 238)
Apple Cinnamon Bread Pudding (page 239)
Fruit Salad

FISH

Salmon Tartare with Orange (page 97)
Scallop Ceviche (page 98)
Potatoes and sugar snaps in Vinaigrette (page 299)
Chilled Parchment-Baked Swordfish (page 123) and Penne
Angel Food Loaf (page 303) with Fruit Glaze (page 270)
Premier Cru Chablis
or
Gevrey-Chambertin

POULTRY AND FISH

Steamed Mussels in Wine and Herbs (page 125)
Turkey Tonnato (page 156)
Corn and Sugar Snap Pea Salad (page 173)
Chilled sliced potatoes with Creamy Vinaigrette Dressing
(page 300)
Cherry Clafouti (page 272)
White Graves
or
Australian Shiraz

---

* Serve with the main course when some of your guests
are vegetarian, giving them a larger portion in place of
the fish.

CHICKEN AND VEGETARIAN

Grilled Spiced Ground Chicken (page 164) and vegetables
Tahini Sauce (page 110)
Cucumber Raita (page 177)
Steamed Rice (page 181)
Naan (page 226)
India pale ale

SEAFOOD AND/OR VEGETARIAN

Caviar or Bell Pepper Spread (page 36) in Buttered New
Potato Cups (page 25)
Paella, Classic Style or Vegetarian (page 142)
Fennel, Orange, and Fig Salad (page 175)
Raspberry Jelly Roll (page 264)
Vintage Champagne

SEAFOOD AND CHICKEN

Salmon and Shrimp Terrine (page 91)
Chicken with Apricots and Pine Nuts (page 163)
Mashed Sweet Potatoes (page 192)
Barley with Apples (page 186)
Steamed broccoli rabe
Chocolate Cake (page 260) with Chocolate Bavarian
Cream Filling (page 267) and
Raspberry Glaze (page 270)
Macon
or
Savigny Lès Beaume

ADAPTABLE FOR ANYONE

Bite-Sized Corn Bits (page 38) with Guacamole (page 39)
and Salsa
All Kinds of Chili with Beans and Mushrooms, Chicken, or
Seafood (page 106)
Brown Rice with Cheddar (page 182)
Lavash (page 228) or flour tortillas
Apple-Ginger Custard (page 272)

Albariño Rias Baixaz
or
Rioja Criziana

VEGETARIAN

Three-Vegetable Terrine (page 92)
Potato Focaccia (page 227)
Sweet Bell Pepper Soup with Rice (page 56)
Fresh Fruit and Sour Cream (page 276)
Arneis
or
Chianti Classico Reserva

SEAFOOD

Reblochon
Calamari Filled with Fish (page 131)
Risotto with Fennel, Saffron, and Tomato (page 76)
Beet and Radish Salad (page 178)
Chocolate Angel Food Loaf (page 303) with Fruit Glaze
(page 270)
Montrachet
or
Vosne-Romanée

SEAFOOD

Steamed Vegetable Dumplings with Ginger-Soy Dipping
Sauce (page 40)
Mussels and snow peas on mixed greens
Tender Ginger-Flavored Steamed Fish Fillets (page 153)
Steamed Rice (page 181)
Steamed Buns (page 232)
Ginger Angel Food Loaf (page 303) with Real Vanilla Glacé
(page 279)
Chaumes

SPRING BRUNCH
VEGETARIAN AND CHICKEN

Frittata Crepes (page 112)

Avocado Salad with Chicken, Apples, and Walnuts
(page 174)

Sweet and Nutty Bulgur Salad (page 182)

Pane al Latte (page 223)

Just Plain Cake (page 304) with Raspberry Cream Filling
(page 268)

South African Chardonnay

or

South African Pinotage

PASSOVER
ADAPTABLE FOR ANYONE

Curried Lentil Soup with Mango (page 62)

Date-Nut Charoseth (page 325)

All Kinds of Curry with Chicken and/or Chickpeas
(page 108)

Rice (page 181)

Spinach Sauce* (page 201)

Matzos

Pureed frozen banana with pineapple and toasted almonds

Israeli kosher wines from the Galil district

BIRTHDAY PARTY

Heart-shaped jelly sandwiches on Peanut Butter Bread
(page 220)

Mini pitas with tuna salad (page 147)

Birthday Cake (page 271)

Normandy sparkling nonalcoholic cider

PICNIC OR SUMMER SUPPER
SEAFOOD

Cherry Bread with Havarti

Scallop Ceviche (page 98)

Shrimp Tabbouleh (page 130)

Scallop and Potato Salad (page 143)

Steamed beets, corn, and sugar snap peas mixed with lime
juice, yogurt, and sesame seeds

Blueberries with sour cream and yogurt

Rosé

GUESTS AT SHORT NOTICE
VEGETARIAN

Penne with Rich Tomato and Spinach Sauce (page 88)

Avocado and Apple Salad (page 174)

Steamed asparagus with toasted sesame seeds

Bread

Sweet Potato or Banana Soufflés (page 274)

Chenin Blanc

or

Crozes Hermitage

CHICKEN

Chicken in Wine (page 160)

Cauliflower Broiled with Cheese (page 198)

Rice (page 181)

Salad greens or steamed greens with Vinaigrette (page 299)

Chocolate Bread Pudding (page 339)

Alsace Pinot Blanc

or

Cru Beaujolais

———

Spaghetti and Eggs (page 337)

———

Piperade (page 113)

———

* Serve with the main course when some of your guests are vegetarian, giving them a larger portion in place of the fish.

And Then Some

ON RESERVE

If you have these in the house, you can make something good and substantial without going to the store, or going only to dash through the express lane.

On the spice rack

Sesame seeds: Toast and toss them on steamed vegetables for a quick side dish.

To toast them, spread the seeds in an even layer on a piece of foil. Place in the toaster oven or oven at 350° F. until golden, about 2 minutes, stirring them once. Watch carefully to make sure they don't burn.

Dried basil

Dried oregano

Ground cumin

Vanilla extract

Peppercorns: Buy whole peppercorns, fill a peppermill, and grind it fresh yourself as you need it. It's a world away from the preground pepper that comes in jars or tins.

Salt: I like to keep coarse or kosher salt on hand to use for most savory cooking, and finer table salt for baking. If you'd like to put salt on the table for your guests to season their food, you can use whichever you prefer.

In a cupboard

Olive oil (see Note)

Balsamic vinegar

Canned chickpeas

Canned kidney beans

Pasta: Keep a variety of shapes on hand, such as penne, orrechiette, and spaghetti.

Canned tomatoes: (In 14- and 28-ounce cans; no salt or seasoning, so you can control the flavor.

Rice (long-grain white or brown): You can cook it according to package directions or the directions on page 181, then toss it with kidney beans and the cumin-seasoned oil and balsamic vinegar dressing on page 336. You can also stir pesto into hot cooked rice. Make a well in the center and fill with tomato sauce mixed with chickpeas. Also, see broth, below.

In the freezer

Broth (chicken and vegetable): Yours (pages 285, 286) or a good commercial brand (low-sodium, no added sugar or seasonings). Substitute broth for water in rice, couscous, or bulgur wheat. For fuller flavor, sauté an onion in extra virgin olive oil before adding the grain and broth. For even more flavor, sauté the onion, add the grain, cook it in broth, then toss with grated cheese just before serving.

Pesto: Freeze yours or a good commercial brand in small batches (about 2 tablespoons) in snack-sized zip-lock bags. You can use an ice tray to make cubes, then keep them in a plastic bag in the freezer. Spread it on toasted bread; toss it with hot pasta or rice. Stir it into store-bought tomato sauce to enhance the flavor.

Tomato sauce: Yours (page 337) or a good commercial brand (low-sodium, with minimal seasoning so you can adjust it with fresh or dried herbs to taste). Freeze in small batches so you can use as much or as little as you need.

Pita bread: Heat it in foil in the oven until thawed enough to split (don't defrost before putting it in the oven). Split and toast. Rub with garlic and brush with olive oil. You can go a step further and sprinkle with grated cheese while the bread is still warm.

Spread with Quick! Chickpea Spread (see page 335).

French, Italian, or sourdough bread: Keep the bread in the freezer, tightly wrapped. You can toast it and rub it with a garlic clove, brush with oil, and sprinkle with crumbled dried basil. If you slice the bread before you freeze it, you can take out as much or as little as you need.

Soak it in water and balsamic vinegar (1 part vinegar to 4 parts water), squeeze dry, crumble, and toss into a salad with lettuce, tomatoes, cucumber, celery, and the Multipurpose Oil and Vinegar Dressing on page 336.

Unsweetened cocoa powder: Keep it in an airtight container in the freezer.

Grated Parmesan cheese: Keep it in an airtight container in the freezer.

Shredded sharp cheddar: Keep it in an airtight container in the freezer.

In the refrigerator

Check often to make sure nothing's dated, mushy, or moldy. Food has been known to go bad before its use-by date, so if the label says it's still good but your nose or eyes say otherwise, trust yourself.

Garlic: Should last 3 weeks.

Onion: Should last 3 weeks.

Lemons: Should last 2 to 3 weeks.

Eggs: Store according to the date on the carton.

Milk: Store according to the date on the carton.

Dijon mustard: Keeps indefinitely.

Tahini: Store according to the date on the label.

NOTE: If you have an excellent olive oil, the quality of your other ingredients *almost* doesn't matter. Similarly, because olive oil lays the foundation for the dishes that call for it, a bad one could ruin the whole thing. Connoisseurs like to make trouble for the rest of us by issuing elaborate lists of the traits of good olive oil. In fact, choosing a good one is simple. First, check the color. It should be golden or sea-green, but most important, it should be clear, not cloudy. Next, smell it. If you enjoy the aroma, chances are you will like the taste. Third, take a drop on the tip of your tongue. It should taste smooth, without a bitter bite or aftertaste, and the flavor should echo down your throat.

Fast, Simple Recipes Using Only *What's "On Reserve"*

Quick! Chickpea Spread

S ERVES 4 TO 6

  1 cup canned chickpeas, rinsed and drained
  1 ½ tablespoons tahini
  1 teaspoon ground cumin
  1 ½ teaspoons fresh lemon juice (optional)
  Pinch coarse salt
  1 tablespoon sesame seeds, toasted
     (optional)

Place the chickpeas, tahini, and cumin in the work bowl of a food processor or blender. Add 1 tablespoon hot water and the lemon juice, if using. Process until smooth. Season with salt and place in a serving bowl, sprinkled with toasted sesame seeds, if you'd like.

Quick! Garlic Bread

S ERVES 8 TO 10

  1 loaf Italian or French bread, sliced
  1 garlic clove
  Extra virgin olive oil
  Crumbled dried basil and/or oregano
  Grated Parmesan cheese (optional)

Toast the bread lightly.

  Slice the garlic clove in half lengthwise. Rub the toasted bread slices with the cut side of the garlic clove and brush with the olive oil. Sprinkle with crumbled dried basil and/or oregano.

  Heat the broiler, place the toast on a broiler sheet, sprinkle with cheese, if desired, and put it under the broiler, 2 inches from the heat, until browned and the cheese has melted, about 30 seconds.

More than a
Toasted Cheese Sandwich

FOR EACH SANDWICH

1 large egg
²/₃ cup milk
Generous pinch crumbled dried basil and/or
    oregano
Pinch coarse salt
¼ cup grated or shredded cheese
2 slices bread

In a mixing bowl, beat together the egg and the milk. Stir in the basil and/or oregano and the salt. Place the cheese between the slices of bread. Carefully dip the sandwich in the milk mixture. Place on a nonstick baking sheet and bake at 375°F. until browned, about 15 minutes, turning over after 10 minutes. Or lightly grease a non-stick skillet or griddle with vegetable oil, or squirt it with nonstick spray, and place over medium-high heat. When hot, add the sandwich and cook until the underside is golden brown, about 4 minutes. Turn over and cook to brown the other side and melt the cheese, about 3 minutes.

Multipurpose Oil and Vinegar Dressing

SERVES 4

Use basil if the seasonings in your main course are basically Mediterranean; cumin if they're Southwestern, Mexican, or Indian.

2 tablespoons extra virgin olive oil
1 tablespoon balsamic vinegar
½ teaspoon Dijon mustard
Pinch crumbled dried oregano
Pinch crumbled dried basil or ground cumin
Coarse salt

Combine the oil, vinegar, Dijon mustard, oregano, and basil or cumin. Whisk vigorously, or blend in a blender or with an immersion blender. Season with salt, and toss with steamed vegetables, rinsed drained canned chickpeas, or kidney beans.

Spaghetti and Eggs

F O R   E A C H   S E R V I N G

2 to 4 ounces dried spaghetti
1 large egg
2 tablespoons milk
2 tablespoons grated cheese
Generous pinch crumbled dried basil and/or
    oregano
1 teaspoon extra virgin olive oil
Salt and freshly ground black pepper

Cook the pasta according to package directions.

Meanwhile, in a mixing bowl, beat together the egg, milk, grated cheese, and basil and/or oregano.

Drain the pasta in a colander, but don't rinse out the pot. Put the oil in the pot and toss the drained pasta back into it, tossing quickly to coat with the olive oil. Place over low heat and stir in the egg mixture. Stir constantly until creamy. Season with salt and pepper. (The egg sauce may scramble a bit—don't worry, it will still taste great.) Serve right away.

When You Really Need
Tomato Sauce

M A K E S   A B O U T   2   C U P S

1 tablespoon extra virgin olive oil
1 garlic clove, crushed and minced
1 onion, chopped
Generous pinch crumbled dried oregano
Generous pinch crumbled dried basil
One 14-ounce can chopped tomatoes,
    drained

Heat the oil in a saucepan over medium-high heat. When hot, add the garlic, onion, oregano, and basil. Reduce the heat to medium-low and sauté, stirring often, until the onion is soft and limp, about 7 minutes. Turn up the heat to medium-high, add the tomatoes, and stir until bubbling. Turn down the heat to medium-low and simmer until it breaks down to a thick sauce, about 7 minutes. Serve chunky, or puree in a blender or food processor, processing in short spurts to avoid making it too thin.

Variations
• Stir in rinsed canned chickpeas and grated Parmesan cheese to taste, and serve over pasta.
• Omit the basil and add 1 generous pinch ground cumin. Stir in rinsed canned kidney beans and serve over hot cooked rice.

Savory Bread Pudding

SERVES 2

1 cup tomato sauce
Generous pinch crumbled dried basil and/or
    oregano
2 large eggs
¼ cup grated Parmesan cheese
2 to 3 cups chunks bread, crusts removed

Heat the oven to 425°F.

In a large mixing bowl, combine the tomato sauce, herb(s), eggs, cheese, and bread, tossing to combine well. Let sit for 10 minutes for the bread to soak up the sauce. Lightly grease a 6-inch square baking dish with vegetable oil or squirt it with nonstick spray. Pour the bread mixture into the dish, and bake until puffy and golden brown, about 35 minutes. (If the top starts to brown too quickly, cover loosely with foil.)

Frittata Wedges

SERVES 2 TO 3

2 teaspoons extra virgin olive oil
1 onion, chopped
4 large eggs
¼ cup tomato sauce
¼ cup grated Parmesan or shredded
    cheddar cheese
Generous pinch crumbled dried basil and/or
    oregano (with Parmesan) or generous
    pinch crumbled dried oregano and
    generous pinch ground cumin (with
    cheddar)

Heat the oven to 450°F.

Heat the oil in an ovenproof 8-inch nonstick skillet over medium-high heat. When hot, add the onion, reduce the heat to medium-low, and sauté, stirring often, until soft and limp, about 7 minutes.

Meanwhile, in a large mixing bowl, beat the eggs. Pour half of the egg mixture into the skillet and rotate the pan so it covers the bottom evenly. Cook over medium heat until the bottom is set.

Place in the oven and bake until the top is set, about 4 minutes. Turn out onto a plate and repeat with the remaining egg mixture.

When the second frittata has set, spread it with the tomato sauce. Sprinkle evenly with the cheese and top with the herbs and/or cumin. Place the other frittata on top, and place the skillet back into the oven until the cheese has melted and the halves are fused, about 5 minutes.

Carefully turn out onto a large plate, cut into wedges, and serve.

Chocolate Bread Pudding

1 cup milk

$\frac{1}{4}$ cup unsweetened cocoa powder

$\frac{1}{2}$ cup sugar

2 eggs, lightly beaten

1 teaspoon vanilla extract

2 cups bread chunks, crust removed

In a large mixing bowl, combine the milk, cocoa powder, sugar, eggs, and vanilla. Add the bread and dunk to soak it thoroughly.

Heat the oven to 375°F. Lightly grease a 3- to 4-cup baking dish with vegetable oil or squirt it with nonstick spray. Add the bread mixture and bake until crusty on top and set throughout, about 20 minutes. (If the top starts to darken too fast, cover loosely with foil.)

Quick! Rice Pudding

SERVES 4

$\frac{1}{2}$ cup short-grain rice

2 cups milk

$\frac{1}{4}$ cup sugar

2 large egg yolks

1 teaspoon vanilla extract

Pinch each ground cinnamon and nutmeg or
1 teaspoon grated lemon zest (optional)

In a heavy saucepan (preferably enamel), combine the rice, $1\frac{3}{4}$ cups milk, and sugar. Bring to a simmer over medium heat, stirring often. Cover, turn down the heat, and let simmer until thickened, about 25 to 30 minutes. Check often to make sure the mixture isn't sticking. When most of the milk has been absorbed, remove from the heat and take off the cover.

In a medium-sized bowl, stir together the egg yolks and remaining $\frac{1}{4}$ cup milk. Add a small spoonful of the hot rice mixture and stir well to blend. Add another spoonful and stir again. Finally, add one more spoonful of rice to the yolk mixture and stir. Then slowly stir the yolk mixture into the saucepan with the rest of the rice. Return to medium heat and stir until very thick.

Add the vanilla, and the cinnamon and nutmeg or lemon zest (if using) and stir well to blend. Remove from the heat and let sit for about five minutes before serving.

ABOUT THOSE APPLIANCES . . .

"A wise man wants only what he needs."
—Euripides
"HA!"
—Author

Choose appliances according to the foods you enjoy making and serving, and buy whatever will help you do best what you want to do most.

Any appliance worth buying should:

1. Make preparation easier. If the appliance is cumbersome or complicated, you might as well work by hand.
2. Make preparation faster altogether. If a machine works quickly and well at a particular task, such as chopping onions or kneading dough, but takes forever to clean afterward, it may not be a good deal.
3. Produce better results than working without it. If the bread machine makes bland, pasty loaves or the electric pasta maker makes gummy fettuccine, you'll be better off making your bread dough in a mixer and cranking your pasta by hand.

NOTE: Don't buy any appliance for the attachments you can purchase separately—buy it for its basic function. If you want to make pasta, you'll get better results with a machine designed expressly for that purpose than with an adapter for a mixer, which may do a fine job making the dough but far less well pressing and shaping it.

I recommend the following appliances for the recipes in this book:

Pressure Cooker: Life is too short to cook without one.

You can make risotto in seven minutes, and it will taste better than when you stood over it for forty. You'll make full-bodied vegetable broth in thirty minutes instead of over an hour; open a pack of dried legumes and within forty minutes, have them fully cooked and recipe ready (no soaking!); make brown rice or barley in ten minutes; and steamed pudding in forty minutes instead of the two or three hours it normally takes.

What's the trick? The pressure cooker raises the temperature around the food many degrees above the normal boiling point, so everything cooks faster. Pressure-cooked food tastes better because the cooker locks in the steam and the flavors that ordinarily waft out with it.

Since there's no rational reason to resist pressure cookers, the fact that so few people have taken to them suggests that many don't really know what pressure cooking is. If you're under the impression that pressure cooking is a cold and remote process, pressure cooking is real cooking. When you're making risotto, for example, you sauté and season your ingredients as you would in a regular saucepan. Once you've done that, instead of proceeding in the conventional way—standing over it and stirring for forty minutes—you lock on the lid and leave it to cook for seven.

And you may have heard that pressure cookers are dangerous, prone to blow to smithereens, splattering your walls with molten stew, and scalding the hide off anyone within range. But today's pressure cookers won't explode. Many have double or triple safety systems, giving the steam alternative escape routes. The Swiss company Kuhn Rikon makes particularly durable, attractive pressure cookers in a range of sizes, including a heavily promoted four-liter model that makes roughly six portions of soup or risotto. The larger five-liter cooker gives a big batch of beans the requisite room to expand, and makes enough broth to last for a month in this household.

The owner's manual that comes with any pressure cooker will help you convert conventional recipes for use with the appliance.

Is it for you? If you make broth, soup, tomato and other sauces, risotto and brown rice, barley, beans, or steamed puddings, you will come to rely on it.

Immersion Blender: Here's another wonderment often overlooked. Instead of transferring hot soup to a blender or food processor with the hazard that entails, you can bring the blender to it. Plug it in, immerse the blade in the saucepan, turn it on, and you've got smooth, thick soup or sauce. The Cuisinart model comes with attachments for whipping egg whites and making mayonnaise. You can make smooth creamy dressings from oil and vinegar, fresh sauce from raw tomatoes, milkshakes, fruit smoothies, and iced coffee frappes. You clean it by holding it under running water and wiping with a sponge.

Is it for you? If you make soups, sauces, and salad dressings, it's a lot easier to use and clean than a food processor or standup blender.

Food Processor: Look for one with a wide bowl with high sides, wide blades, and a wide feeding tube. The extra surface space makes it easier to clean. Buy one with a small inset bowl for processing smaller amounts.

Is it for you? If you make things calling for thinly sliced ingredients (such as stir-fries and other Far Eastern dishes), or if you're going to be doing a lot of chopping, mincing, pureeing, and bread baking, it's for you. Many people have bought bread machines to avoid kneading, not realizing that a food processor can knead very well.

Heavy-Duty Mixer: From a purely aesthetic point of view, nothing says, "kitchen" better than a gorgeous, gleaming classic KitchenAid Mixmaster on the counter. With their large stainless bowl and bulbous whisk or dough hook, these machines make terrific cake batters, icings, and bread dough. These mixers handle anything that needs to be whipped, creamed, beaten, or kneaded, and are to be recommended to the casual baker. But if you're finicky and prepared to pay extra for superior results, nothing beats the Magic Mill, an industrial-strength megamixer that has the power and mechanical ingenuity to render everything from the lightest angel cake to the heartiest whole wheat bread. It is an imposing machine, but given that it earns its place on the counter with impressive performance, it's not an imposition.

Is it for you? Heavy-duty mixers are for bakers. While a food processor can handle dough and batters, it can't hold as much as one of these. And because you can't adjust the power on a food processor, you can't control the consistency of the contents. Both the KitchenAid and Magic Mill make better bread dough than most bread machines.

Pasta Press: A hand-cranked gadget (some have motors) for rolling and cutting pasta dough.

Is it for you? If you'd like to make pasta occasionally, you'll be glad to have one of these. I prefer to crank by hand because the heat from motorized gizmos makes the pasta too sticky to handle. Also, a manual machine is much less expensive than an electric model, a better investment if you'll be making pasta only several times each year.

Electric Steamer: A good steamer will make perfect rice without guesswork, and cook everything from vegetables and dumplings to chicken and fish without troubling you for anything but adding water at the start and setting the timer. Electric steamers provide steady, even heat, and they're easier to clean than stovetop or bamboo steamers.

Is it for you? If you eat rice often, prefer your vegetables steamed, and enjoy this easy, low-fat cooking method, by all means, buy a steamer.

Electric Griddle: Provides an even, nonstick surface for making pancakes (page 245), French toast (page 246), grilled cheese sandwiches (page 340), frittatas (page 251), fried eggs (page 248), and other things that otherwise require stovetop cooking. The uniform heating helps everything cook evenly, and the nonstick surface makes cleaning easy and fast. (Just let it cool and wipe the surface with a damp sponge.)

Is it for you? Can you resist it? If you serve breakfast or brunch a lot, or you want to be able to make swift suppers without heating up the stove and cleaning a sauté pan, it's hard to imagine how you can.

Ice Cream Maker: While you can buy an inexpensive hand-crank machine, if you're serious about ice cream (*IF?*) a more costly, fully automated ice cream maker will make you happier.

Is it for you? This is a straight up or down question. Do you want real fresh, natural, preserva-tive-free, rich-tasting ice cream at the push of a button?

Bread Machine: A bread machine is supposed to give you all of the satisfaction of eating home-made bread without any of the hassle involved in baking it. Pour your ingredients into a chute, set a timer, and within hours, enjoy the aroma and flavor of a fresh loaf of bread. The machine will have blended, kneaded, fermented, and baked the dough. All you have to do is remove it and slice it. Or you can have the machine blend and knead the dough, leave it in the machine to rise, then take it out to shape for yourself and bake in your oven.

Is it for you? Only if you've tasted bread made in a machine *and* liked it enough to spring for one of your own. Keep in mind that if you can spare the few minutes it takes to supervise a food processor or mixer (see above) while it blends and kneads the dough, and then a few minutes more to shape and bake it, you may prefer to get a more versatile machine and make bread partly by hand.

ALSO HANDY

Cushionaire Baking Sheet: Cookies, bagels, pretzels, and such won't burn on the bottom with this ingenious piece of bakeware.

Baker's Peel/Stone: For crisp-crusted breads. The stone absorbs moisture from the dough, and the peel makes getting breads and pizzas to and from the stone much easier.

Skewers: For appetizers, grilling, and broiling. Wooden ones must be soaked for 30 minutes prior to cooking to prevent burning.

Kitchen Shears: For mincing herbs, separating cauliflower and broccoli florets, and various other odd jobs.

Handheld Electric Mixer: Especially useful if you don't own a Heavy-Duty Mixer.

Vegetable Peeler: Aside from the obvious, it can shave thin slices of cheese and slice vegetables for garnishes.

Cookie Cutters: For cutting small sandwiches for children or canapés for cocktails. Also to use as stencils for decorating cakes. And to make cookies!

English Muffin Rings: For shaping timbales and molding rice, as recommended in several recipes.

Squeeze Bottles: For making patterns on the serving plate and dabs and doodles on top of the food. You can find them in most housewares departments or you can reuse squeezable ketchup or mustard containers, making sure to clean them well first.

Parchment Paper: For lining baking sheets when making cakes such as jelly rolls, and for wrapping around chicken or fish to keep moist when baking.

Medicine Dropper: For garnishing soups with cream. You can use the dropper to make patterns on the surface of soup just before serving.

PET PEEVE

Some fancy champagne flutes force you to sip through pursed lips. Champagne that's drunk from some of those flutes might as well be administered through a medicine dropper. In France people actually *drink* champagne, sometimes from goblets with clear hollow stems that display the bubbles rising into the cup. It's worth searching for something like this if you enjoy champagne.

STRAIGHT TALK ABOUT TABLEWARE

Even if you don't have a limited budget for tableware, you probably have limited space to store it. If you like buying tableware and get bored easily, shop at a place that's so inexpensive, you can buy on impulse and get whole sets of dishes to use for the year until you get sick of them. Restaurant supply stores carry inexpensive practical tableware, and you can often find pieces that will customize your collection. For example, I found a set of large oval plates with matching soup cups that fit into grooves in the plates, perfect for serving soup and salad.

For the Infrequent Shopper

Buy bowls that can do triple duty—soup, cereal, and dessert. Multi-use bowls will be neither as wide and shallow as dedicated soup bowls or as round and deep as cereal bowls.

Buy medium-sized dinner plates, especially if you like to serve courses. Huge plates will look empty if you're using them for an appropriate portion of entrée and side dish after a first course. (But don't buy plates that are so small your guests will embarrass themselves by spilling stuff over the sides.)

And remember, white plates look stark and empty unless you pack them. Darker colors make it seem as if there's more food on the plate.

Have an equal number of water and wineglasses to have at each place. Keep filling those water glasses and you'll find that you go through less wine, and feel a whole lot better the next day.

SUGGESTIONS FOR STORAGE

How Good Food Goes Bad and How to Delay the Inevitable

1. It becomes a host for mold or bacteria. Remove moldy foods from the rest. Mold spreads, and one fuzzy berry will indeed spoil the whole pint. Don't pack produce tightly, or it will bruise and decay.
2. Food succumbs to excessive or prolonged exposure to those elements that accelerate aging in every living thing: light, heat, moisture, and air. Use airtight, moisture-resistant containers, such as zip-lock bags, to shield food from those things as well as you can. But let fresh uncooked vegetables breathe a bit—either by poking holes in plastic bags or buying zip-lock vegetable bags with holes—or they'll succumb to their own fumes.

Better Safe Than . . .

If something's been refrigerated or frozen for a while, smell it, then take a taste to make sure it's still good.

Pack leftovers according to how you plan to serve and/or reheat them. If you've got chicken and rice and you're going to microwave them, pack each separately. Otherwise the chicken may overcook before the rice is warm. If you're going to reheat the food in a conventional oven, you can pack it together because you have more control over the heat distribution. (Use that control . . . stir often!)

Not trying to be difficult! It may seem to you that my defrosting and reheating instructions are complicated. But I assure you they're only what they need to be to preserve the flavor and texture of each dish. If you can do it more easily another way and get good results, ignore my advice!

For Storage

Get yourself to label *everything* with the name of the contents and the date you packed them up.

Pyrex containers in various sizes let you see what's inside, and allow you to go from freezer to oven or microwave oven without transferring. (You will have to replace the cover, which is rubber, with a damp paper towel for microwaving and foil for a conventional oven.)

Zip-lock bags in various sizes don't take up much room. You can see what's inside them, (but do remember to label the bags anyway!) and you can freeze individual portions. Do not microwave! Let the ingredients thaw slightly at room temperature or in a bowl of cold water, open the bag, transfer the ingredients to an appropriate bowl or dish, and microwave in that.

Aluminum foil for food you'll be transferring straight from the freezer to a conventional oven.

If you want to store something very hot very fast, fill your sink with ice and cold water. Put the hot pan into the water, making sure the water doesn't run into the pan, and stir until it stops steaming. Transfer the food to a cool container.

BIBLIOGRAPHY/ RECOMMENDED READING

Baking

BAKING IS a skill, science, art, and for many, a passion. The following emphasize each element to different degrees, and all are instructive, inspiring, and reliable.

Alford, Jeffrey and Duguid, Naomi, *Flatbreads and Flavors* (Morrow)

Clayton, Bernard, *The Complete Book of Bread* (Fireside)

Leader, Daniel, *Bread Alone* (Morrow)

Ortiz, Joe, *The Village Baker* (Ten Speed Press)

Reinhart, Peter, *Brother Juniper's Bread Book* (Addison-Wesley)

Sands, Brinna, *King Arthur Flour 200th Anniversary Cookbook* (Countryman Press)

Indian

MY APPRECIATION of good Indian cookbooks is unbounded; learning how to make fully satisfying curries, flatbreads, and condiments has been one of the great rewards of my life as a vocational home cook. The seasonings, spices, and techniques would be a mystery to me still if it weren't for these dependable, detailed books.

Batra, Neelam, *The Indian Vegetarian* (Macmillan)

Marks, Copeland, *The Varied Kitchens of India* (Evans) and *Indian and Chinese Cooking from the Himalayan Rim* (Donald I. Fine)

Punjabi, Camellia, *The Great Curries of India* (Simon and Schuster)

Solomon, Charmaine, *The Complete Asian Cookbook* (Tuttle)

Fish

I'VE FOUND that I can never cook fish or seafood so well that I have nothing to learn from experts on the subject. Here are my favorites, for substantive instruction and (in Alan Davidson's case) scholarship and wit.

Davidson, Alan, *Mediterranean Seafood* (Penguin edition) and *North Atlantic Seafood* (Penguin edition)

Le Divellec, Jacques, *La Cuisine de La Mer* (Robert Lafont) (in French)

Peterson, James, *Fish and Shellfish* (Morrow)

Middle Eastern

I GREW up eating the food of the Middle East, but continue to learn from books written by authorities on the subject, particularly:

Mallos, Tess, *The Complete Middle Eastern Cookbook* (Tuttle)

Weiss-Armush, Anne Marie, *The Arabian Delights* (Lowell House)

General

Casas, Penelope, *The Foods and Wines of Spain* (Knopf). Perhaps the best single volume on the subject. Simple recipes/superb results.

Cunningham, Marion, *The Fannie Farmer Cookbook* (Knopf). A reliable, diverse, all-purpose cookbook. My favorite general cookbook.

Field, Michael, *All Manner of Food* (Ecco). An instructive and appetizing survey of popular ingredients and cooking techniques.

Sass, Lorna, *Great Vegetarian Cooking Under Pressure* (Morrow). The best introduction to pressure cooking; the author justifies her enthusiasm for the pressure cooker with one wonderful recipe after another.

Spencer, Colin, *The New Vegetarian* (Viking). Long my single favorite vegetarian cookbook.

Reference

FOR INFORMATION about ingredients, manners, customs, and food history, I consulted:

France, Christine, *Cooking Hints and Tips* (Dorling Kindersley). Lots of good preparation and storage advice, plus plenty of imaginative tricks for garnishing and serving. Some superb simple recipes, too, all in a slim, fully illustrated volume.

Herbst, Sharon Tyler, *Food Lovers Companion* (Barrons) and *Food Lovers Tiptionary* (Hearst). Straightforward—but not straitlaced—reference guides to ingredients and how best to use them. The author packs an immense amount of useful, accurate information into these vital reference books.

Jenkins, Steven, *The Cheese Primer* (Workman). The most readable, comprehensive guide to cheese to date. The author's voice is formidable, but fortunately it's easy to distinguish between his vast knowledge and his strident opinions, and come up with a way to choose your favorite cheeses from the hundreds he describes here.

Mariani, John, *The Dictionary of American Food and Drink* (Hearst). Fun facts to know and tell!

Post, Peggy, *Emily Post's Etiquette, 75th Anniversary Edition. The* manners book.

Nissenbaum, Stephen, *The Battle For Christmas* (Knopf). How Christmas came to be what it is.

Owen, Sri, *The Rice Book* (St. Martin's). The author documents the stories—historical and mythical—of the grain that sustains more than half the world. She includes eclectic recipes for everything from risotto to sushi to rice and coconut pudding.

Schivelbusch, Wolfgang, *Tastes of Paradise, A Social History of Stimulants* (Pantheon). Some like coffee, some like tea . . . the author explains how this came to be.

Trager, James, *The Food Chronology* (Owl Books). Two thousand pages of food trivia through the ages.

Toussaint-Samat, Maguelonne, *The History of Food* (Blackwell). Long my favorite single volume dealing with the evolution of foods and the development of European cuisine.

SOURCES

Mail order, by phone or e-mail, makes it possible to obtain virtually any ingredient and cooking implement regardless where you live. I can think of few people who benefit more from access to the Internet than home cooks who'd rather stay close to their kitchens than roam the earth—or even the town—to get high-gluten flour, fenugreek, or springform pans.

The following all-purpose food sites offer infinite links to mail-order sources of food, gear, and cookbooks:

epicurious.com

thekitchenlink.com

For coffee online I go to:

starbucks.com and **peets.com**, not only to purchase smooth, aromatic coffees, but for tips on brewing and storage

For tea online:

specialteas.com

For wine online, check out:

virtualvinyards.com

There is no better single source of baking ingredients and equipment than King Arthur Flour's Baker's Catalogue. Here's where you'll find that high-gluten flour for bagels, as well as some of the best all-purpose and specialty flours milled in the country. King Arthur also sells sugars, seasonings, nuts, dried fruits, and cocoa, as well as a full range of baking utensils from spatulas to high-power mixers.

kingarthurflour.com, or **800-827-6836**

Maid of Scandinavia carries cake pans and decorating equipment for the no-holds-barred approach to everyday and speical-occasion baking. There's no excuse for not making a cake in any shape requested by your child (purple dinosaur included); you can get everything you need to do it from this source.

800-328-6722

You can outfit your kitchen with everything from shelves and lights to pizza ovens, cookware, and grapefruit spoons with one call to Williams-Sonoma. The catalogue is also an excellent source of specialty foods, including rice for paella and risotto, herbs and spices, and wonderful own-label concentrates for broth.

800-541-2233

Kuhn Rikon makes the best pressure cookers I've tried, in a range of sizes.

800-662-5882, kuhnrikon.com/kuhnrikon

INDEX

CONVERSION CHART
Equivalent Imperial and Metric Measurements

American cooks use standard containers, the 8-ounce cup and a tablespoon that takes exactly 16 level fillings to fill that cup level. Measuring by cup makes it very difficult to give weight equivalents, as a cup of densely packed butter will weigh considerably more than a cup of flour. The easiest way therefore to deal with cup measurements in recipes is to take the amount by volume rather than by weight. Thus the equation reads: 1 cup = 240 ml = 8 fl. oz.; $\frac{1}{2}$ cup = 120 ml = 4 fl. oz. It is possible to buy a set of American cup measures in major stores around the world. In the States, butter is often measured in sticks. One stick is the equivalent of 8 tablespoons. One tablespoon of butter is therefore the equivalent to $\frac{1}{2}$ ounce/15 grams.

Liquid Measures

Fluid ounces	U.S.	Imperial	Milliliters
	1 teaspoon	1 teaspoon	5
$\frac{1}{4}$	2 teaspoons	1 dessertspoon	7
$\frac{1}{2}$	1 tablespoon	1 tablespoon	15
1	2 tablespoons	2 tablespoons	28
2	$\frac{1}{4}$ cup	4 tablespoons	56
4	$\frac{1}{2}$ cup or $\frac{1}{4}$ pint		110
5		$\frac{1}{4}$ pint or 1 gill	140
6	$\frac{3}{4}$ cup		170
8	1 cup or $\frac{1}{2}$ pint		225
9			250, $\frac{1}{4}$ liter
10	$1\frac{1}{4}$ cups	$\frac{1}{2}$ pint	280
12	$1\frac{1}{2}$ cups	$\frac{3}{4}$ pint	340
15		$\frac{3}{4}$ pint	420
16	2 cups or 1 pint		450
18	$2\frac{1}{4}$ cups		500, $\frac{1}{2}$ liter
20	$2\frac{1}{2}$ cups	1 pint	560
24	3 cups or $1\frac{1}{2}$ pints		675
25		$1\frac{1}{4}$ pints	700
27	$3\frac{1}{2}$ cups		750, $\frac{3}{4}$ liter
30	$3\frac{3}{4}$ cups	$1\frac{1}{2}$ pints	840
32	4 cups or 2 pints or 1 quart		900

Solid Measures

U.S. and Imperial Measures		Metric Measures	
ounces	pounds	grams	kilos
1		28	
2		56	
$3\frac{1}{2}$		100	
4	$\frac{1}{4}$	112	
5		140	
6		168	
8	$\frac{1}{2}$	225	
9		250	$\frac{1}{4}$
12	$\frac{3}{4}$	340	
16	1	450	
18		500	$\frac{1}{2}$
20	$1\frac{1}{4}$	560	
24	$1\frac{1}{2}$	675	
27		750	$\frac{3}{4}$
28	$1\frac{3}{4}$	780	
32	2	900	
36	$2\frac{1}{4}$	1000	1
40	$2\frac{1}{2}$	1100	
48	3	1350	
54		1500	$1\frac{1}{2}$
64	4	1800	
72	$4\frac{1}{2}$	2000	2

Equivalents for Ingredients

all-purpose flour—plain flour
arugula—rocket
buttermilk—ordinary milk
confectioners' sugar—icing sugar
cornstarch—cornflour
eggplant—aubergine
granulated sugar—caster sugar
half-and-half—12% fat milk
heavy cream—double cream
light cream—single cream
lima beans—broad beans
scallion—spring onion
squash—courgettes or marrow
unbleached flour—strong, white flour
zest—rind
zucchini—courgettes

Oven Temperature Equivalents

Fahrenheit	Celsius	Gas Mark	Description
225	110	$\frac{1}{4}$	Cool
250	130	$\frac{1}{2}$	
275	140	1	Very Slow
300	150	2	
325	170	3	Slow
350	180	4	Moderate
375	190	5	
400	200	6	Moderately Hot
425	220	7	Fairly Hot
450	230	8	Hot
475	240	9	Very Hot
500	250	10	Extremely Hot

Linear and Area Measures

1 inch	2.54 centimeters